THE COLD WAR
U.S. ARMY

THE COLD WAR U.S. ARMY

Building Deterrence for Limited War

Ingo Trauschweizer

UNIVERSITY PRESS OF KANSAS

All photographs, unless noted otherwise, are from Record Group 111: "Signal Corps Photographs of American Military Activity, 1900–1981," National Archives II, College Park, MD.

Published by the University Press of Kansas (Lawrence, Kansas 66045), which was organized by the Kansas Board of Regents and is operated and funded by Emporia State University, Fort Hays State University, Kansas State University, Pittsburg State University, the University of Kansas, and Wichita State University

Library of Congress Cataloging-in-Publication Data

Trauschweizer, Ingo.
The Cold War U.S. Army : building deterrence for limited war /
Ingo Trauschweizer.
p. cm. — (Modern war studies)
Includes bibliographical references and index.
ISBN 978-0-7006-1578-0 (cloth : alk. paper)
1. United States. Army. Europe and Seventh Army—History. 2. United States—Armed Forces—Europe—History. 3. Operational art (Military science)—History—20th century. 4. Europe—Strategic aspects.
5. Deterrence (Strategy) 6. Cold war. I. Title.
UA26.E9T73 2008
355.00973'09045—dc22

2008003947

British Library Cataloguing-in-Publication Data is available.

Printed in the United States of America

10 9 8 7 6 5 4 3 2 1

The paper used in this publication is recycled and contains 30 percent postconsumer waste. It is acid free and meets the minimum requirements of the American National Standard for Permanence of Paper for Printed Library Materials Z39.48-1992.

Contents

A photograph section appears following page 146.

Preface

The following study of the U.S. Army in the Cold War considers recent events, and contemporary history always walks a fine line between past and present. This book is intended as a work of history, but it may also address, indirectly, questions of great current and perhaps even future significance. In that respect, my choice of subject matter was influenced by the seismic changes in international security since the end of the Cold War. Initially, I wanted to participate in the debate over military transformation and military revolution that seemed to dominate both the scholarly and the public policy debates. Soon thereafter, however, the context of my work changed dramatically, due to the events of September 11th and the subsequent global "war on terror." But the resulting monograph should not be misunderstood as a work of contemporary commentary. In addressing the U.S. Army in a particular environment, I am presenting a case for enhanced dialogue between scholars and policymakers. As a work of history, my book may answer some of the questions that it has raised, but I hope that its greater contribution to the future of discourse about international security rests in these very questions. Institutional adaptation to a changing global environment, technological change, bureaucracy and interservice cooperation or rivalry, and the relationship of domestic and international events need to be considered in all their complexity. Recent history, thus, offers an interpretation of the past that may enhance the effectiveness of analysis of the present. It may even influence how we plan for the future.

I was very fortunate to go to graduate school at the University of Maryland. This facilitated access to critical archives without much expense. Moreover, constant exposure to the intellectual and scholarly discourse at the many exciting public policy institutions in Washington, DC, such as the Woodrow Wilson Center and its Cold War International History Project, helped make this a better and more relevant book.

A historical study is ultimately an exercise in solitary writing, but the analysis depends on the professional and personal expertise and support of many people. First, I must thank my parents for so graciously permitting me to pursue my interests overseas and to stay away from Germany for years at a time. I am repaying them with this book—albeit in a language that they will find difficult to read. This book could not have been written without the professional guidance and involvement of Jon Sumida, a true *Doktorvater* and a naval historian who allowed me to pursue a topic on dry land. Our shared interest in strategy and policy has made this a very beneficial relationship. Among other Maryland faculty, Jeffrey Herf, John Lampe, Keith Olson, George Quester, Shu Guang Zhang, and Madeline Zilfi made critical suggestions and offered their support. Outside of the University of Maryland, I am particularly indebted to the comments of Bianka Adams, Alexander Cochran, Kenneth Hamburger, Paul Herbert, David Hogan, Jonathan House, Lawrence Kaplan, Eugenia Kiesling, Brian Linn, Gordon Rudd, Robert Rush, James Wilbanks, and Harold Winton. Finally, I am grateful for the support of Randy Papadopoulos, Douglas Selvage, and Richard Wetzell throughout my career in graduate school.

Many heartfelt thanks are due to the staff of the National Archives in College Park and of all other archives and research libraries in the United States and Europe that I have consulted for this book. I must have taxed their patience over the years, since I have been working on the edges of declassification. I cannot possibly thank all the individuals who made critical contributions, but these archivists and librarians represent all the others who have worked behind the scenes: Rich Boylan, Milt Gustafsson, Larry MacDonald, Wilbert Mahoney, Cliff Snyder, and John Taylor at the National Archives; David Keough and Richard Sommers at the U.S. Army Military History Institute; Mike Browne and Virginia Navarro at the Combined Arms Research Library; Barbara Constable, Charlaine McCauley, Stephen Plotkin, Randy Sowell, and John Wilson at various presidential libraries; Joanne Hartog at the George C. Marshall Research Library; Johannes Geertz, Chris Lennaerts, and Annemarie Smith at NATO's new archive in Brussels; and the late Charles Kirkpatrick and Bruce Siemon at the V Corps and USAREUR historians' offices in Heidelberg.

For financial support, I would like to acknowledge the Department of the Army, the John F. Kennedy Foundation, the Lyndon B. Johnson Foundation, the Department of History at the University of Maryland, Norwich University's faculty development program, and, particularly, the George C. Marshall Foundation and the Baruch family. These generous grants and fellowships made extensive travel and research possible. Without these, I could not have written this book.

Final thanks are due to the late General Andrew Goodpaster and to General Donn Starry for their willingness to give of their time for interviews and in additional communication and to generally follow the progress of my work. Thanks also to the readers and editors at the University Press of Kansas for the thorough and caring process by which they transformed my manuscript into a book. Naturally, even all of this expertise and support could not avoid all errors and oversights. These are mine entirely.

Abbreviations

ACE	Allied Command, Europe
ACAV	armored cavalry assault vehicle
ADM	atomic demolition munition
AFCENT	Allied Forces, Central Europe
AIAS	Army's Institute of Advanced Studies
APC	armored personnel carrier
ATFA	Atomic Field Army
BAOR	British Army of the Rhine
BMP	*boyevaia mashina pekhoty* (Soviet infantry combat vehicle)
CAC	Combined Arms Center
CARS	Combat Arms Regimental System
CBR	chemical, bacteriological, and radiological
CENTAG	Central Army Group
CINCENT	Commander in Chief, Allied Forces, Central Europe
CINCUSAREUR	Commander in Chief, U.S. Army, Europe
CONARC	Continental Army Command
CPX	command post exercise
EDC	European Defense Community
EDP	Emergency Defense Plan
FADAC	Field Artillery Digital Automatic Computer
FTX	field training exercise
G-2	intelligence
G-3	operations
IFV	infantry fighting vehicle
IRBM	intermediate-range ballistic missile
JCS	Joint Chiefs of Staff
LANDCENT	Allied Land Forces, Central Europe
MACOV	Mechanized and Armor Combat Operations, Vietnam
MBT	main battle tank
MICV	mechanized infantry combat vehicle

MLF	multilateral force
MLRS	Multiple-Launch Rocket System
MOMAR	Modern Mobile Army
NATO	North Atlantic Treaty Organization
NBC	nuclear, bacteriological, and chemical
NORTHAG	Northern Army Group
NSC	National Security Council
REFORGER	Redeployment of Forces to Germany
ROAD	Reorganization Objective Army Division
ROCAD	Reorganization of the Current Armored Division
ROCID	Reorganization of the Current Infantry Division
ROTAD	Reorganization of the Airborne Division
SACEUR	Supreme Allied Commander, Europe
SHAPE	Supreme Headquarters Allied Powers, Europe
STRAC	Strategic Army Corps
TACFIRE	Tactical Fire Direction System
TOW	tube-launched, optically tracked, wire-guided missile
TRADOC	Training and Doctrine Command
TRICAP	triple capability
USAREUR	U.S. Army, Europe
USCINCEUR	U.S. Commander in Chief, Europe
USEUCOM	U.S. European Command

Maps

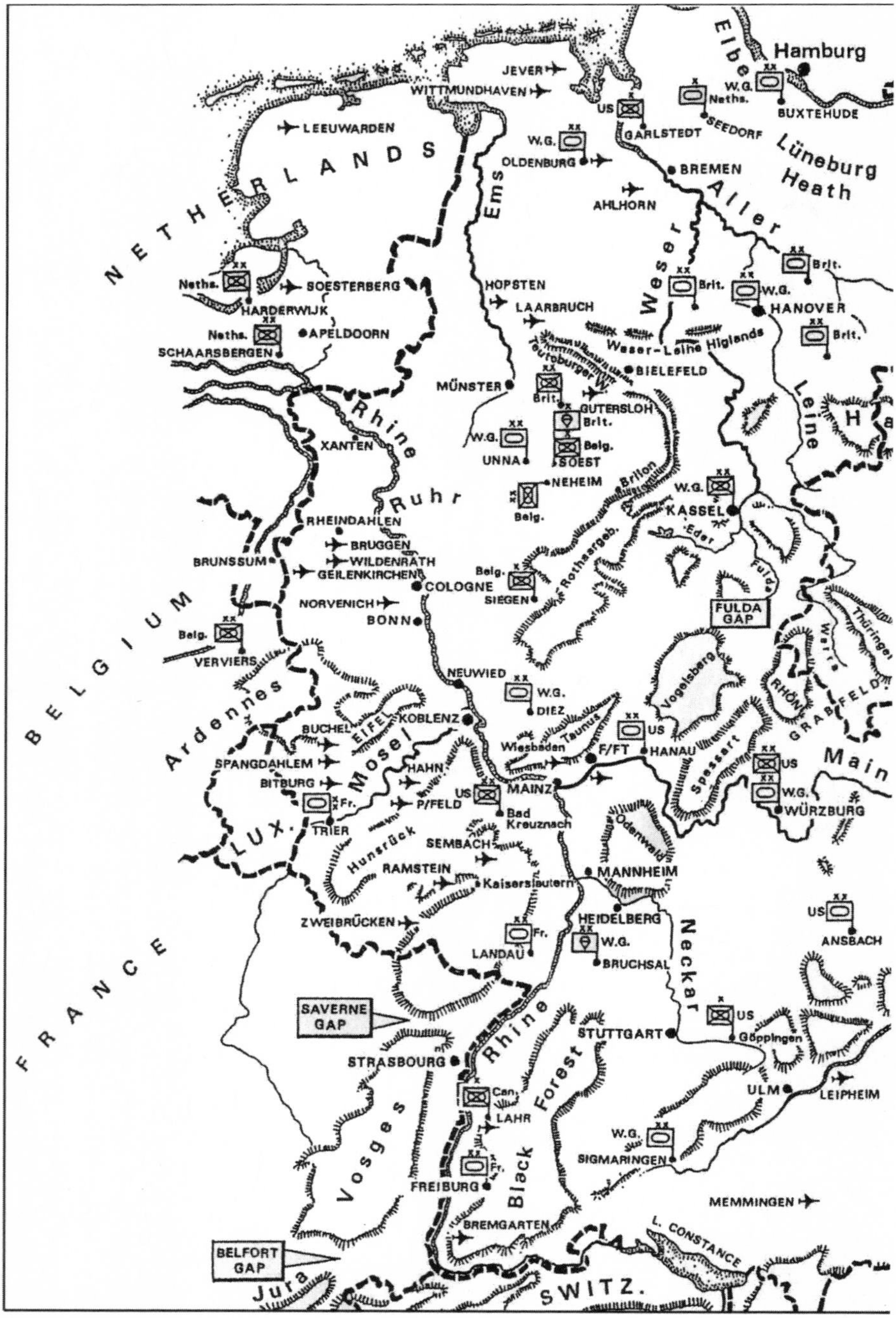

Map 1. Germany, Central Europe, and the Central Front in 1980s

Source: Hugh Faringdon, *Strategic Geography: NATO, The Warsaw Pact, and the Superpowers*, 2nd ed. (London: Routledge, 1989). Reproduced by permission of Taylor & Francis Books UK.

Sov.
E.G.
SCHWERIN
PARCHIM
E.G.
EGGESIN
TROLLENHAGEN
Sov.
NEUSTRELITZ
MIROW
Pol.
SZCZECIN
GOLENIOW
Sov.
STARGARD
WITTSTOCK
Sov.
PERLEBERG
Fürstenberge
Sov.
Sov.
NEURUPPIN
Sov.
TEMPLIN
F.R.G.
G.D.R.
FINOW
CHOJNA
Sov.
STENDAL
ORANIENBURG
Foerswalde
Sov.
WERNEUCHEN
BERNAU
MARXWALDE
POLAND
Döberitz
Sov.
DALLGOW
Berlin
Sov.
HILLERSLEBEN
Sov.
ALTENGRABOW
E.G.
POTSDAM
Wunsdorf
BRAND
FÜRSTENWALDE
MAGDEBURG
Sov.
Oder
Pol.
GUBIN
Pol.
KROSNO
ZERBST
Sov.
ROSSLAU
JÜTERBOG
DREWITZ
Saale
Elbe
KÖTHEN
Sov.
E.G.
HALLE
COTTBUS
FINSTERWALDE
WELZOW
FALKENBERG
SPREMBERG
Pol.
ZAGAN
SZPROTAWA
Sov.
LEGNICA
OSLA
MERSEBURG
Sov.
LEIPZIG
GRIMMA
RIESA
Sov.
GROSSENHAIN
NAUMBURG
E.G.
WEIMAR
ERFURT
Sov.
JENA
Sov.
E.G.
DRESDEN
ALTENBURG
Sov.
OHRDRUF
WROCZLAW
TURNOW
Sov.
MLADA BOLESLAV
Wald
Frankenwald
ERZGEB
Cz.
KARLOVY VARY
Cz.
SLANY
Sov.
MILOVICE
Prague
Fichtelgeb.
HOF CORRIDOR
Sov.
VYSOKE MYTO
CHOTUSICE
CZECHOSLOVAKIA
Cz.
HAVLÍČKUV BROD
Cz.
PLZEŇ
WEIDEN
Cz.
TABOR
Oberpfälzer Wald
NUREMBERG
Cz.
SUŠICE
BECHYNE
CHAM
BÖHMERWALD
Cz.
Č. BUDĚJOVICE
W.G.
REGENSBURG
Bayerischer Wald
Danube
W.G.
NEUBURG
Isar
Lech
PASSAU
Inn
FÜRSTENFELDBRUCK
Munich
LECHFELD
SALZACH
SALZBURG
W.G.
GARMISCH
AUSTRIA
BRIGADE
DIVISION
ARMOURED (TANK)
MECHANIZED (MOTOR RIFLE)
AIRMOBILE
MOUNTAIN
TERRITORIAL under NATO command
0
200

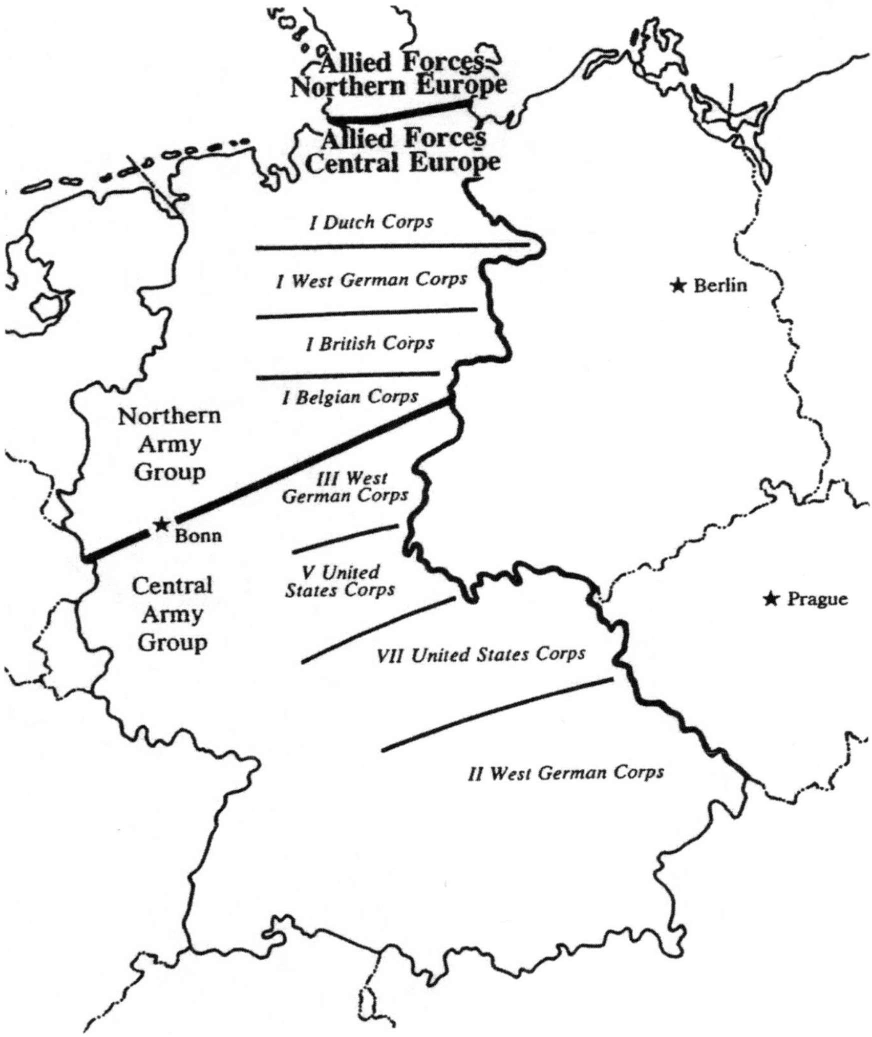

Map 2. Corps Sectors at NATO's Central Front

Source: William P. Mako, *U.S. Ground Forces and the Defense of Central Europe*, (Washington, D.C.: Brookings Institution, 1983), p. 33. Reprinted with permission from The Brookings Institution.

THE COLD WAR
U.S. ARMY

Introduction

Defense is a stronger form of fighting than attack.
—Clausewitz, *On War*

This book provides an empirical study of the evolution of the Cold War U.S. Army. It is not intended as a comprehensive history of the U.S. Army during that era.[1] Rather, it is an institutional history that focuses on doctrine, strategy, operational planning, organizational structure, and technology. After the Korean War, the army defined its primary mission as the deterrence of war in Central Europe.[2] The global nature of the Cold War, however, demanded general-purpose forces that could be deployed to fight elsewhere as well. The creation of such general-purpose forces proved to be unattainable. The requirements of an army capable of fighting effectively in Europe against Soviet armed forces and those of its satellites were in important respects different from those of a force capable of dealing with irregular opponents in underdeveloped countries. Army leadership therefore made the decision to emphasize preparedness in Europe and neglect preparing for the contingencies in other parts of the world.[3] This process began with the reorientation from purely conventional to conventional and nuclear forces at the end of the Korean War and culminated in the 1980s with the close alignment of operational doctrine with mission, force structure, organization of the combat division, and weapons technology. The Cold War army did not just happen. It had to be created through a protracted and difficult process that was shaped by internal conflict and external imperatives.

At this point, it is necessary to describe deterrence as a concept. In general terms, deterrence was equated with dissuasion. During the Cold War, and in historical and scientific scholarship since its conclusion, deterrence has generally been understood as a function of nuclear arsenals.[4] Some scholars have discussed a theoretical model of conventional deterrence based on historical case studies or the strategic situation in Europe in the late 1970s and 1980s.[5] They are a small minority, however, and did not consider the specific circumstances of Central Europe in the first decades of the Cold

War.[6] The intricate interplay of nuclear and conventional deterrence has received short shrift in the literature on the subject. The critical question may be stated as follows: What role, if any, did conventional force play with respect to the deterrence of Soviet aggression? European leaders, most notably Charles de Gaulle and Konrad Adenauer, did not believe that the United States would have been willing to fight a nuclear war in the event that Western Europe came under conventional attack. Thus, it would appear that historians and political scientists have posited a much more clear-cut conception about deterrence as practiced than the evidence suggests.

This book focuses on the experience of the U.S. Army in the Cold War. The contribution of air force, navy, and Marines to the defense of Western Europe will be discussed only with respect to its impact upon ground forces. It will acknowledge the usefulness of strategic nuclear weapons in deterring general war at the outset of hostilities. Tactical nuclear weapons will be taken into account, as they greatly influenced tactics and operational planning for conventional as well as nuclear war and deterrence. This book argues that the capacity for war fighting and deterrence are very closely related. The nuclear deterrent was immediately apparent to the enemy, but effective territorial defense depended on readiness and structure of ground forces as well as on integration of tactical nuclear weapons. Consequently, army leaders adopted a concept of limited war that allowed for the use of tactical nuclear weapons but offered an alternative to Massive Retaliation, the strategy of nuclear deterrence that was adopted in 1953. The capacity to wage limited war became the main focus of the army's political struggle for survival in the Eisenhower years. War in Europe could have remained in the realm of the tactical forces for a short period of time in which deterrence—of general nuclear war—was still a useful concept.

The army, the Kennedy and Johnson administrations, and academic theorists in the 1950s and 1960s each had a somewhat different understanding of limited war. The army defined it as any war below the level of strategic nuclear exchange. Defense officials of the Kennedy and Johnson administrations considered a more specific type of conflict: counterinsurgency warfare in places such as Laos, Indonesia, or Vietnam. Scholars thought in terms of a conflict such as the Korean War, where political objectives were limited and use of nuclear weapons was avoided.[7] This ambiguity led to serious misunderstandings. The army's suggested strategy of flexible response was based on the fundamental belief that the United States needed an alternative to strategic nuclear weapons for the defense of Europe. General Maxwell Taylor, U.S. Army chief of staff from 1955 to 1959, publicly expressed the army's concerns.[8] John F. Kennedy's enthusiastic response to Maxwell Taylor's work, however, indicated that he did not grasp fully the difference between flexible response and limited war, as the army perceived it, and Flexible Response, as Kennedy installed it as national military strategy. Taylor defined the army's mission as creating a credible deterrent with respect to a limited war in Europe. Kennedy, on the other hand, believed that the army's ability to wage limited war made it suitable for deployment in Europe and elsewhere.[9]

Taylor concluded that in order to create the proper force for the defense of Western Europe, the army needed to acquire nuclear weapons and alter its organizational structure and doctrine.[10] But there was never a master plan to achieve such a transformation. The army responded to crises, pressures, and influences, ranging from the Soviet threat to national strategy, interservice rivalry, budgetary concerns, technological innovation, and European military and political developments. The Cold War army, whose capacity to wage limited war against a Soviet-style opponent was made manifestly evident in the Gulf War in 1991, matured over three decades. This transition process was evolutionary and occurred in several stages.

First, a new basic purpose for the army had to be found in order to adapt to the realities of the nuclear age and to ensure the survival of the institution as a premier fighting force. By the end of the Eisenhower administration, limited war, without use of the most destructive nuclear weapons in the arsenals of the United States or the Soviet Union, was widely debated in military and political circles. With the notable exception of the air force, all military services agreed that limited war was possible. As a consequence, strategic nuclear deterrence expressed in the threat of Massive Retaliation had lost much of its initial appeal. Thus, by the end of 1960, the army had secured a role as a primary contributor to the national security and strategy of the United States.

The second phase of the transition process brought a fundamental reorganization of the army's combat divisions. The pentomic division, introduced in 1956 and so called because it consisted of a pentagonal unit with five battle groups armed with conventional and atomic weapons, had been designed to address bureaucratic pressure for reform and provide dual capability for conventional and nuclear war. It provided a rationale for the army's own nuclear weapons. Although it was impractical from an operational perspective, it marked a sharp break from the traditional combat division, thus opening the way for future change. Its successor, the Reorganization Objective Army Division (ROAD), served as the basic divisional organization of the Cold War army. The result of the organizational change was a flexible combat division with three brigade headquarters to which a varying number of maneuver battalions could be attached. ROAD was developed in 1960 and 1961 by generals who had served in senior command positions in Germany.

It was greatly influenced by the structure of West German army divisions. Despite the focus on war in Europe, the inherent flexibility of the ROAD division also was a significant step toward preparing the army for challenges in secondary theaters of the Cold War.

The third crucial step was the adjustment of operational and tactical doctrine to suit both the new mission and the new combat division as well as address the fighting methods of the Soviets. This was achieved only in the post-Vietnam recovery of the army. Here, the institution discovered the concept of operational art. Once more, examples in Germany, both contemporary and historical, served as useful points of reference. Active Defense, the tactical doctrine of 1976, was modeled upon West German concepts of mechanized conventional and tactical nuclear warfare. Its successor, the operational doctrine of AirLand Battle, introduced in 1982, drew heavily upon the Reichswehr conception of command and control of combined arms in battle that had emerged between 1920 and 1932. The German influence was augmented by attention paid to Soviet intentions and capabilities, based upon study of Soviet manuals and military journals as well as of the Yom Kippur War of 1973.

The critical points in time of the army's transition were the mid-1950s, when the service redefined its mission, the early 1960s, when the organizational structure of the combat division was improved, and the late 1970s, when operational doctrine specifically tailored to the threat and circumstances in Central Europe was written.[11] Official historians of various army commands have addressed changes in doctrine in great detail.[12] It is not the purpose of this book to restate their arguments. It will be necessary, however, to show the crucial links to the first two stages of the transition process. Military historians have neglected the two decades from the end of the war in Korea to the withdrawal of American ground forces from Vietnam. Instead they have been preoccupied with the study of the Vietnam War in order to explain the defeat of the U.S. military at the hands of a poorly equipped irregular enemy. The army in particular has been criticized for its lack of readiness for the conflict and its unwillingness to make fundamental changes necessary to win the war. In the larger context of the Cold War, however, the Vietnam War was merely an episode. It is difficult to conceive how else the army could have acted in fulfillment of its mission to prevent nuclear war between the superpowers.

The central question of this book is the role of a military institution within a nation's strategy. Strategy is defined as the proper relationship of means to ends in order to achieve a political objective. It would be unwise to equate civilian oversight of the military with civilian control of strategy. It would be foolish to argue that military services should be permitted to define national strategy. Strategy is neither dictated from the top nor shaped from the bottom of the chain of command. Instead, it is arrived at in the intricate interplay of several layers of the state and its defense establishment.[13] As a consequence of the primary research focus on the army, it might at times appear that the argument was made that military means define the ends of strategy. Such a conclusion would be unfortunate. A comprehensive study has to consider all aspects that shaped the strategy of the United States. But while much of the diplomatic, economic, financial, social, and cultural context of the Cold War has been addressed in many articles and monographs, the military means that helped the United States achieve the objective of its policy of containment have been largely ignored or taken for granted.[14]

In addition, this book pursues the subject of operational art as a binding link between strategy and tactics.[15] Military strategy is concerned with the use of battles to win a campaign or a war. Tactics are concerned with fighting a battle. Operational art combines the need to coordinate multiple battles and apportion resources, both men and materiel.[16] This book argues that early in the Cold War the U.S. Army conceived of war in tactical terms and began to consider operational art only after its defeat in Vietnam. Moreover, it offers evidence of developments in Europe that will show to what extent the army's attitude toward conflict in general was determined by the particular requirements of Central Europe. The very presence of five combat divisions in Germany altered the nature of the institution, but, more dramatically, so did the close interaction with the German army, with each institution drawing upon the ideas, concepts, and traditions of the other to a much greater extent than has been acknowledged thus far.[17]

This book reconsiders German-American defense relations. Historians have addressed aspects thereof, such as rearmament, nuclear weapons, alliance relations, economics, and finance, but little has been done to analyze the overarching issue of the defense of West Germany.[18] Most scholars have accepted the argument that nuclear deterrence worked.[19] Historian Marc Trachtenberg has put forth a somewhat different explanation. He identifies the German question as the central issue of the Cold War but argues that the United States and the Soviet Union came to a tacit agreement, which assured that the United States would control German ambitions in Europe. Trachtenberg contends that Soviet Cold War policy was driven by the fear of a militarily powerful Germany, which would threaten Soviet security, either as an instrument of Western aggression or after severing ties with the North Atlantic Treaty Organization (NATO).[20] The agreement was the result of crises in Berlin and Cuba and of failed attempts of the Western alliance to create a European nuclear force. The Soviets may have had good reason to fear a resurgent Germany, but Trachtenberg treats West Germany as a client state, which did little more than respond to American initiatives. A close reading of military and political records, however, reveals that West German politicians greatly influenced the debates of NATO strategy; that Bundeswehr combat division served as a model for the U.S. Army; and that German doctrine became a critical measuring stick for the army's operational philosophy.

At the heart of the exposition stand U.S. Army, Europe (USAREUR), and its operational arm, Seventh Army, the largest and best-prepared field army the United States ever deployed abroad in peacetime.[21] The mere fact that the crises on the periphery of the Cold War have taken on great prominence serves as an illustration of the quiet effectiveness of deterrence in Europe. The difficulty for the army lay in the need to be prepared for both conventional and tactical nuclear war. This dual capability became a dominating issue of civil-military relations and interservice rivalry in the United States. This dynamic also drove the development of tactical and operational doctrine within the army. A temporary solution was found in the reorganization of army divisions, first to the pentomic division and then to ROAD. This, however, was an attempt to solve a very complex problem without addressing all of its component parts. Doctrine lagged behind, especially in the 1950s. It was really only after the Vietnam War that the army found itself in a strategic environment that permitted the linkage of doctrine to operational necessity rather than bureaucratic, fiscal, or technological pressures. Nevertheless, the reforms of the 1950s and 1960s must not be overlooked. They constituted the first serious steps toward transformation of the U.S. Army.

Military histories of the Cold War are scarce.[22] Army historiography of the 1950s and 1960s has been preoccupied with the wars in Asia. Studies of the Vietnam War stand out, but the Korean War has also received a share of attention.[23] And, yet, Andrew Bacevich's study, *The Pentomic Era,* offers the only comprehensive treatment of the army in the 1950s.[24] He argues that the army had to find a way to survive within the strategic doctrine of Massive Retaliation while at the same trying to obtain major changes in national military strategy. He concludes that the army introduced force structure for political reasons that only served as a deterrent but had little actual fighting capability. This book will show, however, that one could not be achieved without the other. Bacevich's conclusions are limited by the chronological focus on the Eisenhower years, which did not allow him to consider ROAD and its relationship to Flexible Response. Army historian John B. Wilson takes a chronologically broader view. He provides the most comprehensive treatment of the pentomic division and ROAD, but the scope of his study does not allow for discussion beyond the structural changes.[25]

There is an inexplicable absence of considerations of operational doctrine in most histories of the Cold War army before 1973. This may reflect the contemporary bias within the army toward doctrine, but it is apparent that unified tactical and operational concepts did exist and were widely accepted, even prior to the wide-ranging discussion of doctrine in the wake of the defeat in Vietnam. The most comprehensive treatment remains Robert A. Doughty's *The Evolution of U.S. Army Tactical Doctrine, 1946–76*.[26] Studies on army nuclear doctrine also provide useful insight.[27] But contemporary publications of army officers struggling with the lack of a coherent tactical doctrine for atomic warfare are quite revealing in their own right. In 1953, two colonels on the faculty of the U.S. Army Command and General Staff College provided a semiofficial expression of doctrinal thinking.[28] Their book is permeated by cautious optimism about the deployment of nuclear weapons, their usability at the tactical level, and even their offensive value, but the authors lamented that the army had not implemented any of the methods suggested in the book. In 1958, two instructors at the Infantry Training School published a manual for tactical nuclear warfare of the pentomic division.[29] They noted that many pertinent articles had appeared in service journals, but that analysis was scattered and that commanding officers had nowhere to turn to keep up with the dynamic changes required by nuclear weapons. While the book praised the value of the pentomic division on the nuclear battlefield, it was written as a substitute for official doctrine.

At this point, it is necessary to introduce terms of army organization, weapon systems, and operational concepts for conventional and nuclear war. Specific developments will be discussed in greater detail in subsequent chapters, but this broad outline provides essential background information to administrative, institutional, and operational decisions made by army leaders in the course of the Cold War. Throughout the twentieth century, the division was the principal operational and administrative unit in the U.S. Army. It served as the smallest combined-arms force that was capable of sustained independent combat operations. During World War II, there were three types of army divisions in the European theater of operations: infantry (14,000 officers and men in combat and combat support units), armor (11,000 officers and men), and airborne infantry (13,000 officers and men). These were grouped into corps of two or more divisions, armies of several corps, and army groups of two or more armies. For tactical deployment, infantry divisions had three regiments (3,200 officers and men)—each of which had three maneuver battalions (870 officers and men), a cannon company, an antitank company, and other combat support forces—four artillery battalions (520 to 530 officers and men), and logistical and administrative units. Armored divisions were essentially similar, except that they had two combat command headquarters under which tank battalions could be combined with armored infantry and self-propelled artillery to operate as semi-independent mobile task forces.[30]

During the Cold War, army combat units were adjusted to the requirements of conventional and nuclear warfare. In the mid-1950s, battle groups of 1,500 officers and men in five companies replaced regiments and battalions. They were intended to function as autonomous tactical formations on a nuclear battlefield for several days or even weeks. Five battle groups and supporting artillery battalions and logistical units formed an infantry or airborne division. Armored divisions remained similar to those of World War II. In the 1960s, brigades supplanted the battle-group concept. Divisions had three brigade headquarters and a flexible number of maneuver battalions of between 800 and 1,000 officers and men in three or four line companies. At the same time, mechanized infantry as well as airmobile and air assault formations were added to the order of battle. For most of the Cold War, the army deployed in Germany five combat divisions and several independent brigades and armored cavalry regiments. These were grouped in two corps, which in the event of war would have been combined with two German army corps and French forces in southern Germany to form Central Army Group (CENTAG).[31]

Conventional arms were improved significantly. During World War II, the army relied upon riflemen who moved on trucks, half-tracks, or foot. Infantry had no armored personnel carriers (APCs) besides M3 half-tracks, which were ill suited to operate alongside tanks. Army commanders used infantry primarily to assault strongpoints, traverse rivers and establish bridgeheads, fight in urban environments, and defeat enemy formations that had been bypassed by American tanks. During the Cold War, armored and mechanized infantry replaced conventional infantry.[32] In the early 1950s, American infantry battalions and battle groups received M59 APCs, but it was impossible to provide enough of them to equip entire divisions. Moreover, while it could transport ten soldiers into battle, its .50 caliber machine gun did not provide much fire support for riflemen who had to fight dismounted. The M59 had a cruising range of 120 miles and maximum speed of 30 miles per hour. It was replaced in the early 1960s by the M113 APC, which could transport a squad of eleven. The M113 moved at greater speed than main battle tanks and matched their range, but its armor was weak and the machine gun remained its main armament.[33]

Soviet APCs matched American models in speed and range and could transport between sixteen and twenty-two officers and men. Unlike the M59 and the M113, Soviet APCs provided protection against nuclear, bacteriological, and chemical (NBC) weapons. In 1967, the Soviet army introduced the

BMP (*boyevaia mashina pekhoty*, or infantry combat vehicle), an infantry fighting vehicle (IFV) that could transport a squad of eleven officers and men into battle, who could then fight mounted or dismounted. It was armed with a 73-mm gun and an antitank gun with a range of 3,000 meters.[34] The Germans had also adopted an IFV. The U.S. Army, on the other hand, tried without success to develop an armored IFV throughout the 1960s and 1970s. It finally adopted the Bradley in 1981. Infantry was still supposed to fight dismounted, but the Bradley was armed with a 25-mm Bushmaster gun, which could fire 200 rounds per minute at ranges of up to 2,000 meters. The Bradley also could engage enemy tanks with its antitank missile launcher. At the end of the Cold War, the army had an IFV that could transport infantrymen and provide fire support for their dismounted operations and that had enough firepower to destroy enemy tanks and other armored vehicles.[35]

Tanks were the primary weapon system of maneuver forces.[36] The army intended light tanks to perform primarily screening and reconnaissance functions, but they could also serve as mobile weapons to attack enemy infantry. In this role, they were sometimes supported by assault guns, that is, infantry guns mounted on light tank chassis. Direct assault of enemy tanks and other forces was to be conducted by medium tanks. American light tanks of World War II were the M3A1 Stuart, primarily used for reconnaissance operations, which weighed 14.3 tons, had a 37-mm gun, a maximum speed of 30 miles per hour, and a cruising range of 70 miles, and the M24 Chaffee, which arrived in Europe in late 1944 and provided greater fire support with its 75-mm gun. The M4 Sherman was the principal American medium tank. It was armed with a 75-mm (1942 model) or 76-mm (1945 model) gun, weighed 30 tons, had a maximum speed of 24 (1942 model) or 29 (1945 model) miles per hour, and a cruising range of 100 miles. While the Sherman tank did not match armor or armament of the modern German Tiger and Panther tanks and could defeat them only in extraordinary circumstances, it was mechanically reliable and could be produced in much greater numbers than the German tanks.[37]

The lethality of tanks increased significantly throughout the Cold War. A medium tank during World War II had to fire thirteen rounds to achieve a 50 percent likelihood of hitting a standing target at 1,500 meters, but a main battle tank of the 1970s needed only one round.[38] This was the result both of more powerful tank guns, which fired high velocity rounds that were much more destructive than the shells used in World War II, and of improved sights and range-finding technology.[39] But at the same time, infantry fielded greatly improved antiarmor weapons, such as tube-launched, optically tracked, wire-guided (TOW) missiles and Dragon lightweight shoulder-fired guided missiles, and posed a greater threat to tanks.

During the Cold War, tank battalions and armored cavalry regiments received new light- and medium-gun tanks. The M41 Walker Bulldog replaced the M24 Chaffee at the end of the Korean War. It was armed with a 76-mm gun, weighed 23.5 tons, and had a maximum speed of 45 miles per hour and a cruising range of 100 miles. The M41 was later replaced by the M551 Sheridan, a lightweight assault vehicle that could be transported by air. The Sheridan was strongly armed with a 152-mm gun and a Shillelagh antitank missile launcher, although the gun was not fully reliable when used to dispense high-explosive conventional ammunition. The Sheridan weighed 17 tons, could reach speeds up to 43 miles per hour, and had a cruising range of 375 miles, a result of the shift from gasoline to diesel engines. It was a hybrid vehicle that was intended to function as a light tank as well as an assault vehicle for armored cavalry, which had previously relied upon a modified version of the M113 APC. The Sheridan was used in combat in Vietnam and introduced briefly in Europe, but although it was a capable antitank weapon system, it could not effectively perform other missions of light tanks and required more maintenance than commanders in Germany deemed worthwhile.[40]

For medium-gun and main battle tanks, USAREUR received M47 and M48 Patton tanks with 90-mm guns. Although their armament and armor were sufficient, they weighed over 50 tons and had maximum speeds of only 30 miles per hour and cruising ranges well below 100 miles, although the M48A2 tank model of 1956 increased the latter to 160 miles. Patton tanks were replaced after 1961 by M60 main battle tanks propelled by diesel engines, which increased the operating range to 300 miles. The M60 had a 105-mm gun with an effective range of 2,000 meters.[41] In the early 1980s, M60 tanks were replaced by Abrams tanks, which were armed with a 105-mm gun, could reach speeds of 45 miles per hour, and provided protection against NBC attacks.[42] Abrams tanks also had a much more sophisticated laser range finder system, which improved the likelihood of hitting enemy tanks with the first round. Against this stood Soviet T-55, T-62, and T-75 main battle tanks, armed after 1962 with 115-mm guns (1,500-meter range). All Soviet main battle tanks since the late 1950s provided NBC protection.[43] Heavy tanks, such as the M26 Pershing tank and the M103 heavy tank, designed for direct assault and to support main battle tanks against Soviet armor, played no significant role in official plans for the defense of Western Europe but offered the only viable antitank weapon in Seventh Army's arsenal against Soviet armor in the late 1950s and early 1960s, until the deployment of sufficient numbers of M60 tanks in Europe.

Field artillery provided indirect fire support for offensive and defensive operations of armor and infantry formations. Direct support came from mortars and antitank guns organic to maneuver battalions. At the outset of combat operations in World War II, U.S. Army divisions had towed 75-mm guns, towed and self-propelled 105-mm howitzers (with a range of 12,150 yards), and towed 155-mm howitzers (with a range of 16,350 yards).[44] In the course of 1942, corps began to receive 155-mm guns, 8-inch howitzers, and 240-mm howitzers (all of them towed). Field artillery was modernized further throughout the war and a new generation of towed and self-propelled 105-mm howitzers, 4.5-inch guns (20,500 yards), towed and self-propelled 155-mm guns (ranges of 20,100 and 18,750 yards, respectively), 8-inch howitzers (18,510 yards), and towed 8-inch guns (35,000 yards) became the most effective weapons in the American arsenal. These guns fired high-explosive shells, steel shrapnel rounds, or armor-piercing ammunition.[45]

At the outset of the Korean War, the army still relied on guns that had been available at the end of World War II: 105- and 155-mm howitzers, 155-mm guns, 8-inch howitzers, 8-inch guns, and tractor-pulled 240-mm howitzers.[46] But nuclear weapons made concentration of forces dangerous and required greater mobility. Consequently, the army attempted to design artillery pieces that were self-propelled, could be transported by air, provided NBC protection, and could traverse 360 degrees in order to fight in all directions. Although some aspects of the ambitious rearmament program were unattainable, the army introduced a new generation of artillery pieces in the 1960s. These 105-mm, 155-mm, and 8-inch howitzers, as well as 175-mm guns, increased range, traverses, and mobility. Their detonating methods and high-explosive shells also increased lethality.[47] In Europe, army combat divisions relied primarily upon self-propelled 105-mm (11,500 meters) and 155-mm howitzers (14,500 meters and 18,000 meters, depending on the type of ammunition). Self-propelled howitzers moved at a maximum speed of 35 miles per hour and had cruising ranges of 220 miles. In the mid-1950s, divisional artillery obtained nuclear capability with a composite battalion of self-propelled 8-inch howitzers, which could fire conventional or nuclear shells at ranges between 16,800 and 20,600 meters, and four Honest John missile launchers.[48] Later generations of 155-mm howitzers were to be capable of firing nuclear ammunition. In addition, towed 8-inch howitzers were distributed to USAREUR primarily for nuclear fire. Corps and army group also had self-propelled 175-mm guns, which fired conventional shells for 32,800 meters. Soviet artillery had towed and self-propelled 122-mm howitzers, towed and self-propelled 152-mm guns, and towed 180-mm guns with a range of 30 kilometers (probably nuclear capable). Both the towed 8-inch gun and the towed and self-propelled 240-mm howitzer could fire nuclear shells.[49]

Towed guns remained part of the army's arsenal in locations outside of Europe. The light M102 105-mm howitzer (1.6 tons) was introduced during the Vietnam War. It was transportable by utility helicopters and could be air-dropped by parachute. Its rate of fire was higher than that of heavier howitzers (three rounds per minute sustained fire and ten rounds per minute maximum). The fundamental differences between towed and self-propelled guns lay in the size of the crew, rate of fire, and mobility. The American M109 self-propelled 155-mm howitzer required a crew of six, moved at 35 miles per hour with a cruising range of 216 miles, and could fire four rounds per minute for a short period of time or one round per minute sustained. The M114-towed 155-mm howitzer required a crew of eleven, needed to be emplaced, and could sustain a rate of fire of forty rounds per hour. Fire control was improved significantly with the adoption of the Field Artillery Digital Automatic Computer (FADAC) in the early 1960s and the Tactical Fire Direction System (TACFIRE) in the mid-1970s, which allowed forward observers to communicate directly with the fire-control computer.[50] In the late 1960s and 1970s, the army intended to employ most of its firepower against tanks, but artillery officers found that more cost-effective rocket launchers could achieve the same effect on enemy armor as long-range howitzer fire. As a result, the army adopted the Multiple-Launch Rocket System (MLRS), which could fire hundreds of antitank bomblets over 30 kilometers in less than one minute.[51] Today, the army relies primarily on the MLRS as well as on 105-mm and 155-mm howitzers.

Besides conventional artillery, the army adopted tactical nuclear weapons. The earliest atomic weapon system was the 280-mm cannon, which was introduced in USAREUR in 1953. Soon thereafter, rockets and missiles replaced atomic cannons. First among them was the Honest John, a truck-mounted rocket launcher that could fire conventional and atomic ammunition. In its heaviest version, it could launch a 47-kiloton warhead up to 38 miles. Its smaller cousin, the air-transportable Little John rocket launcher, could fire warheads of up to 10 kilotons, for a range of 11.3 miles.[52] For close combat, the army adopted the Davy Crockett, fired by jeep-mounted recoilless rifles, with a maximum range of 4 kilometers and an atomic warhead with a yield of 0.4 kilotons. Its reliability on target was questionable, and soldiers in Seventh Army liked to point out that the range of the weapon barely exceeded the burst radius of the warhead. Historian Sean Maloney applauded the decision of the Canadian army not to adopt the weapon system.[53] It was deployed briefly in Germany in the first half of the 1960s. At the end of the 1950s, the army deployed surface-to-surface missiles. The Corporal guided missile had a range of 75 miles and could carry warheads of up to 40 kilotons. It was replaced in the 1960s by the Sergeant ballistic missile, which had the same range but an improved target acquisition mechanism. The Redstone, designed by Wernher von Braun and his engineering team in Huntsville, Alabama, had a

200-mile range and could carry a 3-megaton warhead. After 1963, the even more lethal Pershing I replaced the Redstone.[54] As the first line of defense, in the mid-1960s, atomic demolition munitions (ADMs) were placed at the intra-German border. Medium nuclear land mines had yields of between 1 and 15 kilotons. In comparison, the atom bombs exploded over Hiroshima and Nagasaki in August 1945 had yields of 13 and 25 kilotons, respectively.

The army had no clear guidance for the use of tactical nuclear weapons. Army leaders assumed that forward defense near the intra-German border would force the Soviets to mass troop formations on East German territory. These massed formations would present lucrative targets for atomic strikes. On the defense, forces expected to disperse in order to avoid presenting an equally lucrative target to Soviet nuclear weapons. Planning for conventional as well as nuclear war in Europe acknowledged the lethality of firepower and assumed that only fast mobile formations could operate effectively. Army operational concepts of the 1960s and early 1970s centered on channeling the enemy attack into prepared killing zones, in which conventional and atomic fire could be brought to bear with maximum effect. Toward the end of the Cold War, concepts of airmobility and deep battle added to the depth of the battlefield and the tempo of anticipated operations. In 1982, the army adopted AirLand Battle doctrine, which was designed to take advantage of technology in an attempt to retain initiative in defensive and offensive operations.

Chapter One discusses the army's marginal role in nuclear deterrence strategy of the 1950s. Eisenhower's New Look defense policy with its threat of Massive Retaliation raised serious questions about the utility of ground forces in the atomic age. The Army Staff, under the leadership of Matthew B. Ridgway, was put on the defensive in domestic discussions of defense budgets, military strategy, and availability of new technology for ground forces. In the Western alliance, meanwhile, the sense of urgency that had been displayed after the outbreak of the Korean War had waned. NATO adopted Massive Retaliation in 1954 and shifted its emphasis from conventional rearmament to nuclear deterrence. On the operational level, alliance commanders developed sophisticated concepts for the atomic battlefield. These doctrinal considerations were advanced in contrast to the army's emphasis on large formations and firepower. But although American tactical and operational doctrine may have been ill suited to the military circumstance in Central Europe because it treated atomic weapons merely as a more powerful and destructive form of artillery, the ideas developed in NATO headquarters were much too advanced to be adopted by any existing army of the alliance.

Chapter Two discusses the army's operational and political response to the New Look. It focuses on Maxwell Taylor, Ridgway's successor, and his attempt to transform the army. The air force and navy had adopted nuclear weapons and were widely regarded as the principal military means for nuclear strategy. The army had been slow to adjust, and its budgets did not allow it to respond to the increasing cost of land warfare with conventional and nuclear means. Therefore, Taylor believed that nothing short of radical reform would suffice to improve the army's standing. It found new purpose in creating the concept of a deterrent for conventional and tactical nuclear limited war in Europe, and Taylor initiated a fundamental reform of the combat division. His pentomic division was impractical, but it secured the army's hold on tactical nuclear weapons and provided political leverage that allowed the service to reclaim a premier position among the armed forces of the United States. NATO's supreme military commander, General Lauris Norstad, also approached the issue of limited war and credibility of deterrence in Central Europe. He believed that conventional and tactical nuclear defense could force the Soviets to consider the consequences of escalation to higher levels of nuclear war and reconsider their resort to war. The chapter shows that Massive Retaliation remained the strategic concept of the alliance throughout the 1950s, but that the deterrent value of NATO ground forces was strengthened by the integration of conventional and tactical nuclear weapons.

Chapter Three discusses the reorganization of Seventh Army into pentomic divisions, their reception by commanders in the field, and the ultimate rejection of the concept. It shows parallel developments in Germany and NATO that led army generals to believe that European combat divisions were structurally superior. The tendency toward dispersion, mobility, and mechanization continued, as brigades and maneuver battalions replaced regimental combat teams and battle groups. Eventually, generals Bruce Clarke and Clyde Eddleman, both with recent command experience in Germany, introduced concepts to replace the pentomic division. Eddleman's ROAD concept proved better suited to the changing global perception of the army. Clarke had introduced a universal combat division that could operate in the mechanized, and potentially nuclear, operational environment of Central Europe. But as the pressures of the New Look on the army were reduced in the late 1950s, army leadership began to consider seriously the possibility of military intervention in crises on the periphery of the Cold War. This new approach never challenged the deterrence of war in Europe as the primary mission of the service, but it did contribute to the introduction of combat divisions built around three brigade headquarters and a flexible number of maneuver battalions.

Chapter Four discusses the adoption of the ROAD concept and its relation to changing national and alliance strategy. It considers the strategy of Flexible Response, introduced by the Kennedy administration in 1961, and describes the impact of ROAD on Seventh Army and on the deterrence posture of NATO ground forces in the Central Region. The army did not fully embrace Flexible Response, despite agreement with the notion that greater strategic flexibility was necessary. In order to maintain uncertainty about the kind of American response to Soviet aggression and thus enhance the deterrent effect of Flexible Response, the strategy was left vaguely defined. This led to distinctly different interpretations even within the Kennedy administration. Large parts of the administration believed that conventional defense of Western Europe could be sustained for several weeks. The army's operational concept, on the other hand, did not include protracted conventional operations. Both the secretary of defense and NATO's new supreme commander supported the position of the army, although Robert McNamara was less convinced of the absolute need to employ tactical nuclear weapons than was General Lyman Lemnitzer. Lemnitzer feared that increased emphasis on conventional defense threatened the concept of forward defense at or near the intra-German border, which was predicated on the notion that nuclear weapons would be used to destroy massed Soviet or Warsaw Pact formations that were trying to cross the border. NATO commanders believed that their forces were too small for defensive operations without nuclear weapons.

Chapter Five addresses the global nature of the Cold War and the fundamental strategic dilemma of the army in the 1960s. Its primary mission remained the deterrence of war in Europe, but secondary missions included preparedness for different kinds of limited war in the Third World. The chapter discusses why the army found it impossible to fulfill both aspects of its mission. It shows that ground forces built for armored and mechanized warfare were ill suited for counterinsurgency operations in an environment with poor infrastructure. The chapter explains why ROAD contributed greatly to deterrence in Europe but could not win the Vietnam War. As the war dragged on, light infantry divisions had to be created, the development of critical weapon systems and equipment items for use in Europe was delayed, and officers and skilled personnel had to be withdrawn from Europe. Nevertheless, the United States maintained the equivalent of five combat divisions in Germany, and the German army achieved a degree of readiness that compensated for some of the weaknesses of USAREUR. National strategic demands exceeded army capability, but deterrence in Europe remained the priority of army leaders. This contributed to the defeat in Vietnam, but unlike Western Europe, Southeast Asia was never a critical theater of the Cold War nor was there much danger of escalation to nuclear war.

The final chapter discusses the recovery of the army in the decade following the war in Vietnam. The focus of the institution almost immediately returned to Germany. Soviet intentions, capabilities, and operational plans were considered as the basis for U.S. Army planning. The Yom Kippur War of 1973 between Israel and Egypt and Syria had shown the effects of modern armor and antitank weaponry. It also served as an illustration that Soviet armored weapons were equal to those of the Western alliance. As a result of such observations, the army published new doctrine in 1976. Active Defense was advocated as the operational future of the army, but the concept drew much criticism from inside and outside the service for its emphasis on the first battle and on the defensive. General Donn Starry and other doctrinal planners realized that the Soviets had perfected ideas of deep battle, characterized by several echelons of attacking forces that could be fed onto a battlefield with precise timing. In order to counter skill, brute force, and superior numbers, the army could not rely upon tactical expertise and firepower alone. In 1982, Active Defense was replaced by AirLand Battle doctrine. Now the Cold War army had come into its own, through the marriage of mission, organizational structure of the combat elements, weapons technology, and operational doctrine geared toward a specific type of warfare in Germany. But this was only possible because, in the decade after the Vietnam War, national strategic objectives and army operational objectives were fully aligned.

The primary sources for many aspects of this book were difficult to assemble, and by its very nature no work on national-security questions in the twentieth century could reasonably claim to be complete. Presidential, foreign, defense, and alliance politics since World War II have created a vast store of public records, but a great number of documents remain classified. In addition, this book cuts very close to current affairs, and some of the protagonists of the later chapters are still alive. This has offered the opportunity for oral history interviews, but it has also limited access to personal papers. Research for this book has been conducted in government and military archives in the United States and Western Europe, although American records naturally make up the bulk of the evidence presented. It is an empirical, multiarchival study, but the available record cannot answer all questions. At times, it has proven necessary to employ carefully crafted theory to explain specific courses of action and their alternatives. These sections have been clearly identified.

The study of the Cold War army has become timely and even pressing. The U.S. military, presumably in the midst of transformation to face the challenges of the twenty-first century, is once again encountering many of the questions addressed in this book. Technology, skill, and the tendency toward specialized forces may be enticing, but the question, to what extent a small and specialized force can serve its purpose in a global context, needs to be raised. The army's experience during the Cold War offers an interesting and important American case study of transformation. The reform, at first driven by budgetary pressure and new technology, was not an immediate success. Deterrence suffered from the introduction of the pentomic division. It is true that ROAD was a vast improvement, but tactics, operations, and military strategy remained unconnected due to the lack of applicable doctrine and conflicting strategic objectives. The United States had allowed itself to believe that its army could fight anywhere in the world and win under difficult circumstances. This book suggests that an army will fight as well as it has been prepared. But the degree of preparation is conditioned by the policies of the state, by national and military strategy, by civil-military relations, and by society's willingness to contribute the immense human and materiel resources necessary for postmodern war.

1

The U.S. Army in National and Alliance Strategy

In 1953, Dwight D. Eisenhower became president of the United States and hostilities in Korea ended. Both events—the election of an army general to the White House and the conclusion of a grueling war—promised better times for the army. But it soon became apparent that its position as the primary agent of American national security was in danger. Eisenhower's fiscal conservatism favored nuclear deterrence, which was in theory no less effective and much cheaper than the maintenance of large conventional ground forces. Massive Retaliation thus came to replace defense of territory as the preferred means to meet the threat of Soviet expansion during the 1950s. In effect, this required reductions in spending on the army in order to enhance the strategic offensive capabilities of the U.S. Air Force and, to a lesser degree, the U.S. Navy. Political leaders in the United States and Western Europe questioned the utility of conventional forces. By 1955, airpower was seen as the dominant form of war, with land power relegated to the status of an auxiliary service.

From World War II to Korea

After World War II, the general public regarded ground forces as unfashionable. Although the army had fought valiantly, the advent of atomic weapons made land forces appear to be of limited utility. Consequently, the army was dramatically reduced in size, from the wartime high of eight million officers and men in eighty-nine divisions to a mere ten combat divisions and 591,000 officers and men on the eve of the Korean War.[1] Even the army's own first postwar operational doctrinal manual was self-effacing. Its mission statement emphasized training and proper equipment of combat units for the defense of the United States, but it also pointed at the provision "of Army units for attachment to the Air Force for performance of prescribed functions; to provide common type support for Navy and Air Force as directed."[2] For land-warfare tactics, it prescribed offensive spirit and emphasized firepower. Both infantry and armor would be best employed offensively. Defensive operations were to be employed only where dictated by the circumstances. Divisions on the defensive were advised to choose strongpoints and attempt to defend in place.[3] In general, the manual left little doubt that army planners strongly favored the offensive as the best way to preserve freedom of action and dictate the course of a battle.[4]

According to the doctrinal manual, offensive operations had both physical and psychological effects on the enemy. Assault of defensive positions and aggressive pursuit of retreating units were to result in attrition of the enemy force. Rapid attacks on command and logistics functions were to degrade the enemy's ability to coordinate operations of forward-deployed combat units. The goal was to direct a well-planned effort against dominating terrain, supply lines, and vital areas in the enemy's rear.[5] There, he would have to stand and fight. Army doctrine held that decisive battle was to be sought in a war of movement, but that ultimately it would be necessary to reduce enemy strongpoints. In operations against fortified positions, commanders needed to allow for sufficient time to assemble the right combination of firepower and maneuver capability, signal communications, and other vital support. Once the force had been assembled, and reconnaissance had revealed the weak points in the defensive position, the attack would commence under the assumption that fire superiority had to be established before combat units could launch an assault. Armored reserves had to be prepared to exploit a breakthrough and drive into the rear of the enemy's frontline positions.[6] Their objective was to attack enemy command and control functions, to cause confusion, and to kill or capture large numbers of enemy troops.[7]

The defensive was primarily for the purpose of gaining time, "pending the development of more favorable conditions for undertaking the offensive, or to economize forces on one front for the purpose of concentrating superior forces for a decisive action elsewhere." Based on hard-fought defensive battles of World War II, such as the defense of Bastogne during the Battle of the Bulge, the army recognized only positional defense as a legitimate form of the defensive. There was awareness, of course, of successful German employment of mobile defense in depth on the Eastern Front, but that did not yet have a significant place in official doctrine. For the time being,

> defensive doctrine contemplates the selection and organization of a battle position which is to be held at all costs. Forward of that position maximum use is made of covering forces to delay and disorganize the advance of the enemy and deceive him as to the true location of the battle posi-

tion. Strong reserves are held out to destroy the enemy by counterattack if he penetrates the battle position and after the momentum of the attack has been spent.[8]

The main line of resistance was considered the last resort, while forward units added depth to otherwise linear defense.[9] Atomic weapons did not yet enter into operational doctrine beyond a few veiled remarks about technological advances. As the manual was published, in August of 1949, the United States government still believed that it possessed a monopoly on the weapon. Pentagon officials had only just begun to contemplate tactical use of atomic weapons.

The Korean War shifted army attitudes that had prevailed in the immediate postwar period. After World War II, the U.S. Army had been demobilized rapidly. Its main task became the occupation of Germany and Japan. By the end of the 1940s, increasing tension between the United States and the Soviet Union had polarized international relations, and war was again considered possible. But there seemed little use for large fighting formations of men armed with the weapons of World War II. The Korean War revealed the fallacy of such arguments. It showed that war could be limited, even in the atomic age. It also demonstrated that the army had been reduced to a point where it was difficult to function as an effective fighting force. At the beginning of the war, North Korean troops held the advantage in manpower, equipment, and readiness. The army had four infantry divisions in Japan, but all of them were severely under strength and lacked even basic weaponry and equipment.[10] The first American soldiers that encountered the enemy were barely able to delay the North Korean advance so that other elements of Eighth Army could take up suitable defensive positions.[11]

The defense of the Pusan Perimeter offers several interesting examples of tactics that did not correspond to the official doctrine promulgated in 1949. Of course, the divisions, regiments, and battalions defending Taegu and other critical points also bore little resemblance to the tables of organization and equipment prescribed by the army. In practice, while relying on linear defense of the southeastern tip of the Korean Peninsula, General Walton Walker installed a system in which mobile, centrally located reserves could stop any infiltration. Walker's ad hoc defense resembled German battle group actions in World War II.[12] As Eighth Army gathered strength and found its footing, its tactical behavior changed accordingly.

In September and October 1950, army units recovered the initiative and conducted offensive operations that were more in accordance with current doctrine. When Chinese troops entered the war and forced the Americans onto the defensive, army units conducted area defense, based on strong positions and high grounds. This was a response to the numerical superiority of the Chinese forces, but it was also a consequence of the quality of available personnel. Reservists, who had not received much training before being sent to Korea as individual replacements, could more easily learn basic skills for the defense of strongpoints than those required for attack. In spite of the much longer duration of offensive operations and the war of posts from September 1950 until 1953, it was the experience of defensive operations and near defeat in the summer of 1950 that was to contribute more greatly to the development of doctrine for war in Europe.

Once American forces had established superiority in firepower on the ground and in the air, the course of the Korean War reinforced the army's tendency to rely on heavy firepower rather than maneuver.[13] This appears to have originated in the American Expeditionary Force of World War I. Moreover, the influence of tactical ideology of the French army, which was widely admired by American officers before World War II, should not be underestimated. It is generally assumed that the quick defeat of French arms in 1940, coupled with the stunning operational success of German war of movement, prompted a shift in American thinking, but the events of World War II, as well as those of the Korean War, do not support such a conclusion. U.S. Army doctrine continued to emphasize a methodical offensive in which firepower was seen as the means to reduce enemy strongpoints and collapse the enemy's front line. Armored and mechanized maneuver elements of the army were supposed to support infantry, although it was acknowledged that they could become the main instrument of offensive action if the enemy was disorganized or could not hold its fortifications. Conversely, on the defensive, the enemy was to be forced to expend vast amounts of manpower in assaults on fortified positions covered by concentrations of artillery and machine guns. The Korean War did not challenge this line of thinking because American artillery was superior to that of the enemy and terrain and weather conditions favored the use of infantry.

With the introduction of the 280-mm atomic cannon in 1953, tactical use of atomic weapons by ground forces became possible. This amplified the predilection to rely on heavy firepower both as a means of fighting a numerically superior enemy and of minimizing friendly casualties. In practice, however, it was unclear what changes atomic weapons would bring to tactics and operational planning. For the next few years, atomic weapons were regarded as a more powerful form of artillery rather than as a basis for a different kind of tactics, operations, and strategy. In 1953, the Weapons System Evaluation Group in the Pentagon prepared a study that "analyzes critical phases of the assault by a USSR mechanized army (reinforced) on prepared defenses of the U.S. type corps deployed on a wide front on representative terrain in Western Germany." While all major weapons systems of the corps were being evaluated, attention was focused on atomic capabilities. The Joint Strategic Plans Committee concluded in January 1954 that the study was not ready to be shown to allied officers.[14]

Nuclear weapons would also affect the ability of the United States to move reinforcements and supplies to Europe by air and sea. At a Joint Chiefs of Staff (JCS) meeting on 14 May 1954, the question was raised "as to the feasibility of re-enforcing ground forces in Western Europe from North America during the first 30 days of a general war." Thirty days were deemed to be the critical time period, but it was unclear whether the United States and its allies had sufficient transport. Moreover, bomb damage to ports and radiation in general could seriously limit the capability to unload and distribute men and materiel.[15]

In 1954, new army operational doctrine was published that attempted to integrate the recent experience of the Korean War and the availability of atomic weapons for tactical purposes. Concern about the emphasis of the Eisenhower administration on nuclear deterrence was manifest. The manual left no doubt that only land forces could win wars. For that purpose they had to be supported by the other services, while "Army combat forces do not support the operations of any other component." There was also a stern warning not to neglect ground forces in peacetime: "Their [army, air force, and navy] maintenance in proper balance is essential if the objectives of national policy are to be attained." Limited wars against Soviet satellite states were possible, as demonstrated by the Korean War. Strategic mobility and the ability to fight on a conventional or atomic battlefield, therefore, were essential. Unlike the more enthusiastic advocates of atomic weapons, the authors of the manual reminded army officers that the final objective of war had to be political and that "victory alone as an aim of war cannot be justified, since in itself victory does not always assure the realization of national objectives. If the policy objectives are to be realized, policy and not interim expediency must govern the application of military power." Still, the manual stressed the quest for decisive victory on the battlefield through offensive action.[16]

The offensive depended on the massing of superior force at the point of decision and the effective application of firepower. To achieve numerical superiority in one sector of the battlefield, strength had to be conserved in other sectors and it might be necessary to accept a defensive position temporarily.[17] Once the assault force had been assembled, heavy artillery was expected to subdue the defenders and enable the ground attack to proceed at a deliberate pace. But the manual failed to prescribe proper employment of tactical atomic weapons. Instead, division commanders were left with the options to "consider atomic fires as additional firepower of large magnitude to complement other available fire support . . . [or] fit his maneuver plans to the use of atomic fires."[18] It was stated that atomic weapons were more suitable for attacks with deep objectives, but there was no mention of the potential negative effects of their use on the movement of friendly forces.[19] Commanders were reminded that it was critical to maintain a sufficient reserve to exploit a breakthrough and to commit that reserve decisively rather than piecemeal. Otherwise, the defenders might recover and force the attacker into a battle of attrition.[20]

The expected primary role of infantry was to reduce enemy strongpoints or to defend favorable ground or critical positions. Commanding officers had to keep in mind, however, that defense or conquest of terrain features were not ends in themselves.[21] The objective was to destroy the enemy force. Natural and man-made obstacles could help to achieve that by rendering the enemy more vulnerable to the application of heavy conventional or atomic firepower. Commanders had to prepare methodically for offensive action, albeit not quite as deliberately as had been the case prior to the Korean War.[22] They were asked to concentrate their main effort on a narrow front, with as much support as could be spared. In order to draw enemy forces away from the point of decision, they were also encouraged to develop diversionary attacks on wider fronts. Once the attack was under way, the commander was to influence the course of action mainly by committing his reserves and directing artillery fire.[23] There was little doubt that the army considered fire support to be decisive.[24]

Plans for the offensive were characterized by great hope that war of movement, for the purpose of applying overwhelming firepower, would break the cohesion of enemy forces. The defensive, on the other hand, was still treated as the stepchild of tactical and operational thought.[25] There was some movement toward more active defense, but positional defense was still regarded as more universally applicable, especially for infantry units. For the first time, the authors of operational doctrine recognized the mobile defense as a separate form of the defensive, particularly in situations and terrain that would allow the defender to maneuver and defend in depth.[26] In the positional defense, most available combat units would deploy well forward in order to deny the enemy critical terrain features. Within the operations branch of the U.S. Army, Europe (USAREUR), there was a great degree of skepticism about the applicability of static defensive tactics. Major Melbourne C. Chandler expected the tactical situation in Europe to be reminiscent of the initial phase of the Korean War, during which American forces tried to maintain cohesive defensive positions but were repeatedly attacked from the flanks and forced to abandon their positions. He concluded that Seventh Army needed to emphasize mobile defense and maneuver in depth.[27]

Mobile defense in current doctrine featured a small forward-deployed combat force with the bulk of the defenders in reserve for local counterattacks. Defense was conducted either to gain time while conditions more favorable to offensive actions would develop or as an economy of force while offensive operations were under way in other parts of the combat zone.[28] As in the offensive, the proper utilization of terrain was critical. To improve on natural obstacles, field fortifications and barriers might have to be built. In the balance, however, the enemy could only be contained on the defensive. Counterattack was necessary to destroy him.[29]

In preparing for the threat of atomic weapons, commanders had to "intensify appropriate individual and unit training," disperse their forces in order to avoid offering a "lucrative target," seek shelter, intercept enemy reconnaissance, and conduct counterintelligence operations. During mobile defensive operations, it was crucial to disperse the reserve to the greatest degree possible without impeding its ability to strike at the appropriate moment. Field Manual 100-5 described enemy atomic attacks "as a warning signal for mobile reserves to prepare for employment in counterattacks or in blocking roles," since the enemy would surely use atomic weapons in preparation for ground attacks. For higher command echelons, the "threat of enemy use of atomic requires that plans be prepared for replacement of complete tactical units."[30] The army was wary of the degree of destruction that enemy atomic fire could bring on its units, but army leaders were optimistic that properly concealed defensive positions, mobility, and initiative would be sufficient means to avoid offering concentrated and exposed targets.

National Strategy and the Army

The basic principle underlying the grand strategy of the United States during the Cold War was attrition. In the late 1940s, the Soviet Union had yet to recover its economic strength. The United States, on the other hand, had become the dominant economic power. Despite fear of Soviet military aggression, American leaders recognized that in protracted peaceful competition the more robust economic and social system of liberal capitalism would outlast the repressive authoritarianism of the Kremlin.[31] This was the belief of George Kennan, a policy analyst in the U.S. embassy in Moscow and subsequently director of the State Department's Policy Planning Staff, who first introduced the policy of containment. Containment of communism ultimately meant denial of any further Soviet, and after 1949 also Chinese, territorial advances, while waiting for the much inferior economic and social system of the dictatorships to crumble under the strains of the competition with the West.[32]

Soviet control of the rich resources and skilled manpower of Western Europe would have redressed the economic imbalance and thus compromised the assumptions of American grand strategy. Thus, the defense of Western Europe was not only desirable. It was necessary. The basis of defense was economic, political, and military cooperation. The Marshall Plan of 1947 furthered economic integration, both within Western Europe and of Europe with the United States. The resulting European Recovery Program became a symbol for the economic recovery of the western half of the continent, including the occupation zones in Germany that were soon to form the Federal Republic.[33] This course of action addressed two significant problems of the late 1940s: the danger of communist electoral victories, particularly in France and Italy, and the gradual filling of a power vacuum in Europe left by the destruction of Germany as a great power and by the weakening of France and Great Britain. Militarily, Western Europe felt vulnerable to Soviet attack despite the American monopoly of atomic weapons. On the other hand, the great manpower base, economic strength, and social and political cohesion of the United States and Western Europe favored long-term success. To achieve greater political ties and increase the defensive posture of the region, the United States abandoned a founding principle of its foreign policy and entered into a military alliance in peacetime.

The United States and its European allies formed the North Atlantic Treaty Organization (NATO) in 1949 as a step toward the creation of a more credible military deterrent to Soviet aggression. Prior to the outbreak of the Korean War, there had been little realistic hope of defending Western Europe with conventional forces. Atomic weapons were, as a consequence, by default the basis of deterrence. The Soviets were warned that aggression in Europe would result in serious repercussions, and American war plans of the period revolved around atomic attacks by the air force. But in the summer of 1949 the Soviet Union successfully tested its first atomic bomb. The loss of the atomic monopoly altered the theoretical underpinnings of deterrence. Until then, strategic deterrence had been theoretically plausible. In reality, the small size of the stockpile of atomic bombs in the United States precluded the liberal use of them that was suggested in several plans for war against the Soviets.[34] Hundreds of atomic bombs would have been needed to achieve the objectives, but only dozens were available. Ground defense as an element of deterrence became even more important once the Soviets had the means to launch atomic attacks of their own. Nonetheless, in spite of the need for much greater spending on the army, Secretary of Defense Louis Johnson intended to comply with the ceiling for the defense budget that President Truman had set at $13 billion.[35]

The State Department's Policy Planning Staff moved the process of conventional rearmament along, with the formulation of NSC-68 in the spring of 1950. Historian David Fautua argues that this critical document of U.S. Cold War strategy saved the army. But it is unlikely that the policy paper would have led to major changes in defense policy without the outbreak of the Korean War and the fear in the United States and Europe that this event signaled more aggressive tactics on the part of the Soviet Union.[36] In response to the war, both atomic and conventional rearmament were accelerated and NSC-68 became the blueprint for defense policy in the second term of the Truman administration. Paul Nitze, the primary author of the study, estimated a need for annual defense budgets of about $40 billion.[37] A National Security Council (NSC) estimate concurred. The U.S. military could achieve the objectives of NSC-68 with less than $30 billion per year, but $10 billion to $12 billion were needed for other defense-related expenditures, including military assistance to allies.[38] The justification for higher defense spending was that the atomic monopoly had been lost and with it the security that had been provided by strategic deterrence. In order to deter war, it would be necessary to provide sufficient military force to convince the Soviets that an attack would not succeed. To this end, both atomic weapons and conventional forces were needed, and the bulk of them would have to be prepared for the defense of Western Europe.[39]

NSC-68 projected the year of maximum danger of a Soviet attack to be 1954. Force planners had hoped to achieve their force objectives by that year, although, in the event, their realization had to be postponed until the end of 1955. The JCS recommended an army of twenty-one combat divisions.[40] The price tag for balanced atomic and conventional military forces was high. Because of the outbreak of the Korean War, the defense budget for 1951 soared from the initial appropriation of $13 billion to $48 billion. The army's share of the original budget was only $4 billion. This was raised to $19 billion, which exceeded the money spent on the other services. The Truman administration set the final 1952 defense budget at over $60 billion, with spending on the air force surpassing that spent on the army. But in absolute figures the army budget still increased to more than $21 billion. The administration lowered the 1953 defense budget to approximately $47 billion. The army received only $13 billion, even though the war in Korea continued. The air force received more than $20 billion in the same year, and the navy had almost caught up to the army. The final defense budget proposal of the Truman administration, for 1954, requested $41 billion.[41]

In 1951, the United States deployed four army divisions to augment the lone division stationed on occupation duty in Germany. This was largely a political signal, as even five American divisions had little hope of containing a determined Soviet offensive. The Soviet Union was credited by Western intelligence with 175 active divisions and the potential to mobilize 500 divisions. While there were questions about the combat readiness of these divisions, which were significantly smaller and less well supported than their American counterparts, the force was regarded as overwhelmingly superior.[42] Clearly, West Germany would have to be rearmed to take advantage of its military and economic potential and of the experience of veterans of World War II.[43] While there had been tentative private conversations before, it was the Korean War that made German rearmament possible.[44] Despite French reluctance, British concerns, and Soviet fear of a resurgent Germany, NATO governments decided in 1950 that a West Germany contribution to the defense of Western Europe was necessary. The French government proposed an integrated European force as a politically acceptable solution. This was ultimately a distraction that delayed West Germany's entry into NATO, but by late 1954 it was decided that twelve West German army divisions, a small air force, and a navy in the Baltic Sea should be created to augment the existing and planned forces of the Western alliance.[45]

For the time being, the U.S. military was guided by war plans that called for the defense of the Rhine River but prepared fallback positions on the Iberian and Italian peninsulas.[46] The anticipated worst cases projected the loss of all continental territory, as the result of a shortage of combat divisions. Sixty divisions at the outbreak of war were deemed necessary to defend the Rhine, but only twenty-six were available as of August 1949 and only two measured up to American standards.[47] An intelligence report of late 1949 put the combat effectiveness of French army divisions at 70 percent that of a U.S. Army division. The other continental European armies ranged between 40 and 60 percent.[48] There was hope that greater defense spending in the United States and an increased sense of urgency in Europe would create the means to defend the Rhine. This was expressed in REAPER, the first American war plan that was largely written against the backdrop of NSC-68.[49] In the event, European rearmament was slow and there were insufficient troops to achieve the goals set in REAPER. Even the U.S. Army planned to contribute only two infantry divisions in the first days of defensive operations.

Soviet superiority on the ground forced the allies to re-adopt a strategy of nuclear deterrence. The Eisenhower administration quickly abandoned the parallel buildup of conventional and nuclear forces that had been at the core of NSC-68 in favor of Massive Retaliation. British military and civilian leadership had called for nuclear deterrence even prior to Eisenhower's election.[50] Nevertheless, the British Chiefs of Staff, who had been very pessimistic about the defense of Europe, were more optimistic in late 1952. Plan FAIRFAX, the outline of intentions for the first half of 1953, was based on the assumption that both sides would use atomic weapons. The plan stated that "survival of the United Kingdom base and western Europe in the initial intense phase is of overriding importance." This included "the holding of the front in western Europe."[51] Such a feat could not be accomplished with conventional forces alone, but the development of atomic weapons that could be used for tactical purposes was on the brink of fruition.

Dwight D. Eisenhower entered the White House with the conviction that American and NATO strategy needed to be overhauled. The alliance required a military buildup in the short term, prompted by concerns generated by the Communist attack in Korea. NATO leaders had agreed to very ambitious force goals at the Lisbon summit in 1952, but Eisenhower doubted the ability or willingness of the signatories to deliver on their promise.[52] Ultimately, the American contribution to the buildup would necessitate a high level of defense spending that could slow or even reverse the growth of the U.S. economy. Eisenhower assumed that the Cold War would be a protracted struggle over decades, and he believed that the United States would prevail because of its much stronger economy. The deterrence of war, the security of the United States, and the defense of America's allies were essential, but they could not come at the price of weakening the American economy. Hence, the New Look defense policy was introduced in 1954 after thorough review. The basic premise was that U.S. overseas deployments had to be reduced if a suitable strategic reserve was to be built within a sustainable defense budget. Military leaders warned that this policy would endanger the credibility of the NATO alliance and weaken the deterrence posture of the United States.[53]

Eisenhower proposed a reduction of the armed services from 3.5 million officers and men to 2.5 million. In his view, a sufficient stockpile of atomic weapons and technologically advanced delivery vehicles were the most credible deterrent that could be afforded. The allies would have to carry a greater share of the burden of regional territorial defense. The United States would provide strategic and tactical nuclear weapons, maintain a strong mobilization base, and control the essential lines of maritime communication, but existing overseas force deployments could not be maintained indefinitely. In the long run, Eisenhower hoped to withdraw most American troops, leaving only a token ground force. The New Look also introduced covert operations behind enemy lines and in unstable states as a significant element of strategy. The policy was driven by fiscal and economic considerations. It would have been possible, from the vantage point of 1953, to build up nuclear and conventional forces to a degree that would have increased deterrence on all levels of war. But the price tag was too great, and Eisenhower was afraid that such a policy would corrupt American democracy by placing too much power into the hands of the federal government.[54]

Eisenhower and his advisers believed that Massive Retaliation, in spite of the risk of nuclear annihilation, was the price that had to be paid for prosperity, freedom, and security.[55] Nuclear deterrence was deemed more affordable and sustainable in the long run than the defense program outlined in NSC-68. But by placing such great emphasis on nuclear weapons, the Eisenhower administration greatly reduced its options of response to Soviet aggression. Should war break out despite the threat of Massive Retaliation, the only alternative to executing the strategy was to surrender Western Europe to the Soviets. NSC-162/2, the policy paper that defined the New Look as national security policy, emphasized diplomatic, political, economic, and covert measures to contain Soviet aggression or subversion. Militarily, airpower was the essential tool of deterrence. The role of the ground forces in national strategy was left undefined. It was suggested that the army might serve as an occupation force after nuclear weapons had driven away the defenders, and that it could maintain order at home if the United States itself ever came under nuclear attack. Major combat operations, however, were deemed unlikely. Consequently, the service was relegated to third place with respect to the allocation of defense funds.[56]

Initially, Eisenhower was more generous to the army than was Harry Truman. Eisenhower's 1954 defense budget was $5 billion less than Truman's $41 billion proposal for the same year. However, while the army was to receive only $12 billion under Truman, or just below 30 percent of the defense budget, Eisenhower asked Congress for an army budget of almost $13.7 billion. Congress appropriated a defense budget of $34.4 billion, with an army share of $13 billion. The air force received $11 billion and the navy $9.4 billion. But after the Korean War, the army's budget and its share in overall defense appropriations declined sharply. The 1955 defense budget was reduced by $5.5 billion. The army bore the brunt of the reduction and its budget dropped to $7.6 billion, about one quarter of overall defense appropriations. This reduction, and the fact that the army was the only service to receive less money in 1955 than in the previous year, contributed greatly to the subsequent drive to reform the service. By 1957, the fiscal situation had worsened. The army received $7.5 billion, less than half of the $16.5 billion granted to the air force. In fact, the air force received almost as much as army and navy ($10 billion) combined. Within three years, the army's share of the budget had declined from 38 percent to less than 22 percent.[57]

Eisenhower's defense budgets were within the range envisioned by NSC-68, but strong emphasis on airpower indicated a significant shift of emphasis. The air force budget more than tripled between 1950 and 1957 (from $5.2 billion to $16.5 billion). The army budget increased by $3.4 billion between 1950 and 1957 (from $4.1 billion to $7.5), but budgets prior to the Korean

War did not have to provide for atomic armament, while the post-1950 budgets had to cover the high acquisition costs of extensive atomic weapons procurement. The cost for research and development of rockets and missiles was added to conventional armaments, as well as personnel and operating costs. As a result, the army faced severe reductions in manpower and in the number of active divisions. In December 1953, the JCS approved new force objectives for 1957, which called for a reduction of the army from 1.5 million to one million men, in fourteen rather than twenty combat divisions.[58] The Army Staff accepted the guideline, based on the assumption that eight Japanese divisions would be created, that most American divisions in the Far East could be withdrawn, and that West German rearmament would commence quickly.[59]

Despite the agreement in principle, General Matthew B. Ridgway, the army chief of staff, had serious reservations about the new force goals. He considered it a grave mistake to cut the size of the army prior to the actual achievement of certain force levels by West Germany and Japan. Moreover, he questioned whether new weapon systems would indeed reduce the need for manpower. The great philosophical difference between Admiral Arthur Radford, the chairman of the JCS and outspoken proponent of the New Look, and Ridgway rested on their interpretations of economics and the role of military leadership. Radford viewed economic stability as a crucial element of military preparedness, whereas Ridgway thought that soldiers should stay out of economic questions and focus on sound military advice to their civilian superiors.[60] The question for Ridgway was how he could gain sufficient financial resources, within a limited defense budget, for an army of fourteen or even seventeen active divisions.[61]

Ridgway had been appointed army chief of staff in 1953, after one year as Supreme Allied Commander, Europe (SACEUR).[62] He was a decorated World War II airborne general and had commanded Eighth Army and the U.S./UN forces in Korea. But although Ridgway was a distinguished combat leader, he lacked the diplomatic sensibility required to execute his difficult task. To some extent this had already shown up during his tenure in Europe, which had produced thinly veiled complaints about "the American headquarters at Paris." He found that his time as chief of staff "was to be spent in the unhappy task of defending the U.S. Army from actions by my superiors which, to my mind, would weaken it, physically and spiritually."[63] Ridgway was caught between two fundamental pillars of his professional ethic: military professionalism and adherence to civilian control of the military.[64]

General Ridgway discovered that Secretary of Defense Charles Wilson was adamantly opposed to a large army. His relationship with Wilson was difficult from the beginning. He had hoped that Eisenhower would retain

Truman's last defense secretary, Robert Lovett, in the Pentagon because of Lovett's proven ability to see beyond partisan issues.[65] Instead, Eisenhower chose Wilson, a former General Motors director, whom Ridgway regarded as dangerously simplistic in his reliance on nuclear deterrence.[66] Ridgway did not reject the need for a capability of massive retaliation, but he noted that the capacity to respond flexibly was of no less importance. He doubted that strategic bombing could defeat the enemy. The Soviet Union and China were large landmasses and the attacking planes would have to penetrate deep into enemy airspace to find significant targets, which would be guarded by capable air defense systems. He warned that the destruction of the enemy's economy and will to fight by strategic bombing campaigns would take time, while Soviet ground forces might well be able to advance across Western Europe quickly. There was, moreover, a strong religious undertone in Ridgway's rejection of the objective of Massive Retaliation: "Such mass destruction is repugnant to the ideals of a Christian nation. It is incompatible with the basic aim of the free world in war, which is to win a just and enduring peace."[67]

The army chief of staff found it difficult to accept that a former army general—President Eisenhower—directed defense policy that was detrimental to the army.[68] Ridgway's relationship with Eisenhower had changed: "The old informal Ike and Matt relationship" was gone. He may still have been "Matt," but Eisenhower was now "Mr. President."[69] The apparent abandonment of his old service by the president contributed to an overall decline in morale that found its expression in a large number of resignations. Between 1954 and 1956, 132,000 junior grade officers quit the service. Major General Gerald Higgins prefaced his letter of retirement with the words that "if present trends continue the Army will soon become a service support agency for the other armed services." Contemporary articles in service journals indicated that many officers who stayed in the army agreed with Higgins. They felt a sharp decline in their status and resented the public admiration for bomber pilots and naval aviators. Among the most extreme responses was that of an army major, who questioned whether an institution that had become an auxiliary service should be retained in the first place. His ironic suggestion was unification of army and air force.[70]

Motions for a unified chief of staff to control all armed forces had in fact been army policy in the early 1950s. They were shelved for fear that such a position would be filled by an air force general and that it would accelerate the marginalization of the army into a civil defense force that would uphold law and order.[71] Maxwell Taylor, Ridgway's successor as chief of staff, made it clear that the army would not accept the civil defense mission as its primary raison d'être. He argued that deterrence offered an alternative mission, because conventional and even tactical nuclear deterrence relied heavily on the combat readiness of active forces, while the nuclear deterrent looked imposing at any rate. But this did not draw a positive response from the other service chiefs or the administration. General Lyman Lemnitzer summed up the feelings of many senior officers in the mid-1950s when he wrote: “Today it seems to me that the very survival of the Army . . . is at stake.”[72]

The Korean War had done little to improve the public's opinion of the army. The war had been fought in a remote geographic locale that was of no consequence to most Americans. Moreover, the war had not been won. Instead, a stalemate had developed that seemed to resemble the senseless slaughter of the western front in World War I. As in the 1920s and 1930s, common sense appeared to dictate that land forces were too slow and ponderous for the warfare of the twentieth century. Airpower, especially when equipped with atomic weapons, afforded a faster and cheaper way to fight. It also reduced the likelihood of American casualties. As long as the Soviet Union did not possess a large long-range bomber force or intercontinental missiles, the American homeland appeared safe. And once the Soviet Union acquired the means to strike at the United States, there seemed even less use for ground forces. The army itself devoted much energy and resources to developing antiaircraft defense systems. Such systems could of course be useful in the defense of Western Europe, but in the mid-1950s, even prior to the Sputnik shock of 1957, they were largely connected to considerations of nuclear war.

Ridgway argued that balanced conventional and atomic military forces were required to prevent war. Therefore, he was distressed about the permanent reduction of army expenditures and the force cuts that had been agreed upon in 1953. The goal of a one-million-man army remained in place, but Secretary Wilson moved up the schedule from 1957 to 1956. He suggested that this could be achieved by reducing all army units to 85 percent of their current personnel strength, coupled with the deactivation of some units. Ridgway objected on the grounds that a balanced and ready force was the best, and the only credible, deterrent. Tactical atomic weapons offered greater firepower, but there was little evidence to suggest that a combat unit so equipped would need fewer men. Ridgway also strongly advised against placing great expectations in the combat readiness of the reserve in the crucial opening months of war. Wilson's allies argued that West German troops would fill the gap, but the decision to allow rearmament had been delayed until 1954 and the subsequent military buildup proceeded at a slow pace.

General Ridgway was surprised to hear President Eisenhower claim in his 1954 State of the Union address that the defense budget proposal for 1955 had been unanimously recommended by the JCS.[73] He was particularly embittered by the political nature of the process. Ridgway emphasized that he believed in civilian control of the military and thus supported any decision once it had been made, but he also clarified that the unanimous agreement had in fact been about force objectives for 1957 and not the 1955 defense budget, as the president had claimed.[74]

There was in fact significant opposition to the proposed budget and personnel cuts. The secretary of the army, Robert Stevens, had informed Wilson in October 1953 that the ceilings mandated by economic considerations would force the army to eliminate two divisions and to withdraw four divisions from the Far East by June 1955. The planned general reserve force in the United States would have only one of eight intended divisions, one regimental combat team, and several antiaircraft batteries ready for combat.[75] Wilson himself had raised the possibility of withdrawing all but a token U.S. ground force from Europe in an NSC meeting on 1 October. The secretary of the treasury supported Wilson's position, but Eisenhower insisted that the presence of American forces boosted the morale of the allies and that any immediate force withdrawal would have a negative psychological effect. He hoped that the proposed personnel cuts could be achieved without further reduction in the number of combat units.[76]

Ridgway explained the army's situation in a congressional hearing in February 1954. He agreed to achieve the one-million-man army by June 1956.[77] As a result, there were to be sixteen combat and two training divisions. The combat divisions could be maintained only if a greater proportion of army personnel went into combat units. That would leave support and logistics units short of personnel, but it might be possible to employ civilian contractors for some positions. Ridgway questioned whether the smaller army could maintain sufficient forces for a major crisis outside of Europe. Greater strength and proficiency of the reserve may have helped to assure that the army could still fulfill its global requirements, but there was no provision for recalling discharged servicemen, who were technically part of the reserve, to their reserve or national guard divisions.

Ridgway also stated that the army had begun to modernize during the Korean War. He estimated that by 1956 all combat units would command the most advanced weapons technology. He noted that "the dollar value of our inventory of weapons, including artillery, tanks, and combat vehicles, will be more than double that of June 1954." In addition, major support equipment had been greatly enhanced and there was a greater number of army aircraft that were better integrated into strategy and tactics. But while Ridgway expressed pride in the improvement of technology, he fundamentally believed that wars were won by men, and not by machines.[78] Moreover, there was a significant downside to the modernization of weapon systems based on the tactical, operational, and even strategic conceptions of 1950. Most of the new equipment had been conceived for conventional warfare. Some of it might still be useful on an atomic battlefield, but most was already outdated. The army did not have enough money to replace it, and Congress, having just spent funds on the modernization of the army, would be loath to allocate more funds unless the army staff conceived a persuasive new concept for the nuclear age.

Muzzled by his superiors in the Pentagon and the White House, Ridgway defended publicly policies that he was convinced were dangerous.[79] The army was overextended geographically, and soldiers could soon expect to spend half of their time in the service overseas. But the real problem, as Ridgway saw it, lay in the mobilization potential. The active forces were good, albeit too small, but in both world wars the major bottleneck had been military and economic mobilization. Ridgway feared that the manpower of the reserve would be available but that the capacity of the army to absorb the reservists would be insufficient, from a standpoint of both training and equipment. Soldiers could be trained relatively quickly, but weapons and equipment would have to be produced with equal rapidity. Not only did the army not have sufficient stockpiles of critical materiel, but even more serious was the lack of an up-to-date industrial mobilization plan. In addition to the armed services of the United States, allied forces would also require American weapons and equipment should war break out.[80] The U.S. economy was strong, of course, and the industrial potential of the nation had overcome a similar predicament in World War II, but then there had been enough time to react. The next war could be decided within days.

Ridgway did not propose that increases in army budget, maintenance of a sufficient force, and greater stockpiles of weapons and equipment for the reserve should be taken from the other services. He did not concern himself with the overall defense budget. It was his job to give the president the best advice that he could. What disturbed him most was the unquestioning belief of many military officers, politicians, and private citizens in strategic bombing as the method to win the next war. Ridgway would have liked a more balanced air force that contained strong strategic and tactical capabilities, long-range transports for intercontinental deployment of army units, and specialized aircraft for employment on the battlefield. The army itself could have provided much of the latter, if only disputes with the air force over mission could be resolved. Atomic weapons had changed the timetable of war. Movement in force by sea was no longer fast enough. For the army, strategic airlift and close air support were the most essential aspects of the air force. In Korea, Ridgway had observed operations of the Marine Corps that were greatly aided by its possession of tactical aircraft of its own. Ideally, the army should have such support, or its equivalent, from the air force in the next war.[81]

In March 1955, the JCS sent new recommendations with respect to prospective force levels to the secretary of defense. The Joint Chiefs proposed a gradual reduction of the army to seventeen divisions by 1957 but also suggested that a thinning out of the divisions could prevent further cuts. Thirteen divisions should be mobile, one should be static, and three should be for training purposes. In that way, the army could be cut to one million officers and men by 1957. By June 1956, the army had indeed been reduced to eighteen divisions, ten regimental combat teams, and 133 antiaircraft battalions.[82] In 1961, at the end of the Eisenhower administration, there were fourteen army divisions, and only eleven were combat-ready.

In the mid-1950s, the army's role in national strategy remained poorly defined. General Ridgway thought it should be as "an Army trained, equipped, and organized to fight and win in an atomic war,"[83] but he had little time and energy to deal with the practical implications of this objective.[84] Naturally, the army studied the problem at hand. The form and shape of its combat elements would have to be radically different from the fighting forces in existence. Ridgway initiated medium-term studies, hoping to shape the army of the 1960s. His preferred solution was a streamlined force that would be built around small combined-arms battle groups that could fight semi-independently from the division. All but the heaviest forces should be transportable by air to assure transcontinental reinforcement and in-theater mobility. Fire and maneuver remained the basic tenets of land combat, but there would be little use for preconceived concepts of battle. Instead, commanders had to apply initiative and imagination. Atomic weapons would force the units to disperse on the defensive so as not to offer a lucrative target, but the capacity to reassemble swiftly to prevent enemy infiltration had to be retained. This would also allow for offensive capabilities in the exploitation of friendly atomic strikes.[85]

Ridgway interpreted the mission of the army as one of readiness and deterrence, but he questioned a strategy that could serve no political purpose if war broke out. Army generals also feared the implications of radiation and nuclear fallout for ground forces that were to occupy enemy territory.[86] War in general, and atomic war in particular, were not very likely, but the intelligence community expected that the Soviets would use the years from 1954 to 1957 to increase their atomic-weapons stockpile while maintaining their conventional superiority. Most likely, U.S. strategic deterrence would dissuade the Soviet leadership from starting a war in Central Europe. Nevertheless, it was possible that NATO's activities could be misread as aggressive and that the Soviet response might lead to general war. It was also possible that the Soviet Union or an Eastern European satellite state could trigger war inadvertently.[87]

Ridgway retired on 30 June 1955. Once more, he expressed his views to the secretary of defense. Wilson decreed that Ridgway's parting letter should not be made public, as it was quite critical of national defense policy. A copy was leaked to the *New York Times* shortly afterward, but it is unlikely that the general himself had a hand in this. The letter emphasized Soviet superiority in ground forces that would force the United States under its current policies to strike first with atomic weapons. To Ridgway, this was politically unwise and morally reprehensible. He believed that the United States should have the option of meeting conventional attack with conventional forces. Ridgway judged U.S. forces to be "inadequate in strength and improperly proportioned to meet [alliance] commitments." He cautioned that the atomic superiority of the United States was temporary. Furthermore, the United States was lacking the "mobile-ready" force called for by defense officials in public statements, and America's allies would be defeated in detail if the Soviets waged a global war.[88]

Beginning in January 1956, Ridgway's memoirs were published in the *Saturday Evening Post*. The general pulled few punches, sharply attacked Secretary Wilson, blamed a sinister conspiracy within the administration for having decided upon cuts in the army even prior to listening to Ridgway's advice, and stopped just short of openly attacking Eisenhower. The quick publication of such a critical account was in itself an unusual occurrence. The public reaction showed that the army had friends among the media. While conservative and isolationist papers, such as the *Washington Star*, the *Chicago Tribune*, and the *New York Sunday News*, predictably dismissed Ridgway's account and criticized the army's internationalism, more liberal papers, including the *New York Times*, the *Washington Post*, the *Atlanta Constitution*, and the *St. Louis Post-Dispatch* agreed with some or all of Ridgway's criticism. Army officers also gleefully observed the outpouring of support from Democrats in Congress.[89]

Maxwell Taylor, Ridgway's successor, publicly defended the administration against the charge of political meddling. But he championed a limited-war strategy and privately urged retired generals to help the army maintain the momentum created by Ridgway's retirement and memoirs. Specifically, Taylor believed it was necessary to educate the public about "the proper composition and strength of our defense forces. In the discussions of new weapons there is the danger that the continued indispensability of land forces may be obscured in visions of more attractive solutions to national security."[90] Taylor's efforts could not change the fact, however, that the army faced an official attitude best summarized in the words of the secretary of defense: "Maximize air power and minimize the foot soldier."[91] As a result, planning for the defense of Western Europe commenced in a climate that favored atomic over conventional weapons.

Strategy and Operations: The North Atlantic Alliance

When NATO was founded in 1949, leaders of the alliance endorsed deterrence as the primary military objective, but they also realized that measures to ensure the forward defense of NATO terrain had to be taken in case deterrence should fail.[92] Beyond statements of intent, however, there was very little military substance. In 1949, NATO was a political alliance, a diplomatic deterrent. In case of war, the atomic umbrella extended by the United States would have to protect Western Europe. There was little doubt, despite the unfavorable military balance of power on the ground, that the West would win a general war against the Soviets. But how exactly atomic weapons would stop the Soviet military offensive was left unsaid.

NATO members envisioned that a war would be fought in several phases. The first objective was to contain the Soviet offensive. Use of atomic weapons by both sides was expected. American planners believed that the determining factor in the medium term—that is between 1951 and 1954—was the economic weakness of the Soviet Union, which would preclude a protracted war. The main thrust of the Soviet offensive was expected to sweep through the North German plains to the English Channel and proceed due south into France and the Iberian Peninsula. Simultaneously, attacks would occur in Northern and Southern Europe. To counter the threat in Central Region (West Germany, France, and the Benelux countries), NATO envisioned forward defense in Germany. Ground forces were to buy time for the mobilization of the alliance's great military potential and protect air bases from which the strategic atomic counteroffensive was to be launched. NATO estimated that ninety divisions would be necessary by 1954 for this purpose.[93] Throughout the conflict it would be crucial to maintain open maritime traffic between Western Europe and North America.

When General Eisenhower took command in 1951 as the first NATO supreme commander, he found that his force consisted of only eighteen divisions. Upon mobilization, he could count on eleven additional divisions. This added up to only one-third of the ground force required to implement the alliance's medium-term defense plan for Central Europe, which called for the employment of fifty-four combat divisions.[94] The United States hoped to provide over two-thirds of its promised commitment by the end of the year. This was within reason, as the buildup plan called for only 40 percent of the 1954 objective forces by July 1951.[95] On the other hand, there was no strategic guidance beyond the medium-term defense plan, and operational planning was scant. Even placing a telephone call from Paris to Oslo, one of the future regional NATO headquarters, took 12 hours and could only be completed with Soviet assistance, as the lines ran through East Germany.[96]

Nevertheless, NATO intended to build ground forces that would serve as a credible deterrent, bolstered with the American atomic potential. At the very least, ground forces had to provide the shield behind which the atomic forces—NATO's sword for offensive operations deep into enemy territory—could be employed. This has become known as NATO's shield-and-sword strategy. The force goals that the political leaders of the NATO member states agreed upon in 1952 at Lisbon were an ambitious step toward establishing such a conventional shield. If they had been implemented, NATO would have increased its ground forces from twenty-five combat divisions to over forty-one active divisions in 1954, with the potential to mobilize forty-nine reserve divisions within one month. Eleven of these ninety divisions were supposed to be American and Canadian. Although the mechanics of West German rearmament had not yet been agreed upon, it was expected that the Germans would contribute eight active and four ready-reserve divisions. In reality, the Bundeswehr did not reach twelve divisions until well into the 1960s.[97]

The Lisbon agreement revealed a bias toward infantry. Including the reserve, there were thirty-eight infantry divisions and division equivalents in the firm commitments for 1952. This number would rise to sixty-two divisions in 1954, with twenty-one armored divisions to provide mobility and striking power.[98] That would have been a formidable fighting force and a very credible deterrent, but, unfortunately, NATO's actual strength never approached this level. The cost of the commitment was prohibitive. Aggregate defense expenditures of European NATO countries stood at $7.4 billion in 1951. To fulfill their commitment, the European allies would have had to quadruple defense spending.[99] NATO military commanders suspected that the force commitment was never intended to be more than the expression of an ideal and the basis for further negotiations.[100] Still, the military capability of NATO in the course of the 1950s began to reach levels that caused the Soviets to worry about the cost of victory. The main contributors to the increase in forces were the United States and West Germany.

Both General Ridgway and his successor, General Gruenther, had to concede that territorial defense would be difficult. Ridgway established a unified headquarters for Central Region and appointed French Marshal Alphonse Juin as commanding general of all allied land forces in the region.[101] Ridgway stressed that deterrence was the primary mission of NATO and that its success depended on "strong, balanced, combat-ready forces, capable of challenging aggression, or at least of rendering its success doubtful."[102] NATO began to consider the effect of atomic warfare on the tactics of land forces.[103] But the relaxation of the European military buildup led Ridgway to conclude at the end of his tenure in 1953 that "a full-scale Soviet attack within the near future would find Allied Command Europe critically weak to accomplish its present mission."[104] Allied Command Europe (ACE) comprised seventeen active divisions and a significant reserve. In addition, tactical atomic weapons had made their appearance in U.S. Seventh Army, in the form of the 280-mm atomic cannon. The political alliance had been able to generate a military force that could be seen as a significant deterrent. Central Europe could be contested, if not defended, if the European allies took decisive steps to maintain the momentum of the military buildup and if West German rearmament was permitted soon.[105]

General Gruenther urged that "atomic weapons must be used in a major war, by the Allies, without delay, and regardless of initial Soviet use thereof." He believed that only the combination of tactical atomic weapons and increased ground forces with a German contingent would give NATO the ability to arrest a Soviet offensive. In nuclear war, ground forces were needed for counterattacks and to retake lost ground. Gruenther expected that both sides would expend most of their atomic arsenal within the first thirty days of a war. If the initial atomic phase was not decisive, war was expected to drag on. The first thirty days were critical because it was the length of time that NATO required to complete its mobilization. In addition, NATO planners expected that the bombing campaign of the first month would interdict or at least impede the Soviet supply system, and thus disrupt their offensive operations for the first four months of the war.[106] The plans of Supreme Headquarters Allied Powers, Europe (SHAPE) included the preemptive use of atomic weapons. Indeed, the Eisenhower administration had advanced plans for the predelegation of nuclear weapons to SACEUR.[107]

No one should have been more opposed to an atomic strategy than the Germans. But the defense of Germany on the ground posed tremendous difficulties. This is borne out in SHAPE's general assessment of the defense of Western Europe. General Gruenther's staff listed several problems with executing operational plans. Operations east of the Rhine would be hard to support given that the ammunition dumps were west of the river and the lines of communication still stopped at its banks. Furthermore, West Germany lacked strong enough natural obstacles. To complicate matters, current U.S. Army doctrine emphasized concentration of force, which would lead to great vulnerability to atomic weapons because massed formations offered a better and more lucrative target than dispersed units. Finally, there still was no definite assurance when German troops would become available and how effective they would be. SHAPE planners added that they worried about "the psychological effect on civilian population and military personnel of mass use of atomic weapons, both in the battle area and rear areas, and in particular, its effect on the refugee problem."[108]

Still, NATO plans provided for forward defense east of the Rhine, as soon as a good number of West German divisions would become available. At the very least, the Soviet advance had to be delayed to assure mobilization of the ready reserve within the first thirty days of war. Minimum objective was to hold a line along the Rhine and IJssel rivers. Naturally, there was also the realization that the alliance could only expect a German defense contribution if it actually attempted to defend Germany. SHAPE hoped to deny to the Soviets the Rhine and Ruhr industrial areas as well as large parts of Bavaria, but planners warned that strong mobile self-contained forces were needed to hold significant portions of West Germany and add to the depth of allied defenses. In addition, operations between the Weser and Rhine rivers would have to be treated as one coherent battle.[109] Overall, Gruenther hoped to hold a line from the Weser to the Main River, running through Fulda, and extending to the Ludwig Canal.

U.S. European Command (USEUCOM) generated a secret operational concept that could not be revealed to the allies. It largely agreed with SHAPE planning, for thirty days of atomic war, but suggested that the Soviets might seek terms for a cease-fire. If they did not, subsequent operations would be far-reaching. American planners expected that a large-scale counteroffensive could begin four months into the war, after sufficient buildup of Western ground forces. This counteroffensive would move with two pincers out of Central and Southeastern Europe. A force of armored units, motorized assault units, and airborne units, aided by an amphibious landing near Rostock, was to sweep Germany clean of all Soviet troops in three months of hard fighting. From the Oder and Neisse rivers, NATO land forces would advance from Frankfurt/Oder to Warsaw by way of Posen and Kutno. USEUCOM planners predicted that allied forces would hold a line deep inside Poland running from Gdansk at the Baltic Sea to the Vistula River and on to Krakow at the end of the first year of the war. Finally, they were expected to reach the Polish-Soviet border area within one year of the beginning of the counteroffensive. Meanwhile, forces advancing from Greece, Northern Italy, and Turkey were supposed to sweep through Austria, take the Balkans, aided by the Yugoslavian army, and threaten the Ukraine and the Black Sea from Romania and Bessarabia.[110]

The practicality of the American plan was doubtful. General Gruenther, who served both as SACEUR and as U.S. Commander in Chief, Europe (USCINCEUR), insisted that he had to issue the plan according to the guidance of the U.S. Joint Strategic Capabilities Plan. Personally he saw little use for it. Gruenther concluded that "the concept of a large-scale, more or less conventional penetration of the heartland of Russia in a war extending over some two or more years is open to serious question from an economic as well as military standpoint." Gruenther doubted that the NATO partners would support the plan. He favored "limited advance to protect and recapture NATO territory pending further guidance as to the role of SACEUR's forces in concluding a general war." In response, the JCS clarified that no international approval of the plan should be sought at this point. First, the alliance would have to agree on a concept on how to defeat the Soviet Union rather than merely contain its armed forces. Until such a decision was made, "[U.S. and USEUCOM] planning must be accomplished on a unilateral basis."[111]

Bowing to reality, SHAPE was more concerned with defensive operations. Gruenther expected Soviet and satellite armies to attack Central Region with seventy divisions, twenty in tactical reserve, and sixty more to follow within thirty days of mobilization. Four Soviet and four Polish divisions were expected to attack from Mecklenburg into Jutland. Fifteen Soviet, thirteen Polish, and four East German divisions were expected to move across the Elbe River. In the area of operations of Seventh Army, ten Soviet, six Czech, and four East German divisions were expected to attack from Thuringia, through the Fulda Gap, and two Soviet and eight Czech divisions were expected to attack from Bohemia, and possibly Austria, into Bavaria.[112] Against that stood thirty-two active and twenty ready reserve divisions. However, SHAPE estimated that ten of its infantry divisions would not be effective.[113] This raised several questions. If the bulk of the attack was expected north of Kassel, why were the best NATO forces, the two corps of Seventh Army, deployed further south? Who was supposed to stop the onslaught of thirty-two Soviet and Eastern Bloc divisions at the Weser, or at least between the Weser, Rhine, and IJssel rivers? There were no German troops yet, and British Army of the Rhine (BAOR) was smaller and less effective than Seventh Army. The Belgian and Dutch troops in the area were of low quality, and Canada deployed only one brigade.

Of course, these were force projections for 1957. But at the end of 1954, SACEUR commanded only forty-four active divisions in all of Europe. Of these, eighteen were deployed in Central Region.[114] Even with eight German divisions, Gruenther would be nearly 20 percent short, and it was doubtful that four French divisions could disengage from the war in Algeria as promised. It was certainly unrealistic to list sixteen French divisions under command of SACEUR within one month of mobilization.[115] SHAPE planners clearly understood that known measures of force ratio were of little use since "the conduct of the land operations will be so different from the past, that it would be unwise to judge their course and eventual outcome solely by conventional standards and comparison with experiences from the last war." Tactics and operations were based primarily on the employment of tactical and strategic nuclear weapons. Ultimately, NATO operational planning rested on the assumption that atomic weapons could arrest a ground offensive because the ability of Soviet land forces to move and be supplied would be disrupted.[116]

SHAPE proposed new tactics and organization for ground forces on the atomic battlefield. Field Marshal Montgomery, the deputy SACEUR, lamented that Western armies were still designed for set-piece attacks of artillery and infantry supported by tanks, with a pace of 2.5 miles per hour. In this he saw very little evolution since World War I.[117] In contrast, General Gruenther advised his field commanders to conduct defensive operations from behind a natural or artificial obstacle, with the forward edge of the defensive zone based at the obstacle itself. In order to traverse the obstacle, the enemy would have to concentrate forces and would thus offer a suitable target for atomic weapons. It was not stated how the necessary dispersion of the defending forces at the time of atomic strikes could be assured without risk of losing control or ability to mass for counterattacks. The key operative terms were dispersion and mobility, somehow to be achieved by smaller formations, better control, rapid command decisions, and a small park of vehicles. Should the enemy still advance, mobile striking forces had to counterattack in order to prevent a breakout from the established bridgehead.[118]

Defense in depth was envisioned to begin with a covering force of one infantry battalion, which was to be supported by a battery of light artillery or mortars, one squadron of light armor, possibly a troop of combat engineers, and a small signal element. This task force would be deployed right at the obstacle. The reinforced battalion of less than 1,000 officers and men would have to defend a front of 12,000 to 15,000 yards. The strike force for the counterattack was to consist of two armored divisions, possibly organized in two groups. This task force would have two infantry battalions, two armored battalions or regiments, two artillery battalions or regiments, one engineer battalion or two companies, and one special signal unit. In addition, the corps was to hold one infantry division in reserve, whose regiments or battalions had to be capable of independent operations. Moreover, there was to be a central reserve, wherever possible, of one armored and two infantry divisions to repel infiltration that exceeded the strength of the striking force. Reserve formations were to defend vital installations in the rear area against deep penetration or airborne attacks.[119] In general, forces were to be prepared to operate as battalions or as brigades or as regiments. Divisional actions were to be conducted only in desperate situations.

U.S. Army doctrine was much more conventional at this point and ill suited to the tactics proposed by ACE. That is to say, even though atomic weapons were to be employed under the guidelines of Field Manual 100-5, the tactical deployment of forces had changed very little and the offensive remained the focal point of command thinking. SHAPE emphasized active defense, somewhat comparable to the mobile defense portions of U.S. Army doctrine. But there was no suggestion of linear positional defense in the NATO plans. This is surprising, given that political pressure from the West German administration forced SHAPE to consider forward defense to begin further east than militarily prudent, and in less suitable terrain. Like U.S. Army doctrine, NATO plans also featured counterattacks, but in General Gruenther's thinking it was atomic firepower that would kill the enemy, most effectively where he was on the attack and had been forced to mass troops to overcome defensive obstacles.

The difference in tactical and operational thinking between SHAPE and the army rested to a large degree on the political objectives of the respective manuals and plans. The army needed to prove that ground forces could still make a valuable, even decisive, contribution to war. NATO, on the other hand, was a defensive alliance. It was thus only natural for SHAPE to outline how defensive operations would lead to the defeat of the Soviet offensive. For the army to do the same would have played into the hands of advocates of Massive Retaliation, who saw airpower as the future of war. There is also a measure of doubt about the defense of Western Europe that can be inferred from army doctrine. Large-scale amphibious landings are discussed in great detail. In part, this may have stemmed from the recent history of the Normandy and Inchon operations, but it is surprising to see nearly as much discussion of such operations as of the defensive, particularly because landing forces would be exposed to attacks with nuclear weapons.[120] Finally, army doctrine was tailored toward an existing force while SHAPE attempted to initiate a transformation of the NATO armies. It has to be added, of course, that most of the thinking that went into army doctrine was shaped during the Korean War and before the formal adoption of the New Look and Massive Retaliation.

In essence, SHAPE suggested active defense in depth, with mobile units for counterattacks. But SHAPE planners failed to attune their suggested operations to political objectives. If pursued, their plans would have almost certainly led to the destruction of large parts of Western and Central Europe.[121] Exercise CARTE BLANCHE in June 1955, which featured large-scale use of air forces and atomic weapons, revealed that the loss of lives and destruction of territory in Germany would be horrific.[122] The British Chiefs of Staff seriously doubted the feasibility of forward defense as stated by SHAPE but recognized Gruenther's dilemma. For political reasons, SACEUR had to provide operational plans for forward defense. Moreover, he could not expect to receive additional divisions in the current political climate that favored nuclear deterrence. The British Chiefs of Staff doubted that NATO forces could arrest a Soviet offensive. Consequently, they suggested that the ground forces of the alliance should be considered as supplement to the nuclear deterrent rather than as a capable first line of defense.[123]

NATO evaluated the capabilities study for war occurring in 1957 and saw it as essentially sound. For the first time, SACEUR's plan outlined a strategy based on unrestricted use of atomic weapons.[124] SHAPE expected that the intensive atomic exchange in the first month of the war would deny Soviet reinforcements from moving west, that the enemy tactical air force could be grounded, and that enemy logistics would be disrupted severely if not severed altogether. The notion that NATO might employ atomic weapons first raised questions in the minds of the political leaders of the alliance, but given the lack of sufficient forces for a conventional defense there was tacit agreement on its necessity. The organizational and tactical changes suggested by SACEUR were scrutinized more closely by NATO military committees, which called for further study: "For example, the organization, disposition, depth, and strength of the sample 'yardstick' must be examined thoroughly in light of enemy mass infiltration tactics over a broad front." The imminent German defense contribution, coupled with the tactical use of atomic weapons, offered the prospect of the Rhine River being held and suggested that forward defense in West Germany could be attempted. The NATO Standing Group of the Military Committee concluded that ACE had presented a proposal that provided a credible deterrent and allowed for realistic operational defense while the strategic offensive would ensure that the West won the war.[125]

The timetable of the German military buildup was critical, yet it remained uncertain. Officially, NATO expected all twelve German divisions to be committed to ACE by 1957. General Gruenther, however, feared that German forces might not be effective until the end of the decade. Still, in Gruenther's own words,

> we should defend with a forward strategy. . . . We will be able to implement such a strategy when we have a German contribution. We are trying to create a force with sufficient strength, land and air, to create a shield which will force an enemy to concentrate as he comes against it. As he concentrates, he becomes very vulnerable to atomic weapons.[126]

But whether forward defense could be achieved in 1957, as originally intended, had been put into doubt. The Standing Group no longer believed that it was possible unless the NATO partners increased their defense contributions. The delayed buildup of the Bundeswehr had serious consequences for NATO strategy. In addition, the committee complained that military forces of other NATO members had been temporarily redeployed, obviously a reference to French forces in Algeria.[127] Later in 1955, the Military Committee once more defended the crucial importance of forward defense to NATO strategy, but it was quite clear that the forces at hand did not correspond with the commitments for 1956.[128]

The United States meanwhile was in the midst of reappraising its policy for the defense of Western Europe in the wake of the rejection of the European Defense Community (EDC) by the French.[129] Military officers were aware that a choice between Germany and France might be looming.[130] The army leadership did not think that the alliance was politically or militarily feasible without both countries, but navy and air force indicated that they would be comfortable with relying on West Germany as the primary continental European defense partner even if that meant that France would withdraw from the alliance.[131] In any case, German entry into NATO would allow the implementation of SACEUR's forward-defense concept. Of course, NATO infrastructure and force dispositions had been "based on the assumption that German military forces, under EDC or otherwise, would be available to lend the essential strength to a forward strategy, so vital to a successful defense of Western Europe."[132] The JCS concluded that basic U.S. defense policy toward Western Europe remained valid and that West German territory should be defended.

With regard to German rearmament, the Joint Chiefs recommended retaining the force objective of the EDC proposal, which foresaw eight infantry and four armored divisions. The JCS supported a German proposal to mechanize two of the infantry divisions. This was thought suitable "in view of the probable tactical employment of the German Army."[133] In addition, Germany was to create four corps and one field army headquarters. It was believed that this could be achieved within two years, but the Joint Chiefs suspected that another six months might have to be granted in addition.[134] The Joint Chiefs assumed that this force could later be increased. For the rearmament period, the Germans could rely on the U.S.-type field army and modified tables of organization and equipment.[135] In the event, the Bundeswehr needed the better part of a decade to create all twelve of its divisions, manpower goals were drastically reduced by the late 1950s, and there was no intention to create additional active divisions at a later point. The field army was also never created. Instead, two German corps were integrated into Seventh Army—one served in Northern Army Group (NORTHAG) and one under Allied Forces, Northern Europe, in Schleswig-Holstein.

In November 1954, NATO adopted the strategy of Massive Retaliation. Central Europe was indefensible on the ground with the forces available or likely to become available. It remained crucial to convince the Soviets that quick victory in Europe was impossible. To this end, and in line with the position of the Eisenhower administration in Washington, NATO certified the immediate use of atomic weapons even if the Soviets attacked with conventional forces. The initial phase of war, intended to blunt and arrest the Soviet offensive, rested on good intelligence of Soviet capabilities, intentions, and operations, on the secure operations of NATO air forces from European bases, on defensive and retaliatory use of atomic weapons, and on the development of highly trained and mobile ground forces, deployed in depth and ready to confront the Soviets without delay. The ground forces also had to have atomic capability, defined as "the ability to integrate the delivery of atomic weapons with the delivery of present type weapons. This involves the integration of intelligence and communications systems, and a common tactical doctrine."[136]

Reliance on nuclear deterrence did not absolve the allies from providing ground forces. Lauris Norstad, a U.S. Air Force general serving as deputy SACEUR for air operations, explained the function of the shield under Massive Retaliation:

> In contributing to the deterrent, our forces in being, adjacent to our frontiers, impose upon the Soviets the critical decision of initiating hostilities by employing armed forces and carrying out any active aggression against ACE. This decision to use force, involving as it does consideration of the real threat of instant, large-scale atomic retaliation, could not be taken except as a last resort. Regardless of the advantages to be gained by an act of aggression, the price would be the destruction of Russia.[137]

MC 48, NATO's strategic planning paper of November 1954, called for fifty-eight active combat divisions. The firm commitments for 1955 stood at forty-four divisions and those for 1956 at forty-one.[138] Part of the discrepancy stemmed from the inclusion of twelve German divisions in the MC 48 force objectives. But these could not yet be counted toward the firm commitments, and German rearmament proceeded much slower than expected. When the Military Committee approved MC 70 in 1958, a revised strategic guidance report, force requirements were increased. Active-force objectives and the forces of the first and second echelon of reinforcements should total over eighty divisions for 1958 and almost ninety by 1963. All twelve German divisions were to be committed to SACEUR by 1961.[139] Once again, this was a force objective that could be met by the United States but not by its European allies.

NATO struggled with the implementation of forward defense throughout the 1950s. The forward-defense line only reached the intra-German border in 1963. But the U.S. Army discovered that the deterrent value of forward defense in Germany afforded the best argument for the utility of ground forces in the atomic age. Upon General Ridgway's retirement in 1955, General Maxwell Taylor set about to transform the army and alter national strategy.

2

Atomic Weapons and Limited War

In 1956, the Army Staff introduced a new divisional structure for operations on conventional and nuclear battlefields. The existing divisions were triangular—that is, they consisted of three regiments or regimental combat teams. The new divisions were made up of five battle groups and were thus called pentagonal. They were to be equipped with atomic weapons. The common assessment of these pentomic divisions is that they were hastily designed, prematurely adopted, and operationally impracticable. Most scholars have taken the view that the reorganization constituted the army's attempt to adjust its combat organization and tactics to nuclear war.[1] Others have pointed out that the reorganization was driven by budgetary as well as technological considerations.[2] Such concerns indeed influenced the thinking of General Maxwell Taylor, the army chief of staff. But Taylor had a more radical objective. He intended to transform the army into a modern, dual-capable force, armed with conventional and atomic weapons. Taylor defined the army's mission to be the prevention of war in Central Europe. If war broke out, it would be the army's objective to prevent escalation from limited to all-out nuclear war. In creating a combat force that could fulfill this mission, Taylor intended to shift the emphasis of national strategy from reliance on nuclear deterrence to war-fighting based on flexible and proportional response.

Designing the Atomic Army

The first practical steps toward redesigned ground forces for the atomic age were taken overseas. General Maxwell Taylor, in command of Eighth U.S. Army in Korea, advised the South Korean ground forces to experiment with a division that had five instead of three major combat elements in order to facilitate greater dispersion and flexibility on the battlefield.[3] General James Gavin, who, like Taylor, had commanded airborne forces in World War II, also considered a new force structure. He had been an innovator in the field of airborne operations during World War II, and after the war had become interested in rocket and missile technology as well as tactical applications of atomic weapons.[4] In 1951 and 1952, Gavin took part in the joint-service VISTA project, a study of future atomic ground and air warfare in Europe.[5] In December 1952, he took command of U.S. VII Corps in Germany. There, he presided over map exercises and maneuvers, during which a new structure for combat divisions was developed. Gavin concluded that existing infantry and airborne divisions could not function in atomic war. The armored division, on the other hand, seemed adaptable, due to its preexisting task-force structure, the combat commands.[6]

Gavin and his staff proposed a fundamental reorganization of combat elements of the army for nuclear war. Cavalry units, forward deployed at the intra-German border, needed to possess tactical airmobility. Gavin argued that helicopters offered a proven method of providing airmobility for infantry divisions. Missiles could replace conventional artillery, thus increasing range and adding tactical atomic capability to the division where necessary. As the depth of the battlefield increased, communications would become even more important than ever. Gavin suggested that battalions and regiments now needed the kind of equipment that regiments and divisions had had in their inventories during World War II. Moreover, Gavin argued that linear defense, with its fixed lines of communications, was no longer appropriate. The atomic battlefield would be much deeper, wider, and less structured than the one of World War II; it would be "amorphous." Infantry divisions for such an environment would have to be built around battle groups that were smaller than the existing regimental combat teams. These were to be dispersed widely in order to present less of a target to atomic attacks.[7] But Gavin concluded that the new divisions had to be larger than the triangular ones.[8] Upon concluding his command tenure in Germany, General Gavin became assistant chief of staff for operations.

The army chief of staff, General Matthew B. Ridgway, agreed that the combat division should be built on semi-independent combined-arms battle groups that could move by air. Ridgway explained to General Gruenther:

> I am . . . very much concerned with our readiness to air move intra-theater and inter-theater forces. Specifically, I envision our being confronted with problems of considerable magnitude in the event that a major portion of the European Peninsula falls to the enemy. The ability to move across large bodies of water and reestablish a lodgment in Europe through the combined use of special weapons and airborne assault forces may well be decisive.[9]

Ridgway endorsed the concept of the battle group because he recognized that atomic weapons made essential the ability to disperse rapidly, but he insisted that it was also necessary to be able to mass quickly to strike at enemy formations. Firepower would be decisive in future battles, but maneuver remained crucial in order to concentrate all available forces at the point of decision.

General Ridgway initiated studies on how to organize the combat elements of the army for the 1960s. Pressure from the Defense Department directed the outcome to favor smaller combat units, even though all available evidence pointed to the need to increase the size of the division. Ridgway nevertheless believed that increased mobility, greater flexibility, and a decline in vulnerability to atomic attacks could be achieved if several basic tenets were adhered to in future reorganizations of the division. Personnel cuts necessitated a better ratio of combat to support manpower and units. Combat units needed to gain mobility and flexibility. Technological improvements were to be the backbone of reorganization. Overall, the army had to improve its capability for protracted war. Tactical doctrine would have to be reconsidered accordingly. Ridgway thought that reorganization should not be delayed beyond 1956.[10]

The schedule was tight, since many of the guidelines, as well as the shift in emphasis to smaller units, were only announced in April 1954. By the fall, Army Field Forces, supported by the Command and General Staff College, presented plans for the Atomic Field Army (ATFA-1). The proposal had a great degree of built-in flexibility. Infantry divisions were to resemble current armored divisions in that they would gain task force organizations that could respond to changing situations. ATFA-1 suggested a building-block structure, based on three combat command headquarters, maneuver battalions, and support units. Every infantry division should have seven infantry battalions, as well as tank, signal, and engineer battalions and a support command, which included medical, maintenance, supply, transport, and service companies. Division artillery would be one 4.2-inch mortar battalion, capable of firing both conventional and atomic ammunition, and two towed 105-mm howitzer battalions. ATFA-1 also suggested that staffs could be reduced and administrative functions could be lessened by moving tasks from division headquarters to battalion and support command. Proposed personnel strength was 13,500 officers and men, a reduction of almost 4,000. Little change was deemed necessary for the armored division, but it would still be possible to eliminate over 2,500 personnel slots and present a leaner division of 12,000 officers and men. Moreover, all aircraft generic to combat divisions were to be gathered in an aviation company, attached to the divisional headquarters battalion. Command over atomic weapons rested with the field army commander rather than the commanding generals of the divisions.[11]

In February 1955, 3rd Infantry Division and 1st Armored Division tested ATFA-1 in exercises FOLLOW ME and BLUE BOLT. The results were negative. While the infantry division stood to gain flexibility from adding combat commands, it was not suitable for sustained combat. The likely conditions of nuclear war were such as to require more manpower and an increase particularly in reconnaissance functions, because frontages would be extended and the battlefield would be deep. The division also lacked antitank and artillery weapons. The personnel reduction compromised the performance of important staff functions, and staffs at division, combat command, and battalion levels were simply too small. BLUE BOLT proved inconclusive as to whether the new armored division would be less vulnerable to atomic attacks. Renewed testing in SAGEBRUSH, a joint army and air force exercise in November and December 1955, showed that the infantry division was salvageable if its staff was increased and an infantry battalion was added. All told, the strength of the infantry division had increased to 17,027 officers and men, only slightly less than the pre–ATFA-1 division. The personnel strength of the suggested armored division stood at 13,971.[12]

Such an increase ran counter to the basic principles of defense policy in the Eisenhower years, and the army would have invited severe criticism if it had endorsed the concept. From an operational standpoint, the situation was even worse. Major General George Lynch, who had commanded 3rd Infantry Division during SAGEBRUSH, concluded that the improvements over the traditional division were not significant enough to justify the changes, with the possible exception of more serviceable logistics. He argued that the existing regimental combat teams had greater inherent flexibility than the proposed combat commands. Lynch suggested retaining the structure of the old infantry division and increasing its personnel to 21,678 officers and men. Major General Robert Howze, commander of 1st Armored Division, found the suggested armored division generally acceptable, albeit with minor changes. Howze did not specify the personnel increase that his alterations would require, but the commanding general of Fourth Army, John Collier, estimated that the armored division needed 15,819 officers and men.[13]

During this period of testing and debate, Army Field Forces had been disbanded and replaced by Continental Army Command (CONARC). In 1956, CONARC circulated tables of organization for ATFA divisions. The infantry division remained controversial, but CONARC had reinstated the three regiments and stressed improvements made in flexibility and protection against atomic attack. It was to have 17,460 officers and men, an increase of eight personnel slots over the old infantry division.[14] As envisioned by General Ridgway in 1954, ATFA could have been a fundamental transformation, but by 1956 the study had been altered to a more conservative reform proposal and exercises had revealed that tactical atomic war could not be simulated.[15] The army still lacked a clear understanding of the effects of atomic weapons on command and control of large formations. In April 1956, army chief of staff General Taylor rejected ATFA-1. For political reasons, the army needed smaller divisions with integrated atomic weapons.

In June, Taylor outlined his conception of future army organization to the service chiefs and leaders of the defense establishment. He argued that the proper combination of firepower, movement, and skilled personnel would determine the success of ground forces. Heavy firepower would come mainly from rockets and guided missiles. But the launchers had to be protected and they had to be maneuvered to critical points on the battlefield. Mobility was also significant, because rapid dispersion and concentration of force would be the most important tactical principle on the atomic battlefield. Taylor stated that lightweight equipment, thin-skinned troop and weapon carriers, and army aviation were crucial to achieve greater tactical mobility. He pleaded that the army needed capable and intelligent personnel, attempting to reverse a trend that led most young men to consider the more glamorous options in the air force and navy, generally leaving the army with the bottom of the recruitment pool. Taylor concluded that limited regional aggression would pose the greatest military threat once the Soviet Union had achieved nuclear parity with the United States.[16]

To some, the immediate application of Taylor's proposal seemed unlikely. Willard G. Wyman, commanding general of CONARC, noted in July, three months after Taylor had rejected ATFA, that "the army, of late, has been criticized for failing to organize its forces to fit existing developments of weapons." He reassured his audience, however, that the results of recent maneuvers in which the ATFA concept had been tested were being evaluated. He cautioned that "whatever the outcome, reorganization cannot take place over night." Wyman considered the possibility of modernizing existing units, such as platoons, companies, and battalions.[17]

Taylor disagreed. He found that a doctrinal and organizational study of the Army War College, which had been undertaken in response to General Ridgway's request of November 1954, offered a basis for immediate reorganization. "Doctrinal and Organizational Concepts for Atomic-Nonatomic Army during the Period 1960–1970," commonly referred to as the PENTANA study, provided a broad perspective on sustained ground operations in Europe. It called for fully air-transportable divisions. There should be no more infantry, armor, or airborne divisions, but instead one standard combat division built upon five battle groups that were self-sufficient and contained their own artillery. The new division was set at only 8,600 officers and men. Tactical atomic weapons were to be controlled at the division level. There was immediate widespread criticism in the army of the PENTANA study, ranging from not enough armor to insufficient conventional artillery and doubts about staying power.[18]

While Taylor liked the dynamic and forward-looking PENTANA concept because it could be portrayed to the civilian leadership as a lean combat division for the nuclear age, he did not find that the universal division was entirely practical.[19] More important, Taylor did not believe that dual capability could be achieved. The Army Staff resolved to develop separate proposals for atomic and nonatomic armies. Once completed, the differences could be adjudicated under the guidelines of the PENTANA study. Taylor concurred but feared that such a force could be created only on paper unless the army's budget was significantly increased.[20] He nevertheless approved the concept on 1 June 1956 as a long-term objective.[21]

Even prior to approving the PENTANA study, Taylor had called for a reorganized airborne division of 10,000 to 12,000 officers and men, with five battle groups and tactical atomic weapons.[22] Expanding the self-contained combat elements from three to five was perceived necessary in order to carry out a new approach to area defense. Each battle group was to have the capability to fight in all directions, thus creating islands that would cause the enemy to amass forces and present targets for atomic weapons.[23] Questions remained, however, as to whether the commander of a division could effectively control five battle groups and the battle group commander five companies. Colonel James Shepherd, then teaching at the Command and General Staff College, argued that even the attachment of a tank company to a battle group would overtax the commander.[24] Taylor pressed ahead despite such criticism, mostly because he felt that making tactical atomic weapons organic to the division would lead to more intense consideration of their proper employment, which was still largely unexplored.[25] Contemporary critics charged that the pentomic division was at least in part a public-relations stunt. Taylor himself coined the term "pentomic," combining the pentagonal structure and atomic armaments, because the army needed to appear less stodgy and more in tune with advances in cutting-edge technology.[26]

In August 1956, CONARC called for an airborne division of 11,500 officers and men, a personnel decrease of 5,600 from the triangular airborne division. It consisted of five battle groups with five infantry companies apiece. Each battle group also had a mortar battery and a headquarters and service company. Aviation and reconnaissance companies, along with headquarters and service companies, as well as a signal battalion and combat engineers, were attached to the division. Division artillery fielded twenty-five 105-mm howitzers and four Honest John rocket launchers. But conventional firepower was limited by the desire to transport the entire division by air. This meant that the division did not have any 155-mm howitzers. The Honest Johns also could not be transported by air in the theater of operations, but they offered the only way to incorporate atomic capability at the division level. The new airborne division needed only half of the airlift required to move the triangular division.[27] One army captain summed up the basic idea: "Concentrate to fight—disperse to live."[28]

Dispersion, mobility, and flexibility became the central features of the combat division in the nuclear age. PENTANA was the long-term model, but in the short term, the pentomic division was introduced as a five-year experiment to be conducted in the field. The risk was obvious. The experimentation period was short—most reorganizations need more time to develop—especially given that much of the equipment for more mobile land forces, such as armored personnel carriers (APCs), better tanks, more reliable helicopters, and crucial communication systems, were not yet available.[29] The end of the experimentation period would, however, coincide with the termination of the expected second term of the Eisenhower administration. It is possible that Taylor had already gauged the need to reform the reorganized division at the beginning of the next decade and was hoping for a more congenial strategic and political environment.

Unlike ATFA, the Reorganization of the Airborne Division (ROTAD) was not tested in a large-scale field exercise. Instead, the capabilities of individual units of the division were evaluated separately by elements of the 101st Airborne Division. The result was sobering. Although the division was suitable for airborne assaults of short duration, there were questions about the artillery. The lighter field guns that could be moved by air transport suffered from short range and lack of lethality. The division leadership thus requested that 155-mm howitzers should be returned to the division, except for parachute assaults. Also, the logistics of the division were deemed less effective than those of the old triangular formation. Manpower, logistics capacity, and support elements had dropped to a level where garrison duty and the maintenance of combat readiness were mutually exclusive. The test director proposed a 10 percent increase in personnel strength to the base division and a garrison complement at the home station. He also noted that commanding officers of rifle companies, mortar batteries, and howitzer batteries would bear much greater responsibility and had to be capable of independent actions. CONARC and the Army Staff, unwilling to sacrifice air-transportability of the direct support guns, rejected the suggested changes in artillery. ROTAD was finally adopted in the summer of 1958, with an increase in mortar strength but without heavy howitzers or additional manpower.[30]

In the meantime, Taylor and CONARC had set their sights on the reorganization of the infantry division along the lines of the pentomic concept. In December 1956, CONARC presented organization and equipment charts for the Reorganization of the Current Infantry Division (ROCID). Taylor had provided guidelines that included five battle groups, conventional and atomic artillery organic to the division, tank, signal, and engineer battalions, and a reconnaissance squadron that could move on the ground and in the air. CONARC found that it was possible to provide the division with the necessary and requested elements, but only if it was slightly larger than Taylor had intended. CONARC proposed an infantry division of 13,700 officers and men. It had five infantry battle groups, one tank battalion, a light artillery battalion with thirty 105-mm howitzers, and a heavy and atomic artillery battalion with two Honest John rocket launchers, four heavy 8-inch howitzers, and twelve 155-mm howitzers.[31] But not all infantry battle groups in the U.S. Army, Europe (USAREUR) received a fifth rifle company prior to June 1960.[32]

The armored division was left largely intact. The tables of organization and equipment for the Reorganization of the Current Armored Division (ROCAD) also were published in December 1956. ROCAD had more conventional artillery than the infantry division but did not have Honest John rocket launchers and relied entirely on four self-propelled 8-inch howitzers for atomic fire support. CONARC had added a reconnaissance and surveillance platoon to the reconnaissance battalion, supported by additional aircraft in the aviation company. Despite the initial assumption that the number of vehicles should be reduced, due to their vulnerability to nuclear attacks, ROCAD did not actually see such a reduction, mainly because the new division required more transportation resources than the old armored division. ROCAD totaled 14,617 officers and men, 655 more than the proposed ATFA-1 armored division. Its armor strength rested on fifty-four light-gun tanks (M41 Walker Bulldogs) and 324 medium-gun tanks (M47 and M48 Pattons). The latter were grouped in four tank battalions, while the light-gun tanks were utilized in supporting functions.[33] Armored divisions retained armored infantry units, but all M59 APCs were centralized in a transportation unit. While APCs could be assigned to infantry units, only one infantry battle group at a time could be mechanized, a shortage that also affected ROCID. Moreover, only one additional battle group could be motorized if the divisions used all of the light trucks of the transportation battalion. This left the infantry component of three battle groups without armor or trucks.[34]

The pentomic reorganization was far-reaching, and Taylor faced opposition both inside and outside of the army. In the fall of 1956, the Army Staff prepared a demonstration to showcase the capability of the atomic army. It was intended to show government officials how the army would exploit the firepower of tactical nuclear weapons, survive Soviet nuclear strikes, and regain the initiative. General Taylor had ordered the demonstration because "the advent of modern weapons of the massive retaliation variety has created a growing feeling within the government that sizeable Army forces may no longer be required."[35] Fort Benning, Georgia, was the preferred location for the demonstration because there it was possible to showcase an entire battle group. The only problem was that the atomic army was not ready: "It will be necessary for the Army to develop fully before the demonstration date those concepts of the tactical employment of participating troops and equipment which are not yet firmly established."[36]

Internal criticism centered on the battle group, which replaced the traditional battalions and regiments. Proponents of the regimental system were particularly outspoken. The deputy chief of staff for personnel argued that regiments were crucial for the esprit de corps of the entire army.[37] He conceded that questions of tactics were outside of his responsibility, but he suggested that the regiment be kept as an administrative unit. Combat units could then be assembled into battle groups as the situation warranted. He estimated that 185 regular regiments would form the core of the army.[38] This was derived from the 540 active combat battalions in the army, consisting of 159 field artillery, 155 antiaircraft artillery, 123 infantry, 57 armor, 23 armored infantry, and 23 airborne battalions.[39] Furthermore, regiments would make mobilization easier and ensure greater coherence in the reserve. Taylor did not find the objections convincing, but in 1957 he accepted the Combat Arms Regimental System (CARS), which designated distinguished regiments as administrative parent units of battle groups, battalions, and companies.[40]

To persuade doubters, Taylor emphasized the need for dual capability. He pointed out that the pentomic division could fight on an atomic battlefield if strategic deterrence failed. Simultaneously, the new division ensured that the army could also fight in a conventional environment. More importantly, the new division was innovative and would advertise a modern army to the public. Taylor did not stress this point at the time, but in his memoirs he pointed out that the conventional arms needed for limited war lacked glamour. He claims that Defense Secretary Wilson once returned an army budget proposal that included mainly rifles, machine guns, trucks, and "unsophisticated aircraft," directing him "to substitute requests for 'newfangled' items with public appeal instead of the prosaic accoutrements of the foot soldier." Taylor explained that nuclear weapons "were the going thing and, by including some in the division armament, the Army staked out its claim to a share in the nuclear arsenal."[41]

For public consumption, emphasis in re-equipment was put on atomic and tactical nuclear weapons, surface-to-surface missiles such as the Corporal or Redstone, intermediate-range ballistic missiles (IRBMs) such as the Jupiter, and rockets for close-range nuclear combat such as the Honest John, the Little John, and the Davy Crockett.[42] In addition to tactical nuclear weapons, pentomic divisions also needed new conventional weaponry and equipment. An entire host of small arms, the M1 rifle, the carbine, the submachine gun, and the Browning automatic rifle, were to be replaced by the M14 rifle, which fired 7.62-caliber rounds and could be set to either semiautomatic or automatic firing modes. In addition, the M60, a new machine gun, also using 7.62-mm ammunition, was to be substituted for Browning .30-caliber light and heavy machine guns. In August 1957, Taylor approved a program intended to replace light, medium, and heavy tanks with a main battle tank and an airborne assault vehicle.[43] The M113 APC, an air-transportable vehicle, also was to become available.[44] From the perspective of procuring improved weaponry and equipment, the pentomic division proved useful, but most of the new conventional weapons did not reach U.S. forces in Europe before the height of the Berlin Crisis in 1961 and after the termination of the pentomic division had already been announced.[45]

Tactical changes brought about by the reorganization of the combat divisions were not elevated to the level of doctrine.[46] Army doctrine thus still emphasized infantry attacks at deliberate pace, supported by tanks and heavy artillery. Andrew Bacevich, a retired army officer and historian, has shown that atomic weapons deepened the army's belief in the application of firepower. Atomic artillery would blast a hole in the enemy's line of defense, enable ground forces to achieve a breakthrough, and afford armored and motorized formations the opportunity for maneuver. More important, atomic fire would shake the enemy so thoroughly that maneuvering units would encounter little resistance in their task to disrupt command, control, communications, and intelligence. But this was a theoretical conception of the effect of atomic weapons rather than tactical doctrine for their employment. Bacevich doubted that firepower would have been as decisive in a war against the Soviets as it had been in World War II and the Korean War.[47]

Maxwell Taylor predicted that future wars would be fought with atomic and conventional weapons and that the side that applied firepower more effectively would win. Taylor acknowledged the need to be prepared for conventional wars, but his emphasis was on atomic weapons. He explained that strong forward-deployed ground forces in Germany were necessary to ensure that atomic weapons could be used on Soviet tactical formations before they had closed with the bulk of the North Atlantic Treaty Organization (NATO) forces. Taylor believed that "one of the primary purposes of ground combat will be to discover, or to develop, targets for our [atomic] weapons, so that if we are successful in doing that we can virtually destroy any target on our front, so that our movements thereafter will largely be in the nature of exploitation."[48] Maxwell Taylor did not refashion the army to suit the strategy of Massive Retaliation. Instead, he redefined the army's mission, which implied the adoption of a more flexible national strategy.

Limited Nuclear War: Maxwell Taylor and the Army's Mission

Taylor had been appointed army chief of staff in June 1955. Historian Jonathan House described the magnitude of his task: "In order to justify its existence and mission, the U.S. Army had to develop a doctrine and structure that would allow ground forces to function effectively on a nuclear battlefield."[49] Taylor intended to find "ways and means to improve the combat readiness of the Army in support of a strategy of Flexible Response and to improve its morale depressed as it was by the precedence given to the needs of the Navy and Air Force by the ex-Army man in the White House."[50] He hoped to refine a draft paper, "The National Military Program," which he had written in Korea.[51] He argued that in order to deter general war, the army needed the capabilities to respond quickly to limited aggression.[52] Taylor stressed that deterrence required the possession of real strength. Only a strong army would serve as a deterrent to Soviet aggression. It was not enough to deploy five combat divisions to Germany. The U.S. Army also needed sufficient reserves and transportation capacity and an operational concept that reflected the changing face of warfare in the nuclear age.[53]

Taylor's memoirs leave no doubt that he intended to alter national military strategy. An article written for Foreign Affairs in the spring of 1956 outlined the basic tenets of his views on deterrence based on balanced conventional and nuclear forces.[54] Therefore, the argument that Taylor adopted the pentomic division for the purpose of adjusting the army to the strategy of Massive Retaliation is unpersuasive. To the contrary, the reform was pursued for political reasons. Taylor proposed a bold move that showed the army's orientation toward the future of war. Since the army's viewpoints about future war did not match those of the rest of the defense establishment, reform had to be presented as being in compliance with current policy and strategy. Since limited war was not a fashionable concept, the army needed to find a concept that would appear to be well suited for general war while allowing improvement in the capacity to fight limited wars. The pentomic division was intended to enhance the army's position with respect to the other armed services, to help redefine the role of the institution in the Cold War, and to contribute to a change in national military strategy.[55]

Despite contrary evidence provided in the ATFA studies, Taylor publicly supported the notion that increased firepower with atomic weapons would lead to smaller combat units.[56] He also explained the army's push for tactical nuclear weapons under his leadership as a desire to obtain greater deterrent value. He admitted that he believed at the time that once obtained these weapons would stay in the arsenal for a long time and that the army could achieve a sound balance of nuclear and conventional weapons. Taylor later claimed that the great costs associated with tactical nuclear weapons came as a surprise.[57] To complicate matters, the army needed to maintain the ability to fight large and small wars alike. The ideal army, Taylor told the annual conference of service secretaries in 1955, "would include forces that would be readily available to carry out separately any of our various missions." This entailed a ready force to meet the commitment to NATO, as well as a separate force for local contingencies elsewhere. Taylor concluded that the ideal solution would be "exceedingly difficult to attain" and that the army would have to do its best within the available means.[58]

In September 1955, General Taylor told an assembly of the 101st Airborne Division that the army was in a period of revolutionary transition from the gunpowder age to the nuclear age.[59] Strategic mobility, crucial for rapid reinforcement of overseas-deployed forces, was to be achieved through superior airlift. The nuclear battlefield required greater tactical mobility. This was to be achieved through the air-transportability of all infantry combat divisions and their organic equipment.[60] Consequently, the weight of equipment had to be kept low. Although firepower, especially if provided by atomic weapons, was deemed essential to winning defensive and offensive battles alike, it was crucial to concentrate fire and mass at critical points of the battlefield. Furthermore, dispersion was critical so as not to present an attractive target for Soviet nuclear strikes. Taylor stressed that neither firepower nor mobility was sufficient in its own right and that highly skilled soldiers remained essential.

Taylor had little time to consider operational needs as the army was put on the defensive in budget debates. A critical moment came in February 1956 when Taylor and Secretary of the Army Wilbur Brucker appeared in the House of Representatives. The appropriations committee was an ideal forum for the suave and intellectual Taylor, who presented a stark contrast to Matthew Ridgway.[61] Taylor defended the adequacy of the army's budget for 1957, thus calming Republican fears of outright opposition. But he also presented his views on the army's role in deterrence and outlined a strategy that would become known as Flexible Response, based on strategic and local deterrence and the ability to fight limited wars with appropriate means. When the committee chairman asked whether Taylor's acceptance of the budget was "a forced attitude," Taylor replied that he considered "the funds allocated marginally sufficient to maintain the Army I have described." If, however, purely military considerations prevailed, Taylor preferred an army of 1.5 million men in twenty-eight active divisions. He stated that such a force should be balanced and capable of fighting with nuclear and conventional weapons in any environment.[62]

Taylor followed up on his critique and told President Eisenhower that the current emphasis on nuclear weapons should be replaced by deterrence and response proportional to the level of threat or attack. The medium-term war plan for 1960 remained focused on general war with the Soviet Union, characterized by almost immediate resort to nuclear weapons, but Taylor pointed out that the National Security Council (NSC) had already assessed a Soviet attack on the United States as the least likely scenario in future war. Thus, Taylor argued, it was necessary to prepare the armed forces to deal with the more realistic threat of local and proxy Communist attacks. Taylor noted that the U.S. military needed diverse types of forces to deter both small and big wars. Too much emphasis on airpower would leave the free world vulnerable to limited and local aggression that could only be countered by ground forces. He concluded that it was unwise to pursue policies that would alienate potential allies.[63] Eisenhower responded by emphasizing the capability of tactical nuclear weapons, allied ground forces, and strategic deterrence.[64]

From a strategic and operational perspective, the objective was not to defeat the enemy's military forces but to destroy his will to wage general war. It was, of course, generally assumed that the threat of nuclear escalation would be persuasive enough and that war would not break out, but if it did, NATO declared its intention to employ nuclear weapons at the outset. Maxwell Taylor believed that a strategy that risked national survival to counter even limited aggression was unwise and that proper use of the army offered better alternatives. With sufficient capability to wage both conventional and atomic war, the army could extend the concept of deterrence into a war. At the outset, general deterrence might fail, but there was still the possibility that spirited and skillful defense of West Germany could persuade the Soviets to seek an armistice and return to the controlled crisis state of the Cold War. This was important because Western intelligence sources assumed that war could only break out by accident or miscalculation. In either case, it would be crucial to convince the Soviets rapidly that a negotiated settlement was preferable to a protracted war.

The U.S. Army and the ground forces of the European allies would have to be able to contain or delay the Soviet offensive. This would leave the enemy particularly vulnerable to atomic strikes. For Taylor, limited war meant any conflict that did not include the use of strategic nuclear weapons.[65] Hence, deterrence could work at the general level, fueled by the capacity for strategic use of nuclear weapons, but also at the conventional and the tactical nuclear levels. General Lauris Norstad, Supreme Allied Commander, Europe (SACEUR) from 1956 to 1962, suggested that a "pause" before resorting to nuclear weapons would be appropriate. But although army leaders believed that use of tactical nuclear weapons need not lead automatically to general nuclear war, Norstad assumed that it would trigger immediate escalation. Norstad, a proponent of strategic deterrence, nevertheless felt that Massive Retaliation did not provide the proper means to counter limited aggression.[66]

The army position held that the U.S. military should be concerned first with deterring general war, next with deterring local war, third with winning local war, and only last with winning general war. To this avail, it was necessary to maintain the technological edge over the Soviets—build a continental defense system that would reduce U.S. vulnerability to nuclear attacks; deploy adequate armed force abroad with the capacity to sustain protracted combat; form a powerful rapid response force to intervene in local crises, including the capability to employ nuclear weapons; continue military and economic aid to the allies; emphasize rapid mobilization of reserve forces in the United States; increase stockpiles of critical materials at home and abroad; and devise an industrial mobilization plan for protracted war. Unfortunately, "the army's capability to fulfill its role in the national defense structure [was] impaired by serious limitations on its state of readiness, by inadequate strategic and tactical mobility, by the absence of a flexible logistics system, and by a lack of understanding and support for the Army's needs." The first order of the day was therefore to convince the civilian leadership of the army's utility in the nuclear age.[67]

The immediate objective was to reform the army into a "ready, mobile, hard-hitting, modern [force] capable of moving by land, sea, or air, anywhere in the world to deal with any threat the United States government may decide to meet." The report concluded that the army was prepared to fulfill its most important tasks but that there were great risks in the event of active military operations. General Taylor believed that the army constituted a serious deterrent force, but he had doubts about its actual combat capability. Tactical atomic weapons could help to address this problem, but the army had to ensure that this did not lead to reliance on atomic weapons in situations that were best addressed by conventional means. To counter the strategic threat, the West had to continue its military buildup, but greater emphasis needed to be placed on unified and joint commands. Operationally, the army hoped to employ aviation to enhance greatly the mobility of combat units in theater. New missile technology could address some of the weaknesses in tactical air support. Finally, atomic weapons had changed the dimensions of time and space in battle. There would be much greater depth to the combat zone, and events would unfold rapidly. The tactical and operational goal had to be the annihilation of the enemy forces.[68]

The army continued with "an extremely rapid transition to atomics." This was "for a number of reasons, not all of them military." The complex tactical and doctrinal concepts for new kinds of war had not yet been fully developed. Doctrine had to consider that the most modern army would present the best targets for nuclear strikes. This was the result of mechanization, which tied combat formations to their vehicles, and of the sophistication of logistics. Ports, supply stocks, and headquarters would make good targets, and losses could not always be replaced or otherwise redressed. In addition, the army realized that its capability to fire atomic weapons surpassed its target-identification capacity by a wide margin. The army also lacked vehicles needed to achieve the degree of mobility that was deemed necessary. This would not be decisive in Europe, however, as the enemy was in a similar situation. Army leaders found some solace in the belief that tactical atomic weapons were a means of deterrence and war fighting, while strategic nuclear weapons could only deter war or cause annihilation.[69]

General Taylor's assessment of the operational capability of NATO in Central Europe was upbeat. Forty Soviet and Warsaw Pact divisions faced sixteen combat-ready NATO divisions. Seven more NATO divisions were to become available within thirty days of mobilization. In addition, there were forty British, French, Spanish, and Italian divisions that could be mobilized, but only about half were anywhere near combat-ready. It was anyone's guess how many divisions the Soviets would employ in an offensive if they chose to forgo surprise and deliberately built up their forces. In any scenario, Soviet and East European reserves were more plentiful than NATO's. Nevertheless, Taylor expressed confidence that a forty-division attack could be stopped east of the Rhine if NATO forces received sufficient tactical air support and the authority to apply atomic firepower. Chances against an all-out attack were much more doubtful, since the military mobilization base of the European NATO partners was still too small and U.S. reinforcements were far away. Much would depend on the West German military buildup over the course of the next three years. To increase the mobility and flexibility of U.S. forces in Europe, Taylor revealed that a second armored division and an airborne division would replace two of the four infantry divisions presently stationed in Germany.[70]

The Joint Chiefs of Staff (JCS) agreed that atomic weapons had to be used in the defense of Western Europe. The short-term defense plan for 1956 conceded that the Rhine-IJssel line might fall.[71] The defensive phase, possibly holding on to the Pyrenees, would be characterized by strategic nuclear attacks on Soviet targets before the Western allies could commence their offensive. War might last for three years, and the army had to be prepared to deploy eighty-five divisions. The air force chief of staff disagreed with the assumption that there could be major military operations after a prolonged nuclear exchange. Admiral Radford argued that immediate use of tactical nuclear weapons would be necessary if American forces came under attack by the Soviets. Taylor consented, because he saw no alternative to defending crucial areas in Europe and the Middle East without nuclear weapons at that point.[72] He believed that the possession of tactical nuclear weapons served as a deterrent, prevented the enemy from massing forces in war, and limited aggression. Their use would offset the Soviet numerical advantage in ground forces and bring about the stalemate that would force the enemy to decide whether to escalate.[73]

The debates of the JCS about strategic objectives for the medium term afforded Taylor the opportunity to press upon the other service chiefs the need for a more flexible strategy. When Admiral Radford attempted to include the immediate use of atomic weapons in medium-term as well as emergency planning, Taylor formally objected. He argued that the threat of Massive Retaliation would deter Soviet aggression in Europe only as long as the United States had a significant advantage in the number of nuclear warheads and long-range delivery vehicles. Taylor expected that the Soviet Union would catch up to the United States by the end of the decade. Since current contingency plans were based on the principle of rapid escalation from tactical to strategic use of nuclear weapons, limited aggression would lead to general war. Automatic escalation made no sense once the Soviet Union had acquired the means to strike at military and civilian targets inside the United States. Instead, Taylor argued, the U.S. military needed to develop capabilities to respond to limited aggression with measured force.[74]

Taylor's objections were brushed aside in the revised guidance for medium-range and short-term plans, but use of nuclear weapons was only assured in case of an attack on the United States or its armed forces. Admiral Radford decided to resolve the issue once and for all. On 16 May 1956, he forced a vote of the JCS that redefined general war as "any war in which the armed forces of the USSR and the U.S. are overtly engaged." In other words, any Soviet incursion, no matter how limited, would cause the United States to use nuclear weapons. Radford carried a three-to-two majority, with Taylor and Marine Corps commandant Pate in opposition. Taylor and Pate insisted that a limited conventional and atomic conflict with the Soviet Union remained possible because both sides would be restrained by the risk of mutual annihilation. In a meeting with Taylor and Radford on 24 May, President Eisenhower, who did not believe that war in Europe could be controlled, endorsed Radford's position. At the same meeting, Eisenhower also stated that only active armed forces mattered in a general war. The president implied that army reserve divisions committed to reinforce Allied Command, Europe (ACE) could not be moved to Europe fast enough to affect the outcome of the conflict.[75]

The pressure on the army to either conform with or try to force adjustments to national strategy was increased by the Radford Plan of July 1956.[76] Admiral Radford suggested that army combat divisions should be withdrawn from Europe.[77] In their stead, small atomic task forces and European conventional forces could achieve the same deterrent effect as currently did deployed forces. Historian Richard Leighton argues that Eisenhower supported the Radford Plan and that it was the keystone to a revision of strategy, in order to defeat the critics of Massive Retaliation. Within the year, army forces overseas were to be reduced to the aforementioned atomic task forces that could repel limited aggression. The limited-war mission was to be carried out by the air force, the navy, and a smaller Marine Corps. All were to be armed with nuclear weapons. Army strength was to decline significantly, and civil defense was to become the army's main task. Marc Trachtenberg claims that the withdrawal of American armed forces from Europe was a central pillar of Eisenhower's defense policy and global strategy. For that purpose, nuclear weapons had to be shared with the allies.[78]

Taylor opposed Radford's proposal because it was designed for general nuclear war against the Soviets. He thought that it would seriously compromise the ability to fight regional wars. Although the plan, if implemented, might deter the Soviets from initiating nuclear war, it would open the door for limited forms of aggression. Taylor objected forcefully in the meeting of the JCS on 9 July 1956:

> The Chairman's concept represents a program which prepares for one improbable type of war, while leaving the United States weak in its ability to meet the most probable type of threat. It fixes the form of possible military reaction, with a resultant loss of flexibility and adaptability for the political and military policy of the United States. It will frighten and alienate our friends. It will play the Russian game directed at getting our forces out of Europe and of Asia. It substitutes the concept of "Fortress America" for our former strategy based upon forward deployment of deterrent forces in co-operation with our Allies of the Free World. I repeat the opinion that it represents an unacceptable military program for the United States.[79]

The other service chiefs greeted Taylor's statement with silence. It was only the reaction in Congress and in European capitals to the publication of elements of the plan in the *New York Times* on 13 July that caused Eisenhower to bury the Radford Plan.

All of this was not merely a philosophical debate about strategy. The army was in serious danger of being reduced significantly. On 30 June 1956, there had been eighteen active divisions and almost one million men. In July 1957, the services proposed new force objectives. The army hoped to limit personnel cuts to 50,000 officers and men and retain at least fifteen divisions. The air force, in contrast, did not think that the army needed more than eleven active divisions, and both air force and navy agreed that 800,000 officers and men would be sufficient. Admiral Radford even suggested a gradual reduction of the army to eleven divisions and 700,000 officers and men. It was crucial for the survival of the army, both as a significant part of the deterrent force and as a fighting force, to prevent Radford's proposal from being implemented. Eisenhower decided to reduce the army to 850,000 officers and men by 1959 but offered no decision for the longer term. The debate continued well into 1959, but in the end Maxwell Taylor and his successor, General Lyman Lemnitzer, could claim a partial victory, as the army stood at fourteen divisions with 873,000 officers and men on 30 June 1960.[80]

The debate about force structure was defined less by sound strategic thought than by budget constraints.[81] The defense budget—and the army's share—remained contentious through the latter part of the 1950s. When the services provided their estimates for 1958 in the fall of 1956, the total added up to over $48 billion, $10 billion above the ceiling set by the administration. About half of the total was requested by the air force. The army claimed a need for $12 billion to increase manpower and deploy more atomic support forces to Europe. Secretary Wilson, in his final year in the Pentagon, objected and set a firm force goal of one million men for the army. Still, in November, the services requested more than $45 billion. The administration's defense budget request, presented to Congress on 16 January 1957, totaled $38.5 billion in new authority, for an expected $38 billion in obligational expenditures. The army's share was $8.54 billion, or about half of the air force's. In line with President Eisenhower's decision, army force objectives were reduced to 900,000 men by June 1958 and 850,000 men by the following year. Moreover, 1957 saw a movement for greater economy in Congress, and the final appropriation was even lower. On 1 August, Congress approved a defense budget of $33.76 billion. The army's share stood at $7.26 billion; the air force received almost $16 billion.[82]

The pressure on the military in general—and the army in particular—was relaxed in 1958. The budget for 1959 benefited from the changing political climate in the aftermath of the Sputnik shock. Soviet advances in rocketry and missile technology had alerted congressional leaders that the U.S. military might not have the technological edge that had been projected and that the relatively small size of the active armed forces was thus a much bigger problem than had been assumed. Secretary Wilson had initially set the guidelines for the 1959 budget at $37.2 billion, with an army share of $8.6 billion for 850,000 men. Army Secretary Brucker warned that this would force the army to withdraw one division from Korea and two battle groups from Europe. In his budget request of January 1958, President Eisenhower asked for only $8.5 billion for the army. Congress thought this to be inadequate.[83] The two houses compromised on a defense budget of $39.6 billion, including almost $9 billion for the army. The military construction bill that followed pushed the defense budget above $40 billion for the first time since the Korean War.[84]

After Sputnik, defense policy and strategy were reviewed and the JCS were asked to give greater consideration to a force structure adaptable to either general or limited war. The public, and indeed many high-ranking military and civilian officials, assumed that a force capable of fighting general war could cope with more limited conflict. Maxwell Taylor had consistently challenged such views. He argued that armed forces that were well prepared for limited war might be able to function in general war, but that although "there's nothing of use in the little war not applicable to the big war,...the reverse is not true."[85] Even John Foster Dulles, secretary of state and architect of Massive Retaliation, now pushed for limited-war capability in a potential European theater. The threat of massive retaliation was clearly less useful than it had been in 1954.

Neil McElroy, the new secretary of defense, found his hands tied by rising costs. He projected defense expenditures of $41.25 billion in fiscal year 1960. The army could only expect $9.1 billion, which would lead to a further force reduction to 825,000 men. In the service proposals of October 1958, the army had maintained that $10.2 billion were necessary to maintain the approved strength of fourteen divisions through 1960, with a slight increase in manpower to 880,000. President Eisenhower eventually requested a defense budget of $40.95 billion in expenditures, including $9.26 for the army. Congress ultimately approved $39.2 billion for defense and $9.38 billion for the army. Again, this was increased to slightly over $40 billion through a supplementary military construction bill.[86] National military strategy had undergone a subtle change in philosophy, but there were not sufficient funds yet to implement the dual capability for limited and general war across the armed forces.

A divide between the State and Defense Departments characterized the debate of the 1961 defense budget. Dulles urged a thorough review of national strategy, based on the assumption that nuclear deterrence had to be supplemented by a serious capability for conventional war. In many respects, the State Department had returned to the basic premise of NSC-68. To implement Dulles's proposals, a significantly higher budget was required to sustain the necessary force levels or the military would have to reduce the nuclear deterrent and shift funds within the budget. Either option seemed unreasonable and unobtainable to the Defense Department. The service budget requests topped out at $43.6 billion, including $10.3 billion for the army. Secretary McElroy reminded the services of their manpower authorization for 1960, which stood at 870,000 in the army's case. Eventually, the services agreed to lower their request to $41.4 billion, but there was little agreement on the respective shares. The army thought it should get 34 percent, while the air force demanded 56 percent and would have granted only 20 percent to the army. On 18 January 1960, Eisenhower asked Congress for $40.58 billion, including $9.55 billion for the army and a relatively modest $17.74 billion for the air force. The appropriations bill signed by the president on 7 July was just below $40 billion. Appropriations for the army were $9.54 billion.[87]

Early in his tenure as army chief of staff, General Taylor had found little support for his arguments for greater strategic flexibility from the JCS. But in 1958, the navy and the Marine Corps came to support the need for limited-war capability in meetings of the JCS, and State Department representatives made similar arguments in the NSC. The new JCS chairman, air force general Nathan Twining, argued that any military force built for general war would also be useful in a limited-war environment.[88] Taylor, Admiral Arleigh Burke, and Marine Corps commandant Pate contested this proposition. Part of the problem was that limited war was a poorly defined term. Twining defined it as limitations imposed by the political leadership upon military commanders. As an example, he cited the Korean War, where, he believed, President Truman's refusal to authorize the application of airpower north of the Yalu River had negatively affected the course of the war. Taylor, on the other hand, defined limited war as any war in which no strategic nuclear weapons were used.[89] Twining disagreed with Taylor's assumption that war in Central Europe could be limited. He argued that limited war was a "philosophy of weakness."[90] The president supported Twining's position, despite the fact that air force chief of staff General White was the only supporter of Twining on the JCS. The defense of Europe still rested on the assumption that war between the United States and the Soviet Union could only be general.[91]

The discussion of the defense budget and the increasing debate over adjustments to strategy highlight the centrality of fiscal considerations in the Eisenhower years. Even after John Foster Dulles adopted the army's longstanding position on the need for a capability to fight limited wars with an admixture of conventional and tactical nuclear forces, a thorough review was not forthcoming. Discussions of the basic defense reviews for 1958 and 1959 showed greater receptiveness among administration officials to consideration of limited war. But it became obvious that both strategic nuclear deterrence and sufficient military capability for limited war could only be achieved if the defense budget was increased significantly. That, however, was impossible because Eisenhower maintained that sound fiscal policy for economic growth and security were more important than short-term improvements in the defense posture. The fundamental problem was thus fairly simple but impossible to solve, given the fiscal constraints. An increasing number of administration officials understood the army's point about realistic deterrence, and there was a general trend toward the thinking of NSC-68. But Eisenhower and the Defense Department were convinced that it was too expensive to act upon such considerations.

Taylor had never been shy about expressing his concerns about Massive Retaliation, but he was enough of a diplomat to function effectively within a system that he considered to be defective and unlikely to last for much longer. He assumed that the approaching nuclear parity would force the administration and the military services to shift the emphasis of strategy away from strategic nuclear deterrence. Based on the assumption of greater need for limited-war capability and more flexible, dual-capable forces, Taylor outlined his vision of the future army personnel structure in an address to the defense secretary in June 1958. He called for a modest increase from 870,000 to 915,000 officers and men.[92] He also proposed that 15,000 men should be added to the overseas deployments by June 1962. The reductions in manpower in USAREUR from 240,000 in June 1956 to a planned 225,000 by 30 June 1959 had left the ground forces short of combat units and logistical support.

The difference in thinking among the army, the other services, and the administration rested on the assumption that atomic and nuclear weapons would require less manpower. Taylor objected to such estimates on the basis of the complexity of the weapons, the greater need for maintenance and training, the greater need for speed, mobility, and flexibility, and the greater strains on logistics.[93] Yet his pentomic division had been oriented on the principle of smaller combat forces. In the areas of limited war and dual capability, Taylor warned about equating firepower and military capability. He was particularly concerned about the collateral damage that high-yield payloads of atomic weapons could cause. As he pointed out, the after-action analysis of the SAGEBRUSH maneuvers indicated that actual use of such weapons as simulated in the exercise would have destroyed the army forces and killed most if not all inhabitants of Louisiana, Texas, and the entire Southeast.[94]

Maxwell Taylor and the U.S. Army were not alone in identifying the linkage of mutual assured destruction and limited war. Once the Soviets obtained the capability to destroy significant parts of the United States with intercontinental ballistic missiles, the use of strategic nuclear weapons in a regional conflict would become less credible. In other words, while the weapons would be as destructive as before, the psychological impact on the Kremlin leaders would be lessened by their assumption that the United States would not risk its own destruction. Consequently, the capacity to wage limited war would become more important. That was exactly the point made by a Pentagon staffer to a colleague in the State Department in May 1960. The defense analyst claimed that it was present U.S. policy to build as large a force for limited war as possible once the deterrent had been served. In addition, he added that Great Britain, once staunchly supportive of Massive Retaliation, now pursued a similar approach. Moreover, the Pentagon analyst doubted that NATO war plans calling for the immediate use of nuclear weapons in case of a Soviet invasion stood any chance. The U.S. military expected to be called upon to fight a rather prolonged phase of conventional war "while the politicians talked." In addition, prior to the employment of tactical atomic weapons, the president would likely make an unequivocal public statement that the country was not prepared to use strategic nuclear weapons at this point.[95] This acknowledged that the concept of deterrence could extend into war, and that restraint might allow for limitation of tactical nuclear war.

Maxwell Taylor retired in 1959. He followed the example of his predecessor and quickly published an account of his frustrations with national security policy. Ridgway had placed his criticism in the later chapters of his memoirs, but Taylor took a more direct approach. *The Uncertain Trumpet* was a serious indictment of the shortcomings of Massive Retaliation and a passionate plea for a greater role of ground forces in a more flexible strategy. This was to become one of the founding statements of the strategy of Flexible Response, and it paved Taylor's way into the inner circle of the next president of the United States, John F. Kennedy.

Flexible Response was adopted in 1961, but since 1957 American strategy had moved away from a dogmatic interpretation of Massive Retaliation.[96] The army had been the primary agent for change. The arguments of Maxwell Taylor, supported at times by his colleagues in the navy and Marine Corps, had contributed greatly to the transition from Massive Retaliation to

Flexible Response. Moreover, the introduction of the pentomic division and the subsequent debate about organization and doctrine assured that the army was prepared to operate under a new strategy. But the transition of strategy was also driven by operational planning in the NATO alliance, and by the strategic and political considerations of the supreme commander, General Lauris Norstad.

Toward Forward Defense of West Germany

When NATO was formed in the spring of 1949, its military strategy rested upon the nuclear monopoly of the United States. U.S. Army forces in Europe were insufficient to defend Western Europe. European armies had been demobilized after World War II, and remaining troops were often preoccupied with colonial or postcolonial wars. After the successful test of a Soviet atom bomb, forward defense became the expressed objective of NATO force planning, although actual capability would not catch up with rhetoric for several years.[97] Still, Europeans needed to be told that they would be defended rather than abandoned at the outset of war. General Omar Bradley succinctly stated the political, if not military, necessity for forward defense in April 1949, even before the atomic monopoly had been broken: "It must be perfectly apparent to the people of the United States that we cannot count on friends in Western Europe if our strategy in the event of war dictates that we shall first abandon them to the enemy with a promise of later liberation."[98] Despite such considerations, NATO members agreed that immediate use of nuclear weapons in case of a Soviet attack was necessary.

Limited war entered into the discussions of NATO leaders in 1956.[99] The North Atlantic Council decided in December that localized Soviet attacks of any degree of intensity should be met with conventional force. This upset German chancellor Adenauer, who saw it as a step toward American abandonment of Western Europe. To him, only the threat of nuclear retaliation could deter Soviet aggression.[100] Adenauer had spent the year worrying about signs that Massive Retaliation was no longer the basis of policy for the Eisenhower administration. In the event, the chancellor anticipated the softening of the American position.

Maxwell Taylor questioned NATO force structure in Central Europe. On his way to Washington to take command as chief of staff, he had received briefings at Supreme Headquarters Allied Powers, Europe (SHAPE) in Paris and at USAREUR headquarters. Taylor recalled that he was particularly concerned about the fragility of the logistics base, whose failure would compromise the sustenance of combat operations. He concluded that "it was clear to me that we had too many forces in Europe if we were going to depend on the 'trip-wire' strategy supported by the Massive Retaliation school and not enough balanced strength for a sustained non-nuclear defense." Taylor expressed hope that tactical nuclear weapons would make possible the territorial defense of Western Europe.[101] But the question of trip-wire strategy or forward defense raised doubts about the relationship of strategy and policy. Officially, NATO insisted on forward defense as policy objective. The strategy of Massive Retaliation, however, did not support this objective. Why should large combat elements be moved closer to the intra-German border if ground troops were merely meant to trigger a nuclear response?

By 1956, ACE had improved its force posture, and SACEUR called for the defense of large parts of West Germany. Previous NATO contingency plans had foreseen the Rhine and IJssel rivers as the main line of resistance, with varying degrees of defense to the east. Emergency Defense Plan (EDP) 1-57 stated the new objective as "arresting the Soviet land advance in Central Europe as far to the east as possible . . . and contain the Soviet advance forward of the Rhine-Ijssel." SACEUR particularly referred to the defense of Kassel, Frankfurt, Würzburg, and the surrounding areas. Operational planning relied on heavy and early use of atomic weapons.[102]

The new main line of defense extended from Bremen along the Weser River, to the Harz Mountains, the Lech River, and the German-Austrian border.[103] German military officers were disappointed. General Adolf Heusinger complained that this was not the kind of forward defense envisioned when Germany had joined NATO. Norstad replied that deterrence, not forward defense, was the primary mission of the alliance and that a shift of the main line of defense to the Iron Curtain would be ill advised until ACE had enough troops. Until then, forward defense as envisioned by Heusinger and deterrence were incompatible.[104] EDP 1-57 noted the shortage of German forces. This problem was exacerbated by the deployment of French forces from Central Region to Algeria. Still, containing the Soviet offensive east of the Rhine was SACEUR's first priority in the event of land battle.[105]

General Jean Etienne Valluy, Commander in Chief, Allied Forces, Central Europe (CINCENT), referred to the current deployment as "this half-forward strategy" and criticized the lack of logistical preparation. He lamented that ACE had not positioned a large amount of supplies east of the Rhine. Valluy estimated that stockpiles for fifteen days of combat were essential and that depots had to be built to withstand nuclear attacks. Medium-range plans, calling for more divisions to defend a wider area of Germany, required fundamental changes to NATO infrastructure and depot plans as well as to the command organization in Allied Forces, Central Europe (AFCENT). The current structure could not accommodate twelve German divisions stretched across both Northern and Central Army Groups.[106] Valluy suggested that Northern Army Group (NORTHAG) should be responsible for the defense of Denmark and could, in return, hand over the Kassel area to Central Army Group (CENTAG). Currently, the line of demarcation between CENTAG and NORTHAG interfered with his vision of a defensive battle in the Kassel Gap. He suggested that northern and southern portions of CENTAG would have to hold while the counterattack developed out of the center.[107]

Norstad paid no attention to Valluy's suggestions. The Minimum Force Study conducted by SHAPE in 1957 was based on a different concept of war. SACEUR did not think that planning for operations beyond the initial nuclear exchange in a general war was very important. Clearly, Lauris Norstad expected atomic war to be short. Therefore, only active forces and immediately available stockpiles of equipment were critical. The British Chiefs of Staff considered unrealistic the ready forces that Norstad requested. Great Britain was asked to commit an additional 100,000 men to ACE. Furthermore, the British Chiefs of Staff thought that plans for maintaining maritime lines of communication to the United States were absolutely critical and should be better coordinated with Norstad, who was accused of neglecting the issue beyond a general expectation that reinforcements from North America could be obtained. These were minor quibbles, however, compared to the real concern. SACEUR proposed that in the future ground forces might be crucial to deterrence and should be capable of dealing with limited aggression. Britain, on the other hand, had built its national strategy around earlier concepts of Massive Retaliation that emphasized nuclear weapons and airpower.[108]

The emergence of tactical nuclear weapons and the slow buildup of German armed forces caused NATO to amend Massive Retaliation in 1957. Officially, the alliance continued to rest its strategy on the immediate use of nuclear and atomic weapons in a general war, as expressed by NATO's Military Committee in MC 14/2. This document confirmed the strategy of Massive Retaliation but allowed for more independent operational use of tactical nuclear weapons in the territorial defense of Western Europe.[109] Nuclear deterrence, it was argued, all but assured that the Soviets would not embark on general war, but war by accident or miscalculation remained possible. A short section on limited war suggested that localized conventional attacks should be met initially by conventional forces, but that nuclear weapons would be employed as the situation required, since "in no case is there a NATO concept of limited war with the Soviets."[110] Still, there was a degree of ambiguity, largely because an increasing number of military officers wanted an alternative to the immediate use of nuclear weapons. But despite the concession that limited war, defined by NATO's Standing Group as "armed conflict other than unlimited nuclear war," might occur, it was seen as an extra-European phenomenon.[111]

Limited war outside of Europe did not concern NATO planners directly, but the Military Committee realized that the conventional defense of Germany was weakened by the colonial and postcolonial commitments of France and Great Britain and possibly also of the United States: "We should recognize that the forces of certain NATO nations may need to retain the flexibility required to permit action to meet limited military situations short of general war outside the NATO area."[112] It may seem that such commitments and the conventional defense of Western Europe had common characteristics, but wars of the kind fought in Algeria or Southeast Asia required different equipment, weaponry, logistics, and organization of combat units. More important, they required a different approach to operations. The U.S. Army was less than a decade away from discovering this in a very painful manner.

Massive Retaliation was now more deeply set in NATO strategy, while the supreme commander attempted to guide the alliance toward a modified, more graduated responsive capability. General Hans Speidel, who had taken command of Allied Land Forces, Central Europe (LANDCENT) in the spring, explained that tactical nuclear weapons offered a degree of flexibility not found in earlier NATO strategy. Without determination to use them, the credibility of the deterrent would be lessened.[113] U.S. Army intelligence acknowledged that the Soviets might test Western resolve with limited aggression at the border or in Berlin. There was no direct recommendation as to how to counter such actions, but it was implied that all means, including nuclear weapons, should be available from the outset of hostilities.[114]

The state of readiness of European ground forces remained unsatisfactory. In a review of the national security program in the summer of 1957, the JCS concluded that NATO still was far from achieving force posture that could reasonably be expected to defeat the Soviets. The defense of Central Europe had been improved, but shortcomings in logistics of all ground forces except Seventh Army made sustained operations nearly impossible. This was a problem even in case of general war, because the nuclear phase still had to be followed by a counteroffensive on the ground to secure victory. The official opinion of the JCS underscored that the deterrent was nevertheless strong. But earlier drafts had been more pessimistic. There it had been stated that neither combat nor support forces of European armies had achieved the 1956 force goals. In addition, some countries were capable of maintaining internal security but could not defend their borders against a determined enemy. The JCS found that NATO forces in Central Region could conduct substantial defensive operations but were incapable of taking the offensive. Most likely, the JCS decided to omit the more critical portions of the assessment in the final evaluation for political reasons.[115]

Maxwell Taylor lamented the lack of military involvement in the process of deciding upon NATO force objectives. He pointed out that the JCS had not been asked for advice. He proceeded to offer his assessment. In 1957, the U.S. Army deployed five combat divisions to Germany, committed three of its stateside divisions to SACEUR as rapid reinforcements, and promised to move nine divisions to Europe as second-echelon reinforcements. Altogether, seventeen army and National Guard divisions were committed to the defense of Central Europe. Taylor thought that this was sufficient. In 1959, there would be three infantry and two armored divisions in Germany, two more infantry and one airborne division ready to be deployed upon mobilization, and one airborne, six infantry, and two armored divisions in the second echelon.[116]

The Military Committee submitted MC 70 on the same day that Taylor voiced his complaints about the process.[117] It expressed concern about the vulnerability of concentrated forces to Soviet nuclear attacks. Therefore, it was necessary to deploy small battle formations, supported by heavy firepower. Mobility was crucial and communications had to be reliable.[118] Readiness and qualitative superiority of the NATO forces were to contribute greatly to the deterrence of war. Even though MC 70 was based on the strategic guidance of Massive Retaliation, it included orders to SACEUR to prepare responses to any kind of incursion, possibly without having recourse to nuclear weapons.[119] If aggression escalated to war, the land forces of the alliance would be called upon to defend NATO as far to the east as possible in order to safeguard territory, defend the population, and, most importantly, secure the base area from which the nuclear counteroffensive was to be conducted.[120] Balanced conventional and nuclear forces could achieve forward defense. Once suitable local targets had been identified, tactical atomic strikes were likely to be authorized.[121]

The Military Committee believed that combat operations should be conducted by divisions made up of combat groups of all arms, each capable of independent action. This was more advanced than the pentomic concept, in the sense that NATO subdivisional combat groups were to be fully combined-arms forces. The structure of the combat groups was to be flexible. This would allow for specific adjustments to the terrain and the nature of the threat and enemy forces. The committee thought that tactical nuclear weapons systems might be integrated at division level but did not necessarily have to be. The same point was made for ground reconnaissance and air observation, additional armor, and helicopters. In essence, the NATO military planners suggested a division that more closely resembled ROAD, the future U.S. Army divisional organization, than the recently reorganized pentomic division.[122]

The NATO partners had committed forty-two active divisions and sixteen regimental combat teams to SACEUR. Sixteen additional divisions were committed to the first echelon of reinforcements and twenty-four divisions to the second echelon of reinforcements. The Military Committee recommended an increase of eight active and five first-echelon reserve divisions by 1961.[123] Most of them were to be provided by the Bundeswehr.[124] The U.S. Army was not called upon to increase its active forces in Europe or significantly increase its reserve commitment to SACEUR.[125] The question was whether U.S. Army divisions earmarked for SACEUR could be brought into the theater as quickly as they would be needed. The current JCS-approved contingency plan of the U.S. Commander in Chief, Europe (USCINCEUR) called for the rapid deployment of all four divisions of the newly created Strategic Army Corps (STRAC). Maxwell Taylor urged the other service chiefs to draft movement plans to assure that sufficient transportation would be available.[126] Immediately upon mobilization, the United States was committed to deploy two infantry divisions and one airborne division to Europe. The movement of all three divisions was to be concluded within thirty days. NATO was informed that sufficient transportation capacity existed.[127]

Meanwhile, the majority of Western Europeans wanted more balanced forces and greater strategic flexibility, according to a CIA report of November 1957. The exceptions were the governments of Great Britain and West Germany, who found that deterrence beyond Massive Retaliation was unaffordable and that talk of greater flexibility diminished the value of the nuclear deterrent because it signaled unwillingness to use strategic nuclear weapons. Unfortunately, the Europeans were not willing to pay the price for the adjustment in forces. Still, the danger of limited aggression was perceived clearly on both sides of the Atlantic. Lauris Norstad argued that limited war was a much more likely scenario than a full-scale Soviet invasion of Western Europe.[128]

Nevertheless, NATO strategy remained wedded to the assumption that the first phase of war with the Soviets, which was unlikely to exceed thirty days, "would be characterized by the greatest intensity of nuclear exchange." This would be followed by "a longer period of indeterminate duration for reorganization, resupply and the accomplishment of necessary military tasks leading to a conclusion of the war."[129] Air defense was the greatest weakness in Central Region. It remained critically short of the requirements set in MC 70 despite the introduction of new surface-to-air missiles. This could endanger the effectiveness of the nuclear retaliatory force because the Soviets were expected to attack NATO airfields. ACE was seven first-echelon divisions short of the requirements set by MC 70, and SACEUR commanded only thirty of the required forty-seven nuclear delivery units. Current trends pointed at a shortfall of almost two active divisions, nine first-echelon divisions, and thirty-six nuclear delivery units out of a total of eighty-eight, by 1961.[130] This of course threatened both Massive Retaliation and a more flexible strategy, but it seemed particularly harmful to the prospects of the latter.

The divide between expressed strategy and practical operational concepts was widening. General Norstad did not believe that MC 14/2 offered the best answer to a military challenge. He could not change NATO strategy, but it was possible to steer the military posture of the alliance toward a modified form of nuclear deterrence. Norstad thought that the ability to wage limited war in Europe, at least for a short period of time, was an important element of graduated deterrence for the next decade. He referred to it as the need to force a pause in the continuity of military action, thus giving the enemy time to consider the consequences of continued aggression. Toward the end of General Norstad's tenure, SHAPE explained:

> Our forces must be of such a size and composition, and so organized, trained, and equipped, that they can react promptly to and hold an attack short of general war, at least long enough to identify the nature and scope of the enemy effort and the intention behind it, and to establish clearly the fact that the Alliance will defend any part of NATO Europe subjected to aggression, using atomic weapons, if necessary. The resulting pause would make it possible for NATO to determine the degree of force and weaponry necessary to meet the situation. It would also permit the aggressor to make a conscious decision whether to continue the aggression and thus risk general war.[131]

Other senior NATO commanders shared Norstad's argument for graduated deterrence. General Speidel specified that "it is the mission of the 'shield forces' to impose this pause on the enemy."[132] Norstad believed that the pause concept would be enhanced if conventional and nuclear capabilities were separated in lower-level army units, thus reducing the need to employ tactical nuclear weapons.[133]

All senior commanders of LANDCENT participated in a war game in Paris in November 1958.[134] This was the first AFCENT war game of its kind. Its purpose was to harmonize military thinking among the commanding generals. The scenario was daunting. Within two days, a full-scale conventional Soviet attack had achieved deep penetration at the boundary of NORTHAG and CENTAG. SACEUR had authorized the use of nuclear weapons almost immediately, mostly because it was politically impossible to appear hesitant in the matter. HOSTAGE BLEU proceeded under the assumption that NATO would use nuclear weapons first if necessary. In the specific scenario, intercontinental nuclear exchange rapidly followed upon the instigation of in-theater use of nuclear weapons. In order to ensure the orderly conduct of the war game, it was concluded that the effect of Soviet nuclear attacks on NATO rear areas was weakened significantly by NATO first strikes. War game planners had assumed that too much simulated chaos in the rear area would reduce the benefits of the exercise. The realism of the exercise may thus be questionable, but it was undeniable that SACEUR employed nuclear weapons first, that he did so without much hesitation within hours of the outbreak of war, and that strategic nuclear war followed swiftly.

Turning to operational concerns, the LANDCENT commanders agreed that salients were attractive targets for nuclear strikes; thus, the formation of enemy salients should be encouraged under certain circumstances. The use of nuclear weapons allowed for a quicker start of the counteroffensive than would be the case on an entirely conventional battlefield. Weaker forces could attack after nuclear preparation. Speed was of the essence, since radioactive fallout would slow attacking units if they were not mounted in armored vehicles and could not cross the contaminated area quickly. There was less agreement on the deployment of the two army groups. The boundary was troublesome, and it was unclear whether LANDCENT could indeed coordinate converging attacks on enemy forces that had penetrated the area. While both army group commanders felt that General Speidel could do so, several of the lower-tier commanders thought that one of the army groups should direct the campaign. Potential problems with the command arrangement would be magnified if either army group had been given atomic weapons of relatively high yield. The problem was not solved during the war game or at discussions in Paris.[135]

Corps commanders were concerned that counterattacks would depend on rapid deployment of forces over a wide area and almost immediate offensive actions without spending much time in assembly areas. Simultaneously, targets in the infantry combat zone needed to be struck with atomic weapons, and atomic strikes should also neutralize the enemy artillery. Once atomic fire had been applied, any resurgence of enemy forces was to be suppressed by continuous conventional artillery fire. The priority of targets was unclear. One corps commander suggested that the physical damage created by atomic strikes on the infantry combat zone would be so great as to slow the momentum of the counterattack. Therefore, it would be better to target the enemy's local reserve areas and use conventional artillery at the point of break-in. Another corps commander, however, considered the advantage of using atomic weapons at the break-in point as so great that even the risk of casualties among his own forward troops was acceptable.[136]

To introduce additional land forces into the battle, helicopters were deemed better than parachuting, since parachuting operations required more time and extremely good communications. On the other hand, helicopters were vulnerable and atomic bursts might neutralize landing zones. The corps commanders agreed that the offensive in atomic warfare required command of the airspace in order to deny the enemy full reconnaissance. By the same token, friendly intelligence about enemy formations, particularly pertaining to the reserve, was vital. One could then work out detailed atomic fire plans and advance behind the barrage. Friendly troops, of course, had to remain dispersed as much as possible, and therefore communications and mobility remained critical. In the unfolding scenario, General Speidel ordered CENTAG to advance to Leipzig after seven days of fighting, while NORTHAG had yet to reach the Weser River. Admittedly, this war game was not intended to test specific operational plans, but the timing of the counteroffensive is curious. The most optimistic American plans foresaw months on the defensive, yet here NATO forces were invading East German territory in the second week of the war.[137]

One and a half years later, forward defense remained in doubt. In April 1960, the Military Committee submitted an evaluation of progress toward the attainment of the MC 70 force goals. The conclusions were unsatisfactory. Overall, the commitments of the NATO partners were not commensurate with actual capabilities. The situation in Central Region was particularly problematic because there was a significant shortage of atomic delivery means, resulting in inadequate short- and medium-range ground atomic fire support. The shortfall in atomic weapons made it difficult to compensate for minimum force levels. Manning levels of active divisions stood at 85 percent of wartime requirements. Ammunition reserves and back-up missiles for atomic delivery units were also well below expectations. Under such circumstances, sustained combat would be difficult if not impossible. The Military Committee concluded that "the ground forces in the Central Region have deficiencies which are substantial and critical." The outlook for 1963 revealed that critical shortcomings would remain in the areas of modernization of strike forces, timely provision of ground atomic delivery means, manning of the shield forces, and modernization of the air defense system.[138]

The NATO Council of Ministers also expressed concern about the effects of nuclear parity on deterrence. At its December 1959 meeting, the Council of Ministers initiated a thorough review of the tasks of the alliance in the coming decade. For the United States, the State Department asked Robert Bowie to draft a report, which was completed in the summer of 1960. Bowie emphasized that the strategic deterrent remained credible for general war. He agreed with General Norstad that thirty combat divisions in Central Europe would offer a reasonable regional deterrent. This force, however, needed to be tied to a European nuclear deterrent such as the multilateral force (MLF), then under consideration. Bowie implied that President Eisenhower agreed with the greater flexibility for NATO that was entailed in the report. Later he would argue that it was the failure to realize the MLF proposal that forced NATO to maintain its strong reliance on strategic deterrence well into the 1960s.[139]

General Norstad agreed with the thesis of the Bowie Report that NATO had to enhance the non-nuclear capabilities of the shield forces in order to assure deterrence in the future.[140] But he also indicated that a set of principles had to be established for adequate non-nuclear defense. First, SACEUR should command sufficient ground forces to "defend successfully against the readily available Communist Bloc forces arrayed against ACE, without recourse to nuclear weapons." Second, "the measure of success in this defense would be the prevention of significant loss of ACE territory." Third, tactical nuclear weapons had to be provided in sufficient numbers to ensure strong defense against the Soviets even if they brought reinforcements into the battle or resorted to the use of tactical nuclear weapons. This is intriguing because Norstad admitted that NATO would use nuclear weapons preemptively, but he also implied that there might be a pause between conventional and tactical nuclear war, as well as between tactical and strategic nuclear war. Discussion of the fourth principle remains classified in part, but it can be surmised on the basis of the available record that Norstad wanted a force structure that included a clear distinction between conventional and nuclear weapons. He stated that this could be achieved by providing no nuclear weapons to any echelon below the division.[141]

In December, Norstad reiterated that there could indeed be a firebreak between limited use of tactical nuclear weapons and general nuclear war.[142] He explained the basic tenets of his position to the Defense Department:

> The NATO forces must be organized and equipped to insure a high level of conventional response and should operate under policies which will guarantee that atomic weapons will be introduced into the battle only after a particular decision taken by an authority at a higher level than that of the basic combat unit. These forces must have a balanced capability, nuclear and non-nuclear, which will provide a flexibility of response,

> ranging from the capability (1) to meet any overt Soviet Bloc military action with sufficient strength and determination to force the Soviets either to withdraw or continue the military action with the full knowledge that such continuation will constitute general war and that NATO will retaliate with all weapons and forces, to the capability (2) to destroy, in conjunction with external retaliatory forces, the will and ability of the Soviet Bloc to wage general nuclear war.[143]

Thus the Bowie Report and Lauris Norstad's pause concept both stand as examples for attempts to strengthen regional nuclear and conventional elements of deterrence under a modified concept of Massive Retaliation, although Norstad suggested stronger modifications than Bowie.

Maxwell Taylor realized in his retirement that Massive Retaliation had evolved "from its early purity to a hybrid which . . . bore some resemblance to the strategy of Flexible Response soon to be adopted by the Kennedy Administration."[144] The debate of appropriate strategy for the United States and NATO had indeed revealed that ground forces were to play an important role. Both Maxwell Taylor and Lauris Norstad advanced concepts of proportional response to initial Soviet aggression. They disagreed on the possibility of limiting nuclear war, but even Norstad's pause concept afforded the army strong arguments in the strategic and budgetary debates of the second term of the Eisenhower administration. At the end of the decade, it was the air force chief of staff who found himself isolated on the JCS.[145] But with the approach of greater strategic flexibility, the defects of the pentomic division took on additional significance, and the army had to find ways to improve the operational capability of its forces deployed in Germany.

3

The Pentomic Army in Germany

The assessment of the pentomic division in Seventh Army was ultimately negative. At first, there was optimism that use of atomic weapons by the division might compensate for the numerical inferiority of the North Atlantic Treaty Organization (NATO) ground forces in Central Europe. Hope was transformed into disappointment as army commanders discovered a number of practical difficulties. Communications were cumbersome, and effective control by the division commander of five battle groups as well as division artillery and support units was difficult to achieve. As a result, steps were undertaken in the field to address the most glaring problems, and the practical effect of the reorganization on operational deployment and tactical plans in the theater was negligible. The pentomic division failed to improve fighting capability, but it served its political purpose by halting the downward spiral in funding and manpower that had threatened the army's future. In the meantime, the German army introduced combat divisions based on brigades and a flexible number of battalions. Just as U.S. Army commanders were considering the replacement of the pentomic division, the new German division was accepted as the model NATO combat division. At the end of the 1950s, army leaders moved from adjustments to an unsatisfactory basic model toward structural changes, and in 1961 the army was prepared to present a new combat division to the Kennedy administration.

Seventh Army and the Defense of Western Europe before the Reform

Prior to the outbreak of the Korean War, the army had not played a prominent role in U.S. war plans for the defense of Western Europe. Only two infantry divisions were to be deployed to the theater. Korea, however, provided politicians and military leaders in Washington with the incentive to improve the defenses of NATO territories. Within less than two years, the lone infantry division on occupation duty in Germany became part of a five-division force. The U.S. Army, Europe (USAREUR) was created as a theater army headquarters, and its operational arm, Seventh Army, was reinstated into the list of active field armies. This was the beginning of the largest permanent overseas deployment of American armed forces in peacetime.

Planning for a significant increase in U.S. ground forces in Western Europe was already well advanced in military circles by the summer of 1950. In early September, the Joint Strategic Plans Committee stated that its "planning now envisages over-all U.S. forces in Europe on the order of four infantry and the equivalent of one and a half armored divisions . . . to be in place and combat ready as expeditiously as possible."[1] Moreover, the committee recommended that the Joint Chiefs of Staff (JCS) discuss how many additional combat divisions could be deployed at the outbreak of war in Europe. At this point, western forces in Korea were still confined to the Pusan Perimeter. By mid-October, U.S. representatives to NATO estimated that the current figure of eight army divisions and two division equivalents earmarked for the alliance would rise to fourteen divisions and four division equivalents by 1 July 1952. These would be ten infantry, two armored, and two airborne divisions, as well as five infantry and airborne regimental combat teams and six reconnaissance regiments and armored combat commands.[2]

Seventh Army quickly grew into the most potent combat force in Allied Command, Europe (ACE). By the end of 1953, army forces deployed to Germany included V Corps with headquarters in Frankfurt and VII Corps with headquarters in Stuttgart. V Corps, guarding the approaches into Hesse, had two infantry divisions and one armored division, as well as 14th Armored Cavalry Regiment and 19th Armored Cavalry Group. VII Corps, guarding Bavaria and Baden-Württemberg, consisted of two infantry divisions and two armored cavalry regiments, but 2nd Armored Cavalry Regiment was stationed in Fulda and thus would have likely been appropriated by a hard-pressed V Corps. Within one month of mobilization, one armored, seven infantry, and two airborne divisions were to arrive in the command. One of the infantry divisions would come from the Far East and the remainder from the United States.[3] The order of battle that can be derived from the force deployment list allows for the conclusion that USAREUR expected to fight for Hesse and the Rhine, while the defense of large parts of Bavaria was to be left to French First Army. But the rapid reinforcement schedule raised questions. There was no indication that the U.S. military had the means to transport ten combat divisions to Western Europe in such a short period of time. The discrepancy between the largely political force-deployment planning and available air- and sealift was addressed more prudently in subsequent deployment plans.

One year later, both timing and force deployment had been adjusted. The two corps remained, of course, as did the five combat divisions, three under V Corps and two under VII Corps. V Corps had gained 373rd Armored Infantry Battalion and three heavy tank battalions. VII Corps now had two armored infantry battalions and 2nd Armored Cavalry Regiment had moved from Fulda to Nuremberg, in the VII Corps sector. Both corps had a generous helping of field artillery. V Corps had four field artillery groups and fourteen battalions, and VII Corps commanded two field artillery groups and twelve battalions. The mass of U.S. Army forces remained in the north of the Central Army Group (CENTAG) sector. Seventh Army could expect to be reinforced by 2nd Infantry Division, 1st Armored Division, and 82nd Airborne Division within one month of mobilization. Two months later, one armored, one airborne, and four infantry divisions were to follow. This amounted to one fewer divisions than in 1953, and the timetable had been extended significantly.[4] On the other hand, USAREUR had received its first atomic weapons in December 1953, and by the end of 1954 it had five 280-mm atomic cannon battalions and was awaiting the arrival of the first Corporal battalion and four Honest John batteries.[5]

The JCS were unable to resolve major differences over strategy and operational planning. In March 1955, the JCS earmarked seventeen divisions and one regimental combat team, as well as four tank battalions, for assignment to ACE within the first half year of a war. All but one of the Joint Chiefs found this to be a realistic expectation. General Ridgway dissented.[6] He stated that the army could send only thirteen combat-ready divisions to Europe in that period of time. He rejected the notion that National Guard and Reserve divisions could attain combat readiness and be deployed within less than six months. In addition, one tank battalion should be dropped from the list as a consequence of internal army reorganization. But there was no compromise, and the report was forwarded to the Supreme Allied Commander (SACEUR) with the split opinions of Ridgway and the other chiefs.[7]

In the spring of 1956, 2nd Armored Division replaced 4th Infantry Division in V Corps, and 11th Airborne Division replaced an infantry division in VII Corps. The first echelon of reinforcements, to arrive in theater within one month of mobilization, still consisted of three divisions, but the airborne division that had previously been in this group had been replaced by an infantry division. 82nd Airborne Division now was to arrive within four months of mobilization. Within the following month, 4th Armored and 25th Infantry Divisions were to arrive in Europe, and within another thirty days, five more infantry and one additional armored division could be expected. Still, the reinforcement schedule had again been pushed back, which raised the question of whether the JCS expected a long war.[8] This deployment schedule cast further doubt on the cooperation between JCS and ACE, with U.S. European

Command (USEUCOM) and Seventh Army caught in the middle. Current USEUCOM planning, based on JCS guidance, called for the counteroffensive to begin four months into the war. But only nine of the earmarked seventeen U.S. Army combat divisions were to be available at that point. On the other hand, a sixth battalion of 280-mm atomic cannons and two additional Honest John batteries increased atomic capability.[9] The question was now how Seventh Army envisioned the operational use of these forces.

A series of command post (CPX) and field-training exercises (FTX) in VII Corps in the mid-1950s offered a rare glimpse at operational implications of doctrine on the eve of the pentomic reorganization.[10] CPX WOLF CALL was conducted in July 1955. Emphasis was placed on communications, liaison, and the planning and use of "special weapons." All major tactical formations of VII Corps, except for 2nd Armored Cavalry Regiment, participated in the exercise, but it is well to bear in mind that the corps did not sit across the most worrisome terrain feature in the CENTAG sector, the Fulda Gap. The basic concept of the exercise was "an Army Group in defense of a wide front with the possibility of a withdrawal to a second defensive position." The scenario stipulated that WOLF CALL would begin thirty days after the enemy had first attacked CENTAG.[11] It would be unwise to make too much of a scenario for an exercise that essentially amounted to a war game, but it is nonetheless curious to consider that an entire month would pass before the corps became engaged.

The southern boundary of Seventh Army was set from Erlangen in Franconia to Rothenburg, Heilbronn, Durlach, and the Franco-German border at the Rhine River. French First Army was responsible for points south, including most of Bavaria, Württemberg south of Heilbronn, and the Black Forest region of Baden. The boundary between V and VII Corps ran along the Main River, traversed the hills of the Odenwald, and ended near Heppenheim in the Palatinate. CENTAG had specified two defense lines for VII Corps: GANDER from Gemunden to the Main River, south to Ochsenfurt and Lipprichhausen, and from there to Neustett and Rothenburg; and TURKEY, from the Main River south to Miltenberg, Erlenbach, and Neuenstein.[12] The corps was to practice defense of line GANDER and fighting withdrawal to line TURKEY. The defense of line GANDER would force the enemy to mass his forces. Consequently, "enemy penetration will be reduced by counterattacks, or by the use of atomic weapons followed immediately by counterattacks to destroy the STYGIAN forces and restore line GANDER."[13] The corps reserve was weak, consisting of one armored cavalry regiment with only two combat battalions and two more battalions as reinforcements.[14] But the main force for the counterattack was 2nd Armored Division, which was held in reserve by Seventh Army.[15]

WOLF CALL was followed by FTX CORDON BLEU in October, part of the annual CENTAG fall maneuver. Seventh Army was to execute the counteroffensive, whose objective was seizure of the entire area from the Fulda Gap through the Thüringerwald to the Hof Gap. Subsequently, Seventh Army was to continue the attack to the northeast. For training purposes, this exercise was conducted along a north-south axis. It tested premises for the counteroffensive by pitting two American and two French divisions in deep operations against a simulated aggressor force. All new weapons systems in ACE were made available, including 280-mm atomic cannons, Honest John rockets, and Corporal missiles. Simulation of atomic strikes against tactical targets in West Germany was planned. Overall, "the NATO forces in central Europe will be given an opportunity to practice coordination, cooperation and liaison between inter-allied forces as well as to gain further experience in improving techniques and staff procedures in the employment of special weapons and utilization of airborne troops."[16]

VII Corps, reinforced by 7th French Mechanized Division and two armored infantry battalions, was charged with attacking across the Jagst River toward Rothenburg and preparing to cross the Main River between Ochsenfurt and Kitzingen, while linking up with 5th French Division and 16th British Independent Parachute Brigade.[17] The city of Würzburg was to be recaptured, and the attack would drive on to Karlstadt and Schweinfurt. Eventually, VII Corps would cross the intra-German border and drive toward Eisenach. Atomic weapons were to be used "where remunerative targets are available and to assist in maintaining the momentum of the attack."[18]

Intelligence reports estimated enemy forces to be at only 65 to 78 percent of personnel strength and equipment, leading to a morale rating of "fair." VII Corps would have to conduct its drive into East Germany against XII Corps of Sixth Soviet Army, consisting of two tank divisions, one mechanized and one artillery division, and a rifle brigade. There was, of course, the risk that the enemy would deploy its strategic reserve: 1st Airborne Division in the vicinity of Berlin and two divisions from the Thüringerwald. In addition, five divisions were reportedly in the vicinity of Eisenach, Erfurt, Ilmenau, and Bad Salzungen.[19] At least NATO forces could assume that air superiority had been secured by the time they were to cross the border. This would make the movement of Soviet reserve divisions more difficult. V Corps was to operate to the north and east of VII Corps. But a new U.S. Army element also appeared in the plans of the exercise. U.S. XX Corps had the task of seizing Nuremberg and then driving to the northeast.[20] For the purposes of this maneuver, play of XX Corps had to be simulated. The VII Corps orders give no definitive clues as to the composition of XX Corps, but it is likely that some of the reinforcements earmarked for Seventh Army were to be assembled in a separate corps in order to launch the counterattack on a wider front.

In its evaluation of the exercise, Supreme Headquarters Allied Powers, Europe (SHAPE) stressed the high level of leadership and excellent state of equipment of U.S. Army forces but also noted that the effectiveness of atomic firepower was crucial to the attacker. Here, the NATO command staff insisted that "the effectiveness of atomic weapons against troop concentrations is dependent in large measure upon timely processing and approval of requests."[21] In order to get permission to launch rockets armed with nuclear warheads or fire atomic artillery shells, the division commander would have to ask permission from SACEUR through the chain of command. But by the time permission to engage had been granted, a target of opportunity might well have been lost. It is difficult to imagine that the field artillery commander would withhold atomic weapons if his batteries were on the brink of destruction. There is no evidence that any arrangements for predelegation of authority to use atomic weapons had been made within ACE.[22]

The operational concept for the counteroffensive was outlined in even greater detail in FTX WAR HAWK in the fall of 1956. Objective of Seventh Army was to seize the hill mass between Zwickau in East Germany, Cheb in Czechoslovakia, and Fürth and Zwiesel in northeastern Bavaria. VII Corps was to attack with main effort along the axis Weissenburg-Regensburg-Fürth-Pilsen. The maneuver forces were to be supported by atomic and conventional artillery, as well as air support and additional nuclear weapons from field army. Orders for WAR HAWK called for "atomic and massed conventional artillery preparation followed by a coordinated attack to achieve a breakthrough between Ellwangen and Wasseralfingen." The main effort of the VII Corps offensive was to come from 4th Armor Group, while 8th Infantry Division and 11th Airborne Division were supposed to attack to the right and left, respectively, of 4th Armor Group, in order to seize the shoulders of the penetration area. Once the three objectives had been achieved, 2nd Armored Division, deployed from CENTAG reserve, was to pass through 4th Armor Group and drive into the area between the intra-German border and the German-Czech border. 8th Infantry Division was to follow 2nd Armored Division and mop up bypassed enemy formations, while 11th Airborne Divisions was to protect the southern flank of the corps.[23]

CPX LION NOIR in the spring of 1957 was the first major exercise that included Bundeswehr divisions and the last CENTAG exercise prior to the conversion of Seventh Army divisions into pentomic formations. It was a comprehensive exercise that mirrored the aggressive mind-set of General Bruce C. Clarke, the new commander of Seventh Army. CENTAG was to keep 2nd Armored Division and 1st French Armored Division in reserve for employment against airborne attacks on critical terrain features but also for later counterattacks on the axes Frankfurt-Leipzig and Stuttgart-Nuremberg. Seventh Army was to defend its sector, directing the main effort along the axis Frankfurt-Leipzig. Armored cavalry screening the border, supported by atomic demolition mines as well as atomic and conventional artillery fire, was to delay the enemy advance. Meanwhile, the bulk of Seventh Army was to conduct a coordinated mobile defense by establishing a strongpoint system in depth at the Weser-Lech line, from south of Kassel along the Fulda River in a crescent to Schweinfurt, very close to the border, that would force the enemy to channel its advance into selected killing zones. There, enemy force concentrations could be destroyed by massed atomic and conventional fire as well as by counterattacks on the ground.[24]

This initial defensive phase was to be followed, on order from CENTAG, by a coordinated delaying action from the Weser-Lech line to the Ems-Neckar position, which ran from north of Marburg through the Spessart to Frankfurt, and on south through the Odenwald to the Neckar River. Again, the combination of strongpoint and mobile defense was to force the enemy into killing zones. All along, the northern flank of Seventh Army would be protected by II German Corps, which was to engage the enemy in delaying actions east of the Weser-Lech line, participate in the mobile defense of that position, and repeat the process of forward delaying actions and position defense during the withdrawal to the Ems-Neckar line. V Corps to the south and VII Corps even further south had been given similar tasks.[25] V Corps, of course, had lost 2nd Armored Division to Army Group reserve, but VII Corps expected 3rd Portuguese Infantry Division to become available within fifteen days of mobilization.[26]

The assessment of LION NOIR raised doubts that NATO forces in the defensive phase of the war would be as organized and cohesive as the CENTAG planners anticipated. Soviet ground forces attacked behind a cloud of nuclear explosions that destroyed West German cities all the way to the Rhine River. Eighth Guards Army broke through the disorganized defense at the Fulda Gap and reached Frankfurt and the Rhine near Mainz and Wiesbaden within days. At that point, CINCENT, already played by General Hans Speidel, who was about to take over the command, requested the use of tactical nuclear weapons. The president granted the request, and SACEUR ordered the immediate employment of 100 warheads on Soviet spearheads. Simultaneously, the strategic nuclear counteroffensive had gotten under way. In West Germany, the employment of tactical nuclear weapons became the starting point of a counteroffensive of the remaining ground forces. Play of LION NOIR ended with the reestablishment of West German territorial integrity.[27]

The objectives for the counteroffensive expressed in pre-exercise orders had been more ambitious. CENTAG ground forces, supported by 4th Allied Tactical Air Force, would seize the Eisenach area and link up with Northern Army Group (NORTHAG) forces southeast of Kassel. In preparation for further operations to the east, CENTAG planned to capture the Thüringerwald. Seventh Army was to attack on the axis Wertheim–Bad Kissingen–Eisenach. The entire counteroffensive was to be "strongly supported by air and ground delivered atomic fire power." The rapid seizing of the Eisenach Gap and the linking up with NORTHAG forces were critical. The planners hoped to prevent enemy withdrawal by the speed and shock of the advance, thus allowing for the physical destruction of its combat forces. VII Corps, now with 2nd Armored Division attached, and with orders to drive into East Germany to the south and east of Gotha, had first priority of reinforcement. At this stage, 11th Airborne Division, having traded assignments with 2nd Armored Division, provided the bulk of the army reserve.[28] Further objectives for CENTAG were the crossing of the Saale River in the vicinity of Halle and Jena and ultimately the crossing of the Oder River into Poland.

To sustain the offensive, "strongly supported by air and ground delivered atomic fire power," two corps abreast were to "rapidly seize and secure principal crossings over the Saale River between Halle and Kahla to establish a lodgment area." The objective was to envelop enemy forces in the Eisenach-Jena-Bayreuth triangle by linking up with elements of First French Army at Triptis. Once the bridgeheads northeast of the Saale had been established, the offensive was to drive on to the Elbe River. V Corps was to carry the brunt of the attack on the Mühlhausen-Halle axis, while VII Corps was to function as the northern pincer of the envelopment. This counteroffensive, intended to drive beyond the East German–Polish border, was to be aided by the arrival of fresh U.S. Army divisions. The 20th and 21st Infantry Divisions were to become available, and 10th Infantry Division could then be taken out of the front lines and recover in army reserve. V Corps was to gain a regimental combat team from Luxembourg. VII Corps was to gain 2nd Armored Division from army reserve.[29] Overall, the plan for LION NOIR revealed a reliance on tactical nuclear weapons as compensation for numerical inferiority. There is very little operational detail about how such weapons were to have been employed without interfering with the counteroffensive.

These were the last European maneuvers of the old army divisions. The spirit that pervaded them seemed overly optimistic. They also showed little understanding of exactly how nuclear weapons were to be integrated into a campaign, other than as an extension of heavy artillery. Moreover, beyond speed and dispersion, there were no new ideas on how to address the threat of Soviet nuclear weapons. This is not surprising given the lack of nuclear tactical doctrine in the army in general. That in itself, however, is difficult to explain because army commanders in the United States and Europe expected that tactical nuclear weapons would have to be used early in a war against the Soviets. General Maxwell Taylor hoped that the shift to pentomic divisions would consolidate the army's claim to be a major user of nuclear weapons—a position strongly attacked by the air force—which would as a matter of course lead to the development of proper doctrine for their use. This was indeed central to his conception of army transformation.

Seventh Army, the Pentomic Division, and Operational Planning

At the end of 1956, the Seventh Army retained its command structure of two corps with five combat divisions, but the reinforcement schedule had been accelerated. There still were to be one armored and two infantry divisions arriving in Europe within thirty days of mobilization, but then 25th Infantry Division was to follow within the month. The 4th Armored Division and 82nd Airborne Division were expected to be in theater within 120 days, and the 3rd Infantry Division within the following month. Five National Guard divisions, four infantry and one armored, were to follow within six months of mobilization. This was, at least to some extent, an expression of good faith to the alliance partners. Army generals doubted that guard divisions would be ready and deployed in such a short span of time. This force deployment list was the first year-end statement that explicitly noted that the last earmarked echelon of reinforcements came from the National Guard.[30] Questions about transportation capacities raised by the Army Staff remained unanswered. The timing of the reinforcement schedule was based on availability and expected combat readiness of the divisions, rather than on a thorough assessment of logistics, supply, and transportation. Army, navy, and air force maintained separate planning staffs for overseas deployment. Maxwell Taylor recalled that lack of coordination posed a serious problem for the army. Strategic mobility was perceived as a given by the political leadership in the Pentagon, but the army doubted that all requirements of transportation could be fulfilled in a crisis.[31]

The JCS expected that the reorganization of army divisions, despite the resulting reduction of manpower in combat divisions, would not lead to a significant change in U.S. Army personnel in Germany. This was partly due to the greater need for technical support brought about by the more widespread deployment of atomic weapons systems. The atomic armament of

USAREUR had grown to six Corporal battalions, one Honest John battalion, as well as five batteries that were directly assigned to the combat divisions, and six 280-mm atomic cannon battalions.[32] The personnel cut from combat divisions was to be redeployed in combat support elements at the corps level. At the end of November 1956, there were 202,580 officers and men in army units in Germany. The personnel ceiling for USAREUR after the pentomic reorganization, which was to be concluded in the spring of 1958, was set at 230,000 officers and men, of which 202,200 were to be deployed in Germany.[33]

In 1957, Seventh Army proposed a restationing of its units, hoping to vacate the region south of the Danube, which was to be defended by French and German forces. The proposed forward sector to be covered by Seventh Army would thus be reduced by 100 miles. In addition, flank security and the combat-readiness posture of U.S. ground forces in Germany would be improved in the process. Four of five U.S. Army divisions were to be moved. The main problem was the cost of such an operation. The German government would have to pay for the necessary new installations north of the Danube and could expect only old installations south of the river in return. General Taylor approved of the plan in principle, but he preferred a simpler version involving the movement of fewer American divisions. General Speidel at Allied Land Forces, Central Europe (LANDCENT) was also in agreement but could not say whether the Adenauer administration would approve of the plan. Moreover, approval was needed from the governments of the United States and France as well as from SACEUR.[34] General Valluy, Speidel's predecessor at LANDCENT, previously had suggested creation of a Franco-German army of eight divisions south of the Danube and another Franco-German army in the Koblenz-Trier region.[35]

The proposal to move Seventh Army units north of the Danube stemmed from the threat of atomic warfare that called for a more effective readiness posture of all combat and support elements. Full combat readiness was seen as closely related to the development of fully operational atomic capabilities. Operation SEVENTH HEAVEN, which accomplished some elements of the restationing proposal, began in 1957 but was only completed in the early 1960s when responsibility for the defense of large parts of Bavaria was given to II German Corps. First French Army, which was stationed in the southern parts of Baden-Württemberg, presumably would have moved forward to battle stations in Bavaria upon alert. Although many elements of the original plan were achieved through routine stationing actions, the operation could not be completed in the 1950s because USAREUR headquarters and the German Ministry of Defense could not agree on proper financing. Nevertheless, SEVENTH HEAVEN contributed to the redeployment of American troops further forward and to the north, as well as to the realignment of supplies and equipment that brought fast-moving items closer to the projected front line.[36]

Maxwell Taylor urged deployment of combat units east of the Rhine. In October, General Clarke explained to Andrew O'Meara, commanding general of 4th Armored Division, a unit soon to be deployed to Germany, that the originally intended area of deployment near Baumholder at the Saar River was no longer considered to be appropriate. Instead, the division was to take over an area in northern Württemberg that was to be vacated by 8th Infantry Division, which in turn would take over the area of 2nd Armored Division, a unit that was to return to the United States. Clarke explained that "this is a part of a plan that has been cooking for several months and is in furtherance of General Taylor's expressed desire to get two Armored Divisions east of the Rhine River." This move, involving three divisions on two continents and depending on well-timed air- and sealift, would be complicated.[37] Approval of the plan had only come less than three months before the scheduled movement of 4th Armored Division.[38] It stands as an indication for the greater urgency of the Army Staff to move U.S. combat divisions closer to the intra-German border. It illustrated the desire to shift the main line of resistance from the Rhine River into West Germany. Both armored divisions were now stationed well to the east of the Rhine. Only two of the fifteen infantry and airborne battle groups remained west of the river, while three were stationed at its banks.

The forward-defense concept found further expression in CENTAG's Emergency Defense Plan (EDP) of July 1958. This came in response to a new Allied Forces, Central Europe (AFCENT) operational directive that envisioned a more forward deployment, made feasible by the increased effectiveness of German land forces assigned to CENTAG, as well as by the considerable increase in atomic weapons that was scheduled to become available after 1 July. In the course of 1958, Seventh Army added one Redstone and three Honest John battalions to its armaments. In addition, there were nine 8-inch howitzer battalions and five composite battalions armed with Honest John rocket launchers and 8-inch howitzers.[39] The new EDP served as guidance for all American, French, and German forces assigned to the command. For First French Army in southern Germany, it meant a much greater area of responsibility as the initial defensive positions were moved forward and the focus of American ground forces shifted to the north and east.[40]

CENTAG EDP 2-58 provided for forward defense along four separate lines, all of them to the east of the Rhine River. General Speidel embraced this eastward shift of the defensive positions.[41] Upon taking command of LANDCENT in April 1957, he had proclaimed forward defense to be a critical objective. NATO had to be steered away from viewing West Germany merely as the battlefield in a forward defense of France and the Benelux countries.[42] The new lines of resistance began in Fritzlar at the boundary with NORTHAG and ran to the Vogelsberg, just west of Fulda. There they branched off. Line ETHNOLOGIST continued southeast, passing to the east of Bad Kissingen, Schweinfurt, Bamberg, and Nuremberg, before turning south and east to Landshut. From there it veered south to the Inn River and the Austrian border. Line RUMOR was further to the west, running from the town of Schluechtern to Augsburg, passing to the east of Würzburg. It followed the Lech River to the Austrian border. Line OINTMENT, projected as the position that was to be defended 48 hours after the invasion, ran due south from Schluechtern to Ulm. South of Ulm, the French would be responsible for the defense of Württemberg and southwestern Bavaria. The battle plans were built around the objective of delaying, neutralizing, and destroying enemy forces along their main axes of penetration in order to create the conditions necessary for the NATO counteroffensive.[43]

The army forces charged with these tasks were largely similar to those of 1956. At the end of 1957, V Corps commanded one infantry and two armored divisions, and VII Corps had one infantry and an airborne division. The reinforcement schedule had been slightly altered, affecting the later echelons and ensuring that a tenth combat division would be in theater within four months of mobilization. The first echelon of reinforcements, two infantry divisions and the Screaming Eagles of the 101st Airborne, was slated to arrive within thirty days. The 82nd Airborne Division was to arrive after three months, 2nd Armored Division one month later, 3rd Infantry Division after 150 days, and, finally, one armored and five infantry divisions of the National Guard after six months. Thus there were still seventeen divisions earmarked for deployment to Central Europe, but more than one third were National Guard divisions.[44]

Active divisions deployed to Europe had gone through the process of reorganization into the pentomic format in the course of 1957. 10th Infantry Division and 2nd Armored Division became pentomic organizations by 1 July. The 8th Infantry Division followed on 1 August, and 3rd Armored Division completed what little reorganization it needed by the end of September. Shortly thereafter, in December and January, 4th Armored replaced 2nd Armored Division, and in the spring of 1958, 3rd Infantry replaced 10th Infantry Division.[45] The incoming units had previously been reconstituted as pentomic divisions in the United States. Under the new organization, the infantry divisions in Germany lost one 155-mm and two 105-mm howitzer battalions. They gained a nuclear-capable composite artillery battalion, consisting of one 8-inch howitzer battery, one Honest John rocket battery, and two 155-mm howitzer batteries. Infantry divisions also lost their regimental tank companies but gained an armored cavalry battalion that replaced the former reconnaissance company. Each infantry division lost 3,400 men, but only 450 of them were cut from front-line infantry elements.[46] General Taylor, and the proponents of the pentomic division and tactical nuclear warfare, assumed that atomic weapons would give the division overwhelming firepower. Army requirement studies of the time called for the employment of 151,000 tactical nuclear weapons in the defense of Western Europe.[47]

With the conversion of all major combat units of Seventh Army to pentomic organizations came the need to adjust training practices. On paper, Seventh Army was now a streamlined, highly mobile force that would soon possess even greater atomic capability. It became necessary to translate the theoretical mobility and dispersion capability into actual coordination of all arms and all battle groups of a division. A point of emphasis was the defense against tactical air forces. USAREUR had recognized that the close integration of Soviet ground and air forces in East Germany, coupled with a shortage of effective antiaircraft artillery east of the Rhine, gave the Soviets air superiority at the outset of war. Hence, U.S. Army forces had to be prepared to take defensive and evasive actions. This led to an emphasis on evasion, camouflage, and massed small arms fire. At any point in training tests and exercises, enemy air superiority was stressed and included in the tactical scenarios.[48] NATO exercises, such as COUNTER PUNCH, a SHAPE joint atomic exercise in September 1957, underscored the shortcomings of allied air defenses as well as the expected slow reaction of NATO air forces that would allow the Soviets to sustain the initial advantage. Largely, this was due to the projected destruction of airfields and difficulties in their repair.[49]

Other exercises showed that tactical conceptions had to be reconsidered fundamentally. LION BLEU, an AFCENT command post exercise in March 1958 that involved all major headquarters in Central Region to the level of divisions, emphasized SACEUR's atomic procedures and the adjustment of tactical thinking to the atomic battlefield. Critical communications and logistics capabilities were tested. The atomic scenario revealed significant differences between major commands, such as CENTAG and Seventh Army, whose atomic plans needed to be coordinated better. More problematic was the philosophical difference in target selection of air and ground commanders. Air force generals recommended implementation of preconceived strike plans, targeting fixed structures such as bridges, the destruction of which would slow down the enemy. Ground commanders preferred to expend the atomic arsenal mainly on enemy force concentrations and feared that the preconceived target lists would lead to a rapid depletion of the arsenal. Commanders of ground forces also were hesitant to destroy fixed installations because operational plans for the counteroffensive assumed that many of these features remained intact.[50]

LION BLEU revealed that traditional notions of established lines, protected flanks, and attack en masse "were best forgotten." Atomic battlefield tactics would have to be adjusted to a combat area of great depth and fluidity. Certainly, the density of forces had to be reduced. This was indeed a major feature of the pentomic battle-group concept. In general, LION BLEU underscored the need for mobility, dispersion, and ability to reassemble and strike quickly.[51] As a result of both COUNTER PUNCH and LION BLEU, ground-force commanders concluded that atomic weapons were best used against enemy reserve formations. For the purpose of target acquisition and rapid processing of requests to employ atomic weapons on specific targets, a special targeting section was created within the CENTAG operations center of G-2 (Intelligence) and G-3 (Operations). Seventh Army tested small-unit tactics under simulated atomic conditions in the biggest maneuver to date, field training exercise SABRE HAWK in February 1958. Both corps were involved, V Corps as defender and VII Corps as aggressor, and 125,000 troops participated in the exercise. To assure the same training benefits to all troops, both sides assumed offensive and defensive, including delay and withdrawal operations. Neither side scored a maneuver victory.[52]

At the beginning of 1959, V Corps in the northern sector of the Seventh Army had the 3rd Infantry, the 3rd and 4th Armored Divisions, one armored cavalry regiment, and three independent tank battalions. VII Corps had 8th and 24th Infantry Divisions and two armored cavalry regiments. All three U.S. Army divisions of SACEUR's strategic reserve were earmarked as reinforcements for Seventh Army, although they could also be called upon to react to other crises if necessary. Currently, these were 4th Infantry and 101st and 82nd Airborne Divisions. They were to arrive in Germany within thirty days of mobilization. Additionally, Seventh Army could expect 1st Infantry Division to arrive four months after mobilization. Thirty days later, it was supposed to receive an armored division and three infantry divisions, two of which would be from the National Guard. After six months, four more National Guard divisions would arrive, three of them infantry and one armored.[53] The force deployment plans were left nearly unchanged in the course of the year, but the two corps in Germany traded divisions. V Corps lost 4th Armored Division to VII Corps but gained 8th Infantry Division in its stead.[54] In 1959, USAREUR added a second Redstone battalion, a fifth Honest John battalion, and five composite Honest John and 8-inch howitzer battalions.[55]

The forces earmarked as reinforcements for SACEUR underscored the primary significance of the European theater in the event of war. In 1957, the Strategic Army Corps (STRAC) had been created under Continental Army

Command (CONARC) in order to increase the strategic mobility of the army. Four divisions, 82nd and 101st Airborne and 1st and 4th Infantry, were attached to the new corps. Ideally, STRAC forces would respond rapidly to crises and conflicts around the globe. In actuality, however, all four divisions were part of the first and second echelon of reinforcements earmarked for SACEUR. Three quarters of the corps would be in Europe within the first month of a crisis or war. The army thus retained the possibility for deployment of STRAC divisions outside of Europe but left no doubt that they were to be deployed to Europe immediately in case of mobilization of NATO forces. The strategic reserve was degraded in January 1959. Due to the general force reduction of the army, only three combat divisions could be maintained in ready reserve.[56]

American war plans for Central Europe envisioned a multiphased course of operations. A study for field army logistics, released in May 1959, was based on the assumption that Seventh Army would conduct a delay-withdrawal action of twenty to thirty days.[57] Given the shortness of the east-west axis in Western Europe, such a withdrawal would have to be slow. At the waist of West Germany, the distance from the intra-German border to the Rhine was only about 90 miles, and the total distance between the English Channel and the Rhine was approximately 250 miles. The delay-and-withdrawal phase would be followed by a period of defensive action along a front that might not be stabilized. This meant local attacks and counterattacks to wear down the enemy forces. This indicated that mobile, active defense was now included in operational planning. The defensive phase was estimated at three months at the minimum, but it might last ten to eighteen months. Eventually, the war was to be won in a period of offensive action characterized by rapid movement over long distances. The duration of this third phase could not be anticipated. All along, both sides would probably use atomic weapons. This was indeed consistent with the large-scale exercises within USAREUR in the mid-1950s. It is nevertheless puzzling, as none of the publicized defense plans of ACE or the JCS considered more than two phases, defense-delay and counteroffensive. Furthermore, the defensive alone could last one year. But over a year of atomic warfare, without stable front lines, on German, and possibly on other Western European, territory would not leave much inhabitable land and few civilians to inhabit it.

Unfortunately, the staying power of pentomic divisions for such extended operations was questionable. Most observers within the army doubted whether the battle groups amounted to much in the first place, but they were certainly not capable of sustained operations in a protracted war. Seventh Army found the new divisions wanting in some of the most critical aspects of modern warfare: fire support, mobility, and communications. The insufficient number of armored personal carriers (APCs) and trucks was particularly problematic.[58] Communication systems were insufficient for the complex coordination of five battle groups. Most damagingly for an army that relied upon the application of heavy firepower, the commanding general of Seventh Army artillery concluded that the pentomic infantry division had insufficient conventional and atomic firepower. He believed that the 4.2-inch mortar battery could not provide adequate direct fire support for the battle group. He concluded that the reorganization had taken away the strength of American artillery: centralized command, flexibility, and massing capability.[59]

Logistics were not mobile enough to maintain a network of small general supply points in the forward areas, of which at least two were necessary for a corps of three divisions. Each general supply point carried enough stocks for three days, but obviously such a delicate timed-delivery resupply system was very dangerous. Yet the only alternatives were to amass larger forward supply depots that could easily be destroyed by enemy nuclear fire or to have no forward depots and rely entirely on same-day delivery of supplies. Other aspects of logistics, such as maintenance, suffered from the same problems of mobility and exposure due to the need for forward deployment. General Williston Palmer raised the urgent problem of lack of manpower in a discussion with General Norstad: "Logistical support forces have already been cut below the safety point. If we were involved in a shooting war, it is doubtful that our combat forces could be supported by the current logistical support forces."[60]

USAREUR planners concluded that significant changes to the current system of field army logistics were needed. Every support unit that was at least 100 miles forward of the army rear area had to be fully mobile.[61] If that could be achieved, the forward general-supply-point concept might be feasible. It remained doubtful, however, whether such delicate operations, depending on timing and communications, could have been sustained in a protracted atomic war. No one knew how atomic weapons changed the role of support units and the environment in which they would have to operate. A related question was how supplies were to reach the rear area distribution centers once the thirty or sixty day stocks that were in the theater had been expended. Naturally, maritime communications across the Atlantic Ocean were stressed as critical to the defense of Western Europe, but it was unclear to what extent ports would be functional after nuclear attacks. Pentagon reports of beaching operations for logistics purposes abounded but left vague how such operations would work and how a line of communication from beach to rear area centers was to be established and maintained.

SACEUR doubted that Seventh Army had the logistical means to conduct sustained combat operations. In his Combat Effectiveness Report of 1958,

General Norstad criticized the insufficient number of trucks, ammunition handling units, and chemical, bacteriological, and radiological (CBR) defense capability. This exposed the anomalous position of NATO's supreme commander also being the U.S. Commander in Chief, Europe (USCINCEUR). In essence, SACEUR Norstad criticized his direct subordinate, USCINCEUR Norstad, for being remiss in this area, since theater logistics fell within the realm of USEUCOM. This assessment must have reflected badly upon his alternate headquarters. Of course, this was merely thinly veiled criticism of the army brass, the Defense Department, and the civilian leadership in Washington for generally misplaced priorities. The army acknowledged the lack of trucks, but it was assumed that mobilization and subsequent deployment would provide adequate means of transportation. Other deficiencies could be quickly addressed, in part through the reassignment of former combat troops to support roles.[62]

CONARC evaluated the pentomic division more positively. It was well suited for both conventional and atomic warfare. Consequently, the modified table of organization and equipment for infantry divisions in 1960 did not entail major changes. Overall, manpower remained below 14,000 officers and men, although the personnel of division artillery was increased by nearly 25 percent.[63] Armored and airborne divisions were left intact. In the field, however, the pentomic division still elicited little enthusiasm. General Harold K. Johnson, just prior to becoming army chief of staff, voiced the opinion that this division "would have had a difficult time fighting its way out of a wet paper bag."[64] He particularly mentioned problems with communications, conventional fire support, and transportation. Other soldiers, like Anthony B. Herbert, a platoon leader of an infantry battle group in Germany in 1959, thought that the reorganization made no sense from an operational perspective and thus had to be a publicity ploy. Herbert argued that greater dispersion was of little help on an atomic or even nuclear battlefield, as blast radii and subsequent radiation would destroy all life in a wide area. Herbert also recognized a problem that had been largely ignored in the planning stages, namely the gap between senior commanders and junior officers once the regimental and battalion command levels were combined at battle group. Quite possibly, this could have been made to work with an as yet to be invented communications system, but not with existing technology.[65] Moreover, it removed one command level and reduced the chances for timely promotion of junior grade officers.

Army internal studies of the 1960s concluded that the pentomic division lacked organizational flexibility and committed the U.S. Army to a particular kind of warfare in Central Europe with great reliance on atomic weapons. Tactical mobility was restricted by its cumbersome organization, and the division commander was overtaxed with the control of five battle groups, the division artillery, the tank battalion, and the reconnaissance squadron. Finally, conventional firepower had been reduced to less than that of the division of World War II and Korea.[66] Army officer and historian Robert Doughty concluded that "the resulting unpreparedness of the Army illustrates the dangers of a strategic concept dictating tactical doctrine without consideration of the technical and intellectual capability to follow the doctrine."[67]

Command structure under certain circumstances was also a concern. In peacetime, the NATO military structure did not become operational, and USAREUR's mission statement for 1959 foresaw the possibility that fighting might occur under the auspices of army command in Europe without direct involvement of NATO. Geographically limited crises would then have to be dealt with unilaterally.[68] For such a contingency, USAREUR had three operational plans, one addressing the transition from peace to war and the other two outlining combat operations. OPLAN 302 delineated how USAREUR would deploy Seventh Army if SACEUR failed to take control. OPLAN 303 addressed the most dire situation, a rapid Soviet advance across the Rhine-IJssel line that did not leave enough time for SHAPE to take command of NATO forces in Central Europe. In such a case, USAREUR forces would be ordered to retreat to prepared defensive positions in the Pyrenees.[69]

U.S. forces in Europe were also called upon to prepare for political crises short of war. In 1958 and 1959, USAREUR developed an emergency plan that offered military countermeasures to a potential blocking of Western access to Berlin. 11th Armored Cavalry Regiment was instructed to prepare for actions to reopen access on the ground. Most likely, a battalion-size task force would escort a convoy through Soviet control points and proceed to the city, but in February 1959 more aggressive alternatives were revealed. New plans included the deployment of an armored combat command or even an entire armored division.[70] The latter would have been a provocation that might have caused nuclear war. A Special National Intelligence Estimate, SNIE 100-6-59, pursued the question of how the Soviets and others would react if the United States, Britain, and France undertook military actions to resolve the Berlin crisis. This could range from "a substantial effort to reopen ground access to West Berlin by local action," meaning the dispatch of a reinforced battalion with a reinforced division and tactical air support in ready reserve, to "preparations for general war."[71] Maxwell Taylor was appalled by the discussion of military options. The army did not yet possess sufficient capability to fight a limited nuclear war. Hence, even a skirmish of patrols on the access routes to Berlin might result either in general nuclear war or a political surrender of the U.S. government to Soviet pressure tactics. Taylor thought that the Berlin Crisis underscored the need to develop greater flexibility to respond to local emergencies.[72]

USAREUR suffered from the consequences of the Lebanon operation in 1958 far more than it did from the Berlin Crisis. Eisenhower's decision to contain actively the spread of support for the policies of the Egyptian leader, Gamal Abdel Nasser, and his desire to maintain stability in the Middle East need not have affected troops in Europe very much, as STRAC had the means to deploy ample force to Lebanon or anywhere else in the region. But operations in the Near East and the Middle East fell under the auspices of USEUCOM, and when the crisis in Lebanon became acute, American forces intervened. The United States deployed one reinforced airborne battle group of the 24th Infantry Division, more than 2,200 men, thus degrading the division's infantry strength by 20 percent. A second airborne battle group was put on 12-hour alert, but was ultimately not deployed. USEUCOM and USAREUR also had plans for deployment of emergency-response forces in North Africa.[73]

By 1960, USAREUR was stretched thin. When the Defense Department indicated that five Hawk antiaircraft missile battalions would be attached to USAREUR, General Clyde D. Eddleman, the commander in chief, plainly told SACEUR that these could not be absorbed without negative effect to the combat capability of Seventh Army. General Norstad endorsed the position of the Army Staff that the battalions could be manned entirely by German personnel. Nuclear warheads, however, had to be guarded and maintained by American troops. Eddleman suggested that a rotation system of airborne brigades could alleviate the strain on USAREUR. He proposed to send the airborne brigade of the 8th Division to the United States and in return deploy two battle groups from the airborne corps, which could then form a new airborne brigade in Germany. This would guarantee that at least one airborne brigade was in the theater at any time. Two of the four separate armored infantry battalions in Seventh Army would be sent west of the Rhine to bolster 8th Division. General Norstad expressed his opposition to any action that would lead to a reduction of U.S. forces in Europe, particularly with respect to conventional forces, which were already "pared to the bone." Norstad hoped that an increase in conventional capability of Seventh Army could be achieved and the threshold of nuclear war adjusted accordingly.[74]

FTX WINTERSHIELD II, a large maneuver in Bavaria in February 1961, demonstrated the difficulty of simulating tactical nuclear operations. It included the two corps headquarters and their artillery, 8th Infantry and 4th Armored divisions, one German Panzergrenadier division, a French mechanized brigade, 4th Armor Group, and two armored cavalry regiments. The exercise was carefully controlled and unrealistic in the nuclear simulation, in the interest of training efficiency. To keep the exercise moving, all effects and nuclear casualties were erased after 6 hours. Tactically, the defenders were charged with establishing contact with the aggressor as far forward as possible and then delaying the advance, holding the enemy east of the defensive line at Grafenwöhr for at least 48 hours, defending the Grafenwöhr position, and eventually delaying and preparing to defend a secondary line between Bamberg and Bayreuth. The weather conditions made aerial surveillance impossible. The difficult conditions imposed a heavy responsibility on ground surveillance assets. For useful intelligence and targets for atomic strikes, corps commanders had to rely mainly on long-range patrols and agents behind enemy lines. Once the targets had been determined, corps artillery performed well. The most immediate problem arising from the exercise was the realization that there was neither doctrine nor stated policy for guidance on nuclear target designation and that too much time was lost in obtaining authority to fire. General Clarke concluded that winter maneuvers of this scale should not be repeated.[75]

Clarke had returned to Germany in October 1960 to take command of USAREUR. His command philosophy was based on constant realistic training. But this assumed reliable organizational structure, whereas the pentomic divisions were supposed to be tested and adjusted in the field. Clarke argued that exercises should be conducted to train men and not to test unit structures. Within the year, however, he expressed considerable satisfaction about the strides made by his troops. Marksmanship and the ability of tank crews to engage rapidly an identified enemy target with the appropriate weapon received special mention. Field exercises of Seventh Army were now "realistic."[76] Clarke thus implicitly criticized the tendency of his predecessor, General Eddleman, to experiment with division and battle groups on such occasions. He overlooked, however, that his command would have been much less operationally capable had it not been for the alterations to the divisional structure made by Eddleman. By late 1961, Clarke was satisfied that USAREUR had achieved a very high state of combat readiness, but he nevertheless warned that Germany could become "a second 'Bataan' in case [Seventh Army] is hit without the essential tactical strength and mobility and without the essential logistical requirements for an adequate time and without logistical mobility and flexibility."[77]

The Bundeswehr, LANDCENT, and the Brigade

The buildup of German forces was critical to the forward-defense posture of the alliance. In September 1955, Chancellor Konrad Adenauer publicly insisted that all twelve divisions would be ready in three years time, but various U.S. agencies that monitored German rearmament were highly skeptical. In a review of U.S. policy toward West Germany, the State Department noted in May 1956 that "disappointingly little progress is being made." Sticking points were the deliberate parliamentary investigation into the assurance of civilian control of the military, the unwillingness of the Adenauer administration to raise the defense budget above nine billion German marks, and the increasing support in political circles for shortened conscription of twelve rather than eighteen months.[78] The debate of the Radford Plan did not help in the matter. As Bundeswehr inspector-general Adolf Heusinger pointed out to the NATO Standing Group, it provided the political opposition in Germany with ample ammunition. Nevertheless, Heusinger believed that by the end of 1956 nearly 100,000 men would be under arms. The biggest military problem was the lack of qualified and experienced noncommissioned officers. World War II had ended more than a decade before and many career soldiers who were not politically tainted had aged to the point of being ineffective.[79]

The gap between promised NATO commitments and Bundeswehr forces actually in existence only grew wider. On 14 February 1957, Admiral Radford expressed his concern about inconsistencies in statements by the new German minister of defense, Franz-Josef Strauss, who had been in office since mid-October.[80] Strauss advocated a reduction of the West German manpower objective, while retaining the goal of twelve active army divisions. In December 1956, Radford had learned that only five German divisions were to be combat-ready by June 1957, two more by January 1958, and the rest at an undetermined date in the future. Under the original timetable, the Bundeswehr should have had 96,000 men under arms at the end of 1956, but by late fall there had been only 68,000 men in five divisions and two regimental combat teams. By the end of 1957, only 135,000 men were to be expected, even though the objective had been set at twice as many. Only three of the five promised divisions had indeed been committed to ACE.[81] In the event, Strauss had already adjusted the force objective from 500,000 to 350,000 officers and men, without informing West Germany's NATO partners. He argued that the 500,000-man force objective was based on the creation of a European Defense Community, a plan that had failed in 1954. Strauss wanted to see what changes the ongoing NATO strategy review might bring. Radford deduced from Strauss's public statements that the new force objective might be below 350,000.

The Germans followed the lead of the New Look and began to consider to what extent atomic weapons could compensate for smaller ground forces. Behind such contemplation was the fundamental question of whether a conventionally equipped force still had major utility. The tendency toward smaller units, greater flexibility and mobility, dispersion, and integration of tactical atomic weapons was undeniable. On the other hand, Germany had agreed not to seek production capability for atomic weapons, and it was unlikely that the European NATO partners would concede the point. Even more, complete nuclear sharing was ultimately a political liability, despite efforts of the Eisenhower administration to promote the idea.[82] The West German public viewed nuclear weapons with a great degree of skepticism and gave little support to the idea of atomic weapons for the Bundeswehr. German land forces were designed for a defensive mission, supported by atomic weapons that would have to be obtained from the Americans in case of war. Although the reduction by about 150,000 men in the active force diminished the staying power of the German army, the U.S. government still hoped that twelve fully functional divisions could be fielded nevertheless by the beginning of the 1960s.[83]

German army divisions were intended to be significantly smaller than the triangular U.S. Army divisions and smaller even than the combat divisions under the pentomic concept. A German infantry division had 13,000 officers and men and an armored division only 12,000. By October 1957, the three existing infantry and two armored divisions had reached between 60 and 70 percent of their targeted strength. Two regimental combat teams, one airborne and one mountain, formed the nucleus of the planned airborne and mountain divisions. They stood at about half of their expected final strength of 8,000 men.[84]

Bundeswehr land forces had been organized along the same principles as their American counterparts in the first half of the 1950s, with divisions consisting of three regiments or combat groups. As early as February 1956, German generals suggested that NATO divisions should have a more flexible command structure. This would allow for the tailoring of forces by adding or subtracting combat battalions to task force headquarters. It also expressed the German command philosophy that afforded a great degree of autonomy to junior officers.[85] German planners also were uncertain about the tactical employment of atomic weapons. As more detailed information became available, Bundeswehr commanders began to consider the practical implications of tactical atomic warfare.[86]

German military leaders drew the same basic conclusion as their American allies: the nuclear battlefield required greater dispersion and smaller maneuver units. But while Maxwell Taylor introduced pentomic divisions and battle groups, most German generals preferred a brigade structure in which battalions were the fundamental combat formations. In 1956, some former general staff officers who were involved in devising the guiding principles and structures of the Bundeswehr had advocated integration of tactical atomic weapons and adoption of the pentomic system. General Adolf Heusinger and the majority of Bundeswehr commanders, however, believed that adopting the pentomic division would put into question German operational philosophy, which was based on flexible command, tactical and operational mobility, and massed firepower.[87] Therefore, the Bundeswehr did not follow the example of the U.S. Army. Instead, the German generals introduced a different combat division.

German general officers assessed initial Bundeswehr divisions as too heavy, and they were concerned about the complexity of the command structure in a potential atomic war. German army leaders thus introduced a new divisional organization for 1959.[88] The new division was built upon three self-contained tactical headquarters. Simultaneously, battalions were reduced in size to improve mobility and command and control. To compensate, infantry divisions received twelve rather than nine maneuver battalions. But there was also a fundamental shift in operational and structural thinking. In the old system, the division had been the essential combined-arms tactical unit. After the reorganization of 1958 and 1959, brigades of several maneuver battalions were to be the new self-contained combat formations capable of independent action.[89] They were loosely attached to divisional headquarters, which functioned primarily as administrative units.[90] Brigades could disperse more widely on the battlefield than regimental combat teams, which reduced vulnerability to atomic weapons while maintaining the combat power of the traditional division.[91] Moreover, all infantry units were converted to armored infantry. But tactical atomic weapons were to be integrated only at the corps level in an organizational structure that still was designed primarily for conventional warfare.[92] The Germans envisioned that two or three combined-arms brigades could operate in the geographic area of one division.[93]

German armored infantry divisions had one tank and two infantry brigades. Armored divisions, conversely, had two tank brigades and one infantry brigade. The German army intended to fight mounted as much as possible, relying on tanks, APCs, and Schützenpanzer, or infantry fighting vehicles (IFVs), an area in which the U.S. Army lagged far behind. Bundeswehr leaders doubled the number of combat units by splitting existing tank and artillery battalions in half and then bringing them back up to strength with conscripts and reservists. One-third of each infantry battalion provided the cadre for a new battalion. Battalions were reduced in size and their command structure was simplified to adjust to the projected nature of a nuclear battlefield. The tank battalion was reduced from seventy-seven to fifty-four medium-gun tanks in three companies. Armored infantry battalions retained thirty-nine IFVs. The tank battalion of an armored infantry division had an additional antitank capability of sixteen self-propelled rocket launchers. The bulk of artillery was controlled at the division level, but one artillery battalion was assigned to each brigade.[94]

All German infantry divisions implemented this reorganization simultaneously because of the great urgency to create additional units. Observers in CENTAG feared that doing so weakened the German forces at a time when such weakness could be ill afforded, but there seemed no alternative short of expanding the defense budget dramatically.[95] Unlike later U.S. Army models, the German brigades were largely self-sufficient and would be grouped under existing divisions, which served as administrative units, on an ad hoc basis rather than by permanent assignment. This meant that any Bundeswehr division could interchangeably be armored, mechanized, or infantry.[96]

On 27 October 1959, General Heusinger, now chief of the German Armed Forces Staff, met with the NATO Standing Group to discuss Germany's current military problems. At the time, the Bundeswehr had 146,000 officers and men in eleven understrength divisions. Seven of the armored and mechanized divisions were at approximately 50 to 80 percent personnel strength, while the other two were only at cadre strength, slightly above one-third of their allotment. Heusinger provided no details on either the mountain or the airborne division. He did say, however, that the twelfth division would be activated in 1962. The shortage of young officers and noncommissioned officers had not been addressed. But Heusinger looked beyond immediate problems and pondered the future of deterrence, as nuclear parity was approaching. Much like Maxwell Taylor, Matthew Ridgway, or James Gavin, he concluded that the danger of limited war was growing. Heusinger suggested that it would be better for political leaders to have a degree of flexibility than to be faced with the alternative of nuclear war or surrender. The threat of limited war would have to be addressed by ground forces, but Heusinger thought it unlikely that the Soviets would be deterred by purely conventional combat formations. NATO ground forces needed atomic weapons.[97]

In the course of the ensuing discussion, Heusinger expressed concern about the territorial defense of his country. NATO forces were insufficient for forward defense as far east as intended. This had forced a concept of the defense of fixed lines upon the Germans, a situation that would only change once all twelve divisions were at full strength and increased airpower was made available. Presently, every division would be responsible for a frontage of between 40 and 50 kilometers, which constituted a dangerous extension even for forces armed with atomic weapons. Heusinger argued that the territory between the Main River and Kassel had to be defended rigidly, while areas to the south of the Main and north of Kassel might afford more flexibility. Any hope for success depended upon the cohesion of the defensive forces and on the rapid onset of the counteroffensive. But he feared that the three German brigades deployed east of the Weser River might not hold. SHAPE and LANDCENT were also considering this problem. Additional dangers existed in the likely separation of forces in Denmark and Schleswig-Holstein from Central Region and in the vulnerability of the lines of communication across the Rhine.[98]

In the event, Heusinger had been generous in his accounting of active German army divisions. According to the 1960 NATO review, the Germans had only seven divisions assigned to ACE. Another four divisions and an independent brigade were in various stages of recruitment and training. By the end of the year, the airborne division was expected to be committed to ACE, and in the course of 1961, a fifth infantry division was to follow. But there were only two armored divisions, well short of the six requested in the MC 70 force goals. Eleven German army divisions were to be committed to ACE by the end of 1962, but seven of them would be infantry, rather than four, as had been intended. This was tempered to some extent by the conversion of infantry into mechanized infantry divisions, and there was hope that a third armored division would be in an advanced state of training in 1963. The delay in committing forces to ACE was in part the result of a change of heart. Germany had intended to commit less-than-ready divisions, but now only combat-ready units were assigned to NATO commands. It was also apparent that the Germans considered the brigade rather than the division to be the essential operational formation in the future.[99]

By the turn of the decade, the German understanding of deterrence resembled in most respects that of Maxwell Taylor and Lauris Norstad. It was clear that NATO could not renounce the use of tactical nuclear weapons by its shield forces in the defense of West Germany. But at the same time, the alliance need not pursue an all-or-nothing policy. Naturally, the Bundeswehr aspired to be equal in weaponry and equipment to allies and enemy alike. German generals argued that deterrence had distinct phases. They stated the need for balanced forces, conventional, tactical nuclear, and strategic nuclear. The shield forces were necessary to deter limited aggression or allow for the defense against limited incursion, but they were still regarded as supplementary to the strategic deterrent.[100]

In the late 1950s, LANDCENT adopted the brigade structure as the basis for a standardized NATO division for conventional and nuclear warfare. The driving force behind this project was SACEUR's belief that all ground forces needed to have a high degree of operational compatibility. The LANDCENT division could be assigned up to four self-contained brigades, and it could favor armor or infantry, depending on the situation. This was quite different from the pentomic division of the U.S. Army. That in itself is revealing, as earlier European advocates of the NATO division had argued that the U.S. combat division should be the model for standardization since American planners had a fuller appreciation for the effects of nuclear weapons.[101] General Speidel explained the concept to an American audience in September 1960: "This division is based on the brigade concept and divisional troops. In the infantry division two of the three brigades are capable of engaging in combat for a certain length of time independent of the division. The composition of our division can be changed to meet the developments of the situation."[102] General Valluy, now commanding all allied forces in Central Region, believed that brigades allowed for an excellent admixture of infantry and armor. He expected that the brigade would over time take on the tasks of a current division, including intelligence and atomic fire, while the division would resemble a corps.[103]

The NATO Standing Group concluded that the LANDCENT divisional concept was very well suited to combat in Europe, that it was compatible with the forces in existence, and that it should be accepted as NATO's standard division. This could be achieved if all NATO partners adopted the concept as guidance for future reorganization of their army divisions. The extent to which the standard division would be adopted remained in the realm of national responsibility. The Standing Group cautioned that warfare was evolving and that the standard division needed to be reviewed periodically. As new weapons became available and tactics were adjusted, the structure of the division might have to be altered accordingly.[104] By the end of the decade, France had stated her intention to reorganize army divisions along the lines of the LANDCENT proposal. Belgium intended to adopt the concept for its two active divisions, Portugal seemed willing to do the same for its active division, and Denmark had also embraced the idea.[105] At this point, the U.S. Army was in the planning stages of the second major structural reorganization of combat divisions within five years.

Designing the Army for Limited War? Bruce Clarke and Clyde Eddleman

Bruce Clarke had fought valiantly in World War II, achieving lasting fame as the leader of an armored combat command that delayed the German Ardennes offensive at the village of St. Vith in the vicinity of Bastogne in December 1944.[106] There, Combat Command B of 7th Armored Division had held a crucial road junction for six days, despite being attacked by more than five German divisions. Clarke was later assigned to Seventh Army in Bavaria and missed most of the Korean War, receiving command of I U.S. Corps only in the spring of 1953, three months before the cease-fire agreement was signed.[107] This did not allow him to get a full taste of corps command in wartime, but he nevertheless rose to command the army forces in the Pacific region. Clarke returned to Germany in 1956, chosen by the secretary of the army to straighten out Seventh Army, which appeared to lack strong direction. Clarke took charge, reminded the troops that they were in Germany because the Soviets maintained a threatening presence within striking distance, overhauled training and alert measures, and weeded out ineffective officers to the greatest extent possible.[108]

Clarke's military philosophy was formed during World War II and codified in the lessons he drew from the defense of St. Vith. He believed that tanks lost their strength if they were strung out in support of several units. Therefore, it was his central conviction that tanks should always be massed. Clarke favored an aggressive style of command, but he had made his name in defensive operations. He concluded that concentrated rapid counterattacks threw off the enemy and altered his perception of the defensive forces. At St. Vith, the German commander, General Hasso von Manteuffel, had assumed that he was facing at least one corps rather than merely half an armored division. On the offensive, it was crucial to keep moving, as enemy command and control functions would be more deeply disrupted with every mile that one advanced in the enemy's rear. This operational philosophy ran counter to current doctrine, which featured more deliberate offensive operations and a more static defense. But as his biographers put it, "Clarke was essentially an armored attack officer. And he believed armor should attack on a narrow front—fast and in depth, a spear. . . . His defense was an unending series of swift counterattacks."[109] Between 1956 and 1958, Clarke was in a position to instill this philosophy into Seventh Army and remake army operations in his image.

While the pentomic divisions made their way to Seventh Army, Clarke was worried about the armored cavalry regiments on border duty. The battalions had revealed their weaknesses in training exercises, such as SABRE KNOT and WAR HAWK in 1956. Clarke was convinced that they had to be reorganized. At the same time, however, he argued that the regiment should be maintained, at least as an administrative unit. His suggestion was a structure of three self-contained battalions per regiment.[110] Clarke also voiced reservations about the artillery support of the Reorganization of the Current Infantry Division (ROCID). In April 1958 he reported that the results of the recently concluded field training exercise SABRE HAWK showed that the division artillery was not strong enough to provide adequate conventional or atomic firepower. Clarke criticized the lack of centralized command of the artillery at the division level. Consequently, the flexibility and concentrated fire of division artillery, the strength of U.S. Army artillery in World War II and Korea, had been lost.

As for the battle groups, their direct fire support, provided by a mortar battery, was deemed inadequate and the 4.2-inch mortar unsatisfactory. Clarke was not one to complain without constructive ideas, however. He submitted a proposal to CONARC to remedy the weaknesses. Centralized command of the artillery at the division level, a direct fire-support battalion for each battle group, and elimination of the mortar from the artillery direct-support role would fix the problems. Clarke also called for an additional medium-gun battery and more Honest John rocket launchers for each battery. It would be necessary to cut the battalions and batteries of the division artillery to the bone, but the required number of guns could be manned without reducing the strength of other arms or exceeding the present strength of the ROCID division. This might sacrifice some staying power, but it would solve the immediate problem.[111] Clarke's proposal was realistic as far as atomic firepower went, since the army had just begun to provide atomic weapons to the division instead of retaining all at army and corps levels, but conventional artillery posed a different problem. To Clarke, it appeared crucial to mass the fire of the entire division under the command of the division leader. This ran contrary to the intended semi-independent nature of the battle groups.

Clarke did not reject outright the battle group as a fighting formation. However, he began to ponder the question of the proper design for an atomic army more seriously. He outlined his thoughts in an article in January 1958. Essentially, Clarke offered his plans to overhaul Seventh Army. The purpose of publishing his preliminary ideas was to provide a "guide for a group of staff officers directed to design a field army to fight an atomic war in the North Temperate Zone . . . to stimulate them to come up with the optimum organization for a field army to be employed in the time frame 1965–70." Clarke wanted to eliminate the corps in order to streamline command. He proposed a field army of 200,000 officers and men in six divisions, four in contact with the enemy, one in an intermediate reserve location and thus probably relatively quickly also in contact with the enemy, and one in the rear area, simultaneously recovering and providing security. Ideally, the divisions should be half infantry and half tank forces, with enough flexibility built in to address particular circumstances. Such a field army was to defend an area 100 miles in width and 200 miles in depth. It needed four or five armored cavalry regiments for flank security, target acquisition, surveillance, screening, and a variety of other tasks. Medium-range atomic fire support of about 200 miles was to be provided by the field army artillery command.[112]

Shortly thereafter, Clarke moved from Seventh Army to CONARC, then the hub of future-oriented thinking in the army. The likelihood of atomic war reinforced Clarke's concept to rely on armored formations, supported by centralized division artillery, but it was critical to eliminate the corps-level of command.[113] The result of his tenure as CONARC commander was the concept for a Modern Mobile Army 1965–70 (MOMAR-1).[114] The study was based on the urgent necessity for the army to develop a comprehensive organizational, technological, and operational plan for reform in the 1960s that could be applied toward the army's role in American defense strategy. In essence, Clarke attempted to salvage the usable parts of the PENTANA studies while trying to develop a model that was operationally more practicable. CONARC suggested that limited war, as defined in the 1950s by the army, was a more likely scenario than general war against the Soviets, that limited war could occur anywhere in the world, and that deterrence of general war remained a crucial objective even after limited war had broken out.[115] Western and Central Europe, however, were not listed as one of the regions where U.S. forces might have to fight a limited war in the 1960s.[116]

Based on his recent experience in Germany, Clarke might have assumed that any war directly involving American and Soviet forces would be unrestricted. But the stated objective of the army was to be capable of deterring general war even during a limited war. Other senior American officers in Europe at the time agreed with Maxwell Taylor's conception of limited nuclear war. James Polk, in succession, commanding general of 4th Armored Division, Berlin Command, V Corps, and USAREUR, serves as an example. In recalling his experience in Europe from 1957 to 1971, he told students at the Army War College that he disagreed with the nuclear-firebreak theory developed by Defense Department analysts in the 1960s because all war games showed that the use of tactical nuclear weapons was necessary to defend the Fulda Gap against a full-scale Soviet attack. This, however, would not automatically lead to general nuclear war. Polk reasoned that the "surgical" employment of twenty to thirty low-yield nuclear weapons in the V Corps sector might delay Soviet penetration of NATO defense lines for two to three days. He thought that such a course of events would leave the Soviets with three alternatives: they could quit, retaliate in kind, or escalate. Polk assumed that if "you make it very disagreeable for [them] to escalate," the Soviets were unlikely to do so, since they were rational people interested in their own survival.[117]

Clarke based the MOMAR concept on the assumption that the army of the future had to be capable of operations anywhere in the world, on nuclear and non-nuclear battlefields alike. He believed that the pentomic division did not have enough conventional firepower and that the dispersion of five battle groups critically reduced tactical mobility and maneuverability due to problems with command and control. Specifically, the divisions required more armored vehicles and aircraft to enhance mobility. Following earlier proposals of a universal division, the CONARC study called for two types of divisions, heavy and medium. Either type division was to consist of five combat commands, but there also were to be three task force headquarters that allowed for a return to the triangular structure. This was leaning heavily on the command structure of armored divisions and introduced the notion of building blocks, as the task forces could be assembled from a variety of tank, infantry, and support companies, with fire support from a proposed new battery of "moritzers," a cross between a mortar and a howitzer that had been considered since the PENTANA study of 1955. These divisions should be entirely mechanized or at least motorized.[118] The standard MOMAR field army was to contain two heavy and four medium divisions, but the organization was flexible. A field army operating in Europe, for instance, might have four or even five heavy and only one or two medium divisions, while the proportion would be inverted in Southeast Asia and other regions of the Third World.[119]

The downside to the MOMAR division was its heavy reliance on tanks and armored vehicles. In accordance with current tactical doctrine, both heavy and medium divisions were designed primarily for the offensive and for counterattacks during mobile defense.[120] This was well suited to conditions in Europe, but despite the original purpose of the study to create a general-purpose force, the heavy division did not fit the bill in other potential theaters of war, and the suitability of the medium division was questionable. Army historian John Wilson stated that this weakness was clearly revealed in several theoretical war games. As a result, the concept never made it past the drawing board. It was not tested in the field. Before its three intended follow-up studies could be concluded, MOMAR-1 was rejected in December 1960 by the army's vice chief of staff, General Clyde D. Eddleman, who thought that it lacked the "simplicity, homogeneity, versatility, and flexibility required by the Army for its diverse, worldwide tasks in the coming decade."[121] MOMAR was the expression of a more pragmatic form of the pentomic division, as it had emerged in Seventh Army after 1958, albeit with greater emphasis on armor. Clarke thus attempted to advance the transformation of the army that had been initiated by Maxwell Taylor.[122]

Clarke's concept of universal armor-heavy and mechanized divisions, somewhat reminiscent of the German Panzer and Panzergrenadier divisions of World War II and the Bundeswehr armored and mechanized divisions that had just been introduced, was dismissed as impracticable. It would have tied the army entirely to the plains and hills of Germany. Two observations should be made at this point. First, Clarke was a practitioner, a World War II veteran, a hero of the Battle of the Bulge. In many respects he never developed further as a planner.[123] Bruce Clarke is an example of a general who did attempt to transfer the principal lessons learned in World War II to his conception of a major war in Central Europe. The result was suited only to the situation faced by Seventh Army. This makes it even more puzzling that he excluded Germany from the potential areas of limited war in the 1960s. Second, the army's unwillingness to adopt the MOMAR concept indicated increased concern with deployment outside of Europe. This has been dismissed by critics of the institution who blamed the defeat in Vietnam on the lack of forethought put into planning for non-European war.[124]

The counterproposal for divisional reorganization also came from a general who had gained his most recent command experience in Germany, and it did adopt some of the ideas recommended in the MOMAR concept, most notably the principle of tactical units as building blocks. General Clyde D. Eddleman had been deputy chief of staff for operations under Maxwell Taylor when the pentomic division was designed, but he was dissatisfied with the product. In 1958 Eddleman succeeded Clarke as commanding general of Seventh Army. Thus, he had to make the battle-group concept work in the field. In October he asked General Henry I. Hodes, then Commander in Chief, U.S. Army, Europe (CINCUSAREUR), to approve an experiment during which Seventh Army would reorganize two infantry battle groups in order to test various organizational concepts. Hodes approved the experiment. The artillery structure in ROCID was of particular concern to both Eddleman and Hodes.[125] Soon thereafter, units resembling brigades that combined battle groups made their appearance in Seventh Army, essentially reconverting the pentomic division to a triangular division of two brigades and one battle group. In 1959, Eddleman succeeded General Hodes. On 23 December, he outlined the prospects for the upcoming year to his staff. One of the main events would be "reorganization in all our divisions and the Berlin Command."[126]

Eddleman was appointed army vice chief of staff in November 1960. One of his first actions was the rejection of the MOMAR concept. Subsequently, he directed Clarke's successor at CONARC, General Herbert Powell, to develop divisions to replace the pentomic structure. Clarke had attempted to provide a new division for 1965, but Eddleman wanted a much faster reorganization, which was to begin in 1961. The pentomic division had indeed been devised as a five-year experiment in the field, but it had only recently been fully implemented and some of its new equipment had not even reached the troops. Such rapid turnaround with little time to test any proposal that CONARC advanced served as an indicator of Eddleman's unhappiness with the current divisional structure. Nor did the army chief of staff, General George Decker, interfere. Eddleman's instructions to Powell were very precise, based on his experiences and considerations during his command tenure in Germany. Given that his superiors in Washington must have been aware of Eddleman's views, his appointment as vice chief of staff indicated that the leadership of the army supported rapid reorganization of the combat divisions.[127]

Eddleman instructed CONARC to discard plans for universal divisions and instead devise outlines for separate infantry, armored, and mechanized divisions. Mechanized divisions were deemed particularly well suited to the nuclear battlefield. They formed the core of West German operational doctrine, but the U.S. Army lacked the necessary IFVs, which would not be available for several years. Eddleman nonetheless pushed for the inclusion of such combat divisions in the order of battle, hoping that this would accelerate the development of IFVs. In the meantime, mechanized divisions would have to rely on M113 APCs and M60 main battle tanks. Of course, all divisions needed to have both conventional and nuclear capability. The unpredictability of deployment, to any one of several regions around the globe, led Eddleman to believe that the new divisions should be flexible in their composition. For reasons of training, equipment, and interoperability, it was impossible to create specific divisions for projected tasks. Even the battle group was not automatically out of the question for the new organizational structure. Eddleman suggested that its merits be weighed against those of the battalion as the combat maneuver element. As in the case of the pentomic reorganization, the armored division remained essentially unchanged. In fact, it was the example of the armored division command structure that led Eddleman to consider whether a command level between division and battalion should be reinstated, either as a regiment, a combat command, or a brigade. Eddleman hoped that none of the proposals would increase division size to more than 15,000 men.[128]

The pentomic army never came into existence as a practicable operational force. But Taylor had not intended for the pentomic infantry, airborne, and armored divisions to be the ultimate product of transformation. Instead, they were experimental units that were to be evaluated in the field. This opened the door to more creative thinking among senior commanders. As Massive Retaliation gave way to greater strategic flexibility, it was no longer necessary to adhere to bureaucratic and fiscal concerns quite as much as in 1955 or 1956. Operational necessity was considered more thoroughly. Planning continued to emphasize war in Germany, but operations in Vietnam and other places received greater consideration. The result was the rejection of Bruce Clarke's MOMAR division that too closely resembled the PENTANA roots of the pentomic division. Clyde Eddleman meanwhile initiated a new divisional structure, based on the example set by LANDCENT and the

German army that integrated brigades and divisions. The rapid adoption of Eddleman's division by the Kennedy administration indicated that the army was ready to sell the second phase of its Cold War transition. It was indeed a much stronger product. However, to dismiss the pentomic division as a failure would be simplistic. It did not have much value from an operational perspective, but it had been crucial in sustaining the army through a very difficult phase of fiscal limitations. The key issue now was whether the new division would have sufficient time to come into its own.

4

The ROAD Army and Flexible Response

The strategy of Flexible Response followed by the Kennedy and Johnson administrations was a deliberately ambiguous doctrine that has puzzled historians of the Cold War.[1] In principle, it called for the United States to respond to political or military challenges with means that were proportionate to circumstances. Flexible Response was put to the test in Europe, the Caribbean, and Southeast Asia. The maintenance of equilibrium in Europe in the face of chronic tension constituted the greatest success of the foreign policy of Kennedy and Lyndon B. Johnson. The new strategy enhanced the role of the army through its dependence on ground forces to deter war in Europe and contain the spread of Communism worldwide. How ground forces were to achieve both was left undefined. Most American political leaders favored planning for conventional defensive operations in Europe, but European leaders retained belief in the deterrent value of nuclear weapons. The army found that the new emphasis on conventional war was not well suited to the Central European environment. Questions of conventional or tactical nuclear war were debated throughout the Kennedy and early Johnson administrations, and ultimately the army's position of preparing for limited war that could be either conventional or nuclear gained the upper hand. Nevertheless, army leaders feared that strategic dogma and reliance on nuclear weapons had been replaced by strategic ambiguity and academic theories of conventional war in the nuclear age.

The ROAD Reorganization

On 25 May 1961, John F. Kennedy informed Congress that army divisions needed more conventional firepower, greater mobility, and flexibility to fight in any environment. He found that the Reorganization Objective Army Division (ROAD) offered the kind of army division that addressed the challenges of the new decade. Continental Army Command (CONARC) had submitted the ROAD study to the army chief of staff, General George Decker, in March. It outlined the future organization of airborne, armored, infantry, and mechanized divisions. CONARC had argued that army divisions had to be able to adjust their combat elements according to the tactical and operational situation. To accomplish this, the division had three brigade headquarters and could add or subtract maneuver battalions in order to increase armor or infantry strength as circumstances required. Hence, a nominal infantry division could join the battle as a mechanized or even armored division, depending on the predominant maneuver element.[2]

The CONARC proposal installed the battalion as the basic combat formation of the division, which afforded better control than the battle group and simplified training. It also allowed for greater dispersion on the battlefield. One-fifth of the combat strength of a pentomic division had rested in one battle group. The new infantry division, however, had nine battalions in its base formation. Therefore, the loss of a battalion would reduce the fighting power of the ROAD division much less than the loss of a battle group would have affected the pentomic division. The return of the battalion and the formal reintroduction of the brigade added a second command echelon between division and company, thus providing a sturdier hierarchy and more command positions for junior officers. In order to maintain flexibility in assembling the building blocks of a division, the battalions were designed uniformly. Infantry, mechanized, and armored battalions consisted of three line companies, headquarters, and a headquarters and service company. The reconnaissance platoons were similar in all three types of battalions. It was thus possible to build task forces around available companies and platoons without much delay or confusion.[3]

General Decker approved the concept in April 1961 but expressed certain reservations.[4] ROAD solved a critical problem that had arisen from the general-purpose force requirement of the Defense Department. It allowed for "strategic tailoring" (the ability to assemble divisions for specific missions), "internal tactical tailoring" (the ability to build combat teams within the division), and "external tactical tailoring," allowing army or corps commanders to react to an evolving combat situation by requesting specific battalions from the strategic reserve. But Decker believed that standard divisions with permanently assigned battalions remained necessary. The army did not have the means to maintain the large number of independent battalions that were required to exploit the ROAD concept fully. He approved of the principle of interchangeability of units but specified that it would have to be restricted to divisions within a theater of operations. Permanent assignment of battalions to brigades also fostered personal relationships between brigade commanders and subordinate officers and created a more robust and reliable chain of command.

General Decker wondered whether all artillery had to be self-propelled, given that the army still possessed many towed artillery pieces. In addition, the chief of staff questioned whether two Davy Crockett systems per infantry battalion were sufficient, and he argued that divisional transportation could be reduced. Most important, he pushed for changes in doctrine, specifically pointing at unresolved issues connected with the employment of nuclear weapons. In response, CONARC reinstated towed guns to the division and reduced the transportation capacity of infantry battalions by 30 percent. CONARC also added a third Davy Crockett launcher to infantry battalions and reconnaissance squads. In addition, CONARC began to draw up specific plans for a ROAD airborne division and a separate airborne brigade.[5]

The ROAD concept offered significant improvements in conventional firepower and mobility over the pentomic division. Armored, infantry, and mechanized divisions had identical artillery: fifty-four 105-mm howitzers, eighteen 155-mm howitzers, four 8-inch howitzers, and four missile launchers. The only exception was the airborne division, which had only six 155-mm howitzers and no 8-inch howitzers. Moreover, battalions had some artillery capability of their own, including heavy 155-mm howitzers. Each division also had 100 light and medium helicopters or substitute fixed-wing aircraft. The infantry division had 108 main battle tanks (an increase of 16 over the pentomic infantry division), 195 recoilless rifles (an increase of 145), 131 mortars (an increase of 12), 1,897 machine guns (an increase of 1,236), 93 APCs (a reduction of 95), 1,725 light trucks (an increase of 265), and 1,063 cargo trucks (an increase of 232). The airborne divisions, highly mobile formations to respond to crises anywhere in the world, had fifty-four 105-mm assault guns (an increase of 24), 249 recoilless rifles (an increase of 194), 132 mortars (an increase of 17), 925 machine guns (an increase of 483), 1,411 light trucks (an increase of 71), and 523 cargo trucks (an increase of 371).[6]

The divisions primarily designed for combat in Germany reflected a similar development. The newly created mechanized division had 162 main battle tanks, 171 recoilless rifles, 122 mortars, 1,970 machine guns, 798 APCs, 1,286 light trucks, and 1,127 cargo trucks. The armored division had 324 main battle tanks (an increase of 18), 123 recoilless rifles (the pentomic armored division had none), 109 mortars (an increase of 17), 2,235 machine guns (a reduction of 221), 718 APCs (an increase of 157), 1,302 light trucks (an increase of 41), and 1,192 cargo trucks (an increase of 135).[7]

The Defense Department quickly endorsed the ROAD concept. On 10 May 1961, Secretary McNamara informed President Kennedy that the reorganization would greatly increase the operational capability of army divisions. He criticized the pentomic division for its reliance on nuclear weapons. The new divisions possessed greater conventional firepower, which would increase the range of options short of nuclear war. McNamara stressed the flexibility of ROAD and its compatibility with the Allied Land Forces, Central Europe (LANDCENT) division. He particularly emphasized improvement in mobility and means to counter Soviet mechanized warfare that was afforded by the proposed mechanized division. McNamara concluded that although the reorganization might be expensive, it should nevertheless commence as early as 1962.[8]

In the event, the Berlin Crisis delayed the reorganization of army divisions. The Army Staff decided to use the additional time to test the concept more thoroughly. The Infantry School at Fort Benning was instructed to convert all training plans to reflect the ROAD organization by 1 July 1962. For that purpose it received 197th Infantry Brigade as its model unit. The brigade had an artillery battalion, an armor battalion, a mechanized battalion, two infantry battalions, engineers, and chemical troops. In the course of 1962, 1st Armored and 5th Infantry Divisions, both assigned to the strategic reserve forces, were converted into ROAD units. General Decker was pleased to report to the secretary of the army that both divisions found the new structure to be superior to the pentomic organization. He told Cyrus Vance that "ROAD provides substantial improvements in command structure, organization flexibility, capability for sustained combat, tactical mobility (ground and air), balanced firepower (nuclear and nonnuclear), logistical support, and compatibility with Allied forces (particularly NATO)." This was achieved without increasing the personnel strength of infantry divisions by more than 2 percent, although General Decker worried about the much higher operating costs.[9]

As requested by the chief of staff, ROAD divisions became standardized, at personnel strengths of 14,000 to 16,000 officers and men. Armored divisions contained six tank and five mechanized battalions. Mechanized divisions received three tank and seven mechanized battalions. Infantry divisions had two tank and eight infantry battalions. Airborne divisions had one assault gun battalion and eight airborne infantry battalions.[10] To address concerns about the personnel strength of the army, General Decker recommended that divisions in the United States and Korea make due with a lesser number of battalions. Concerns of the Army Staff that the reorganization would be difficult without personnel authorization above 960,000 officers and men proved valid in 1963 and 1964. Consequently, all divisions that were not stationed in Germany were left at reduced strength. The combat divisions of Seventh Army were converted to the ROAD format between February and October 1963.[11]

ROAD gave the army significant advantage in combat capability over Soviet divisions. The new mechanized division had 5,000 more officers and men in its combat units than a Soviet motorized rifle division. A German mechanized division was even larger, at 19,000 combat troops, but the American division had more combat support units. Overall, a U.S. mechanized division had a peacetime allotment of 25,700 officers and men, versus 14,700 in a Soviet division and 23,000 in a German division. Armored divisions had 25,600 officers and men, as compared to 12,700 in the Soviet division and 21,700 in the German division. A U.S. armored division had nearly twice the number of officers and men in combat units of a Soviet tank division. The Germans and Soviets had a greater number of tanks in mechanized divisions, but the army had more tanks in armored divisions and generally had more APCs in any division. American divisions also held significant advantages in artillery tubes, mortars, aircraft, and, particularly, antitank weapons.[12]

Commanding officers in the U.S. Army, Europe (USAREUR) preferred ROAD to the pentomic division, but the reorganization nevertheless caused concern. General Paul Freeman, who had succeeded Bruce Clarke as commander in chief of USAREUR in 1962, complained that the reorganization entailed the loss of twenty-six line companies in his command. He requested an increase in the number of rifle companies per battalion from three to four. The Army Staff explained that the pentomic infantry division had twenty-five infantry and five tank companies, while ROAD infantry had twenty-one and nine, respectively. The armored division, currently sixteen tank and sixteen armored rifle companies, stood to gain two tank companies at the loss of only one rifle company. Freeman was right, nonetheless, because 4th Armor Group was to be disbanded and its twenty-eight line companies were to be integrated into the ROAD divisions. But the Army Staff concluded that a ROAD division had greater artillery support, increased tactical nuclear capabilities, a division base that could support a greater number of maneuver battalions, improved mobility on the ground and in the air, and improved logistics for sustained combat operations.[13]

James Polk, the commanding general of V Corps, was dissatisfied with the rigidity of the standard ROAD division. He found that 8th Mechanized Division "would be better oriented to its assigned mission if it had one less [mechanized] battalion and one more tank battalion." The ROAD concept permitted for the corps commander to alter his forces, but Polk did not have the means to do so without taking armored strength away from another combat division. Polk also pointed out that the forward-deployed infantry forces, which were to fix the enemy in place, suffered from insufficient antitank capabilities. In the short term, adding tanks to the maneuver battalions could compensate for that weakness, but that solution degraded the capability of the division's armor reserve to counterattack. On the whole, Polk thought that the ROAD divisions were sound but argued that the ability to tailor combat units according to tactical and operational environment had been lost.[14] In the event, USAREUR altered the structure of the mechanized division in 1966 by substituting one tank battalion for a mechanized battalion.[15]

Along with the ROAD reorganization came a shift in the composition of U.S. ground forces in Europe. In 1961, there had been forty-one combat battalion equivalents, almost evenly distributed among tank (fourteen), infantry (thirteen), armored infantry (twelve), and airborne infantry battalions (two). In 1962, Seventh Army received two additional tank battalions. By 1964, the force had changed dramatically, to twenty-two tank, thirty-one mechanized, and three infantry battalions. Both airborne battalions had returned to the United States. The number of maneuver battalions had increased to fifty-six. There was a minor adjustment in 1966, when three mechanized battalions were withdrawn and two tank battalions were added. At the end of the decade, it was projected that USAREUR would command fifty-five maneuver battalions for the foreseeable future.[16]

The return of the battalion and of the triangular division has obscured continuities between the pentomic division and ROAD. The trend toward smaller independent combat elements continued. The battle group of the pentomic division had replaced the regiment as the major combat formation of the army division. Now the battalion was the division's maneuver element, and the Army Staff considered even smaller combat elements for future reorganizations. Whereas the pentomic division was designed primarily for nuclear war, ROAD was a step toward dual capability. But the long-term study Oregon Trail, conducted by CONARC's Combat Developments Command between September 1963 and May 1965, concluded that the ROAD division would suffer great casualties in a nuclear war.[17] Combat Developments Command concluded that even greater dispersion of combat units was necessary and recommended that companies, capable of independent action, should become the army's flexible and mobile combat elements. USAREUR was charged with testing the concept. The 3rd Armored Division was selected to conduct the experiment, and after preliminary testing in May and July 1965, troop units tested the Oregon Trail proposal from 28 August to 2 October.[18]

Exercise FRONTIER SHIELD revealed that the gaps between dispersed companies were too small to permit effective use of friendly nuclear fire in order to accomplish attrition in depth of enemy forces. But the assigned sector of each company already was too large to maintain adequate surveillance.

Means of surveillance could identify larger targets, but small dismounted patrols could not be detected. Small groups of aggressors thus would infiltrate the defensive front and reassemble into potent fighting formations in the rear area. The envisioned degree of dispersion also decentralized firepower of crew-served weapons and did not permit the tailoring of forces to specific missions. The test results showed that companies were too small to operate as self-contained units. Oregon Trail proceeded from the same basic realization as German operational planners had done after 1916: the battlefield was chaotic and could not be controlled. It had to be managed instead. But army field commanders attested that command of dispersed companies and the ability to concentrate force could not be attained. Furthermore, implementation of the Oregon Trail proposal would have meant providing companies with organic nuclear capability. It was questioned whether company commanders could be trusted with such grave responsibility. In the event, the Army Staff ignored the findings of the Oregon Trail study.[19]

ROAD was the end product of the army's opposition to Massive Retaliation and its attempt to achieve greater strategic and operational flexibility for nuclear and conventional war. It served as the basic organizational structure of the army for the remainder of the Cold War. Despite the apparent compatibility of the new division with the strategy of Flexible Response, army leaders found the future to be uncertain. Most of John F. Kennedy's advisers came to Washington in 1961 with the understanding that conventional defense of Western and Central Europe was largely a matter of persuading the allies to maintain a slightly larger number of combat divisions. Consequently, they dismissed the close integration of conventional and limited nuclear means, which army leaders had intended to achieve since 1953. Ironically, the Kennedy administration started out from the same vantage point as Eisenhower's national security team had done: tactical nuclear weapons were a force multiplier. But the new administration was willing to increase defense spending. Intelligence evaluations of Soviet and Warsaw Pact conventional strength that were lower than previous estimates reinforced the conclusion that the North Atlantic Treaty Organization (NATO) ground forces sufficient for forward defense and credible deterrence were within reach.

National Strategy: John F. Kennedy and Flexible Response

Even prior to his election, John F. Kennedy had concluded that the United States and NATO needed a strategy that afforded greater flexibility and appropriate means to address different kinds of challenges. Flexible Response was a deliberately vague concept that evolved over time and has not yet been defined satisfactorily, mostly because, unlike its predecessors, the strategy was not outlined in a memorandum of the National Security Council (NSC).[20] In 1959, Maxwell Taylor, arguing against Massive Retaliation and for a more flexible strategy, wrote that it "would restore to warfare its historic justification as a means to create a better world upon the successful conclusion of hostilities."[21] Senator Kennedy told Taylor in April 1960 that *The Uncertain Trumpet* had greatly influenced his thinking on defense policy and strategy.[22] Kennedy intended to reinstate into national strategy a political objective beyond war avoidance.[23]

Former secretary of state Dean Acheson and his assistant Paul Nitze, two of President Truman's most influential advisers, shaped strategy through their work for the Advisory Council of the Democratic National Committee. In 1959, the council requested unequivocally to replace Massive Retaliation with a more flexible strategic concept. At the end of the Eisenhower administration, the active army had been reduced to eleven combat-ready and three training divisions with a total of 876,000 officers and men. To secure the liberty of the free world through the prudent use of military force, Dean Acheson urged the creation of five new army divisions.[24] Acheson and Nitze argued that nuclear parity would soon create a state of passive deterrence that made the use of strategic nuclear weapons by either superpower less likely. Consequently, ground forces were to play a much greater role in the deterrence of war. But unlike Taylor, Acheson and Nitze doubted the feasibility of limited nuclear war. It was politically unthinkable and would destroy NATO. To them, tactical nuclear weapons were a deterrent and not an employable military means. The objective was to increase the risk to the Soviets inherent in the use of ground forces in an attack on Germany. Acheson and Nitze concluded that this could be achieved by maintaining a balanced force structure in Europe.[25]

Most political analysts in Washington rejected plans for immediate use of nuclear weapons in the forward defense of NATO territory. Those close to the new administration agreed that there had to be substantial use of conventional force prior to a decision to use nuclear weapons.[26] The State Department suggested that "the objective of improving NATO's non-nuclear forces should be to create a capability for halting Soviet forces now in and rapidly deployable to Central Europe for a sufficient period to allow the Soviets to appreciate the wider risks of the course on which they are embarked."[27] This sounded remarkably similar to the objective of Lauris Norstad's pause concept, but unlike NATO's supreme commander, the State Department opposed tactical nuclear weapons. Still, in the event of war in 1961, U.S. ground forces would have had little choice but to use tactical nuclear weapons at the outset of hostilities.

Robert McNamara, the secretary of defense, concluded that the force structure established in the Eisenhower years left the United States without the capability to respond proportionately to local and regional conflicts. In a report to President Kennedy in February 1961, he lamented that U.S. forces overseas "are . . . strongly oriented in their war plans, current capabilities, materiel procurement, and research and development, towards general nuclear war. This is at the expense of their ability to wage limited and especially non-nuclear war." Consequently, the contribution of ground forces to deterrence was modest. McNamara recommended that "the primary mission of our overseas forces should be made non-nuclear warfare."[28] He proposed to increase the budget for army special forces, increase personnel, conduct more readiness and training exercises, enhance air and sea transport, build greater stockpiles of ammunition and equipment, and improve research and development. The immediate cost of this program was estimated at $740 million.[29] In the long term, McNamara suggested increasing the army to sixteen combat-ready divisions.

By 1961, twenty-one active divisions guarded Central Europe, but none of the sixteen European divisions matched the standards of the American units. The Defense Department estimated that the army provided more than half of the actual fighting power of the alliance. How many divisions were necessary, and for what purpose, remained ambiguous. NATO force objectives called for thirty active divisions. General Norstad thought that a thirty-division force could implement his pause concept. The Kennedy administration, however, saw thirty divisions not as a minimum deterrent, but as a force that could defend Germany for several weeks in a conventional war.[30] Few among the army's leaders thought this was feasible, but there was no open dissent to a policy that promised more money, better equipment, and higher status. General Freeman, for instance, heartily embraced Flexible Response but doubted that NATO forces could contain a massive Soviet attack for more than a few hours without resorting to tactical nuclear weapons.[31]

Maxwell Taylor, appointed military adviser to the president in July 1961, also voiced doubts about the emphasis on conventional warfare. Taylor believed that NATO ground forces were too small for purely conventional defense and that conventional forces alone did not pose an ideal territorial deterrent. He conceded that he had "advocated larger conventional forces which would give us some choice other than all-out retaliation or retreat." But he feared that the administration had gone too far:

> My basic reason in the past for pressing for larger conventional forces has been to give us flexibility of response to hostile acts of aggression. It has always seemed to me that the aim of our military policy should be to

increase the available alternatives in the possible uses of military force and thereby achieve a graduated series of possible responses. The development and use of very low yield atomic weapons for battlefield use has always seemed to me to offer the possibility of a very valuable intermediate stage in any escalating series of responses.

Taylor was concerned that current policy directives "would reduce this possibility [of graduated response] to the point of eliminating it."[32]

Between 1961 and 1964, American military strength was greatly increased. The defense budget was raised by $30 billion. It was no longer distributed by share to the armed services. Instead, it was divided between strategic-retaliatory and general-purpose forces. The total payload of nuclear weapons available to the strategic alert force was doubled and the arsenal of strategic-nuclear weapons grew by 150 percent.[33] General-purpose forces, including most of the army, the Marine Corps, and parts of the navy and air force, received about two-thirds of the additional funding. As a result, army size increased to sixteen combat-ready divisions and nearly one million men. Funding for procurement of army equipment rose from $1.5 billion in 1961 to $2.9 billion in 1964. This allowed for modernization and improvement of the equipment of all sixteen active army divisions as well as the six reserve divisions that had first priority. It also provided for the support of the entire twenty-two division force in sustained combat. In addition, the number of tactical nuclear weapons deployed to Western Europe was increased by 60 percent.[34]

While NATO embraced the deployment of greater American armed force to Europe, the alliance did not adopt Flexible Response until 1967. In April 1961, President Kennedy had outlined the basic tenets of his strategy to NATO's Military Committee. He explained that "there should be a re-enforcement of the capabilities of NATO in conventional weapons. NATO needs to be able to respond to any conventional attack with conventional resistance which will be effective at least long enough in General Norstad's phrase, to force a pause." The United States intended to maintain its current troop strength in Europe and increase the conventional capability of its army. Kennedy also stated that NATO needed nuclear weapons, but he had inverted the order of importance. Until that point, conventional forces had been the shield behind which the nuclear sword could be readied and employed. Now they were to take on the offensive functions of the sword, while the nuclear forces prevented escalation.[35]

Dean Rusk, the secretary of state, added that NATO had emphasized the development of nuclear-capable forces for several years and that it was now time "to redress the balance of conventional and nuclear forces so that the

Alliance would in fact have a full range of forces to ensure flexibility of response." Rusk believed that this was essentially what General Norstad had requested. Hence, while NATO strategy needed to be reinterpreted, it did not have to be replaced.[36]

Dean Acheson disagreed with Norstad and Rusk on how to achieve greater flexibility and elevate the nuclear threshold. Acheson, an advocate for a hard line of containment, had returned to the inner circle of foreign policy as a consultant to President Kennedy. In the winter of 1961, he chaired a study group to evaluate NATO strategy, made up of representatives of the departments of State, Defense, and the Treasury, the Joint Chiefs of Staff (JCS), and McGeorge Bundy, the national security adviser. The report submitted in March was almost entirely Acheson's creation. The NSC adopted the Acheson Report as a policy directive in April.[37]

Acheson argued that it was time to build a more balanced force structure for the alliance. The nuclear deterrent was already sufficient. He suggested a modification to the pause concept, urging NATO to strengthen its conventional forces in order to "allow the Soviets to appreciate the wider risk of the course on which they are embarked."[38] But while Norstad was convinced that his ground forces could halt the Soviets only if they had access to tactical nuclear weapons and the authority to use them as required, Acheson believed that purely conventional defense was feasible and urged the buildup of conventional capability to the point where the Soviets were forced to employ nuclear weapons to make gains on the ground.[39]

The JCS was more sympathetic to Norstad's selective use of nuclear weapons than to Acheson's theory of conventional deterrence and war. The Joint Chiefs agreed that it was necessary to be prepared for aggression short of general war, but they made it clear that there must not be any doubt about NATO's willingness to use nuclear weapons even if the enemy did not. A major problem for the JCS was Acheson's recommendation that no tactical nuclear weapons should be forward deployed, to reduce the risk of accidental or unauthorized use. The JCS concluded that the Supreme Allied Commander, Europe (SACEUR) needed the authority to use such weapons immediately if the situation required it and that they would be of no use unless they had been placed close to the main line of resistance.[40] President Kennedy seemed to concur. In a meeting with the JCS in July, he raised the issue of conventional war in Central Europe and stated that he believed that the United States had to be prepared to use nuclear weapons before the Soviets could do so.[41]

German chancellor Konrad Adenauer feared that the Acheson Report indicated a growing unwillingness of the United States to use strategic-nuclear weapons in the defense of Western Europe.[42] German leaders also disagreed with the pause concept, which implied the loss of significant portions of their homeland.[43] Moreover, the German government was convinced that the Soviet Union would not enter into any agreement with NATO after war had broken out.[44] Defense Minister Strauss summed up the German dilemma: "We would be strange and pathological creatures if we, with our 210 people per square mile and with our vulnerability to nuclear attack, wanted to use nuclear weapons unless they were absolutely needed to prevent war, not to make war."[45] The German administration was less concerned about lack of conventional military means than breakdown of deterrence in general.[46] The Kennedy administration believed that a level of deterrence below strategic retaliation was essential, but Adenauer and Strauss warned that the Soviets would interpret this as a sign of weakening resolve.[47]

General Norstad was caught between the European fear of abandonment and the American desire for strategic flexibility. As military commander of all NATO forces, he had to consider European politics. At the same time, he received direct orders from Washington in his role as commander of the American armed forces in Europe. Norstad had managed the delicacies of this situation since 1956, but President Eisenhower had been sympathetic to the general's predicament, as he himself had served in Europe and understood the inconsistency of his New Look with policies to strengthen the bonds of the NATO alliance. Now, Norstad was considered a holdover from the days of Massive Retaliation, and his pro-European arguments came under attack in political circles in Washington. The pause concept had been a significant step toward addressing military crises with appropriate means, but Norstad was unwilling to define the nature and duration of the pause, and he disagreed with those who viewed ground forces as more than supplementary to the nuclear deterrent.

The Joint Chiefs were more aggressive in defining the duration of conventional war. In May 1961, they discussed scenarios for short-term (two to four days) and long-term (one to two months) conventional defense of Western Europe. In either case, penetration of a line from the Kiel Canal to Bremen, Kassel, Würzburg, Nuremberg, Munich, Innsbruck, and Venice by Warsaw Pact forces was unacceptable. In the event of combat operations exceeding one month in duration, the alliance needed twenty-eight active divisions in Central Region, six of them American. A sixth division for USAREUR had already been promised for 1963, and army reinforcements earmarked for Europe had been increased from twelve to thirteen divisions.[48] Within ten days of mobilization, LANDCENT required a seventh U.S. Army division and eight allied reserve divisions. By the end of the first month of the war, NATO needed to have forty-seven divisions in the field in Central Region, nine of them American. The JCS projected that ten

American and forty-seven allied divisions would stand in battle at the end of the second month.[49]

General Norstad discussed the strength of ground forces at the annual Supreme Headquarters Allied Powers, Europe (SHAPE) exercise in May. Only forty-seven of fifty-four required active divisions for the entire command were available. Norstad pointed at improved combat effectiveness of his troops, but he expressed concern about the vulnerability of the air force and the lack of personnel in Central Region. There, twenty-one of the required twenty-seven active divisions were currently under arms, but most of them were under strength. Norstad estimated that their fighting power was equivalent to that of only sixteen full-strength combat divisions.[50] Nevertheless, Bruce Clarke, the commander of Central Army Group (CENTAG), and General Smith, the commander of 4th Allied Tactical Air Force, thought that the ground and tactical air forces at hand were sufficient for forward defense if the use of tactical nuclear weapons was authorized shortly after the outbreak of war.[51]

In addition to unresolved problems with the armed forces of the alliance, military leaders were concerned about Soviet capabilities. The Soviet army had ninety-seven active divisions deployed against NATO, but only seventy of them were rated combat-ready by Western intelligence. Sixty Warsaw Pact divisions, of varying degrees of readiness and reliability, added to the total. That by itself was less daunting than the estimate of 175 Soviet divisions that had been maintained throughout the preceding decade. But Soviet divisions had been reorganized and their combat capability had improved. Intelligence officers believed that there had been a substantial buildup of surface-to-surface missiles aimed at Western Europe. The tactical air force in East Germany had been increased as well. Soviet forces in East Germany, ten tank and ten motorized rifle divisions, constituted an impressive armored striking force, with more than 5,000 tanks.[52]

Allied Command, Europe (ACE) estimated that thirty-two active divisions would compose a credible deterrent. Two-thirds of them were to be American and German. In addition, ACE required a strategic reserve of five American, British, and French divisions. SACEUR also was to receive eight French army divisions shortly after mobilization. Nine U.S. Army divisions were scheduled to arrive with the second wave of reinforcements. Once that group of forces had landed, SACEUR was to have sixty combat divisions for operations in Central Region.[53] But the Military Committee acknowledged that the land-warfare capability of the alliance remained insufficient. Most active and reserve units were short of personnel, there were not enough nonorganic combat and support units, operational stocks were critically short, and obsolescent equipment remained in use. In Central Region the situation was better than in the north, but the desired nuclear delivery capability had not been achieved because of delays in the construction of storage sites and lack of political agreements.[54]

The Berlin Crisis accelerated the buildup of American forces in Germany.[55] The U.S. response to the crisis illustrated the desire to increase and improve NATO ground forces for the long term. On 5 May, Secretary McNamara, supported by the JCS, recommended deployment to Germany of two army divisions, to reopen access to Berlin in the event of a Soviet blockade of the autobahn.[56] But the Defense Department rejected an army proposal to add a fourth combat division to the strategic reserve. As NSC staffer Henry Owen pointed out, deployment of two divisions to Europe would thus leave the United States with only one division in strategic reserve. Owen criticized McNamara in rejecting army recommendations to augment Seventh Army, especially in the critical areas of combat support, conventional artillery, and aviation to provide better reconnaissance, command, and control.[57]

The Vienna summit between President Kennedy and Premier Nikita Khrushchev in June 1961 increased the urgency of a decision. Taken aback by Khrushchev's aggressive rhetoric, Kennedy was convinced that he would have to face a showdown over Berlin.[58] McGeorge Bundy listed the four military options that were available. First, the United States could immediately and substantially reinforce its armed forces. Second, the administration could enact measures short of declaring a national emergency, which would exclude the call-up of reserve units for the time being. Third, a declaration of national emergency could be issued, including limited call-up of reserves. Finally, the United States could postpone a significant military buildup.[59] In July, Kennedy decided to increase the armed forces.[60]

On 25 July, the president addressed the nation. He requested over $3 billion from Congress in additional funds for the armed forces. $1.8 billion were to be used for the procurement of non-nuclear weapons, ammunition, and equipment.[61] As part of the temporary increase of army personnel to one million men, all five divisions in Germany were to be brought to full strength. In the event, 3rd, 8th, and 24th Infantry Divisions each received an additional 1,000 men and enough APCs to allow for their complete mechanization. The influx of personnel was indeed necessary. USAREUR required 18,000 officers and men to ready its five divisions for combat. More than 19,000 additional troops were needed to provide essential nondivisional support to allow for sustained combat operations.[62] In the fall, the army accelerated the distribution of M14 rifles and M60 machine guns and sped up production of the new M60 tank and the M113 APC.[63] Additional steps to increase combat readiness in Europe included the pre-positioning of equipment for one armored and one infantry division as well as several independent battalions.[64] In the event, the Berlin Crisis passed without deployment of additional combat divisions to Germany.[65] The JCS remained convinced that purely conventional war was impracticable.[66]

The July decision to augment Seventh Army was based on the assumption that the Soviets would step up pressure over Berlin in the course of 1961, culminating in a crisis in the winter.[67] Hence, the closing of the sectoral border on 13 August and Soviet threats to cut off all Western access to Berlin came much sooner than expected.[68] But while the administration considered rushing additional forces to Europe, General Norstad believed that the timetable set in July remained sound. Rapid mobilization might preclude negotiations to end the crisis. Norstad believed that all European governments except for the French supported such negotiations.[69] Historian Irwin Wall notes in his study of Franco-American relations: "The United States had called up its reserve, had more troops ready for combat over Berlin than all the other NATO powers combined, and was negotiating from strength."[70]

In Washington, the NSC debated political, psychological, economic, and military measures to prepare particular steps of escalation. The Germans were cautioning that proposals for an airlift or military probes to reopen the autobahn were unrealistic. Defense Minister Strauss had told Norstad in March that Berlin was simply a question of "war or no war."[71] In accordance with U.S. policy, Norstad was planning incursions into East Germany in order to reopen access to Berlin if necessary.[72] On 29 May, he had informed McNamara that "our battalion-sized probe plan has been developed and agreed by the countries concerned."[73] Plans for a division-sized operation were not that advanced. SACEUR had convinced the British to drop their opposition, but he still had to address the lack of French forces. France was to contribute one division to LIVE OAK, but with her forces tied up in Algeria it could not spare more than one battalion.[74]

Like Norstad, Bruce Clarke stressed the need for adequate forward defense. He assumed that the Berlin Crisis was part of a Soviet effort to discredit American leadership and destroy the cohesiveness of the Western alliance. As commander of CENTAG, Clarke was responsible for the defense of the southern half of West Germany. Although he was satisfied with the state of preparedness of Seventh Army, he expressed concern about allied troops. There still were only twenty-one NATO divisions for all of West Germany, and most of them did not have the desired degree of readiness. European armies masked shortfalls of personnel by assigning reservists to frontline divisions upon mobilization. This may have been practicable in the past, but the state of mechanization was now so advanced that capable operators needed constant training. Clarke's greatest concerns were the support units and the logistics system. He pointed out that the European armies relied on combat divisions without sufficient support. There was little he could do about it. Despite NATO's efforts to combine all military and economic power of its members into a coherent defensive system, logistics remained a national responsibility.[75]

Clarke estimated that the Soviets initially might only have twenty-two combat-ready divisions for an offensive against CENTAG. But he stressed that the potential for deployment of twenty-eight additional divisions within ten days of mobilization was unmatched by NATO. At best, SACEUR could hope for six divisions to become available, but it was more likely that none would arrive in the theater of operations in the first two weeks. Clarke deplored the Soviet advantage of shorter supply lines over land. It might take only three to four days to move an armored division from the western parts of the Soviet Union to Germany; the same movement from the United States could take two months.[76] Furthermore, the Soviets had the advantage of initiative, and they could exploit fissures in the NATO alliance, for instance, by announcing that they would not use nuclear weapons.

Clarke doubted that the West could muster the political will to "authorize even the use of tactical nuclear weapons, which in turn might lead to all-out nuclear warfare."[77] NATO, however, would have to resort to nuclear weapons rapidly in the defense of Germany. Clarke also requested more ground forces and close air support. The objective was to present a force strong enough to dissuade the Soviets from believing that they could reach the Rhine River in a rapid war of movement. To that end, USAREUR had to be increased to seven divisions with adequate logistic support. NATO would have to furnish another twenty-three active divisions. These thirty divisions had to be armored or mechanized, to the greatest extent possible. Such a force could adequately guard the most likely axes of invasion in the North German plains and through Hesse toward the Rhine. It could also respond to other contingencies, such as the Berlin Crisis. Clarke feared that current NATO forces could not do either. Therefore, the most aggressive conventional military options debated in Washington were fanciful.[78]

President Kennedy understood that ACE needed more troops if it was to implement LIVE OAK contingency plans and defend Western Europe. Even prior to the erection of the Berlin Wall, the administration had discussed deployment of additional combat divisions to Seventh Army.[79] In September, army generals Lemnitzer and Decker supported deployment of six divisions, but the other service chiefs opposed the idea.[80] It could be perceived as an escalation of the crisis, but there was also the danger that the Soviets might see it as tacit acknowledgment that the use of nuclear weapons in the defense of Berlin was out of the question.[81] General Pierre Jacquot, Commander in Chief, Allied Forces, Central Europe (CINCENT), cautioned that the additional divisions would have to utilize the existing lines of communication, through France or from Bremerhaven to southern Germany. He suggested that one corps of three divisions could reinforce CENTAG while the other corps should be given to the Northern Army Group (NORTHAG). It was to be placed in the area between the Aller and Elbe rivers, to participate in the defense of Hamburg and Bremen.[82]

General Norstad rejected the deployment of American combat troops outside of CENTAG.[83] He feared that separation of American forces would complicate logistics. Moreover, he doubted that northern Germany could be defended in a conventional war unless current operational plans were altered. Norstad criticized British plans that called for withdrawal to the Weser River before using nuclear weapons. He thought that it was unnecessary to give up Hamburg and the advances to Jutland, and he doubted whether tactical nuclear weapons could be used effectively once the Warsaw Pact offensive had gained momentum. Instead, the enemy had to be forced to mass at the border, which would create lucrative targets for nuclear strikes.[84]

Robert McNamara focused on long-term effects of a military buildup. He recognized that six additional divisions in Germany would add options between retreat and nuclear escalation. Unlike Norstad, he thought that several divisions could be stationed in northern Germany, where he expected the bulk of the Soviet attack to develop. As it stood, NATO would have no choice but to respond with nuclear weapons to an incursion aimed at Hamburg, but U.S. forces in NORTHAG might offer a conventional alternative. If NATO fielded thirty-two active divisions in Central Region, McNamara presumed that Western Europe could be defended against a massive conventional attack "for a significant period of time without having to use nuclear weapons." A force of eleven U.S. Army divisions and nine Bundeswehr divisions committed to ACE could be supplied for two months of combat. McNamara estimated that the Soviets could not effectively employ more than fifty-five divisions in an offensive in Germany and that their lines of communication would be vulnerable. He added that thirty-two divisions would be sufficient to defend Germany and allow for implementation of LIVE OAK plans.[85]

The thirty-two-division NATO force for Central Europe seemed within reach. In the summer, the European NATO partners had promised General Norstad to strengthen the posture of his command.[86] Norstad hoped to have twenty-four active divisions deployed in Central Region by the end of the year. He reiterated that the current force counted for only sixteen divisions by American standards, but this too was to be remedied. In addition, the strategic reserve provided by the United States, Canada, and the United Kingdom was to be increased to about ten division equivalents, and France signaled that four combat divisions would be available shortly after mobilization. The six additional divisions under consideration in Washington would increase the total of active divisions to thirty, with a large force in reserve, provided that logistical questions of air and sea transportation could be addressed.[87] The German defense minister thought that thirty-two divisions might be capable of repelling the initial Soviet attack but not the second and third waves. For Europe, he argued, there was still no acceptable alternative to nuclear deterrence.[88]

General Norstad warned the JCS that the escalation from local to general war did not rest entirely with NATO. In case military action was taken, it would be essential to maintain the nuclear capability of ACE. Norstad argued that existing plans for the defense of Germany were applicable in the current crisis. He stated that "the Concept of Operations pertaining to aggression Less than General War establishes the proper courses of action for ACE. Specifically, it would be necessary, if possible, to force a pause in the continuity of military action." This might prevent escalation to general nuclear war.[89] Norstad had modified the official NATO strategy of nuclear deterrence, which stated that no plans for limited war were to be made. Operational plans in 1961 contained the option to fight Soviet and Warsaw Pact forces with conventional weapons for a short period of time during which general nuclear war might still be avoided.

Despite his need for larger ground forces, General Norstad preferred that the six army divisions be held in ready reserve in the United States. He thought their deployment to Europe would send a dangerous signal of escalation to the Soviets. In case the Soviets interfered with Western access to Berlin, or elevated the political pressure otherwise, the divisions still could be deployed, two or three of them within fourteen days and the remainder and two Marine divisions within one month. At the moment, the six divisions were not essential, since "NATO would not agree to a 12 division assault up the Autobahn in an attempt to reach Berlin." Norstad concluded that "the divisions could not make the difference between success and failure in general war." At worst, the United States would have committed all of its combat-ready reserves at the outset.[90] General Taylor questioned Norstad's motives: "This proposal, particularly the six to eight division requirement is very surprising to me. To provide these forces in the time indicated would put great pressure upon our transportation and logistical system and would result in delivering units pell-mell into a strange environment which might soon become one of combat." Taylor concluded that "it is hard for me to view this as a serious proposal."[91]

The medium-term force objective of the army remained undecided until later in the fall. Army leaders proposed sixteen divisions and eight independent brigades. McNamara, who agreed with an ultimate force goal of sixteen divisions, thought that, in the short term, the defense budget would be better spent on improving the quality and equipment of the fourteen active divisions and seven independent brigades as well as the first-line reserve units. But, in October, McNamara tentatively moved toward acceptance of the army's proposal.[92] When the defense budget for 1963 was debated, the crisis in Berlin had convinced most decision makers that fourteen divisions were insufficient for operations outside of Europe in the event of two or more simultaneous crises. By late November, the administration had decided to increase the army to sixteen active divisions. At the same time, plans to deploy additional combat divisions in Europe for the duration of the Berlin Crisis were buried.[93]

On 20 October, President Kennedy specified U.S. policy for military action in the Berlin Crisis. He informed Norstad that interference with access to Berlin short of a full blockade was to be countered by a platoon-sized probe. Kennedy assumed that this would not increase the risk of war. If that did not end the interference, the United States would resort to economic embargo, maritime harassment, and UN action, while mobilizing its armed forces. Next, NATO was to communicate the urgency of the situation once more before embarking upon non-nuclear military operations to regain access to the city on the ground and in the air. In this event, a force larger than a division was to advance to Berlin. This was still a limited military action that aimed at convincing the Soviets to back down. If all else failed, Norstad was told to employ nuclear weapons, at first demonstratively, then in "limited tactical employment . . . to achieve . . . significant tactical advantage such as preservation of the integrity of Allied forces committed, or to extend pressure toward the objective." Kennedy acknowledged the possibility of general nuclear war.[94]

Norstad's relationship with Kennedy deteriorated. Norstad wanted greater flexibility of action, but he opposed the present emphasis on conventional military operations. He tried to convince Washington that greater sensitivity toward allied concerns was needed. When this failed, he refused to alter SHAPE planning in accordance with Kennedy's directive.[95] Norstad supported a kind of flexible response that depended to a much greater extent on the nuclear deterrent than the Kennedy administration in general, and White House and State Department in particular, were willing to concede.[96]

U.S. intelligence agencies predicted that the Soviets would understand that use of nuclear weapons had been selective, but they still would have no choice but to respond in kind. The CIA also cautioned that the European allies would not endorse the use of nuclear weapons over Berlin.[97] Norstad, who believed that the current crisis could be weathered without military escalation, knew that the German military opposed military action by forces larger than one battalion. He suggested a battalion-size or smaller initial probe, to be followed by urgent communication with the Soviets, political pressure by the U.N., maritime operations, a presidential announcement, and direct military action. Military planning centered on a limited-objective offensive in the border area that could be supported by selective use of nuclear weapons. Norstad opposed sending one or more divisions into East Germany.[98] Plans for military operations to reopen access to Berlin remained on the books after the immediate crisis had been diffused in the fall and winter of 1961.[99]

The mobilization during the Berlin Crisis and the reorientation of American strategy also raised questions about the proper composition of the army's reserves. At the time, all six active divisions in the United States were part of the strategic reserve, and three of them were maintained at a high degree of combat readiness. But when Robert McNamara proposed the deployment of all six divisions to Germany in the summer of 1961, he found that the required activation of Army Reserve and National Guard divisions to form a new strategic reserve was difficult since they were short of personnel and equipment. Moreover, the temporary increase in strength of the Active Army from 875,000 to one million officers and men led to plans to reduce the strength of Army Reserve and National Guard. The Defense Department proposed significant cuts, including the elimination of ten nominal reserve divisions, but it encountered heavy political resistance in Congress throughout 1962. Eventually, McNamara accepted a compromise that permitted him to eliminate obsolete divisions while maintaining authorized strength of 400,000 for the National Guard and 300,000 for the Army Reserve. This was the beginning of a fundamental reorganization. Over time, the Army Reserve was turned into a pool of combat support units and trained individual replacements, while the National Guard maintained combat divisions.[100]

The first year of John F. Kennedy's presidency was fraught with crises, ranging from Cuba to Laos to Berlin. Relations with European governments were difficult. Germany and France rejected Flexible Response because of the emphasis placed on conventional forces and limited war. The German and French administrations decried reckless calculations in Washington that pointed at the possibility of war in Europe instead of emphasizing the infallibility of the deterrent. Until 1967, Massive Retaliation remained alliance strategy, even though there were doubts that the United States would expend its nuclear weapons in a European war. The political debate appeared detached from operational planning, however. In 1963, the forward-defense line was moved from the Weser and Lech rivers to the intra-German border.[101]

Strategy and Operations: Forward Defense in Germany

At the beginning of 1961, General Jacquot, the commander of Allied Forces, Central Europe (AFCENT), had informed General Norstad that defense of Germany was impossible. One light battalion of the border guard was to defend 900 square kilometers of the intra-German border. A division was to defend 8,000 square kilometers. Jacquot pointed out that this meant that each soldier was responsible for one square kilometer of ground, and that he had only one tank and one cannon per 80 square kilometers. He concluded that a ten-division covering force could do nothing but withdraw unless it was fighting behind an obstacle. Jacquot continued: "Taking into account the scarcity of our strength, the obstacle we are talking about must be continuous." Moreover, Jacquot was dissatisfied with the command structure, which required him to cede operational command to Norstad in case of war.[102] General Norstad agreed with Jacquot's assessment that the covering force was insufficient in northern Germany. He assured him that the matter would be addressed in the 1966 Force Goals. Norstad ignored the rest of the letter.[103]

General Clarke believed that the troops in Seventh Army and Berlin Command were approaching the peak of readiness. Certain fillers and round-out units were on their way, as was 3rd Armored Cavalry Regiment, so that by the end of the year "USAREUR and all its components will reach a new all-time high in sustained combat capability."[104] Due to the augmentation of 1961, U.S. Army strength in Europe was above the NATO commitment of 232,000.[105] By December 1963, 10,000 troops of the augmentation force were still in Europe, providing three artillery battalions, two armored battalions, and one armored cavalry regiment.[106]

In January 1962, General Norstad advised President Kennedy not to pursue an alteration of NATO strategy at this point.[107] He believed that U.S. objectives could be achieved through "flexible interpretation" of existing documents. He thought that it would be better to present specific proposals about forward defense to the North Atlantic Council than to engage in abstract discussions of strategy. The State Department nevertheless urged Kennedy to "point out that it is difficult to reconcile the present Political Directive, the strategic concept to which it gives rise, and current U.S. strategy." Cosmetic alterations to MC 14/2 were not desirable. The alliance needed a completely new strategic approach.[108]

In May, McNamara explained in detail the guidelines for use of nuclear weapons in the defense of Western Europe.[109] At the North Atlantic Council meeting in Athens, he stated that "alliance nuclear forces are numerically larger than those of the Soviet Union. They are more diversified, better deployed and protected, and on a higher state of alert. They are combat-ready and able to engage in flexible and decisive action."[110] At that point, the United States had more than 5,000 nuclear weapons deployed in Europe.[111] But McNamara explained that tactical nuclear weapons should be the "next-to-last option." Although it might be possible to control and limit tactical nuclear war, it was more likely that it would escalate to general nuclear war. Therefore, it was essential to counter local aggression with conventional means at the outset and to use nuclear weapons only against full-scale attack. However, ACE still had ten fewer divisions in Central Region than the thirty divisions that NATO members had promised. McNamara concluded that the Berlin Crisis offered an example both for the need for conventional forces, backed up by tactical nuclear weapons, and for the effect of NATO troop augmentation on Soviet policy and strategy. He claimed that the Western force buildup during the crisis had caused a policy of restraint in the Soviet leadership.[112]

In the discussion following McNamara's formal statement, the German representatives, Foreign Minister Gerhard Schröder and Defense Minister Strauss, did not express an opinion about NATO defense policy as outlined by McNamara and Dean Rusk, who had spoken prior to McNamara's remarks. Although this silence need not be perceived as outright opposition, the absence of a record is striking.[113] French defense minister Pierre Messmer openly objected to McNamara's statement because it appeared that tactical nuclear weapons were to be taken from frontline forces once the conventional buildup had been concluded. Messmer believed that this would lead to a breakdown of morale among ground forces and would doom them to be destroyed by the better-equipped enemy. McNamara ambiguously retorted that the United States had no intention of withdrawing tactical nuclear weapons from Europe.[114] But in his formal statement, he had indeed warned of the negative effects of "highly dispersed nuclear weapons in the hands of troops" that "would be difficult to control centrally."[115]

In the summer of 1962, news of General Norstad's retirement from NATO, intended for the fall, reached European capitals. Chancellor Adenauer was concerned about the appointment of Maxwell Taylor as chairman of the JCS and added that General Lemnitzer, chosen to succeed Norstad, was an unknown quantity.[116] Norstad replied that although *The Uncertain Trumpet* had been an indictment of Massive Retaliation, Taylor had always supported NATO and the deployment of tactical nuclear weapons. His influence in the Kennedy administration was an asset. Norstad described Lemnitzer as a soldier of strong character, who was a fine choice for SACEUR. Adenauer explained that his concern about eventual American withdrawal was connected to the nature of a democracy in which administrations changed. Presently, there might be enough stability, although Norstad's impending retirement suggested otherwise, but continental Europe had no voice in the Kennedy administration. Adenauer hinted that the friendship of President Kennedy and Harold Macmillan, the British prime minister, might well prove to be counterproductive to the interests of Germany and France.[117]

Uncertainty about Flexible Response was also apparent in SHAPE. General Lemnitzer, who succeeded Norstad as SACEUR on 2 January 1963, was surprised to find that most of his officers equated Flexible Response with conventional defense and graduated deterrence. Instead, he argued, it was a strategy of appropriate response, which could be conventional or nuclear but should not follow a preconceived model of escalation. Lemnitzer found the prevailing interpretation in SHAPE so disturbing that he prohibited the use of the term "flexible response."[118] At the end of the decade, General Andrew Goodpaster (SACEUR from 1969 to 1974), concurred with the substance of Lemnitzer's concern. He endorsed Flexible Response, both as a strategy and as a doctrinal term, but he warned that too many observers still equated it with graduated escalation. Instead, the strategic concept entailed several options: general nuclear response, deliberate escalation including the use of conventional and tactical nuclear forces, and conventional defense. At any point during a war, any of the three responses could be initiated, although Goodpaster conceded that NATO would attempt to rely on conventional defense as long as possible.[119]

To counter widespread trepidation about the weakening of resolve to use the nuclear deterrent, Robert McNamara reminded European leaders shortly after the death of President Kennedy that the number of tactical nuclear warheads deployed in Europe had increased by 60 percent since 1961. Moreover, pre-positioned equipment enabled two divisions to move to Europe in a matter of hours, and the administration had programmed a 400 percent increase of airlift capability by 1968. Even now, the U.S. military was prepared to airlift several divisions and move 1,000 tactical aircraft to Europe within thirty days of mobilization. McNamara concluded that the alliance was strong enough to absorb an initial attack and retain sufficient counterstrike capability. This allowed for a shift of emphasis in the deterrent from reliance on nuclear weapons to a more balanced approach.[120]

Pentagon analysts estimated that NATO forces were approaching the number of Warsaw Pact troops.[121] They did not acknowledge that the Soviets could reinforce their own forward deployed forces much faster because they had come to believe in the speed and reliability of NATO's reinforcement schedule. The key lay in early warning. It was estimated that a Soviet attack could only succeed after a significant buildup of conventional forces. This would be observed and was to sound the alert. That assumption, however, rested on the belief that Soviet actions would be interpreted correctly and that European and American leaders would respond with great urgency and efficiency.

In its estimate for 1962, USAREUR's intelligence division stated that the increasing combat effectiveness of Western armies and the influx of nuclear weapons into NATO had caused the Soviet Union to reconsider the likelihood of success in an attack without previous buildup of forces. But the fall maneuvers of 1961 had shown that the Soviets could move reinforcements to the forward area covertly. USAREUR expected that the enemy could assemble an attacking force of forty-five to sixty divisions in Poland, Hungary, Czechoslovakia, and East Germany, and that this force could be increased to 100 divisions within one month of mobilization. NATO forces could expect only about four days of advance warning. However, intelligence officers reasoned that the Soviet numerical advantage was balanced by the fear that it would cause NATO to use nuclear weapons preemptively. Overall, USAREUR assessed NATO deterrent forces as strong enough to persuade the Soviets that a war could not be won quickly and decisively.[122]

The National Intelligence Estimate of December 1962 found that Soviet military doctrine stressed the use of all types of forces from the outset of war. After extensive debate, Soviet political and military leaders had decided to maintain forces that could fight a protracted war in a nuclear environment, even though this taxed the resources of the country. The ground forces, almost two million men in eighty combat-ready and sixty-five low-strength and cadre divisions, were well trained and equipped. The Soviets placed great emphasis on combined-arms operations with nuclear artillery, qualitatively improved tactical air forces, and other tactical nuclear support. Operational plans stressed rapid movement of armored and mechanized forces to the English Channel, with secondary offensives in Scandinavia, Southeastern Europe, and the Mediterranean, as well as in the Baltic and Black Sea regions. But U.S. intelligence officers perceived limitations to tactical nuclear and air support. Soviet logistics-support groups were much slower than the mechanized strike forces. Also, there were difficulties in command and control that limited supervision of subordinates once the forces had to disperse. The Soviets expected NATO to use nuclear weapons and escalate to general war. Therefore, they lacked doctrine for limited nuclear warfare and would have difficulty with the conduct of operations in limited war.[123]

But the state of readiness of NATO forces in Central Region remained unsatisfactory.[124] Only seven of twenty-three European combat divisions were rated as good or excellent, while the rest were considered fair or poor. Serious deficiencies remained in training, manpower, equipment, and deployments. In November 1962, the NATO Military Committee concluded that "these forces will have only a moderate capability of carrying out their mission."[125] The situation did not improve significantly over the next two years.[126] Consequently, the JCS considered a case in which NATO forces had to withdraw to the Rhine before the counteroffensive could be launched. But in a more optimistic scenario of forward defense, CENTAG forces seized the Thüringerwald, while Soviet troops advanced to the north and west of the Elbe River.[127] It was implied that occupied areas could serve as objects of trade in negotiations. SACEUR now had definite plans for limited war, even without the use of nuclear weapons.[128]

At the end of 1963, U.S. intelligence estimated that between sixty and seventy-five Soviet line divisions were at combat strength, that is, at 85 percent or more of authorized wartime personnel strength. The remainder, fifty to sixty-five divisions, were at reduced or cadre strength. The Soviets still maintained twenty-two combat divisions in East Germany. Moreover, at least 105 Soviet divisions were located west of the Ural Mountains and could be brought onto a European battlefield in several echelons. Sixty-five of them were identified as combat-ready. Between fifty and sixty divisions were expected to conduct the initial attack against Central Region from their assembly areas in East Germany and Czechoslovakia within thirty days under noncombat conditions.[129] The estimate was essentially unchanged in 1964, even though the estimate of Soviet general-purpose forces was lowered to 1.8 million. The Soviet strike force in an attack on Central Region would include between 14,000 and 17,000 tanks, 250 to 350 tactical missiles, and approximately 2,000 tactical aircraft. Mainly because of political pressure on the military, the Soviets had increased their capability to fight a limited war against NATO forces.[130]

In November 1962, the Bundeswehr had assigned its tenth and eleventh division to ACE. 7th Panzerdivision was put under the command of I German Corps in NORTHAG, and 10th Panzerdivision went to II German Corps in CENTAG.[131] NATO now had twenty-six active divisions in Central Region, seventeen of them German and American.[132] The final German division, 12th Panzer, was partially activated in early 1964 and was to be assigned to ACE by the end of the year.[133] The prospects for a successful conventional defense of Germany remained doubtful nevertheless. Defense Department studies of the early 1960s stressed that defense without tactical nuclear weapons could not be conducted east of the Rhine with the means at hand.[134]

Operational planning for most of the 1960s built upon the nuclear-centered concept of the previous decade. In January 1963, General Speidel, the commander of LANDCENT, told Henry Kissinger that his forces could contain an offensive of all Soviet divisions deployed in East Germany only at the Weser. He added that defensive operations would be hampered by uneven logistics. Dutch forces, for instance, were expected to hold their positions for only three days, while U.S. forces had sufficient support for three weeks. Nevertheless, it might be possible to hold the Weser-Lech line for nine days. If NATO had thirty divisions in Central Region, Speidel believed that a Soviet offensive with forty-five divisions could be met initially, but after one week of defensive operations at the intra-German border, tactical nuclear weapons would have to be used or the front would disintegrate. Speidel estimated that it would take thirty-six divisions to contain all Warsaw Pact forces currently in Eastern Europe for up to two weeks without employment of nuclear weapons. Finally, Speidel pointed out that defensive operations with purely conventional forces would limit NATO to fighting exclusively in West Germany. On the other hand, the employment of tactical nuclear weapons might allow for counteroffensive operations in the vicinity of Leipzig.[135]

Despite doubts that northern Germany could be defended, ACE moved the main line of defense in Central Region to the intra-German border in 1963. This followed General Norstad's optimistic assessment of January 1962 that the force buildup during the Berlin Crisis allowed for forward defense of all NATO territory.[136] The official shift of the main line of defense was made to reassure the Germans, who had grown increasingly concerned over the Weser-Lech line and plans for the use of a great number of tactical nuclear weapons on West German territory.[137] Ideally, forward defense should begin east of the border with the interdiction of Warsaw Pact reinforcements. Maneuver exercises of I German Corps in the winter of 1960 indicated plans for delaying actions deep inside East Germany. In a war game, Bundeswehr forces met the Soviets 20 to 40 miles inside East German territory. Both sides renounced first use of nuclear weapons. The German main line of defense was prepared from Lübeck to Braunschweig and into the Harz Mountains, well forward of the northern segment of the Weser-Lech line. The delaying action to the east was to buy enough time to build up forces for the defensive and assemble a force for counterattacks north of the Harz.[138]

Prior to 1963, allied officers had questioned whether Bundeswehr brigades would participate in a fighting withdrawal to the Weser and subsequent defense in depth. Many of them expected that, despite NATO operational plans to the contrary, German troops would attempt to defend the border. But now, officers in SHAPE conceded that it was very likely that the Soviets would penetrate the new forward-defense line. They specified that nuclear weapons were to be used against Soviet formations that had broken through.[139] General Norstad had privately challenged the assumption that use of tactical nuclear weapons had to lead to general nuclear war. After his retirement, SHAPE no longer insisted that there could be no holding back of strategic-nuclear weapons once tactical nuclear weapons had been used. Such a fundamental shift in the understanding of escalation had to be kept secret in order to maintain the credibility of the deterrent.

Protracted war in Germany was undesirable for any party involved. While briefing Secretary McNamara in July 1963, German general Hellmut Bertram argued that even limited aggression would have to be countered with selective use of battlefield nuclear weapons because it would likely be a probe to test NATO's resolve. While the United States did not differentiate between types of tactical nuclear weapons, German doctrine distinguished between battlefield (range of 40 kilometers, yield of up to 10 kilotons), tactical (range up to 600 nautical miles, yields greater than 10 kilotons), medium-range, and strategic-nuclear weapons.[140] Since the German military expected a short war, reserve forces were deemed insignificant.[141] General Taylor warned against the immediate use of low-yield nuclear weapons because it might compel the Soviets to employ medium-range ballistic missiles. He assumed that both sides would attempt to limit armed conflict below the level of strategic-nuclear exchange. Taylor praised the forward-defense strategy, but he recognized that the active forces necessary for conventional and nuclear defense limited to battlefield weapons could not be raised in the near future.[142] The German military believed that a force of thirty to forty divisions at the intra-German border would confront the enemy "with the incalculable hazard of Western nuclear defense."[143]

The State Department was concerned about the support that the German position held among senior officers. Even Secretary McNamara appeared to believe that nuclear war could be controlled.[144] Dean Rusk asked McNamara to review JCS proposals for NATO military strategy, which outlined responses to deliberate Soviet aggression, a scenario regarded to be unlikely even though NATO doctrine still supported the deliberate-war theory. Rusk pointed out that "any strategy paper should . . . stress the more probable type of contingencies, such as unintended conflict arising over Berlin, out of disorders in East Germany or Southern Europe, or by miscalculation." NATO had to be concerned with developing military forces that addressed limited crises without premature use of nuclear weapons. Rusk lamented that the procedure for release of tactical nuclear weapons was ambiguous. This was useful in principle, to enhance the deterrent value of the weapons, but Rusk believed that the strategy paper included early use of tactical nuclear weapons mainly for political reasons, and he was troubled by its implications.[145]

Despite the State Department's pessimistic assessment of conventional defense, Rusk explicitly stated the need to counter a conventional attack with conventional force. He argued that only significant losses of troops or territory warranted first use of nuclear weapons. The secretary of state expressed concern about the lack of emphasis on political control of NATO forces, particularly in the question of pre-delegation of authority to use nuclear weapons. Seymour Weiss of the Policy Planning Staff argued that predelegation was necessary in a combat situation. He and his colleagues did not believe that Germany east of the Rhine could be defended without the use of nuclear weapons, but they did not agree that tactical nuclear war in Europe could be controlled. The Policy Planning Staff concluded that the pause concept remained sound and should be retained, albeit with different terminology. Dual-capable ground forces had raised the threshold of war, but the State Department imposed a highly theoretical separation of war fighting and deterrence.[146]

The Defense Department reached a contrary conclusion. Its studies showed that tactical nuclear warfare could remain limited. Moreover, according to the evaluation of European views of NATO strategy, West German planners considered immediate use of battlefield nuclear weapons to be absolutely necessary due to the lack of space to exploit the advantages of mobile defense and the lack of sufficient mobile reserves. American officers believed that the imbalance of forces in Central Region was the main problem. CENTAG had sufficient conventional and nuclear capability to withstand a Soviet attack, but NORTHAG did not. It was likely that the Soviets would exploit this weakness.[147]

At a December 1963 meeting of the U.S. and German defense ministers and chiefs of staff, General Taylor and his German counterpart, General Friedrich Foertsch, continued the discussion of tactical employment of nuclear weapons. Taylor stated that conventional and tactical nuclear capabilities could not be separated. It was possible to imagine, however, that tactical nuclear weapons might be employed in one sector of the front but not in others. Foertsch agreed that conventional operations might continue even in a nuclear environment. At the least, conventional forces were needed to determine the location of the enemy, conduct reconnaissance in force, and protect nuclear weapons bases and logistics installations. Foertsch concluded that conventional forces in depth were required to prevent infiltration. The defensive would be much more porous in nuclear war than it had been in World War II.[148] The army's assessment of 1953 that nuclear weapons did not lead to lower force requirements still applied.

General Foertsch reiterated the point Bertram had made in July: the United States was planning to withhold battlefield nuclear weapons for too long. He added his personal opinion that there should be no fixed timetables, but he made it clear that nuclear weapons had to be used as necessary. Taylor defended the need to determine the magnitude of the attack. As the situation required, nuclear artillery shells and Honest John rockets could be employed.[149] The U.S. military and the Bundeswehr had similar concepts for the close integration of conventional and tactical nuclear forces but differed in their application. For a decade, the U.S. Army had pursued limited-war capability for the purpose of deterrence, but also to contain a Soviet offensive east of the Rhine, while German generals intended to employ low-yield nuclear weapons almost from the outset of battle. The German concept had the advantage of bringing to bear immediately the most destructive tactical weapons. But it is questionable whether the Germans would have indeed initiated nuclear war on their own territory. The U.S. Army model, on the other hand, assumed that conventional war need not become nuclear, even though the use of tactical nuclear weapons was very likely and that limited-nuclear war might serve to prevent general nuclear war.

By the end of 1963, the split between the departments of State and Defense in interpreting Flexible Response had grown wider. The State Department insisted on sustained conventional operations. Walt Rostow advised Dean Rusk to reject McNamara's proposal for a new military strategy for NATO because it was based on the employment of tactical nuclear weapons. Rostow argued that even the appearance of abandoning the conventional option would cause the Europeans to spend less on defense. It would also embolden those in the United States who wanted to reduce the number of forces that were deployed overseas. Furthermore, de Gaulle's desire to limit U.S. influence over European policies might gain ground among the allies. As a consequence, national nuclear forces would proliferate. Rostow believed that such a chain of events would leave no viable option below the level of general war, and all rationality that the Kennedy administration had introduced to NATO strategic policy would be lost.[150] Scholars of NATO in the 1960s have argued that Washington, Bonn, and Paris fundamentally disagreed on the nature of deterrence.[151] But government records reveal that the Pentagon and the State Department were more deeply split on strategy than were German and American defense officials.

Officials at the State Department were appalled by studies of tactical nuclear warfare conducted by the Army's Institute of Advanced Studies (AIAS), which concluded that nuclear war could be kept limited and that portions of the battlefield could be nuclear and others conventional. State Department officers questioned whether the intended limitation to battlefield targets was practicable. Could population centers be spared? At the very least, there would be significant damage caused by radiation and fallout. Even AIAS analysts admitted that nuclear delivery vehicles were inaccurate. The State Department contended that the amorphous nature of future battlefields made the distinction between battlefield and other targets very difficult. This led to the conclusion that limited nuclear operations, employing only battlefield and selected interdiction weapons, were unrealistic. Moreover, the State Department questioned whether 50 kilotons, the maximum payload called for by AIAS, was a low yield. AIAS clarified that yield could be limited to 10 kilotons for targets in NATO territory. Finally, State Department officers questioned whether the allies could accept the use of tactical nuclear weapons in the defense of major population centers. AIAS projected that both sides might use about 100 nuclear weapons in the vicinity of Hamburg.[152]

The JCS criticized the State Department for interfering with the process of strategic decision making. Its evaluation of strategy was driven by political considerations, while the service chiefs wanted to maintain independence of strategy from politics. The JCS criticized the State Department for adhering to "strategic doctrine developed in 1961 which supports the development and employment of a large conventional force in Europe." The rejection of tactical nuclear war was in any case "unjustified." The JCS agreed that the president had to retain control of the employment of nuclear weapons, but they argued that "any idea of continuing control in full detail is both impractical and dangerous."[153] The JCS, much like McNamara and Lemnitzer, had thus adopted a position that was close to the army's: A balanced territorial deterrent force was to be maintained in Germany for limited war with conventional and nuclear weapons.[154]

Eventually, the State and Defense departments agreed to set their differences aside. The modus vivendi was summed up by Deputy Undersecretary of State Llewelyn Thompson in October 1964: "There is substantial agreement between the two Departments on the principal issues of NATO strategy and specifically on the desirability of increasing the flexibility and capacity of NATO forces to fight conventionally."[155] But this only meant that the two departments would not delve deeply into the question of whether such a force could be created. The United States and West Germany could have attempted to build conventional forces in Central Region that could contain a Soviet offensive near the intra-German border, but that was deemed prohibitively expensive by the German government. Nuclear deterrence had worked thus far, and there seemed to be no political need for major changes in the context of decreasing political tensions.

But military requirements were another matter. By 1964, the German military no longer believed that strategic-nuclear deterrence was credible. General Heinz Trettner, the inspector general of the Bundeswehr, agreed with General Earle Wheeler, the new chairman of the JCS, and Secretary McNamara that graduated deterrence or flexible response was desirable.

McNamara indicated that the U.S. and West German governments broadly agreed on changes to NATO strategy. German defense minister Kai-Uwe von Hassel seemed less concerned with the strategic guidance of the alliance than with its political directives. That was a sensible position, given that SHAPE had interpreted Massive Retaliation pragmatically since the late 1950s. However, as General Freytag von Loringhoven, chief of the operations division of the German Armed Forces Staff, pointed out, Massive Retaliation had to be retained for the unlikely case of a nuclear surprise attack or an all-out conventional offensive by the Warsaw Pact. Thus, Flexible Response had to be tailored to environment and intensity of the conflict. In Germany, due to its population density, there would be less flexibility and operational freedom than in Southern Europe.[156]

General von Loringhoven explained the German operational concept. In the event of an attack on northern Germany, ground and air forces were to engage the enemy with conventional means. Atomic demolition munitions (ADMs) that had already been placed at the border were to be detonated without delay. General Wheeler interjected that not all deployed mines had actually been armed with nuclear explosives because European troops were not fully trained in the use of ADMs. Von Loringhoven then stated that selective use of battlefield nuclear weapons would have to be ordered immediately once NATO forces were in danger of being destroyed. Further escalation could still be prevented if Soviet aggression was contained at that stage. The German concept envisioned the use of nuclear weapons only in Germany and not against the Soviet line of communications.[157] This left room for interpretation. Since the Germans did not believe that the detonation of ADMs would lead to nuclear retaliation, the first phase of the war would be largely fought with conventional force, unless NATO faced imminent defeat. This differed from earlier German concepts that had called for immediate use of battlefield nuclear weapons. General Trettner added that improvements to mobility, conventional artillery, and reserve forces might compensate for some of the shortfall in numbers of NATO ground forces.[158]

The German concept took on a darker connotation once civilian casualties were considered. NATO estimates for the scenario termed "engaged nuclear battle," a two-week battle that resembled the plans outlined by von Loringhoven but expected the use of battlefield nuclear weapons on the second day, assumed civilian casualties of 1.25 million to 1.75 million. In a theater nuclear war with minimal fallout, that is, tactical nuclear attacks at military targets, the nuclear battle could remain restricted to Central Europe, thus excluding both British and Soviet territorial targets. Nevertheless, the civilian casualties in only three days of conflict could be as high as seven million and would certainly be above three million. If there were considerable fallout, casualties would rise to between seventeen and eighteen million dead. Finally, in general nuclear war, the civilian casualties in Central Europe alone would exceed 100 million, and an even greater number of casualties was to be expected in the United States and the Soviet Union.[159] This chilling estimate underscored the need for extended deterrence, even after the outbreak of war.

General Lemnitzer prepared plans for conventional as well as nuclear war. He acknowledged that MC 14/2 did not permit for such a distinction, but he argued that "unavoidable realities of the time required to reach a decision to resort to nuclear war require such considerations." The Military Committee resolved the conflict between strategic guidance and operational planning, while allowing European leaders to reject publicly the strategy of Flexible Response. In essence, the Military Committee agreed with the position of SACEUR. To remedy the immediate clash with MC 14/2, a revised mission statement for SACEUR was drawn up. It no longer included restrictions to operational plans for temporary conventional defense:

> SACEUR will defend the area of Allied Command Europe as far forward as possible, using available forces and weapons of the appropriate strength and kind including, as and when authorized, nuclear weapons. In this regard he is to maintain, until implementation is directed, the capability to carry out nuclear operations.

Official strategy continued to emphasize nuclear deterrence, but for all intents and purposes, NATO had adopted Flexible Response as its military strategy.[160]

The final holdouts against Flexible Response, Germany, Italy, Greece, and Turkey, signaled readiness to change NATO's official strategy only after the release of the alliance-internal Harmel Report, which emphasized deterrence and détente as closely related missions of NATO.[161] Ironically, this shift came at a time when the projections for the defense of Central Region were on the decline. Flexible Response was adopted by NATO in May 1967 and converted into military guidance by January 1968.[162] By the time Flexible Response was finally accepted, the military situation of NATO had grown worse, due to the increased American involvement in the Vietnam War. Consequently, General Lemnitzer assumed that he would have no choice but to rely on tactical nuclear weapons.[163]

In her study on Flexible Response in NATO, Jane Stromseth argued that NATO strategy in the 1960s was a hard-fought compromise that bore little resemblance to the initial proposals of the Kennedy administration. Stromseth recognized that the ambiguity of Flexible Response increased its deterrent value, but she nevertheless believed that Americans preferred conventional defense of NATO territory, while Europeans insisted on the use of nuclear weapons.[164] But NATO military commanders had long adopted the pause concept and other models of graduated and extended deterrence. The nature of the problem was not the question of American commitment to the deterrence of war and to the defense of Europe. Instead, the lack of a clear definition of Flexible Response left administrations in Bonn and Paris wondering whether they could trust those in Washington who professed adherence to nuclear deterrence while advancing arguments for conventional defense. In the event, most European political leaders decided that Flexible Response was a strategy of graduated deterrence rather than a strategy of appropriate response.

General Matthew B. Ridgway, chief of staff, U.S. Army, confers with Secretary of the Army Robert T. Stevens, 26 February 1954. (U.S. Army Military History Institute)

Demonstration of a 280-mm atomic cannon to representatives of several U.S. state governments at Darmstadt, Germany, 19 May 1955.

Honest John being readied during a summer training exercise of U.S. troops at Grafenwöhr, 11 June 1955.

The JCS confer around a globe at the Pentagon, 21 March 1956: left to right, Admiral Arleigh Burke (chief of naval operations), General Nathan Twining (chief of staff, U.S. Air Force), Admiral Arthur Radford (chairman, JCS), General Maxwell D. Taylor (chief of staff, U.S. Army), General Randolph McC. Pate (commandant, U.S. Marine Corps).

Soldiers of the 12th Infantry pause during maneuvers to watch an atomic bomb simulator go off on a far hill on the Baumholder Military Reservation, Germany, 8 April 1958.

General Clyde D. Eddleman, CINCUSAREUR, and Lieutenant General Francis W. Farrell, commanding general, Seventh Army (on right), observe a surveillance unit demonstration of the SD-1 drone at Grafenwöhr, 6 August 1959.

Sergeant Elvis Presley checks the machine gun of a 32nd Armor scout jeep during FTX WINTERSHIELD, Bavaria, 1960.

Secretary of Defense Gates meets with the Unified and Specified Commanders at the Pentagon, 17 August 1960. General Lyman Lemnitzer, chief of staff, U.S. Army, is seated at right; General Lauris Norstad, SACEUR and USCINCEUR, is standing behind Lemnitzer.

A Pershing missile mounted on an XMT 474 carrier demonstrates its mobility in the field at Wackernheim, Germany, 22 August 1960.

An M59 APC traverses a small river during FTX WINTERSHIELD II, Adershausen, Germany, 2 February 1961.

Tanks of 24th Infantry Division on the assault during FTX WINTERSHIELD II, Grafenwöhr, Germany, 3 February 1961.

General Bruce C. Clarke, CINCUSAREUR, bids farewell to his troops at CENTAG headquarters, Hammond Barracks, Heidelberg, Germany, 28 April 1962.

General Sir James Cassels, commander in chief, British Army of the Rhine, and commanding general, NORTHAG (right), and General Paul L. Freeman Jr., CINCUSAREUR, in Freeman's office at Heidelberg, 4 March 1963.

A soldier of C Company, 3rd Armored Battalion, 36th Infantry, manning a .50-cal. machine gun on top of his M113 APC at a roadblock near Fritzlar, Germany, during Operation BIG LIFT, October 1963.

An M60 tank of 3rd Armored Division, part of the aggressor force, scans the area near Halscharf, Germany, for enemy activity, November 1963.

High politics: West German minister of defense Kai-Uwe von Hassel (left) confers with U.S. secretary of defense Robert S. McNamara at the Pentagon, 3 December 1963.

Soldiers of 73rd Artillery stand ready to begin operations with their Sergeant missile during a training exercise in Germany, 11 March 1964.

Self-propelled M110 8-inch howitzer, September 1964.

A Davy Crockett test fired at a NATO artillery show, Hanau, Germany, October 1964.

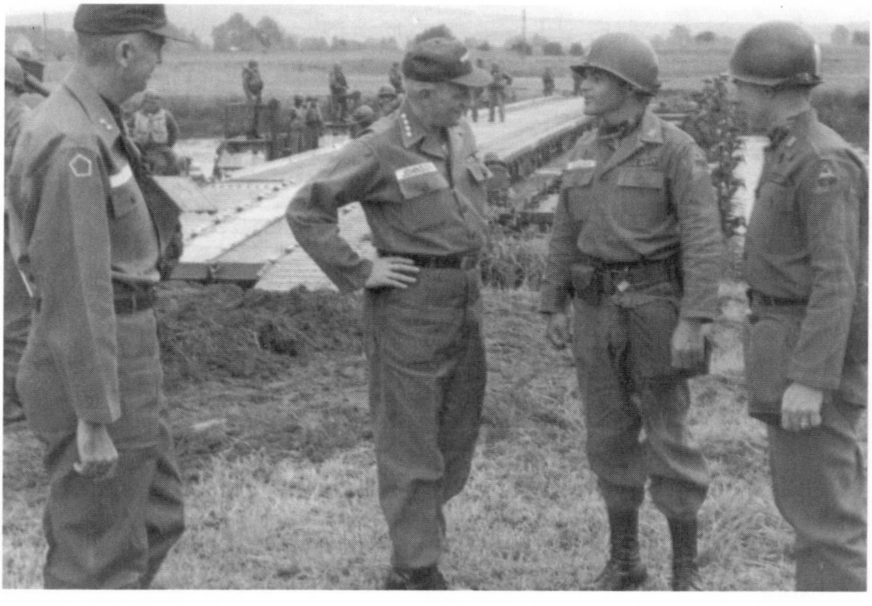

Regnitz River, near Würzburg, Germany, 9 July 1965: U.S. Army chief of staff General Harold K. Johnson discusses river-crossing tactics with 1st Lieutenant Salvatore Zuccalla, commanding officer of 24th Engineer Battalion, as Major General Alexander D. Surles Jr., commanding general of 4th Artillery Division, looks on.

An M113 APC from 1st Infantry Division, Ft. Riley, Kansas, crosses the Main River near Dippach and Rosstadt during Exercise REFORGER II, 19 October 1970. UH-1D helicopters provide air support.

Bundeswehr general Jürgen Bennecke (left) and CINCUSAREUR general James H. Polk prepare to attend a press luncheon to discuss the field training exercise of REFORGER II, Rosstadt, Germany, 20 October 1970.

M551 Sheridans of 4th Cavalry, 1st Infantry Division, Ft. Riley, Kansas, wait to test fire their weapons at the firing range at Grafenwöhr during Exercise REFORGER III, 20 October 1971.

General Michael S. Davison, CINCUSAREUR, and commanding general, Seventh Army, welcomes Lieutenant General Ernst Ferber, chief of staff, Bundesheer, to his office at Heidelberg, 19 November 1971.

General Creighton Abrams Jr., chief of staff, U.S. Army, awards the Distinguished Service Medal to Lieutenant General William E. DePuy at the Pentagon, 26 February 1973. (U.S. Army Military History Institute)

Lieutenant General Donn A. Starry, new commander of V Corps, inspects the honor guard during his welcoming ceremony, Heidelberg, 23 February 1976. Following behind Starry is General George S. Blanchard, CINCEUSAEUR, and commanding general, Seventh Army. (U.S. Army Military History Institute)

An XM-1 tank, a prototype of the Abrams tank, at Detroit Arsenal, Michigan, January 1978.

A TOW missile launcher on an M113 APC at the firing range at Grafenwöhr, 27 October 1979.

Dedication ceremony of the Bradley Fighting Vehicle at Ft. Myer, Virginia, 20 November 1981.

5

The ROAD Army in Germany and Vietnam

The Vietnam War revealed that American political leaders had overestimated the ability of the army to meet contingencies outside of Europe. Recent studies suggest that deterrence and containment of the Soviet Union in Europe remained the critical strategic objective even during the Vietnam War.[1] But operations in Vietnam required substantial adjustment to unit organization and tactical concepts. The army was forced to deploy in Vietnam most of its strategic reserve. The U.S. Army, Europe (USAREUR) became a manpower-reserve pool, particularly for junior officers and noncommissioned officers. The lack of experienced leadership in Germany contributed to a breakdown of morale. Furthermore, the vastly different requirements for the Vietnam War caused delays in the development of new weapon systems and vehicles as well as in the formulation of operational doctrine for mechanized combat in Europe. But although the army had to shift personnel and equipment from Europe to Vietnam and the United States, army leaders carefully maintained a fighting force in Germany that was strong enough to be a credible deterrent. The army decided to retain pre–Vietnam War Reorganization Objective Army Division (ROAD) structures. Practical adjustments to unit organization and tactics were only temporary, which reflected the desire of army leaders to concentrate on deterrence of limited war in Europe. This has been criticized in the wake of military defeat in Vietnam, but it was nevertheless prudent. In the Cold War, the specter of nuclear war in Europe was much more threatening than defeat in a peripheral theater.

The Nature and Requirements of Deterrence in Germany

In the classification of the 1960s, there were three major categories of war: general, limited, and sub-limited war. General war was equated with high intensity war, limited war with mid-intensity war, and sub-limited war with low intensity war. The boundaries between the categories were unclear. Many government officials understood any use of nuclear weapons to qualify as general war or its immediate precursor; others believed that nuclear war could be limited. Political leaders often failed to differentiate between the means for different kinds of limited war, assuming that a capable army could function in any environment. The army's definition of limited war included local aggression, conventional war, and limited nuclear war.[2] The Korean War had proved that conventional war was still possible, even in the nuclear age.

North Atlantic Treaty Organization (NATO) leaders agreed that war in Central Europe would be fought mainly by formations of armor and mechanized infantry, which could employ nuclear as well as conventional weapons. Light infantry seemed of value mainly in static defense of strongpoints and cities. The U.S. Army thus shifted its emphasis from conventional infantry to armored and mechanized divisions. In 1960, eleven of fourteen active divisions had been infantry or airborne infantry. By 1963, half of the army's combat divisions were either armored (four divisions) or mechanized (four divisions).[3] Doctrine reflected the new strategy of proportionate response and the army's mission to deter general war. It stated that even after the outbreak of war, application of measured force could still contribute to the prevention of further escalation.[4] Despite the defensive mission of NATO, army doctrine continued to emphasize offense over defense. The latter "may be forced on the commander, but it should be deliberately adopted only as a temporary expedient." Offensive action, on the other hand, "is necessary to achieve decisive results and to maintain the freedom of action."[5] Army tactics had changed little since 1954, although the army now placed greater emphasis on the combination of mobile defense and heavy firepower to counterbalance the enemy's numerical advantage. It was concluded that it would be more important to maintain one's combat forces than to hold terrain.[6] But the army's doctrinal emphasis on European war raised doubts about its preparedness for operations elsewhere.

The degree of mechanization in the army had risen steadily in the late 1950s and early 1960s. Self-propelled guns replaced towed artillery pieces. Mechanized infantry divisions were built around armored personnel carriers as a temporary solution until infantry fighting vehicles (IFVs) would become available. In the meantime, main battle tanks with greater cruising range and better armament replaced medium-gun tanks. None of these developments was useful for the purpose of combat in Vietnam, but other aspects of technological advance, such as airmobility and the design of attack helicopters, addressed the needs of general-purpose forces. Moreover, the army retained some of the older weaponry, vehicles, and artillery pieces to equip light infantry, mechanized, and armored units that were suitable for deployment in underdeveloped countries.

In the 1950s, army leaders had begun to consider airmobility as an important element of tactical nuclear war. General James Gavin made the first significant proposal during his tenure as deputy chief of staff for operations. He argued that infantry transported into battle by helicopters or light utility planes, that is, airmobile cavalry, was necessary for screening operations and as rapidly deployed reserve to reduce enemy forces or exploit breakthroughs.[7] Considering the results of exercises at the Command and General Staff College, General Hamilton Howze, the first director of Army Aviation, argued in a Pentagon briefing in early 1957 that an air cavalry brigade was better suited than an armored division to delaying the advance of three Soviet tank divisions in Bavaria, as long as it was supported by ample conventional artillery, combat engineers, and tactical aircraft. Since the brigade was not road-bound, all bridges were to be blown up at the outset and air cavalry units would find it easier to disengage and lure enemy formations into established killing zones.[8] Despite Howze's efforts, the Army Staff did not request specific proposals for airmobile divisions, and army aircraft continued to be viewed as a supplementary means to the fighting force, particularly for purposes of transportation and logistics.[9] Still, a structured way to study airmobility was established in the 1950s, and enthusiastic army officers realized that the degree of tactical flexibility that could be achieved might serve the purposes of nuclear, conventional, and antiguerrilla warfare.[10]

During the Kennedy administration, the concept of airmobility evolved rapidly. Robert McNamara thought that aircraft provided a better balance between firepower and maneuver by improving the tactical mobility of infantry units. To study the matter, Continental Army Command (CONARC) appointed a Mobility Requirements Board, chaired by Hamilton Howze.[11] The Howze Board found that it was necessary to give commanders of ground forces the capability to deploy and supply their troops through the air. Howze proposed an air assault division with 459 tactical aircraft, air-transportable 105-mm howitzers, and Little John rocket launchers. It was to be supported by 24 Mohawk and 36 UH-1 helicopters, armed with 2.75-inch rockets.[12] This division was designed to move quickly and fight hard when on the ground. The concept was tested in exercise SWIFT STRIKE II in August 1962.[13] The Howze Board also recommended the creation of air-cavalry combat brigades with 316 aircraft, including 144 attack helicopters.[14] These formations were to fulfill the essential cavalry missions that James Gavin had depicted in 1954: screening, reconnaissance, fire direction, flank protection, and delaying operations. McNamara accepted the army's proposed airmobile units in 1963.

In public imagination, air cavalry and the air assault division have become linked with the Vietnam War, but they were created and indoctrinated for war in Germany.[15] Hamilton Howze envisioned the tactical deployment of combat sections of 50 men that were to be transported into battle by light aircraft.[16] He estimated that three such units, 150 men, could "protect an area which nowadays would be assigned a battle group."[17] The combat sections were to be devoid of artillery, thus placing a greater premium on the performance of division artillery. Tank forces were to be used wherever they could be supplied in the forward area.[18] For purposes of antitank defense, Howze foresaw the utility of helicopters armed with antitank missiles. He concluded that "atomic weapons may be used when they prove suitable."[19]

German observers viewed the experimental air assault division with skepticism. Major General Karl Wilhelm Thilo, the deputy inspector general of the German army, thought that the concept would not work well in Central Europe but might be useful in Korea or Vietnam. Thilo recognized the need for airmobility in military operations, but he feared that the air assault division could only be used once air superiority had been achieved. The Germans also believed that the division was too unwieldy for a nuclear battlefield. They even considered breaking up their own airborne division into three independent brigades, which could then be attached to the three German corps in Central Region.[20] In the event, the Vietnam War delayed the introduction of large airmobile formations into USAREUR.

Germans and Americans concurred in the need for a new main battle tank. As soon as the M60 tank had been distributed to Seventh Army, Franz-Josef Strauss had voiced concern about its shortcomings.[21] Strauss claimed that a Soviet T-10 tank could spot an M60 tank 300 yards before the American tank could see its opponent. The Germans had developed a tank prototype that Strauss believed to be superior to the M60. The German tank weighed 35 tons (almost 10 tons less than the M60), had an 800-horsepower engine, a 200-mile operative radius, a low profile of only 2.4 meters in height (compared to about 3.2 meters of the M60), and was fast and highly maneuverable at speeds above 45 miles per hour. Strauss thought that speed, range, and low profile were the essential criteria of a good tank because antitank guns were so advanced that thicker armor could barely reduce vulnerability.[22] U.S. Army leaders did not agree that the M60 was inferior to Soviet tanks. Its 105-mm gun, using kinetic energy rounds, could defeat a T-54 tank at 2,900 meters, while the Soviet tank had to close to 2,700 meters before its rounds could penetrate the armor of the M60.[23]

In the event, the United States and Germany entered into a joint venture to build a main battle tank for 1970 (MBT-70). The agreement was signed by McNamara and Strauss's successor, Kai-Uwe von Hassel, on 1 August

1963. Both defense ministers realized that the project would be expensive. The United States and Germany were to share equally the research and development costs of the program, up to $80 million. An additional $20 million could be added if both governments agreed.[24] Eventually, the MBT-70 project failed because it became apparent during the Vietnam War that the needs of the two armies were different. The Germans needed a tank for combat in Central Europe, while the U.S. military had to consider requirements for operations worldwide. Resulting differences of opinion about weight limitations, radiation protection, and main armament of the tank could not be resolved. German-American cooperation yielded prototypes, but the project also grew more expensive than anticipated.[25]

In July 1968, German minister of defense Gerhard Schröder and his American counterpart Clark Clifford attempted to resuscitate the MBT-70 project with a supplemental agreement on funding, but neither side wanted to commit to specific production or procurement figures. Moreover, Schröder admitted that "the development project should continue because of its political and symbolic value, whatever the eventual results may be."[26] Design of the MBT-70 was abandoned in 1969 and Congress terminated the program in 1971.[27] The two partners went their separate ways. The United States set out to develop a new tank design to replace the M60 series, ultimately leading to the Abrams tank models of the 1980s.[28] The Germans built the next generation of the Leopard tank.[29]

The German concept of mechanized operations was based on the employment of IFVs alongside tanks.[30] The U.S. Army agreed in principle, but its M113 armored personal carrier (APC) was not an entirely satisfactory vehicle because of its weak armor protection and lack of firepower. Moreover, the vehicle would transport soldiers into battle, but the troops were to fight dismounted.[31] This was not ideal for the deployment of armored and mechanized divisions in mobile operations, particularly on a nuclear battlefield. The army planned to introduce an armored IFV by 1970 (AIFV-70). Both Germany and the United States regarded the IFV as a necessary companion to the MBT-70, but could not agree on the size of the squad to be carried and the extent of protection from radiation.[32] Army leaders hoped that an interim vehicle (AIFV-65) could address urgent needs and serve for experiments toward the design of the AIFV-70. USAREUR required 1,300 AIFV-65s for its armored and mechanized units and an additional 360 for pre-positioned stocks of two additional armored divisions, but the prototype of the AIFV-65 was found inadequate and the vehicle was not mass-produced.[33]

Prior to the deployment of American combat forces in Vietnam, strategic priorities and needs for global military capabilities did not seriously impede development of weapons systems that were designed primarily for European battlefields. There was a widespread perception in Washington that armed forces built to fight the most formidable foe could deal with lesser challenges. But army leaders and administration officials nevertheless found themselves at cross-purposes. The former intended to concentrate on the deterrence of war in Central Europe; the latter believed the United States had to be prepared to oppose aggression on the ground anywhere in the world.[34] Army leaders had assessed Massive Retaliation to be unsound in its reliance on strategic-nuclear deterrence, but now they discovered that the pendulum had swung too far. Instead of trying to fashion general-purpose forces for global contingencies, they continued to focus on limited nuclear war in Europe and the deterrence of general war. This meant that the army would be less than ideally prepared to fight in Vietnam, but given the nature of potential nuclear war in Europe, it was a prudent policy.[35]

The Joint Chiefs of Staff (JCS) also acknowledged the greater importance of the defense of Europe. In the event of a political crisis in Europe, the commander in chief U.S. Pacific would have to dispatch three divisions, even if his forces were engaged in combat in Southeast Asia.[36] The Army Staff hoped to address some of the shortfall in combat divisions for global deployment by increasing the active army from sixteen to eighteen divisions, with seven independent brigades, but in the event, the army saw only a temporary increase to eighteen divisions during the Vietnam War.[37]

JCS studies from 1963 showed that the army would have had difficulty sustaining combat operations in more than one theater. The defense of Central Region east of the Rhine required twenty-six active NATO divisions, as well as twenty-two Ready Reserve divisions that were to join the battle within one month of mobilization. The U.S. Army and Marine Corps were to contribute thirteen of these forty-eight divisions. The counteroffensive, expected to commence half a year after the outbreak of war, required a total of twenty-five American divisions. By then, at least six Army Reserve divisions were to be combat-ready and deployed. As long as conflict was limited to one-theater war, the size of U.S. ground forces was sufficient. In the event of a multitheater war, Europe was the critical region, and even though force requirements and threat perception, as well as friendly capabilities, had not been fully developed for such cases, it was apparent that all available reinforcements would have to be sent to Germany.[38]

This issue was defined more precisely in 1964, when Maxwell Taylor, then chairman of the JCS, informed Secretary McNamara that in case of major hostilities in Europe "we could not continue operations in Southeast Asia beyond a possible holding action employing about four divisions." If planned operations with eight combat divisions in Southeast Asia were continued, "any buildup in Europe, over and above the five divisions now there, would be limited initially to no more than seven divisions for a total of twelve divisions in Western Europe, and this could only be done by transfer of the two divisions from Korea." He concluded that "further expansion of the U.S. ground force contribution in Europe would have to await the availability of the six Army ready reserve divisions," between four and six months from mobilization.[39]

The army had first practiced rapid deployment of strategic reserve forces from the United States to Germany in 1962. Initially, the LONG THRUST exercise, testing the deployment of three battle groups, had been scheduled for May 1961. President Kennedy had cancelled it when it appeared that ground forces might have to be deployed in Laos. But in response to the Berlin Crisis, LONG THRUST was expanded to a strategic mobility exercise during which battle groups were rotated in and out of Germany, from January 1962 to April 1964.[40] LONG THRUST units were not committed to Allied Command, Europe (ACE), in order to indicate the temporary nature of their deployment. LONG THRUST was primarily a political signal to Moscow, but the troop rotation also had operational consequences.[41] One battle group of 4th Infantry Division was sent to Berlin to replace the battle group of 24th Mechanized Division, which in turn reinforced the division in West Germany. V Corps received additional reserves: a second battle group, as well as headquarters and support units of 4th Infantry Division. In the future, the addition of U.S. reserve units to the Central Army Group (CENTAG) was to permit for the shift of a German division to the Northern Army Group (NORTHAG) or a northward adjustment of the border between the army groups. In either case, forward defense near the intra-German border would become feasible.[42]

In 1963, an even larger troop movement accompanied LONG THRUST. Exercise BIG LIFT tested rapid deployment by air of an armored division, whose equipment was pre-positioned in Germany. For the duration of the exercise, the U.S. Army had seven combat divisions and division equivalents in Germany.[43] In December 1964, Secretary McNamara stated that airlift capability had been doubled since 1961, and he estimated that it would triple again by 1970, when the U.S. military was to be able to transport eleven combat divisions to Europe in the first thirty days of war.[44] In 1965, the strategic airlift capability of the U.S. military to Europe and Southeast Asia was sufficient for movement of only one-and-a-half combat divisions with fifteen days worth of supplies.[45] On the other hand, initial response to a Soviet attack in Germany would not require the movement of entire divisions and their equipment, since the weaponry and supply stocks for two combat divisions were pre-positioned. Moreover, there was sufficient sealift capability to move more than ten divisions to Europe within sixty days. This capability was indeed needed, as studies showed that enemy armies could not be destroyed by thermonuclear attacks. Since the ability of European armies to meet their NATO reserve commitments was in doubt, the rapid movement of American reinforcements to Europe was critical.[46]

During the Berlin Crisis, manpower of USAREUR had increased to 273,000 officers and men. But by June 1963, it had been reduced to 256,000, and an additional 16,000 were scheduled for withdrawal.[47] The remaining forces had improved their combat capability. The ROAD reorganization was complete, and more modern equipment had been issued to the troops. This included doubling the number of Honest John rocket launchers per division and adding twelve artillery tubes in mechanized and six in armored divisions. Each armored division had received an additional twenty-nine tanks. USAREUR had seventy-seven heavy Davy Crockett delivery systems. It was planned to replace the remaining 280-mm gun battalions, all Lacrosse battalions, and two of eight Corporal battalions with three Sergeant battalions and two 175-mm gun battalions, both nuclear-capable weapon systems. Coupled with the substitution of 155-mm howitzers for 105-mm howitzers in armored and mechanized divisions as well as armored cavalry regiments, this amounted to an increase in conventional and nuclear firepower over the pentomic division.[48]

Operational planning reached a turning point as the forward-defense line was advanced to the intra-German border. In October 1963, Hans Speidel, who had retired from Allied Land Forces, Central Europe (LANDCENT) and now served as defense consultant to Chancellor Ludwig Erhard, told Taylor that he expected the bulk of the attack against NORTHAG to be in the vicinity of Hannover or of Kassel. The Germans were proposing plans for an immediate counterattack through the Hof Gap against the southern flank of the attacker. This offensive operation was to be conducted by Seventh Army and the two German corps in CENTAG. Speidel argued that the counterattack would have to be anchored by a strong defensive position at the West German–Czechoslovakian border, fortified with atomic demolition mines. Taylor admitted that he had never liked NATO's passive defense planning, but he cautioned that ACE did not have enough reserve forces for a large counteroffensive.[49]

In November, the National Security Council (NSC) circulated a study on management and termination of war with the Soviet Union. The war aim was to be neither unconditional surrender nor complete destruction of the enemy forces, but "a cessation on terms acceptable to the United States." The study concluded that cease-fire and negotiated settlement could be achieved.[50] In the scenario based on initial limitation to conventional weapons, NATO's armies were forced to withdraw slowly, but they were able to contain the Soviet advance east of the Rhine River. Two days after the Soviet invasion, the U.S. military first employed tactical nuclear weapons against battlefield targets and military installations in Eastern Europe. This was done for political more than for military reasons, because it was believed that escalation would force the Soviets to negotiate and withdraw their ground forces to the Soviet Union. The option to terminate war at this stage included the liberation of Eastern Europe. But in the war game, the Soviets responded with nuclear strikes and the U.S. government sent an ultimatum threatening the destruction of military targets inside the Soviet Union.[51]

After two days of deliberations, the Soviets resumed nuclear attacks against targets in Western Europe. The United States immediately retaliated against six military targets in the Soviet Union. On the fifth day of war, Soviet leaders expressed willingness to negotiate, albeit not on the basis of American proposals. Moreover, the attack on the Soviet Union could not go unpunished. Therefore, a counterstrike was conducted against the sites from which ballistic missiles had been launched. The United States maintained that the liberation of Eastern Europe was nonnegotiable and escalated the use of nuclear weapons. The attack was carefully constrained to reduce damage to cities and industrial plants, and no attacks were launched against the Kremlin. Both sides were determined to end the war before it escalated to a full-scale intercontinental nuclear exchange. The Soviets retaliated for nuclear strikes against targets in Russia, but at the same time they broke off the ground offensive in Germany and offered to withdraw their forces to the Soviet Union. It is difficult to determine whether military, intelligence, and political officers in the United States indeed believed that theater nuclear war could be controlled, and it is unclear how they arrived at the conclusion that the Soviet leadership would order retreat. It is nonetheless notable that the war ended on the sixth day with a NATO victory.[52]

Current planning of ACE called for mobile defense at the intra-German border, but maneuvers revealed that counterattacks would open gaps between NATO forces and could destroy the cohesiveness of the front. The Supreme Allied Commander, Europe (SACEUR) expected forward-deployed units to hold or give ground slowly, until it could be determined whether the Soviet attack was a full-scale onslaught or merely a probe. If it were the former, NATO would escalate to nuclear war. American observers were pessimistic about the feasibility of holding operations, since all LANDCENT divisions would be decimated if the Soviets first employed tactical nuclear weapons. Both dispersion and nuclear tactics were insufficient in current doctrine. The crucial problem was that the attacker could mass his forces, while the defender had to cover the entire front and was critically short on reserves. It was also unclear how NATO forces would transition from conventional to nuclear war. Current doctrine might permit for one or the other in a relatively static environment, but not for both in short progression. In addition, LANDCENT forces were deficient in quality and quantity, as training levels remained low, logistics poor, and support troops in short supply.[53] But in its conclusion, the NSC study group pointed out that Warsaw Pact forces faced equally difficult problems, and the prevailing attitude was one of hope rather than frustration.[54]

The NATO fall exercise in September 1964 (FALLEX 64) showed how easily graduated deterrence could fail. Conflict started with rapid Soviet buildup of forces and limited aggression against Germany and Scandinavia, which rapidly escalated to large-scale attacks. NATO responded with conventional force, but it soon became apparent that nuclear weapons had to be used. SACEUR requested authority for their selective release. The North Atlantic Council granted his request on the third day of war in Germany. In response, the Soviets almost immediately escalated to general nuclear war.[55] There is evidence to suggest that this scenario was based more on political guidance than on operational considerations. FALLEX 64 was the first major NATO exercise in which the North Atlantic Council and many national authorities participated. It is difficult to see how SACEUR could have presented a limited-war scenario, which was still excluded in political guidance. FALLEX 64 represented the beliefs of many European political leaders and aspects of the thinking of military officers.

At this time, U.S. Army divisions in Germany were at 100 percent of their authorized personnel strength, and Soviet divisions in East Germany remained at about 80 percent. The Pentagon assumed that an American division had at least twice the combat power of a Soviet division. Intelligence reports estimated Soviet strength at sixty to eighty combat-ready divisions, but in the eyes of the Secretary of Defense this only amounted to between twenty-four and thirty-five U.S. division equivalents, or about twice the size of the Active Army. This assessment was supported by a comparison of manpower. Soviet ground forces had about two million officers and men under arms; the U.S. Army had one million. The army had increased its capability for sustained combat operations by increasing the inventory of equipment for all sixteen divisions to the point where they could be supplied out of existing stocks until the productive capacity of the nation could provide steady supplies. In addition, other NATO divisions were deemed to be slightly better than Soviet divisions. The thirty-four operational Soviet and Warsaw Pact divisions in East Germany and Czechoslovakia could be reinforced to sixty divisions in three or four weeks time, but NATO could expand from thirty-five to fifty-seven Soviet division-equivalents within a month.[56] State Department analysts found the Pentagon position overly optimistic. In their opinion, the United States would find it difficult to supply troops in Europe and Asia while Soviet submarines threatened vital shipping lanes.[57]

Robert McNamara summarized the state of deterrence in his address to the NATO Ministerial Meeting in December 1964. He stated that the threat of all-out nuclear attack had been effectively deterred. He did not think that NATO should prepare specifically for limited nuclear attacks against Western Europe, because any such action would prompt the alliance to implement its plans for general war. McNamara believed that a deliberate Soviet conventional attack was less likely than it had been in 1961. The threat remained significant, and weaknesses in NATO forces still had to be addressed, but the tactical nuclear capability on the ground, coupled with the strategic deterrent, had reduced the risk of war. The United States had deployed or allocated 40 percent of its tactical nuclear stockpile for the defense of the alliance. The aggregate yield of tactical nuclear weapons stored in Germany was 5,000 times greater than the atom bomb dropped on Hiroshima, and this calculation did not even include atomic demolition charges.[58]

Naturally, it was desirable to absorb limited conventional attacks without resort to nuclear weapons, but McNamara's address indicated to what extent the secretary of defense had adopted the concept of integrated conventional and tactical nuclear ground forces. Most of the Soviet experts in the State Department had come to the same conclusion; other analysts, particularly on the Policy Planning Staff, maintained doubts. Former ambassador to Moscow Llewelyn Thompson questioned why a massive conventional Soviet attack against Central Region was still under internal discussion. The Soviets could not possibly believe that they would win quickly and decisively, thus preventing nuclear escalation. Thompson thought it was plausible that the Soviets might believe the West would accept military defeat rather than initiate the use of nuclear weapons. But if that was the case, Soviet plans had to include an option to accept a negotiated end to the conflict if the assumption was proven wrong. In the event, McNamara recommended significant improvements in territorial force posture. He was optimistic about the state of deterrence.[59] Yet a strong deterrent, built for large-scale conventional or nuclear war in Central Europe, did not necessarily translate into a capable force for global deployment.

ROAD, Global Deployment, and the Vietnam War

The Korean War and the nuclear arms race had spawned a debate on the subject of limited war that helped shape the perception of the political leaders who decided to commit American advisers and combat forces to Vietnam. Strategy analysts of the 1950s, such as Bernard Brodie and William W. Kaufman, questioned whether Massive Retaliation could deter limited aggression. Senior army officers and leaders of the opposition Democratic Party also questioned the reliability of Massive Retaliation as deterrence strategy. In 1957, two seminal studies of limited war added to the argument against total deterrence. Robert Osgood argued in *Limited War* that the destructive power of nuclear weapons forced world leaders to limit their aims. The study of history showed that limited objectives translated into limited war. Henry Kissinger, a future national security adviser and secretary of state, reached a wider public with *Nuclear Weapons and Foreign Policy*. Massive Retaliation, he maintained, was strategically problematical because it was reactive rather than active, and thus it forfeited the initiative in the case of lesser threats. He argued that the United States needed to recover the ability to respond to local and limited aggression in order to regain the initiative in the Cold War. Eisenhower's focus on economy of means and reliance on nuclear deterrence had left the United States defenseless to all but the most dangerous forms of aggression.[60]

Army leaders found that the arguments advanced by Osgood and Kissinger were useful for their purposes, but neither provided the army with a solution to the problem of dealing with multiple forms of limited war. Operational requirements and force objectives were clearly defined for war in Europe, but it was less apparent what capabilities were needed against less well-known enemy forces in the Third World. Maxwell Taylor had stated that the ideal Cold War army was to consist of two distinctly different components, a force equipped and trained for nuclear and large-scale conventional war in Europe, and a different kind of force for sub-limited or purely conventional war. The pentomic and ROAD reorganizations were steps in the direction of strategic flexibility of general-purpose forces. But the army was too small to operate with two or more sets of doctrine and equipment, and thus even ROAD formations remained tied to mid-intensity war. As a consequence, the army's ability to fight a sub-limited war was underdeveloped.

ROAD divisions offered greater flexibility for global deployment, but the organizational change in itself did not solve the problem of how a division could operate in Germany and Vietnam. The Operations Research Office, a joint research organization of Johns Hopkins University and the army, suggested that all but a token American ground force should be withdrawn from Europe once the Bundeswehr had gained strength. Otherwise, two types of field armies would have to be created, one with and one without tactical nuclear forces.[61] The Army Staff never seriously considered proposals for a major realignment of forces in Germany. The pursuit of dual capability, on the other hand, became linked to the elementary question of the necessary kinds of combat capability for limited and sub-limited war in the 1960s. In Europe, an "in being" dual capability, that is, the possession of nuclear weapons by maneuver battalions without pre-delegated authority for their use, was desirable. This did not adversely affect the compatibility of army divisions and allied forces, whose tactical formations also were equipped with nuclear-capable weapon systems. But the possession of tactical nuclear weapons by any command echelon from platoon to field army caused concern among U.S. allies outside of Europe. It raised questions about whether such weapons were to be employed in "brushfire wars" in the Middle East or Southeast Asia.[62] Moreover, it was difficult to guarantee the safety and security of nuclear weapons in transport or in unstable regions.[63]

The Operations Research Office suggested that combat units were to be armed with conventional weapons only. They were to be supported by Special Nuclear Groups that could provide tactical nuclear fire support at any command echelon, from company to field army, with weapons systems ranging from Davy Crocketts to Pershing missiles. It was estimated that Seventh Army would require between 100 and 125 such groups on the company level, twenty-five to thirty for the battalions, five to eight for the brigades, two for the corps, and one for the field army. But such theoretical proposals did not resolve the question of whether ROAD divisions were capable of engaging vastly different enemy forces in dissimilar environments. ROAD was more adaptable to counterinsurgency warfare as well as to big-unit war in Europe than the pentomic division, but organization was not the only issue. Doctrine mattered as well.[64]

To conform to the global nature of Flexible Response, the 1962 edition of the army's doctrinal manual for operations contained sections on jungle, desert, and mountain warfare, but these were very general, and none of them exceeded one page in length.[65] There was a more detailed discussion of unconventional war, emphasizing reliance on local personnel as well as economic, political, and psychological means of warfare. But major combat operations by American forces against guerrillas were not intended.[66] That being said, army forces were supposed to be prepared to counter tactics that sought to limit the effect of their superior firepower and technology. This was to be achieved in decisive offensive operations by small task forces; heavy combat support units were to be held at central locations.[67] ROAD divisions, in short, remained calibrated to fight a big-unit war in Europe.

The Kennedy administration assumed that wars of national liberation, conducted mainly by guerrilla forces, posed an imminent threat and that U.S. ground forces had to be capable of addressing developing crises in Laos and Vietnam. But army leaders viewed deterrence of war in Europe as their primary objective and believed that a credible territorial deterrent to Soviet attack had to be maintained. This position was supported by defense experts in Europe, such as Otto Heilbrunn of the Royal United Kingdom Service Institute and Helmut Schmidt of the German opposition party SPD.[68] Seventh Army and the rapidly improving Bundeswehr provided the core of the deterrent forces.[69] Army leaders did not intend to upset the balance of power in Europe by shifting their focus to peripheral areas of the Cold War. For the time being, that is, prior to the 1965 escalation of the Vietnam War, this meant that the bulk of forces deployed in sub-limited war in any Third World country were to be light infantry formations. In the future, the development of airmobile combat forces promised to increase tactical mobility.

As early as 1962, General Earle Wheeler, then army chief of staff, had informed Cyrus Vance that "type" divisions for Europe and Vietnam had been developed because "it is necessary to design packaged forces either to reinforce a well established theater of operations, such as Europe, or to deploy to trouble spots in relatively undeveloped and remote areas of the world such as Southeast Asia." The ideal division for Southeast Asia was to be a reinforced ROAD infantry division of 36,776 officers and men, in seven infantry, two tank, and two mechanized battalions, with 24,000 men in combat elements and over 12,000 in supporting units. Germany was to be defended by standard ROAD armored divisions and by mechanized divisions with 32,732 personnel in three tank and seven mechanized battalions. The projected ratio of combat to support forces organic to the division was nearly four to one.[70] That combat-support ratio did not include nondivisional elements, which later accounted for the bulk of U.S. forces in Vietnam.

ROAD infantry divisions had retained a great number of armored vehicles and heavy artillery in order to fight in mid-intensity war.[71] But it was widely assumed, both within and outside the army, that war in Vietnam was to be fought by infantry on foot and that there would be few targets for heavy guns.[72] Based on the experience of the Korean War, where monsoon rains had made most of the countryside unsuitable for tanks, and a misreading of French operations with mechanized forces in the Indochina War, army leaders were convinced that tanks, APCs, and armored cavalry assault vehicles (ACAVs) would be of little use in Vietnam. Their understanding of French armored and mechanized operations was based on journalistic accounts of the Indochina War rather than on careful study of French after-action reports. French armor had suffered from flawed operational philosophy and outdated equipment. French commanders had dispersed obsolescent armored vehicles over the countryside of Vietnam and had not retained concentrated armored formations to support infantry operations.[73] The prevailing negative attitude in the U.S. Army toward armored operations in Vietnam was reinforced by lack of doctrine for mounted combat outside of Europe.[74]

The Army Staff recognized that the requirements of combat in Vietnam and Germany were vastly different. Besides obvious contrasts in climate and environment, enemy objectives, tactics, mobility, and ability to seize and hold terrain were dissimilar. Warsaw Pact armies were expected to deploy armored spearheads and mechanized army groups in order to defeat NATO ground forces and conquer Western Europe, but Vietnamese guerrilla and regular forces moved on foot, had little artillery support, and conducted raids, ambushes, and attacks on base camps. These forces sought to terrorize the local population and break the spirit of the South Vietnamese government and its American ally. For ground forces in Vietnam, this meant that there would be no fixed front lines or secure rear areas. This was particularly problematic with regard to the artillery support that army units had come to expect. In the event, light and medium artillery was concentrated in fire bases from which all ground operations in the vicinity could be supported.[75] This system, coupled with close air support and the lack of enemy field fortifications, was so effective that the role of artillery changed from softening enemy positions for infantry assault to destruction of enemy formations.[76] The resulting reliance on firepower helped to minimize friendly casualties but contributed to indiscriminate killing of enemy combatants and local civilians. As army officer and historian Robert Doughty pointed out, it maximized the strength of U.S. forces in Vietnam.[77] But at the same time it impeded attempts to pacify large areas of South Vietnam and win the support of the population.[78]

The notion that Vietnam would be entirely an infantryman's war was proven wrong after 1965. Initially, the employment of medium-gun tanks by the Marine Corps and ACAVs by armored cavalry squadrons went largely unnoticed, but as the emphasis of the war shifted from counterinsurgency to operations against National Liberation Front and North Vietnamese regiments, the army called for systematic analysis of the terrain. In 1967, the Mechanized and Armor Combat Operations, Vietnam (MACOV) study found that despite monsoon climate and environmental features, armored vehicles could be deployed in most of the country. The MACOV study assessed two-thirds of Vietnam during the dry season as traversable by tanks and APCs, although planners expected tank operations to be curtailed by the rainy season.[79]

Armor units had begun to employ tanks and ACAVs quite successfully in 1966, but they "had to invent tactics and techniques, and then convince the Army that they worked."[80] Specific deviations from operational conception for war in Europe included the use of M113 APCs as assault vehicles and concentration of force on the defensive. The APC received two machine guns with shields and additional protection for the driver, thus converting it into an armored assault vehicle, which allowed riflemen to remain mounted during a firefight.[81] Dispersion on the defensive, critical in Europe where the enemy had heavy conventional and nuclear firepower at his disposal, was counterproductive in Vietnam. North Vietnamese troops and South Vietnamese guerrillas used infiltration tactics and did not possess much heavy artillery. Therefore, army units in Vietnam resorted to the defense of strong perimeters as a means of avoiding defeat in detail. Once enemy forces attacked such defensive perimeters, they could be annihilated by concentrated artillery and small-arms fire.[82] For offensive operations, the MACOV study strongly suggested combining armored, mechanized, and light infantry units.[83] Eventually, the army deployed one dozen tank and mechanized battalions in Vietnam.[84]

Tank battalions required little structural change. The main adjustment during the Vietnam War was the introduction of the M48A3 medium-gun tank, an improved version of the Patton tank series.[85] The M48A3 was armed with a 90-mm gun, but otherwise it was similar to the M60 tank that was used in Europe. The smaller gun made the M48A3 more suitable for operations in support of infantry, while the M60 was built to combat Soviet tanks and armored vehicles in defensive and offensive operations.[86] The M48A3 was designed for combat in Vietnam, as the era of medium-gun tanks in Europe had already come to a close. Because of the difficult environment and lack of established infrastructure, the tank battalion received a service company in addition to its regular three tank companies and the headquarters company.[87]

In 1969, armored cavalry received the M551 Sheridan. In Vietnam, Sheridans replaced both Patton tanks and ACAVs. Soldiers in the field preferred the new vehicle to the ACAV but found it a poor replacement for the medium-gun tank.[88] As a hybrid vehicle, it ultimately failed to convince the army brass. There was little use for its light-tank functions in Germany. Despite misgivings about poor performance as a scouting vehicle for cavalry, USAREUR welcomed the Sheridan as replacement for the M114 ACAV in its armored cavalry regiments, because of the much greater tank-killing power of the 152-mm gun and missile launcher.[89] But eventually, army leadership recognized that armored cavalry was better equipped with a mixture of M60 tanks and M113 APCs until a mechanized fighting vehicle could be developed.[90]

Despite innovations in armor, the infantry, with much artillery support, fought most of the engagements in Vietnam. The army deployed five infantry divisions, one air cavalry division, and one airborne division, as well as four light infantry brigades, one mechanized brigade, and two airborne infantry brigades.[91] Separate infantry brigades had been created in 1965, with four infantry battalions and a battalion of field artillery with eighteen towed 105-mm howitzers and thirty 3.5-inch rocket launchers. Unlike the division artillery of ROAD infantry, field artillery of the separate brigade did not have 155-mm or heavy 8-inch howitzers.[92] By 1968, rocket launchers had been eliminated from field artillery battalions in Vietnam and Europe.[93] Typical infantry battalions deployed in Vietnam had no armored vehicles and only limited organic artillery. A standard infantry battalion in Vietnam had twelve 81-mm and four 4.2-inch mortars, twelve 90-mm recoilless rifles, twenty-six light machine guns, and 110 40-mm grenade launchers, as well as 841 5.56-mm rifles.[94] An infantry battalion deployed in Europe had forty-nine APCs, forty-nine light and twenty heavy machine guns, eighteen 81-mm mortars (nine of them self-propelled), four 4.2-inch mortars, and four self-propelled 107-mm mortars, as well as eighteen 90-mm and six 106-mm recoilless rifles. Battalions in Europe were issued 606 7.62-mm rifles, which expended standardized NATO ammunition.

Infantry units in Vietnam adjusted tactical doctrine and unit organization to the nature of enemy threat and environment. Stripping away tanks and APCs left lighter formations that could be used in difficult jungle or mountain terrain.[95] Heavy guns and mortars were taken away from the division artillery and integrated at corps level, but they could still be found in fire support bases. Most battalions stripped away other organic items, such as antitank and antiaircraft weapon systems, that impeded the mobility of rifle companies and air assault elements.[96] This freed up personnel, which allowed line battalions to add a fourth rifle company.[97] In some circumstances, however, division and brigade commanders found it useful to retain one heavy battalion, with tanks, APCs, and heavy artillery. Tactically, infantry was deployed in search-and-destroy operations, trying to find, fix, and destroy the enemy during the daytime but then withdrawing into defensive perimeters at night. This had to be supplemented by a force for local security and another for ready reaction. The fourth line company allowed each combat element of the battalion to rotate functions and assured that one company could recover in reserve.[98]

The helicopter was the most important army vehicle of the Vietnam War. Lieutenant General John Hay pointedly summarized the importance of the helicopter: "It extended the infantry unit's area of control at least threefold. A commander could react to opportunities quicker, delay his decision, or even change his plans en route. . . . His entire unit could be shifted to a new area on short notice."[99] Hay concluded that "in a land that favored the easily hidden, lightly loaded foot soldier, the helicopter balanced the odds."[100] It was the employment of air cavalry and the Air Assault Division in Vietnam that convinced army leaders in Washington that the concept of airmobility was sound and should be retained. Helicopters were expected to perform even more effectively in the open countryside of Central Europe.[101] The main tactical difference was that attack helicopters in Europe were intended to increase the antiarmor capability of USAREUR, rather than operate primarily against enemy infantry.

Organizational adjustments to infantry brigades and battalions, as well as the introduction of a new tank model and armored vehicle for combat in Vietnam, led to distinctly different equipment and tactical organizations in the field armies in Vietnam and Germany.[102] Tactics and operations in Vietnam were characterized by reliance on long-range fire support, close air support, helicopter gun ships, and airmobile formations that could be transported into battle by helicopter.[103] Some of the tactical and materiel innovations of the Vietnam War might have been useful in future combat operations in Europe. The helicopter is the obvious example, but equally important were advances in signal communications that allowed division and brigade commanders to direct operations of all their maneuver and combat support elements.[104] The army introduced satellite communications, and manual switchboards were replaced by digital relays. Moreover, radio frequencies were improved over the limited equipment of the 1950s. Employing new technology under combat conditions greatly increased training and the expertise of communications troops.[105] This helped address the command-and-control problem that had haunted the pentomic division. On a European battlefield, it would contribute greatly to the effective employment of dispersed battalions and facilitate rapid-fire support or resupply.

Combat in Vietnam did not change army operational doctrine significantly. The 1968 edition of Field Manual 100-5 emphasized the offensive and remained focused on Europe, limited war, and graduated deterrence, rather than on the ongoing war in Vietnam.[106] Technological developments were addressed, particularly in the areas of electronic warfare and intelligence, but the chapters on "Strategy and Military Force," "The Operational Environment," "Command," "The Principles of War and Operational Concepts," and "Conduct of Battle" appeared essentially unaltered from the 1962 edition. In the latter parts of the manual, Vietnam experience led to an expansion of the discussion on airmobility, which was now treated separately from airborne operations. Surprisingly, there was no longer a chapter on military operations against irregular forces. Its main points were integrated into a short section on guerrilla warfare. The army treated Vietnam as an exceptional case, even as the war escalated. Vietnam drew away much of the resources needed to defend Western Europe and deter war in the first place. The army was unwilling to compound this problem by adjusting operational doctrine to the type of war it had to fight in Southeast Asia.

The army has been criticized for fighting a mid-intensity war in an environment that called for tactics of low-intensity warfare.[107] On the surface, that was certainly true, but it overlooked the strategic and political circumstances that had set the parameters within which army leaders shaped their institution in the decade following the Korean War. It was an expression of the army's single-minded focus on European war. Given the dire consequences of nuclear war, the army's focus on Germany was prudent. But in national strategy, the emphasis on containing the spread of Communism shifted to the periphery of the Cold War, thus divorcing it for several years from military strategy. Containment and attrition remained the grand strategy and the guiding policy of the United States. In light of this basic truth, it is possible to interpret the military defeat in Vietnam in measured terms. Much like tactical and operational success did not translate into strategic victory, local defeat did not lead to a breakdown of grand strategy. But the war itself weakened the deterrent in Europe.

The Army in the Shadow of Vietnam

During the Vietnam War, U.S. military strength in Europe dropped from almost 420,000 to 315,000 by September 1968. Army forces in Europe were reduced from 272,000 officers and men during the Berlin Crisis to less than 170,000 at the end of 1970. USAREUR became a manpower and materiel replacement pool, which caused severe shortages of experienced command personnel and conventional ammunition. General Lyman Lemnitzer, NATO's supreme commander from 1963 to 1969, recognized the need to maintain combat and support units in Vietnam at a high level, but he assumed that the drawdown was temporary. At least the policy to move only individual soldiers out of Europe, and not entire units, assured that the order of battle was unaffected. Lemnitzer reasoned that the return of combat veterans from tours in Vietnam provided expertise, and that the improvement of the Bundeswehr compensated for some of the weakness of USAREUR.[108]

Due to the decision of President Johnson to fight the Vietnam War without calling up the reserve, the U.S. military had to deploy most of its strategic reserve. This could not be sustained without weakening the deterrent force. By March 1966, the JCS called for a more permanent solution. In addition to forces requested by General William C. Westmoreland for Vietnam, the United States needed an adequate strategic reserve, a strong training and rotation base, and enough troops in Pacific Command for tasks not directly related to the war. All this had to be achieved without degrading the American military posture in Europe. Under existing Defense Department plans, USAREUR stood to lose nearly 60,000 officers and men, or twenty-one battalion equivalents of combat effectiveness. This would compromise critical maintenance and support functions. The recovery period of USAREUR logistics would last more than eighteen months. The JCS strongly advised against implementation: "The United States would assume a high-risk posture . . . and would place the security of the remaining forces in jeopardy by degradation of their structure, support, and the capability to reinforce in a timely manner."[109]

The army had enough combat battalions to sustain its posture in Europe and fight the war in Vietnam, but it lacked support units. Maxwell Taylor had warned about the imbalance of combat and support forces as early as 1964.[110] This was particularly problematic because an American mechanized or armored division required twice the amount of support forces of a German or British division.[111] As an alternative to the Defense Department plan, the JCS suggested a more gradual and balanced buildup of forces in Vietnam that would cause USAREUR to lose 55,300 officers and men, 3,500 less than the minimum drawdown under the rejected plan. This was more than a cosmetic change, because these 3,500 men were critical skill personnel whose loss USAREUR could least afford. The JCS plan led to a reduction of the degradation from 100 percent to less than 50 percent in some areas. It could not, however, reduce the loss of combat power, and restoration of the U.S. Army posture in Europe would still take eighteen months.[112]

For 1967, Pacific Command requested twelve additional combat battalions and support forces for deployment in Vietnam. The army could meet the request only on a delayed time schedule, lagging between six and eight months behind the commander in chief of Pacific Command's requirements. Afterward, only two airborne brigades were left to reinforce troops in Europe or react to a crisis elsewhere. In addition, the JCS feared that equipment shortages would keep divisions earmarked as NATO reinforcements from reaching combat-readiness until late 1968. The personnel shortage in USAREUR caused by the immediate drawdown of 1965 and 1966 could still be alleviated, but command effectiveness would continue to be at a reduced level because skilled personnel could not be replaced. To make things worse, combat readiness of the reserve was at a low level because equipment had to be withdrawn from reserve units to support mobilization of forces. The army had a force deficiency of almost three active divisions to maintain the strategic reserve and other base requirements.[113] The JCS feared that the United States would not be able to prosecute the war in Vietnam decisively while also fulfilling its other commitments. The chiefs suggested withdrawal of two brigades from Germany.[114]

In early February 1966, the army had begun to withdraw personnel from all commands in order to increase the training base in the United States. USAREUR had been assured that the Department of the Army did not intend to withdraw more than 50 percent of the authorized strength of any one branch. Nevertheless, USAREUR lost more than 4,500 officers, over 2,500 of them in combat units. By late September, there were so few battalion and company grade officers left that noncommissioned officers were commanding artillery batteries and other units. Although that trend was reversed in October, the result was a force without sufficient leadership. At the end of the year, USAREUR counted only slightly more than 10,000 of its authorized 17,000 officers. In addition, there was a serious shortage of military occupational specialists that degraded artillery, maintenance, and logistics functions. The majority of combat battalions fell below 75 percent of their authorized strength and readiness levels.[115]

Despite the drawdown, Robert McNamara expressed confidence that the army was capable of fulfilling its mission in Germany. In order to compensate for the personnel and skill reduction, greater emphasis was placed on tactical nuclear weapons. McNamara stated in the Senate in January 1967 that NATO might have to use nuclear weapons even in limited war. The United States had about 7,000 tactical nuclear weapons deployed in Western Europe. But McNamara assumed that the theater nuclear capability was a deterrent in itself, keeping the Soviets from using nuclear weapons during a ground offensive. Therefore, use of tactical nuclear weapons by NATO forces would only be authorized at a point where conventional defense was faltering. McNamara believed that the defensive capabilities of NATO forces in Central Europe remained strong enough to contain a major Soviet conventional assault.[116] But despite McNamara's optimism, the criticism of NATO's Military Committee, that "improvement in the modernization of equipment and mechanization of land forces is impeded by the serious shortage of major units," remained valid.[117]

The void in leadership in USAREUR, which continued throughout the 1960s, caused a number of problems. As the war in Vietnam dragged on and opposition to the war grew in the United States, European-American relations soured. In Germany, American bases and personnel became targets for terrorist attacks. Incidents in the late 1960s remained isolated, but by the early 1970s, cells of the Red Army Faction had been formed and the terror campaign became more coordinated.[118] American soldiers did little to endear themselves to their German hosts. USAREUR's crime rate rose dramatically after 1967, and the remaining officers were so heavily taxed that they had few resources to address the problem. Germans became the targets of violent robberies, rape, and homicide. Along with the soaring crime rate and the general decline in morale came increasing drug abuse, a problem that was reduced only after the creation of the all-volunteer force in 1973.[119] Race relations became so poor that pitched battles between white and black soldiers occurred in bars and on the streets of German cities. German newspapers and media outlets took up calls for American forces to go home in the later parts of the 1960s. Overall, morale and leadership in USAREUR were at a low point in 1973. Combat capability had eroded accordingly.[120]

Lemnitzer's fears of declining U.S. military capability in Europe and diminishing defense spending of European states because of political détente were aggravated by further improvement of the Soviet military. In 1965, it had been estimated that there were 108 combat-ready line divisions and that Soviet divisions in Eastern Europe were at 90 percent of war strength. Forty-five Soviet and Warsaw Pact divisions and 2,900 tactical aircraft were immediately available for employment against Central Region. U.S. intelligence analysts explained this as a response to heightened international tensions, directly related to the Vietnam War. Soviet doctrine emphasized nuclear war and saw the proper role of ground forces in the exploitation of nuclear strikes, but it considered conventional operations more prominently than had previously been the case. Intelligence analysts believed that the Soviets could not use more than eighty divisions in their strike force and theater reserve against Central Region. The necessary buildup could be concluded within fifteen days.[121] While the reliability of Western intelligence estimates of Soviet and Warsaw Pact strength in the 1950s has been questioned, recently released records from former Warsaw Pact states indicate that the estimates of the late 1960s and 1970s more accurately represented actual threat.[122]

The intelligence estimate of November 1966 reported 109 combat-ready line divisions and thirty-two cadre divisions. Apparently, the Soviets had eliminated the tier between cadre and combat-ready units. As a consequence, there were more than fifty Soviet and Warsaw Pact divisions in Eastern Europe that could be used at the outset of an attack against Central Region. Thirty-five of these divisions were stationed in East Germany and Czechoslovakia, eleven in Poland, and seven in Hungary. Western intelligence analysts were uncertain whether the divisions in Hungary would be employed against Central or Southern Region. Moreover, the Soviet Union possessed a vast reserve. It was deemed likely that the attack would start only after a striking force of sixty divisions and a theater reserve of twenty divisions had been assembled. This could theoretically be achieved within two weeks, but weakness of the railroad network might extend the buildup period to about one month.[123] In the long run, the U.S. intelligence community assumed, Soviet ground forces would convert to a smaller number of larger divisions.

Western intelligence believed that Soviet doctrine of the mid- and late

1960s was based on ground operations following a nuclear exchange.[124] Thus, USAREUR had to be prepared for nuclear, conventional, and mixed warfare. Combat forces were trained for small-unit tactics on the nuclear battlefield.[125] General Andrew O'Meara, the commander in chief, instructed his troops to advance as the cloud settled after a nuclear burst. That was the moment to close with the enemy and utilize concealment offered by the burst and the disorder that it had caused. O'Meara believed that the nuclear battle would be decided by small units, often acting in isolation. He concluded: "The leader on the nuclear battlefield must be a 20th century Jeb Stuart. He must surprise the enemy with his tactics and his daring, catch him off balance with his initiative, beat him with his aggressiveness and his plain battlefield horse sense."[126]

While the United States was becoming more deeply embroiled in the Vietnam War, France announced its withdrawal from NATO military commands in March 1966. The loss of French combat forces, five active divisions and reserves, reduced NATO ground forces in Central Europe to twenty-two active divisions.[127] Even more damaging to the army was the loss of its primary line of communication from the Atlantic and North Sea ports through France to Germany.[128] Supply depots had to be relocated, leading to a concentration of more than 75 percent of USAREUR's vital materiel in the vicinity of Kaiserslautern. This caused alarm about the vulnerability of the logistics system to nuclear attack.[129] After 1967, USAREUR depended on the pipeline and transportation system from the northern German port of Bremerhaven to the deployment area in the south of the country. This line of communication ran parallel to the intra-German border, in a geographic area that might be overrun by Soviet forces. Plans to build a new line of communication through Belgium and the Netherlands did not come to fruition.

Despite the difficulties, Defense Department analysts claimed that rough parity of forces would exist at the outset of hostilities. In a conventional attack without major preparation, forty-five Warsaw Pact divisions would face twenty-four NATO divisions, but NATO would have 50,000 troops more under arms than the Warsaw Pact. Even if the Eastern Bloc successfully concealed preparation for a major conventional attack, it could only amass a manpower advantage of 300,000, even though it might field eighty divisions to NATO's twenty-six. While Warsaw Pact forces had a higher ratio of tanks to men, NATO forces were superior in the areas of support and combat logistics. The Defense Department conceded that Warsaw Pact forces might swell to 1.625 million troops and 110 divisions after three months of mobilization, but in the same amount of time, NATO could raise 1.42 million officers and men in 37 divisions and a slightly larger number of aircraft than the Warsaw Pact. If French forces came to the aid of NATO, the Soviet manpower advantage would be eradicated.[130]

NATO leaders encouraged plans and exercises for tactical nuclear war. Unlike Pentagon analysts, they deemed existing ground forces inadequate for forward defense and Flexible Response. In July 1967, the Military Committee concluded that the strategy could only be implemented after a transition period of four years, during which proper force structure had to be built. This was disingenuous, given that operational plans since 1957 had been shifted from nuclear deterrence to forward defense and greater flexibility. Nonetheless, the committee members agreed that ACE was incapable of meeting crises without early resort to nuclear weapons. Uncertainty of French military cooperation and possible withdrawal of American and British forces increased the risk that Central Region could fall to a surprise attack. For practical measures, combat capability of the ground forces could be improved by an increase in firepower and in the number of active armored and mechanized units. Second-echelon reserve forces needed to be upgraded to the same status as the first group of reinforcements. Furthermore, personnel levels had to be increased across the board, modern equipment had to be procured in greater numbers, and operational stock levels had to be elevated.[131]

In 1967, the Defense Department announced that, in the following year, two of USAREUR's brigades would redeploy from Germany to the United States. This was the result both of a long-standing debate over the cost of maintaining American forces abroad and of the requirements of the Vietnam War.[132] It was done at least in part to preempt calls in Congress for more drastic force reductions in Europe. Washington tried to mollify its NATO allies by leaving one brigade of 24th Mechanized Division, as well as the heavy equipment for the two withdrawn brigades, in Germany. Technically, the entire division remained part of USAREUR. The concept was called Redeployment of Forces to Germany (REFORGER).[133] It introduced the notion of dual basing, that is, combat and support units that were stationed in the United States but considered to be part of USAREUR. But this was essentially an accounting measure, which withdrew 34,000 combat and support troops while leaving them on the books. USAREUR commanders expressed their dissatisfaction with the solution and pointed out that it made no sense to count units that were not actually present in Europe.[134]

General Lemnitzer protested that the United States was withdrawing most of one combat division, while the Johnson administration explained that combat forces would be returned to Europe as the situation required. Annual REFORGER exercises after 1968 served as valuable training experience for the brigades stationed in the United States and for the military transport system. In those exercises, one brigade moved to Germany, claimed its pre-positioned equipment, took part in a large-scale maneuver, and then returned to the United States. Lemnitzer pointed out that force objectives for 1970 called for approximately fifty-four active divisions, a strategic reserve of five divisions and two brigades, approximately ten divisions as first-echelon reinforcements, and about thirteen divisions as second-echelon reinforcements. For 1972, the aggregate force proposals indicated an increase of one active brigade and the mechanization of two infantry divisions. But, at the same time, the second-echelon reinforcements would drop to less than ten divisions.[135] Without a return of the two brigades and an increase of the U.S. strategic reserve, NATO stood little chance of achieving its objectives.

General Johann Adolf Graf von Kielmansegg, the commander of Allied Forces, Central Europe (AFCENT), also believed that the enemy was improving in quality. Recent Soviet maneuvers indicated more thorough planning for a conventional attack than had formerly been the case. Kielmansegg criticized calculation methods of the Defense Department because mere numerical comparison overlooked the fact that the enemy had the initiative and could amass forces for an attack anywhere between the Baltic Sea and the Alps. The German general assumed that the odds for a Soviet breakthrough were better than 50 percent. Soviet doctrine prescribed an advance of 60 miles per day, without regard for the flanks after a breakthrough. Kielmansegg opposed the American rotation plan. He feared that the withdrawn brigades could not be returned to his command in time. Moreover, he was convinced that early selective use of nuclear weapons was necessary while the defensive front still remained cohesive, but he was pessimistic that release authority would be granted.[136]

Robert McNamara, who championed the REFORGER plan, nevertheless hoped that reliance on the strategic and theater nuclear deterrents could be minimized. Otherwise, the ability to control limited nuclear war was in doubt.[137] Defense analyst Ivo Daalder has shown that the difficulty in defining Flexible Response after 1967 revolved around the role of theater nuclear forces.[138] But there remained a significant conventional force component to the strategy. European leaders depicted the U.S. government as having forced them to accept conventional defense at the expense of credibility of the deterrent, but in fact there was no unified American position. The Europeans warned that Warsaw Pact forces were better armed and equipped for conventional war than NATO forces. Indeed, more than half of the Soviet combat battalions in East Germany were tank battalions, as opposed to only one-third of U.S. Army battalions in West Germany. But McNamara pointed out that the ratio of mechanized to tank forces in USAREUR was derived from operational plans rather than fiscal or materiel limitations.[139]

The JCS was more skeptical than McNamara about rapid deployment of forces to Europe. By 1968, the protracted war in Vietnam had depleted the reserve, and force deployment lists had become impossible to maintain. Two of three army divisions scheduled to reinforce ACE within thirty days of mobilization would need twelve weeks to achieve readiness. One of them, 5th Mechanized Division, was preparing a brigade for combat in Vietnam. The United States had agreed to make 82nd and 101st Airborne divisions available as rapid reserve for Europe, but the entire 101st and one brigade of the 82nd were deployed in Southeast Asia. Finally, only one of the two Marine Corps divisions earmarked for ACE could be sent to Europe without redeployment from Vietnam.[140] NATO planners began to disregard American reinforcement schedules. By 1972, ACE and CENTAG defense plans for the initial phase of the war no longer included the first two American augmentation divisions, even though the JCS insisted that both divisions could be deployed within one month, and the army expected their arrival in Europe within one week of mobilization.[141]

In August 1968, Warsaw Pact forces invaded Czechoslovakia. NATO forces were put on alert. General James Polk, the commander of USAREUR, responded to the invasion by increasing the number of forward observers and helicopter observance flights along the border. To what extent USAREUR could have responded to an attack is uncertain, since the readiness status of combat and support units remained unsatisfactory.[142] Two days after the invasion, General Wheeler, chairman of the JCS, was informed about the army's capability to reinforce NATO. Four combat divisions and the forward-deployed brigade of 24th Mechanized Division were in Germany. The remaining two brigades of 24th and three additional army divisions were scheduled to reinforce ACE for the initial defense of the NATO area. But 1st and 2nd Armored Division were so depleted in manpower and equipment that they would need between fourteen and fifteen weeks to achieve combat readiness, and one brigade of 5th Mechanized Division was deployed in Vietnam. In the event, its two brigades stationed in the United States would not be combat-ready for more than three months. The only forces that could reach Western Europe within one month of mobilization were two brigades of 82nd Airborne Division and 69th Infantry Brigade. In case of war in Europe, the army was to redeploy forces from Vietnam to Germany, but it was estimated that this would take at least four months.[143]

The military chiefs of staff of the NATO countries realized that the invasion of Czechoslovakia did not increase the risk of war.[144] However, the military operation had improved the overall readiness of armed forces in the western USSR, thus reducing the accuracy of recent intelligence assessments. Moreover, with thirteen additional Soviet divisions in Czechoslovakia, Warsaw Pact forces opposite Central Region had grown by five divisions, even after discounting the Czechoslovak forces, which were no longer considered reliable.[145] NATO mobilization plans were based upon receiving early warning, but the new alignment of forces diminished the need for Warsaw Pact force buildup before an attack. Moreover, the Soviets had rapidly brought marginally capable divisions to full strength through a call-up of reserves and the drafting of vehicles from the civilian economy. U.S. intelligence analysts concluded that the Soviet army had between 113 and 126 combat-ready divisions. Overall, the Soviets had 153 divisions under arms, a buildup due to tensions with China. Forces assembled for an attack against Central Region could amount to 1.25 million men, 20,600 tanks, 370 nuclear-capable rocket and missile launchers, 4,900 conventional artillery tubes, and 3,700 aircraft. This force was dual-capable, even though it was primarily designed for nuclear war.[146]

In July 1968, Clark Clifford, the new secretary of defense, submitted a report about U.S. troop levels and the military threat to Europe. He argued that the security of the United States and Western Europe had become fully intertwined since the end of World War II. A significant reduction of ground forces would cause severe damage to the alliance and would endanger the United States. The Europeans had steadily increased their forces, and U.S. ground forces constituted only 12 percent of the manpower in NATO Europe. But in Central Region, ACE still relied heavily on U.S. Army forces. About 600,000 active Warsaw Pact forces were faced by about the same number of NATO troops, about one-fourth of them American. A drastic cut in U.S. force levels would upset that conventional balance. It would be militarily and politically unwise and would endanger the improvement of the deterrent that had been achieved since 1961. Clifford believed that nuclear weapons could not replace soldiers and that conventional weakness might lead the Soviets to engage in acts of local aggression. His report concluded that "NATO's security, and hence our own, requires balanced forces—conventional as well as nuclear. Such balanced forces now exist. We must not abandon them."[147]

Since 1961, the U.S. military had withdrawn more than 100,000 troops from Europe. Further reductions would reduce the credibility of the deterrent. Still, planners in Washington intended to reduce U.S. forces in Europe by 40,000 in 1969, in an attempt to preempt more drastic cuts by Congress. Clark Clifford warned that force reductions must not be equated with savings in expenditures. The withdrawal of REFORGER units had reduced U.S. combat forces in Europe by 13 percent but had reduced costs by only 6 percent. But Clifford's aides feared that up to 100,000 officers and men might have to be withdrawn from Europe in 1968 and 1969, including the two REFORGER brigades.[148] Clifford proposed the return of 41,400 military personnel, 15,300 civilian employees, and 53,000 military dependents to the United States, while making no changes to the order of battle of USAREUR.[149]

The State Department expressed basic agreement: unilateral U.S. force reductions would weaken NATO defenses and precipitate reductions of European military forces. The political consequences would shake the foundations of transatlantic cooperation. Most significantly, a drastic reduction would lead to even greater reliance on nuclear weapons. It could damage disarmament initiatives, such as the nuclear nonproliferation treaty, which many European countries had yet to ratify, and mutual balanced force reduction talks, as unilateral reductions would give the Soviets a favorable result without having to adjust their own force levels. Despite the great strides made by European armies in general, and the Bundeswehr in particular, an unduly hasty withdrawal of American forces would put in doubt whether Europe could be defended.

In his report to Clifford after a tour of Europe in September 1968, General Wheeler pointed out that American forces were not ready for war. General Lemnitzer and the commanders of the U.S. European Command (USEUCOM) had presented Wheeler with a concise analysis of the command's readiness. It showed a dramatic decline since 1965.[150] NATO commitments had remained steady, while U.S. forces had lost 93,000 officers and men and suffered from reduced support and logistics facilities as well as lack of materiel. Combined with the shifting priorities away from Europe and toward Vietnam, this had led to a steep decline in combat readiness. U.S. Air Force, Europe, suffered from a severe shortage of conventional ammunition. Its commander, General Horace M. Wade, estimated that stocks would last for only five days of combat. General Wheeler feared that this was indicative of similar shortfalls in army and navy forces.[151] Wheeler left Europe convinced that USEUCOM had no more nonessential units that could be withdrawn. Any further force reduction would mean the elimination of vital functions.

Wheeler told his colleagues at the November meeting of the Military Committee that they should not forget how easily the Soviet invasion of Czechoslovakia could have spilled across the border. NATO was not prepared to deal with every eventuality that could have resulted. In order to elicit greater enthusiasm for improved military posture, he outlined the steps undertaken by the United States. These included a better fighter-interceptor, other improvements to the air force in Europe, and, most recognizably to the public and the enemy, the upcoming deployment of two brigades of 24th Mechanized Division in the REFORGER exercise in January and February 1969. This showed the will and the capability of the United States to provide rapid reinforcements as required. In addition, the United States planned to increase the manning levels in the strategic reserve. General Wheeler outlined a balanced package of short- and long-term measures to improve NATO's force posture.[152]

LONG THRUST and BIG LIFT had provided some experience with large-scale troop movements to Germany, but the first REFORGER exercise was of a different magnitude. Troop movement began with an advance party on 4 January. The bulk of the troops followed in the course of the next three weeks. Prior to that, there had been four planning and coordination conferences between 7 August and 1 November 1968. The actual field training exercise in Germany lasted seven days. Fifth Army, the coordinating agent for the exercise in the United States, concluded that it had been difficult to provide the necessary training for all troops involved. CONARC recommended that in the future the units scheduled to participate should be furnished with all available personnel to achieve full strength 150 days prior to the exercise. That was a sensible recommendation, but REFORGER was intended as realistic training for rapid response to a crisis, which would not allow for thorough preparations. But otherwise, Fifth Army expressed satisfaction with the course of the exercise. The pre-positioning of equipment was deemed sound, and the deployment and return of forces had progressed smoothly.[153]

In 1969, the Nixon administration reviewed national strategy.[154] Four alternative NATO strategies were proposed for consideration by the NSC. The first strategy would leave only 75,000 American troops in Europe. If these forces came under attack, the United States would use nuclear weapons. The second proposal, initial defense, was based on the assumption that within a period of about three months after a Soviet conventional attack war would have escalated or a cease-fire agreement would have been concluded. This was similar to the assessment of the Kennedy and Johnson administrations. The third option was a strategy of sustained defense, based on the assumption that conventional war could last more than three months and that the United States would not initiate the use of nuclear weapons. Both initial and sustained defense could be achieved with the 300,000 U.S. military personnel currently in Europe, but capability for sustained conventional defense would cost an additional $10 billion per year. The final option was total conventional defense, adding capability to withstand a surprise attack to the requirements for sustained defense. It required at least 425,000 active American personnel in Europe.[155]

The Nixon administration decided to retain the strategy of initial defense.[156] But the dissatisfaction with European complacency that had characterized most of the 1960s did not vanish. Therefore, the United States continued to evaluate ways to reduce its forces in Europe without severely limiting the ability to respond to a Soviet attack.[157] Pressure from the Senate necessitated the consideration of force reductions.[158] But the NSC confirmed in November 1970 that "increased emphasis should be given to defense by conventional forces" because it was "vital that NATO have a credible conventional defense posture" in light of the strategic balance between the United States and the Soviet Union. President Nixon decreed that the authorized level of U.S. forces in Europe by the end of June 1971 should be 319,000 officers and men. He hoped that the allies would also increase and improve their armed forces.[159] This hope was not entirely in vain. The Europeans did indeed promise to maintain their current force levels and "undertake significant improvements over the next five years." What hampered conventional defense and the credibility of the deterrent was "a questionable defense against armored attack, a lack of ready combat reinforcements in the period from M-day to M+30, shortages in selected ammunition reserves, electronic warfare capabilities, and limited effectiveness of air defense." Not all of the weaknesses were addressed in the promises of the allies.[160]

Meanwhile, Soviet capability had increased further. By 1971, there were 58 divisions in East Germany, Poland, and Czechoslovakia, 50 of them combat-ready; 37 of these divisions were stationed close enough to the border for immediate use against Central Region; 70 additional combat divisions could enter the theater of operations against NATO within three weeks. Approximately 80 divisions, 20,000 tanks, 10,000 to 11,000 artillery pieces, more than 2,500 aircraft, and almost 600 nuclear capable rocket and missile launchers were available for an attack against Central Region. Western intelligence still assessed Soviet doctrine as primarily nuclear-war oriented, but it was acknowledged that the Soviets were better prepared for sustained conventional operations than in the preceding decade, although they still had serious shortcomings in logistics. It was not entirely clear to what extent Soviet military capability was affected by tensions with China.[161]

Defense planning for Central Region had adapted to the NATO strategy of Flexible Response. Supreme Headquarters Allied Powers, Europe (SHAPE) called for forward defense "to slow and stop the enemy to force negotiations." To accomplish this, the enemy had to be fixed in place at the outset of battle. Senior commanders in USAREUR did not believe that NATO forces were strong enough for sustained conventional defense. In April 1973, the commander of VII Corps pointed at the weakness in tactical intelligence army units that cast doubt upon target acquisition. General Blanchard was particularly concerned with his counterbattery capability. He feared that "this inability to take on the enemy's artillery could subject us to defeat in detail."[162] The initial phase of conventional defense would have to be brief, but it might still provide enough time to dissuade the Soviets from escalation. General Michael Davison, who commanded both USAREUR and CENTAG, estimated that his forces could execute defensive operations successfully for between three days and two weeks, depending on the arrival of reserve units from the Unites States, until use of tactical nuclear weapons would become necessary.[163] Southern Germany seemed much more defensible than northern Germany, but neither the weakness of the British, Belgian, Dutch, and German defenders nor the strength and capability of Warsaw Pact forces should be understated. Moreover, the North German Plains, while an enticing invasion corridor on a map, had rivers, canals, marshes, and towns and cities that would be difficult obstacles for a large tank force.[164]

In early 1971, USAREUR personnel levels had reached their lowest point. The two corps in Germany were at 88 percent of their authorized strength, but more than one-third of USAREUR's units were below 75 percent of their authorized peacetime personnel strength, resulting in a low readiness condition, that is, not combat-ready.[165] Maneuver analyses determined that V Corps could defend only 48 kilometers of its 82-kilometer defensive frontage, while VII Corps could defend 98 kilometers of its 192 kilometers in conventional and 122 kilometers in "low-intensity nuclear war." Taken together, the two corps could not defend about half of their assigned forward areas.[166] Consequently, General Polk shifted the tactical emphasis of the forward-deployed forces from area to mobile defense. This was aided by the introduction of the tube-launched, optically tracked, wire-guided (TOW) missile, a missile issued to mechanized battalions as a heavy antitank weapon. It was mounted on M113 APCs and had a maximum effective range of 3,000 meters. Each mechanized battalion received twelve TOW launchers. This allowed Polk to group all tank battalions in reserve, while the front line was to be manned by a thin screen of mechanized infantry and armored cavalry, which now had much greater antitank capability.[167]

During the Vietnam War, the design process for a mechanized infantry combat vehicle (MICV) had continued. This was a critical requirement for mobile defense in Germany. In November 1967, the Soviet army had unveiled its first model. Thus both the enemy and the most formidable ally had a decided advantage over U.S. mechanized infantry. The Germans were in the process of replacing the Schützenpanzer with the Marder, which was designed to work closely with the Leopard tank. The U.S. Army did not adopt the Marder because it was too heavy and bulky for air transport and did not possess amphibious capabilities desired by American designers. The lessons of the Yom Kippur War in 1973 underscored the need for mobility, armor, and antitank capability. Consequently, the role and design of tanks and IFVs was reconsidered. Eventually, the army abandoned the MICV design and developed the Bradley Fighting Vehicle, which was brought into service in 1983.[168]

The developments in antitank weaponry, as well as improved armored vehicles and tanks, contributed to the deterrent value of U.S. Army forces in Germany, but General Arthur Collins, deputy commander in chief of USAREUR, questioned the reliance on nuclear weapons. He proposed a review of the long-standing policy to employ tactical nuclear weapons early in a war against the Soviets, even if it was a limited conflict. The army had never unanimously endorsed this approach, but it had nevertheless been prevalent since the early 1950s. Collins argued that the new German political leadership did not agree with the policy. While Adenauer, Strauss, and their successors had advocated the deterrent value of battlefield and tactical nuclear weapons, the Social Democrats, and particularly their defense minister, Helmut Schmidt, considered the dramatic consequences of employment of such weapons on the civilian population and took a different position. Schmidt was a long-standing proponent of conventional deterrence.[169]

General Collins pointed out that "both SHAPE strategy and exercises stress the importance of fighting a conventional war as long as possible." It was widely recognized that the threat to NATO land forces lay in the preponderance of Soviet armor. Collins noted that the antitank capability of USAREUR was the most significant American contribution to the territorial defense of Germany. Increasing numbers of West German reservists provided the opportunity to turn towns and villages into "a hedgehog that would contribute to the delay of advance of Warsaw Pact forces and make the Western armor and aviation combined arms elements more effective."[170] But Collins worried that new antitank weapons, such as the Sheridan, the TOW antitank missile, and the M60A2 tank, had not been integrated into tactical thinking. Thus he proposed a thorough review of operational doctrine.[171]

By June 1972, Collins had gained a clearer appreciation of what needed to be done to adjust USAREUR force structure and the emphasis of its mission. He suggested that the army should reconsider its approach to a balanced force in two respects. First, many of the support and logistics elements could be supplied from local sources in the event of a crisis. There seemed little use in maintaining big support elements for a field army in a friendly country that had great civilian resources in engineering, construction, and maintenance. Moreover, the actual deterrent to impress the Soviets was the combat force. Therefore, Collins proposed a shift in the ratio between combat and support elements. He hoped that this might also address demands for further force reduction.

Second, General Collins believed that the army's tactical nuclear posture could be maintained without outdated weapon systems such as Honest John and Sergeant. He stressed that there would be sufficient nuclear capability on the ground and in the air as long as 8-inch guns, Pershing missiles, and tactical air support were maintained. Overall, Collins described USAREUR's mission as projecting a credible fighting force both outward and inward, to deter the Soviets and reassure the Europeans, while simultaneously regaining congressional and public support in the United States. Collins advocated for a deterrent force first and foremost, but he was convinced that the lack of generic, yet costly American logistics could be compensated for, and that restructured ground forces could fight as well as the current divisions with their heavy logistics tail.[172] This awareness of the armor threat and the resulting emphasis on antitank warfare, ideally with conventional arms, became the centerpiece of U.S. Army doctrinal development in the decade following the Vietnam War.

6

The Cold War Army

At the heart of the army's recovery from the Vietnam War was the newly established Training and Doctrine Command (TRADOC). It came to define the Cold War army.[1] The defeat in Vietnam had made military interventions in the Third World unfashionable. Thus, the army was able to focus on the defense of Germany and deterrence of war.[2] Tactical and operational doctrine in the 1970s and early 1980s was based less on the lessons of the Vietnam War than on analysis of the Yom Kippur War of 1973, which featured a range of American and Soviet weapons and equipment, and of Soviet, German, and Israeli operational concepts of mechanized warfare.[3] The army retained the Reorganization Objective Army Division (ROAD), introduced infantry fighting vehicles and attack helicopters, and designed a new main battle tank to improve its mechanized and armored divisions. More important, the army adopted operational doctrine for war in Germany that emphasized close cooperation with the air force, anticipated fast-moving operations on a deep and chaotic battlefield, and provided methods to engage and defeat Soviet and Warsaw Pact reserves as well as their frontline units. With the publication of AirLand Battle doctrine in 1982, the Cold War army completed its transition, although it was a different force than Maxwell Taylor had envisioned three decades earlier. In the specific circumstance of the late Cold War in Europe, national strategic objective and army operational expertise were finally brought into close alignment.

1973: The Annus Mirabilis of the Cold War Army

Historians of the Western alliance have depicted the early 1970s as a period of severe crisis and near rupture.[4] Different perceptions of détente in Washington and in European capitals, the relative economic decline of the United States and growth of Western Europe, energy crises, a Western European desire for greater independence from the United States, a generally diminishing fear of major war, and public discontent in Western Europe with the

Vietnam War that translated into broader anti-American feelings, posed the most serious threats to the future of the North Atlantic Treaty Organization (NATO). 1973 and 1974 were indeed crisis years for the alliance.[5] But taking a wider view of the evolution of U.S.-European relations throughout the Cold War, the eminent Norwegian historian Geir Lundestad concluded that the alliance remained strong and that the "American-Western European relationship was not redefined." The United States needed its European allies, and the Europeans, "while wanting to strike out more on their own, resisted anything that might reduce the role of the United States in Europe." Lundestad argued that "the emphasis was particularly on the need for the American troops to remain. Europe's dependence on America, especially militarily, endured."[6] Even in the late 1970s and early 1980s, as Western European public opinion turned more sharply against the United States, "European leaders continued to invite American influence" and relied on American armed forces.[7] In the event, the political crisis of the alliance had little effect on the preparedness of the U.S. Army, Europe (USAREUR). The Nixon administration pursued a policy of détente but did not trust the Soviet Union to disarm and therefore did not demand force reductions.

1973 was a year of political and diplomatic tensions between the United States and Western Europe, but it was also a critical point in the development of the Cold War army. First, U.S. participation in the Vietnam War ended. Second, the draft was replaced by volunteer enlistment, resulting in a more highly skilled and generally more professional force. Third, the Yom Kippur War between Israel and an Arab coalition, which was mainly equipped with Warsaw Pact weapons systems, offered valuable insight into the interplay of modern technology, determination, preparedness, and operational doctrine. Finally, directed by the new chief of staff, General Creighton Abrams, the army established a new command that was to direct training and oversee the writing of doctrine.

In January 1973, the United States and North Vietnam signed the Paris Peace Accords after several years of difficult negotiations. The agreement stipulated that all American military operations in Vietnam had to end and that U.S. troops had to withdraw by the end of March. In addition, a cease-fire was announced between the South Vietnamese National Liberation Front and the government of Nguyen Van Thieu. Larry Berman, a political scientist and student of U.S. policy toward Vietnam, argues that Nixon and Henry Kissinger endorsed the peace agreement because it was certain to be violated by the North Vietnamese. Upon such violation of an international treaty, the U.S. government could reenter the battle without facing overwhelming domestic opposition. In the event, the United States did not intervene when North Vietnamese forces launched an offensive in the spring of 1975 that ultimately overthrew the Saigon government and reunified Vietnam by force. For the army, the Paris Peace Accords closed a chapter of the Cold War that had begun with a small group of military advisers in September 1950. During the Vietnam War, the U.S. military lost over 56,000 airmen, Marines, sailors, and soldiers. The army's casualties were 37,895 dead and 208,576 wounded in combat.[8]

Closing the chapter of the Vietnam War, however, did not immediately cure the ills that had befallen the army. The social and racial tensions in the United States of the civil rights movement and the antiwar protests were manifest in the military services. The decline of morale in USAREUR has been discussed already, but the army in its entirety suffered from similar symptoms: poor race relations, drug and alcohol abuse, crime, and a general lack of credible leadership on all levels. By 1973, soldiering was no longer a profession regarded as honorable by the public. Moreover, an entire decade had passed without modernization of doctrine, organization, or training. The defeat in Vietnam weakened the confidence of army leaders in the national political leadership. But Vietnam-era personnel policies were equally destructive, as they left most units ineffective and had caused serious depletion of the noncommissioned officer corps. As a result, combat troops in USAREUR saw themselves as little more than token impediments to a Soviet offensive.[9]

While the United States was preoccupied with the Vietnam War,[10] the Soviet military had advanced concepts of mechanized warfare that blended its superiority in numbers with new equipment for mechanized and armored formations as well as artillery under the doctrine of mass momentum–continuous land combat. In the early 1970s, the balance of forces in Europe favored the Warsaw Pact more clearly than during the preceding decade. General Andrew Goodpaster, Supreme Allied Commander, Europe (SACEUR) from 1969 to 1974, provided a rough tally in an address to the United Kingdom's National Defence College. He credited the Soviet army with 125 divisions, supported by more than 4,000 tactical aircraft. In addition, Warsaw Pact member states had 60 divisions that were closely integrated with Soviet strategy, doctrine, and command. This force was backed by a vast array of tactical nuclear weapons.[11] Warsaw Pact ground forces in Central Europe had added six combat divisions since 1968, and all active divisions had been reequipped with new tanks, armored personnel carriers, missiles, and artillery pieces. Since 1968, Soviet forces in East Germany alone had received 1,500 new tanks.[12]

But Goodpaster nevertheless retained an optimistic outlook. The Vietnam War had drained the strength of the U.S. military, led to delays in mechanization, and made comprehensive programs to strengthen the alliance impossible, but NATO would gain strength in the postwar period:

> During the course of 1974, for example, the defensive strength of NATO's armies will be increased by the introduction of four hundred and seventy-four new main battle tanks, more than a thousand other armored vehicles, and about two hundred medium-range anti-tank weapons. . . . Similarly, air force capabilities will be enhanced by almost two hundred modern combat aircraft, in addition to new tactical transports, and one hundred forty helicopters. NATO's air defense capability will be increased by eight hundred fifty anti-aircraft guns and over eight hundred anti-aircraft guided missiles.[13]

The United States had raised the manning level of its forces in Europe since the end of the Vietnam War, and four additional combat battalions had been created in the theater by restructuring headquarters and logistics units. Other improvements resulted from the increase of tube-launched, optically tracked, wire-guided (TOW) missile launchers and the replacement of older Honest John and Sergeant weapons systems with Lance missiles.[14]

Despite Warsaw Pact superiority in numbers, General Goodpaster concluded that the state of deterrence in Europe was acceptable. In critical categories of weapons systems in Central Region, the Warsaw Pact led NATO by a wide margin. The Eastern Bloc deployed 10,000 more battle tanks and twice as many aircraft in the region as NATO.[15] Nevertheless, this did not prompt despair:

> The Warsaw Pact superiority is not so great that our Soviet military planner could be certain of a quick, easy victory. . . . Everything that we do know, however, indicates that they are a prudent—I might even say a conservative—group. . . . they want clear and overwhelming superiority before risking an attack. . . . Our forces are effective in deterring an attack, and this has always been our primary objective.[16]

The Army Staff also noticed improvement. By the end of the Vietnam War, the army had been reduced to thirteen active divisions, but by 1974 all of them were rated combat-ready, up from only four in 1973. General Abrams cultivated his close professional relationship with Defense Secretary James Schlesinger. Abrams committed the army to sixteen active divisions, although he conceded that this goal would have to be attained within the current manpower allotment of less than 800,000. He argued that this leaner force provided a better ratio of combat-to-support functions, and he called for the integration of Army Reserve and National Guard units with the Active Army in what became known as the Total Force policy. Like many of his peers, Abrams had been appalled by the decision of President Johnson to fight the

Vietnam War without calling up the reserves, and he wanted to ensure that the army could never again be sent to war without crucial support. As a result of the Total Force policy, several National Guard divisions received better equipment and more resources for training. National Guard divisions earmarked to reinforce USAREUR had long been regarded as high-priority reserve forces, but much like the rest of the army, they had been neglected during the Vietnam War. The improved readiness of the reserve helped address General Abrams's fundamental concern. In his experience during World War II, the Korean War, and the Vietnam War, the army had always been poorly prepared. Until his death in September 1974, Abrams worked diligently to build and maintain a well-prepared force.[17]

In 1973, the army established TRADOC in order to centralize the process of reform in training and doctrine. Its first commander, General William E. DePuy, doubted that the ROAD division was heavy enough for war in Germany. He informed General Frederick Weyand, Abrams's successor as chief of staff of the army, that each brigade had to be increased in manpower, should have more armored and mechanized infantry battalions, and needed more fire support, which could be provided by antitank guided-missile companies.[18] Even earlier, in 1971, the Army Staff had initiated tests of the triple capability (TRICAP) concept of mixed armor, airmobile, and air cavalry units. After three years of testing, it was found that TRICAP divisions needed more tanks and less airmobile infantry. The division was too light for combat in Europe, and as the army shifted its focus back to Germany, TRICAP was abandoned, although the air cavalry combat brigade became a separate formation in 1975.[19] In January 1977, Weyand's successor, General Bernard Rogers, approved a Division Restructuring Evaluation as a one-year test. The study was extended upon the request of General Donn Starry, who had taken command of TRADOC. Starry thought that division design should be integrated with changes in the corps or field army. In any case, it had to be closely linked to operational doctrine. But test results were unclear, and it was decided that ROAD remained the best option, especially since it had been updated with a new generation of conventional weapons.[20]

General DePuy was convinced that the unsatisfactory state of the army at the end of the Vietnam War called for drastic measures. Indeed, 1973 offered opportunities for a radical departure from traditional procedures as the termination of the draft had led to the creation of an all-volunteer military. When termination of the draft was first discussed in 1968, army leaders had opposed the idea, assuming that it could only lead to a shallow recruiting pool. In particular, it was feared that an insufficient number of well-educated Americans would choose to join the military. This initial opposition was overcome, and the army underwent a successful transition from draft to volunteer force.[21] Nevertheless, the loss of college graduates as potential officers had an effect on the tactical and operational outlook of the army. DePuy was concerned with the quality of small-unit leadership.[22] He favored a rigid training system that would compensate for a dearth in individual initiative. Even though the doctrinal manual of 1976 emphasized "the ability and willingness of leaders at all levels to act independently,"[23] TRADOC clarified that the army had to train leadership rather than rely on finding natural leaders.[24]

DePuy argued that the best way to rebuild the army was to design tactical and operational doctrine for the most dangerous case: a full-scale Warsaw Pact offensive in Germany. Previously, doctrine had been developed for an already-existing force structure and with consideration of available weapons systems. DePuy believed that TRADOC should design doctrine first and that organizational structures, weapons and equipment, and training were to be tailored to match. Even though DePuy's doctrine was eventually altered fundamentally, the relationship of training and doctrine remained strong. Training was increasingly realistic, and U.S. and NATO forces used their combat equipment more frequently than their Warsaw Pact counterparts.[25] DePuy was convinced that the tank remained the critical weapon but also noted that its defensive capability and new antitank missiles favored the defender. In spite of opposition by proponents of offensive warfare, this approach was more appropriate to the outnumbered forces guarding West Germany.[26]

General DePuy was particularly concerned about the compatibility of German and American operational concepts. He found German tactics superior to those of the U.S. Army. Moreover, DePuy was convinced that his intent to alter fundamentally the tactical and operational approach of the army would face strong opposition from within the service. He hoped that close cooperation with German officers during the process of developing new doctrine would reduce resistance. DePuy believed that the opening battle of the next war had to be fought on the defensive, with armored and mechanized formations bolstered by wire-guided antitank missiles. He agreed with the German concept of forward defense, which put the bulk of the active forces at the forward edge of the battle zone. In 1974, TRADOC initiated permanent consultations between doctrinal planners in the United States and Germany. This served two purposes: it would make tactical doctrine of the two premier NATO armies more compatible and would persuade proponents of maneuver defense that the new concept was tailor-made for conditions in Central Europe.[27]

A comparative study of German and American tactical doctrine conducted by the staff of 1st Infantry Division found that the employment of

German brigades in defensive roles under American command might suffer from the emphasis on "a defend degree of resistance" in German doctrine. In theory, the Bundeswehr had stressed mobile defense, but detractors opposed this because they feared the permanent loss of territory. In the 1970s, the Germans advanced plans in which the bulk of defensive forces were to fight from strong positions, with only a small reserve, perhaps 20 percent of the force, for counterattacks. Differing doctrinal approaches could not be tested in REFORGER 74, the basis of the comparative study, because 1st Infantry Division and 30th German Panzerbrigade had been selected to play the attacking force. Still, despite different doctrinal approaches, dependence on intentions of the American army group commander, and differences in combat task-force organization—the Bundeswehr relied on the brigade as its combined-arms base unit while the U.S. Army maintained the division base[28]—the study concluded that joint operations from the battalion level on up were feasible. U.S. Army officers nevertheless thought that German doctrine overemphasized the need to hold terrain and degraded the tactical reserve.[29] This attitude did not bode well for DePuy, who intended to emulate German defensive tactics.

By 1976, the mission of the U.S. Army was clear. The first post-Vietnam operational doctrine stated bluntly:

> Battle in Central Europe against forces of the Warsaw Pact is the most demanding mission the US Army could be assigned. Because the US Army is structured primarily for that contingency and has large forces deployed in that area, this manual is designed mainly to deal with the realities of such operations.[30]

Based on the lessons drawn from the Yom Kippur War, the authors of the manual emphasized the importance of tank and antitank capability as the centerpiece of modern armies.[31] In October 1973, Egyptian and Syrian forces had attacked Israel. The study of Israeli operations provided examples of both territorial and mobile defense. In the north, Israeli defenders against the Syrian attack had very little room for maneuver, and the defensive positions in the Golan Heights lacked depth.[32] On the Sinai Peninsula, conditions called for mobile defense, which favored the armor-heavy Israeli Defense Force. But political considerations, most notably the fear of an armistice at an early stage of war, had led Israeli leaders to conclude that purely mobile defense in depth risked losing valuable territory that served as a buffer zone between Egypt and Israel. As a result, the Israeli army employed a mixture of strongpoints at the Suez Canal and mobile defensive operations and counterattacks by its elite armored formations.[33]

Army leaders derived from Israeli operations valuable lessons for the defense of West Germany. The Israeli army fought outnumbered against an enemy equipped with weapons systems of similar quality. TRADOC, which focused on the study of tactical and operational implications of the Yom Kippur War, found three fundamental lessons. First of all, modern weapons were far more lethal than earlier generations of weapons systems. Second, the army needed combined-arms teams of armor, mechanized infantry, field artillery, and air defense. These teams were to suppress enemy firepower in order to allow the outnumbered defenders to shift forces to critical areas of the battlefield. General DePuy concluded that movement was the principal tactical desideratum of land warfare. Finally, success in future operations depended on the training of individual soldiers as well as combined-arms teams. DePuy had informed General Creighton Abrams in January 1974 that the most impressive feature of the war had been the performance of Israeli tank crews. Israeli and Arab armor were qualitatively equivalent. The M60 tank and the Soviet T-62 tank, in other words, were "a fair match." DePuy concluded that "therefore, during the next ten years battlefield outcome will depend upon the quality of the troops rather than the quality of the tanks." He deplored that the army was lacking in training ammunition and that the best young noncommissioned officers of the armor branch did not seek assignments as tank commanders.[34]

In the Yom Kippur War, during eighteen days of combat, more than 2,500 Arab and Israeli tanks were destroyed. General DePuy noted that the combined losses of Egyptian and Syrian forces—between 1,500 and 2,000 tanks as well as 500 artillery tubes—equaled the entire American arsenal in Europe.[35] In the Yom Kippur War, 2,500 Israeli soldiers died—more than half were from the armored corps.[36] TRADOC considered the proliferation of modern weapons to be among the primary lessons of the war, and army leaders were concerned about the great lethality of these weapons systems.[37]

The rough parity in quality of Soviet and American weapons systems further emphasized the significance of Soviet numerical superiority in tanks and manpower. But the Israeli army had fought outnumbered, and by the time a cease-fire was reached, it had been well on its way to Cairo and Damascus. General DePuy assumed that the effectiveness of the equally outnumbered NATO forces was a direct function of weapons, tank crew proficiency, and tactics.[38] For USAREUR, it would be essential to create numerical equality or even superiority at critical points. DePuy believed that it would be possible to predict the path of a Soviet breakthrough effort. Drawing upon the tactical situation of 1st Armored Division in Germany, DePuy illustrated defensive operations. The division had to cover a frontage of 60 kilometers, which would overtax its 100 platoons if they were spread out to defend the entire area. Any enemy concentration of force would lead to defeat, unless, "at the critical time and at that critical place, units from the flanks of the 1st Armored Division which are not engaged are moved into the most important blocking position." In order to avoid being outnumbered at any critical point, U.S. forces had to comprehend and exploit the battlefield terrain better than the enemy.[39] Detailed knowledge of the relevant topography thus became a decided advantage of American and German forces in Central Region.

Infantry still had an important role to play in antitank defense and in built-up areas where the mobility and flexibility of individual soldiers were required. Israeli officers expressed great satisfaction with the M113 armored personal carrier (APC), but they used the vehicle for a different purpose than the army, essentially similar to the ad hoc adjustment of assault vehicles in Vietnam. In Israeli practice, the APC, equipped with an additional mounted 7.62-mm machine gun, was employed as an antipersonnel weapon to suppress enemy infantry armed with antitank rocket-propelled grenades.[40] But General DePuy questioned the suitability of APCs for mechanized operations in Germany. The M113 was insufficiently armed, and the .50 caliber machine gun could not be fired effectively on the march because it was not stabilized. Moreover, the vehicle offered a hard ride for its crew that would lead to injuries if it had to operate with tanks at cross-country speed. Finally, its armor was weak. It could not even protect its passengers from 12.7-mm machine guns.[41] De Puy noted that TRADOC wanted to "emulate the Germans[,] but in order to do it well, we need a good tank, an infantry fighting vehicle, self-propelled artillery and effective mobility for the air defense systems." He concluded that "our greatest defect is the infantry vehicle."[42]

By 1975, DePuy was aware that the prospects of the mechanized infantry combat vehicle (MICV) were extremely dim. He implored friends at the Pentagon to discuss the matter privately with Secretary of Defense James Schlesinger, who believed that the MICV was too expensive. DePuy pointed out that it was cheaper than the West German Marder and no more expensive than the Soviet BMP (infantry combat vehicle). The situation required an urgent resolution, as TRADOC drafts of tactical doctrine were evolving toward the German conception. In practice, army units found it difficult to adopt Panzergrenadier tactics without proper equipment. This contributed to general inertia. DePuy acknowledged that only one division of USAREUR had made strides toward new tactics, while all of V Corps seemed to be indifferent to change. He charged that "the German Army believes strongly that the U.S. Army does not know how to fight on a mechanized battlefield against the Soviets. They believe we are too much organized and oriented toward infantry combat. They also believe that our counterattack plans with large forces sweeping across the front are sheer bunk, or at least simply romantic."[43]

Next to tanks and mechanized vehicles with antitank guided missiles, the third critical component of the envisioned fire team was field artillery. By the mid-1970s, all artillery in U.S. armored and mechanized divisions was self-propelled.[44] USAREUR hoped that its tanks and antiarmor weapons systems were sufficient to defeat the much larger Soviet tank force. For that purpose, and advised by Israeli veteran commanders and German generals, TRADOC introduced doctrine that stressed the importance of balanced teams of combined arms that could lay devastating suppressive fire on enemy formations.[45] The new doctrine reflected the temporary technological advantage of the defender. But General DePuy warned of too much enthusiasm for antitank guided missiles. He believed them to be supplementary to the tank, even in defensive operations. He acknowledged their importance, which was reflected in their widespread distribution. Mechanized battalions received eighteen TOW and twenty-seven Dragon launchers. But DePuy criticized that tests of the weapons systems disregarded the most effective countermeasure—smoke. He found it hard to believe that the Soviets had not discovered this rather obvious antidote.[46]

The U.S. Army's organization in Europe was designed to maximize the ability to move and suppress enemy firepower. In 1974, USAREUR commanded thirty-three armor battalions. These were in addition to armor units, twenty-four mechanized battalions, thirty-one field artillery battalions, and fifteen air defense battalions. But combat teams made up only 44 percent of USAREUR's overall strength. They were supported by intelligence (3 percent of USAREUR strength), which allowed USAREUR to see the battlefield better than the enemy, signal communications units (12 percent), which assured close control over all combat units and prompt transmission of orders, combat engineers (9 percent), which supported movement on the battlefield, aviation (2 percent), which supported intelligence and delivered ordnance, and supply and logistics forces (30 percent of USAREUR strength).[47]

Not all senior commanders accepted the doctrinal system proposed by General DePuy. The most politically sensitive was the resistance of Major General John H. Cushman, the commander of the Combined Arms Center (CAC) at Fort Leavenworth, since CAC was to write combat doctrine, a critical component of DePuy's intended tactical system. Cushman, an engineering officer, had the reputation of being an intellectual. Unlike DePuy, he had not commanded large combined-arms organizations in combat. He believed in individual initiative and opposed the rigid system that General

DePuy wanted to impose on the army. As army officer and historian Paul Herbert has argued, the main difference between DePuy and Cushman was that between training and education. Two distinct schools of thought about doctrine swirled around the two generals. DePuy's supporters believed that doctrine had to be simple, clear, and specific. Its substance was less important than its unifying institutional purpose. Cushman, on the other hand, emphasized substance over purpose. In the fall of 1974, Command and General Staff College wrote a draft of Field Manual 100-5 to "indicate and guide but . . . not bind in practice." It was presented at a TRADOC conference in December. To stifle opposition, DePuy rejected the manual, citing the boring nature of its style. He believed that the new capstone manual had to be engaging. He offered Cushman the opportunity to submit a revised draft, but when Cushman failed to deliver it at the meeting in April 1975, DePuy transferred responsibility for the manual from CAC to TRADOC headquarters.[48]

Extensive study of the Yom Kippur War had convinced General DePuy that the next war would be characterized by rapid and decisive battle. He argued that strategists were the heroes of the great wars of the past, including World War II, but that they would play no role in the next major war because combat would be concluded before vast troop movements across continents could affect its outcome. Therefore, modern battle tactics were to be the decisive factor of war.[49] But even if DePuy was right, this did not mean the demise of the art of strategy. If anything, anticipation of a single decisive battle enhanced the need for proper planning, by both military and political leaders. If forces could not be moved into place after the outbreak of war, that is, if NATO mobilization and reinforcement plans were rendered meaningless, then the prewar alignment of forces was critical. Moreover, there was greater need for intrinsic coordination of political guidance, strategic planning, operational conception, and tactics. DePuy suggested that the army should concentrate on the latter.

Active Defense: Doctrine for the First Battle in Germany

Looking back on his career in TRADOC, General DePuy summarized his doctrinal perspective as follows: forward defense at the intra-German border, lack of space for mobile defense in depth in West Germany, an enemy force that outnumbered NATO forces by at least two to one, and the great advantage in reserve forces and reinforcement capability held by the Warsaw Pact. Only the right combination of new weapons technology and defensive tactics afforded NATO the opportunity to succeed. NATO commanders had very little room for error. All of NATO's armies were to adopt a clearly delineated tactical system that would allow them to coordinate closely their operations. Similar tactics of the German and American armies were intended to form the nucleus of a NATO-wide tactical review.[50] To DePuy, the Western alliance held the advantage in close integration of modern weapons systems that could bring lethal firepower on the enemy in a succession of battlefield maneuvers. He concluded: "If ever there was an army that needed an alternative to the long, thin line with its high casualties and dubious prospects it is the weapons intensive, manpower-starved, all-volunteer Army of the 1980s."[51]

Active Defense doctrine stated in great detail how U.S. Army forces should fight the Soviets in Germany. Army leaders knew that their forces would be significantly outnumbered in the crucial opening battle of the war. General DePuy left no doubt that traditional mobilization concepts had lost all meaning, and he advised field commanders to utilize all of their forces at the outset of battle. In past wars, the U.S. military often had lost the opening battle, absorbed the initial attacks, mobilized its vast resources, and recovered to defeat the enemy.[52] But in the next war, U.S. ground forces would find themselves at the end of a vulnerable line of communications. Moreover, modern weapons made protracted war unlikely.

For the opening battle, DePuy prescribed elastic defense, which would maximize the effectiveness of the outnumbered American battalions and their new weapons systems. A reconnaissance screen, deployed forward of the battle area, was to determine where the bulk of the Soviet attack could be expected. Then, six to eight battalions of a division were to be concentrated at the critical point. The remaining three or four battalions would be deployed in mobile operations, screening the remainder of the division's area of responsibility. The main battle would be dominated by armor and antitank weapons. DePuy envisioned defense through the massive application of firepower and maneuver specifically tailored to the anticipated movement of the enemy. Command responsibility was clearly delineated. Corps and division commanders were to concentrate force at the critical point. Brigade and battalion commanders were to direct and control the battle. Company commanders were to fight it.[53]

Army objectives were stated in the opening chapter of Field Manual 100-5. Fundamentally, the army was to "prepare to win the first battle of the next war." If it was necessary to fight more battles "once the war is upon us, we shall aim at emerging triumphant from the second, third, and final battles as well." Army doctrine and organizational structure were conditioned by planned operations in Central Europe. There, "the U.S. Army must prepare its units to fight outnumbered, and to win." This was to be achieved through the proper combination of the best weapons and skilled operators. The doctrinal manual stressed the importance of training leaders as well as their men. The individual soldier had to see himself as a vital member of a team. Therefore, training had to occur in the unit as much as possible, and "collective training in units should aim at maximum effectiveness with combined arms." Advances in technology and changing combat environment and doctrine required constant training to achieve a state of immediate readiness. The authors of the manual, paraphrasing the Roman historian Josephus, demanded: "Our drills must be 'bloodless battles' and our battles 'bloody drills.'" It was the unit commanders' responsibility to "produce a unit ready to fight and win now."[54]

The manual focused on the operations of battalions and brigades. It emphasized the radically changed nature of modern weapons and the modern battlefield in a detailed chapter on the lethality of weapons systems.[55] The doctrine became known as Active Defense, even though DePuy and his collaborators did not favor that phrase and "elastic defense" would have offered a more accurate description.[56] The objective of USAREUR was the attrition by firepower of the Soviet attacking force in the first, conventional battle.[57] The battle was to be won by concentrating sufficient force and firepower at critical times and places, which was to be achieved through superior control and direction of the battle by brigade and battalion commanders. Units engaged in combat had to seek cover and concealment to minimize the effect of enemy fire. Simultaneously, enemy weapons were to be suppressed by combined-arms fire teams.[58] In short, the defense was "a race for time to detect the enemy's main thrust and to concentrate combat power."[59]

Eventually, U.S. ground forces were to take the offensive in order to defeat the numerically superior enemy. But, unlike in previous doctrine, where the offensive had been the primary type of operations, Active Defense prescribed patience and called for the offensive only after enemy forces had been severely bloodied. The basic tactical principles were surprise and deception. Attacks should be planned on the flanks or as narrow penetration, with the goal of destroying enemy support and command and control in order to isolate and decapitate combat units, which could then be defeated in detail.[60] In order to achieve a psychological shock effect, army commanders were to concentrate overwhelming force and firepower at a weak point in the enemy's front. The attack was to proceed on a narrow front and with great depth, so that additional forces could be committed as soon as the initial attack slowed down. Ideally, attacks should be conducted at night, but during the day the shock effect could be enhanced by use of smoke, artillery, and air-dropped mines. Ground forces were to "utilize the cover of the terrain, and suppress or obscure the enemy gunners." This was quite similar to

German tactics of World War II, in that the attack should seek to disrupt command, control, support, and supply lines of the enemy. The effect of a well-coordinated attack would be fear and paralysis.[61]

The ideal formations for offensive operations were combined-arms, battalion-size task forces, based on either tank or mechanized infantry battalions, with additional field and air defense artillery, engineers, attack helicopters, and close air support.[62] Although tanks remained the crucial battlefield weapon system, in spite of the advances in antitank guided missiles, mechanized infantry was to play a vital role in the firepower team. Ideally, mechanized infantry was to fight mounted, even though the army still lacked an infantry fighting vehicle (IFV), or engage the enemy on foot, supported by armored vehicles that could provide firepower. General DePuy reiterated that the M113 APC suffered from weak armor and insufficient armament and stated that the vehicle "cannot keep up with tanks cross country without scrambling the rifle squad inside." Against superior forces, mechanized operations were necessary. The army needed an IFV.[63]

Although offensive operations were necessary to defeat the enemy before he could bring all of his force to bear, the defensive was now stressed more than it had been before. Knowledge of terrain, carefully placed guns and combat units, and a well-prepared defensive area in depth were cited among the main advantages of the defender. However, since initiative rested with the attacker, it was crucial that the defense should not be conducted without counterattacks. Emphasis was placed on understanding the enemy, concentration of force at critical times and places, combat with combined-arms teams, and full exploitation of the natural advantages of the defense. First, the enemy would have to engage a covering force, which could reveal his strength, location, and the general direction of his thrust, while at the same time preventing him from gaining a clearer picture of defensive alignments. The covering force was also tasked with gaining enough time for the main defensive force to deploy to battle stations and improve upon prepared defensive areas. In the main battle area, it was important to maintain coherence at or near the forward edge, to limit the enemy's room for maneuver. It was emphasized that defense had to be elastic in nature but should be anchored by strongpoints, usually terrain features that could be held by a reinforced company or battalion. Counterattacks were important, but they had to be timed precisely because the natural advantages of the defender would be negated once they were under way. Counterattacks were to be conducted with antitank guided missiles and tanks that could hit the enemy in the flank or rear. In elastic defense, army units could shift fluently from defensive to offensive operations.[64]

Most of Field Manual 100-5 was based upon drafts designed by the armor, artillery, and infantry training centers, but USAREUR also contributed.[65] Coalition warfare in Europe posed operational difficulties. Efforts to make doctrine of NATO forces more compatible were not wholly successful. In addition, coordination of unit organization, logistics, weaponry and equipment, and training methods was incomplete. U.S. Army commanders thus had to ensure that their units were "trained in NATO procedures and are alert to the differences in the various armed forces which may affect combat operations."[66] In addition, urban sprawl and infrastructure had altered the landscape of Central Europe. The army had previously considered urban combat and house-to-house fighting, but now it was necessary to develop techniques for operations in "continuous and contiguous built-up areas." USAREUR suggested that adjacent villages and strip areas could be used as defensive strongpoints, with tanks and antitank guided missiles operating in the gaps, while similar areas should be bypassed in an attack. Towns might serve as force multipliers, because a small force could hold out for a long time. But urban areas such as Frankfurt, Stuttgart, or the Ruhr Valley would be difficult to defend, and it was likely that the battle would devolve into infantry combat from street to street. Here it was useful to employ airmobile forces. USAREUR concluded that combat in built-up areas would gain in importance and urged further systematic study.[67]

In 1980, General DePuy recalled the fundamental lines of thought behind the manual. The Vietnam War with its emphasis on light forces was over, and the army could focus on the defense of West Germany. The war had delayed mechanization of the army, but the late 1970s were to be a period of intensive modernization. The keystones of the manual were its focus on European war, almost exclusive emphasis on armored and mechanized combat, and close integration of tactics and modern weapons technology. DePuy and his collaborators prescribed "an elastic defense" that could "cope with Soviet strength and the lack of maneuver room in Germany." This was to be achieved through "superior concentration of combat power in the attack and in the defense through good intelligence, quick decisions, and high mobility . . . as the only solution for an outnumbered force." In retrospect, DePuy maintained that forward defense had to be conducted at or near the intra-German border, with only small reserve forces. He believed that cohesion of the front was critical and that any penetration could spell defeat. He conceded that "all in all, it was a tall order."[68]

Despite DePuy's close adherence to Panzergrenadier tactics, Field Manual 100-5 was not an exact copy of German doctrine. The German and Israeli armies had smaller tank platoons than the U.S. Army; three tanks instead of five. DePuy admitted that this provided for better control by the platoon commander, and he noted that the army could create additional tank battalions with existing materiel by adopting that organization. But he recommended against doing so because the army did not have the additional officers that would be required.[69] German officers criticized the American practice of giving company commanders the main responsibility for directing combat at the tactical level. Both in the German and Israeli armies, tanks were coordinated at the battalion level with other weapons systems, such as infantry, artillery, aviation, mortars, and engineers. But in the U.S. Army, this coordination was called for at company level, thus putting captains in a position of having to control much more than their base company. DePuy concurred with the criticism and stated that future manuals for companies and battalions were to move battalion commanders into a more central role.[70] This appeared to be a qualification to the dogmatic statement that company commanders fought the battle, while battalion commanders directed it. But by the same token, DePuy proudly reported that Bundeswehr leadership endorsed Active Defense after a demonstration at the Grafenwöhr training area in November 1976.[71]

The principal weakness of the doctrine was that it did not address how to defend against additional echelons of attacking forces. It gave the army a clear and concise concept on how, and with what means, to counter the initial Soviet attack. In that sense it was superior to doctrine of the 1950s and 1960s, which had not paid sufficient attention to enemy capabilities and operational thought. Army leaders professed that battles could only be won by ground and air forces in joint operations, but the chapter on "Air-Land Battle" lacked detail. Moreover, the army regarded close air support and interdiction of enemy air forces as supplementary to its own decisive role of employing mobility, speed, and firepower to win the land battle.[72] In retrospect, Active Defense was a transition from earlier doctrine, which was derived from previous experience of the U.S. Army and its current forces and weapons, to operational art, which characterized the approach of the 1980s. The 1982 edition of Field Manual 100-5 would succeed in combining army operational thought with joint and combined operations in order to defeat all enemy forces, and not merely the first echelon. The greatest contributions of Active Defense doctrine were the public debate that began immediately after its publication and the continuation of army-internal studies to improve upon current doctrine, force structure, and weapons systems.

TRADOC's doctrinal system was not universally accepted. A group of army officers and defense analysts criticized the manual as overly defensive. Others pointed at the lack of consideration of combat actions beyond the first battle. Among the most vocal critics was William Lind, an adviser to Senator Gary Hart. Throughout the 1970s, Lind published a series of articles and essays on tactical and operational questions related to land warfare. He argued that the emphasis on the concentration of superior firepower to achieve attrition was misguided. Lind and his fellow reformers, most notably retired air force colonel John Boyd and Steven Canby, a leading defense analyst, suggested that the army should emphasize maneuver over firepower.[73] But Lind's outspoken criticism of Active Defense galvanized the supporters of the doctrine. Consequently, there was a protracted debate between two distinctly different schools of thought. Israeli scholar Shimon Naveh argues that the critical difference between the proponents of firepower and those who favored maneuver rested on their respective approaches to operations. Lind and the proponents of maneuver accused the authors of Active Defense of being rooted in the tactical thinking of the past, thus precluding the necessary reorientation toward operational art as a third level of war that linked tactics and strategy. Naveh believes that the ensuing exchange of opinions was "the longest, most intoxicating and creative professional debate which ever occurred in the history of American military thought."[74]

John Romjue, official historian of TRADOC, discerned six distinct areas of public criticism. Initial opposition centered on the defensive emphasis of Active Defense. William Lind and the maneuver school charged that DePuy had neglected the offensive. But defense analyst Philip Karber noted that Field Manual 100-5 called for counterattacks, and he questioned whether the kind of large-scale counteroffensive favored by Lind could even be conducted in Europe. Military historian Archer Jones believed that the army's rediscovery of the superiority of the defensive was the greatest contribution of the manual. Secondly, critics pointed at the centrality of the opening battle, which would leave the army unprepared for protracted operations. This was indeed a delicate issue, but TRADOC stressed the first battle to combat the traditional notion of the U.S. military that the enemy attack could be absorbed and that mobilization potential of the nation would even the odds. In the event, DePuy's successor, General Donn Starry, redirected emphasis from first to central and later extended battle. Third, critics and defenders of DePuy agreed that Soviet operational thought had evolved beyond the breakthrough maneuver, which remained at the heart of TRADOC's tactical thinking. Philip Karber feared that the Soviet army was prepared to attack on a wide front and seek weak spots of the defensive. Steven Canby added that Soviet doctrine was more opportunistic and less static than Active Defense assumed and could render a line of fortified strongpoints useless.[75]

Army officers and defense analysts alike were uneasy about the apparent reduction of the tactical reserve inherent in TRADOC's presumed order of battle. But this reflected the near overwhelming strength of the enemy and the resulting need to move as many units as possible close to the front. If the army in general, and USAREUR in particular, were to be expanded, combat units could again be held in tactical reserve. On the other hand, Archer Jones believed that the mobile defensive approach delineated in Field Manual 100-5 eliminated the need for a large tactical reserve, which in the past had been necessary to seal off enemy penetration or reinforce eroding defensive positions. Fifth, the adherents of maneuver warfare lamented that the emphasis on firepower rendered all but useless the vehicle technology of the army. But Philip Karber asked why one should not acknowledge the awesome firepower of antitank weapons, and, in the event, Starry's concepts of the late 1970s came to rely even more heavily on firepower. Finally, both Lind and Jones pointed at difficulties arising from the concentration of forces on the defensive. Lind feared that U.S. commanders would have to rely too much on communications systems that could be jammed by the enemy, and Jones questioned whether shifting all but three or four battalions of a division to a critical point would leave enough forces to cover the defensive area. Moreover, concentrating on the defensive would offer lucrative targets for enemy artillery, although none of the critics openly discussed tactical nuclear strikes.[76]

Army-internal criticism of Field Manual 100-5 also stressed the overemphasis of the defensive. Commanders in the field came to realize the dangers inherent in attrition strategy, emphasis on firepower, and static nature of the doctrinal system. NATO's supreme commander, General Alexander Haig, told DePuy that he "would like to see . . . a more explicit reminder that in general the ultimate purpose of any defense is to regain the initiative by taking the offensive." Moreover, Haig feared that the focus on the defense of Germany, however necessary, might lead army officers to embrace defense "for its own sake." He concluded that doctrine should stress "the importance of offensive maneuver in destroying an opponent's will—as opposed to his capacity—to fight."[77] With this last point, Haig raised the question of the psychological impact of combat operations. There appeared to be a belief that the defensive was un-American and that being on the defensive might demoralize American soldiers. As textual analysis of Field Manual 100-5, Haig's critique was unjustified, but as Paul Herbert has pointed out, he correctly gauged the reception of the manual and the likelihood of misinterpretation of its central points.[78]

The criticism that Active Defense was too narrowly focused on war in Europe mirrored the concern with army doctrine prior to 1965. General DePuy believed that army doctrine was adaptable to other geographic locales, such as the Middle East, where the enemy would be equipped with Soviet weapons and indoctrinated in Soviet tactics and operational thought.

The Yom Kippur War indeed had shown that the Egyptian and Syrian armed forces fit that description. Moreover, DePuy expected that the army, if deployed outside of Europe or the Middle East, would face an enemy similar to Warsaw Pact forces in armament and operational concepts.[79]

In November 1980, General DePuy acknowledged that too many army officers still regarded the defensive as inferior to the offensive. DePuy also conceded that too many commanders equated defense with delaying action and thus renounced the multitude of defensive courses of action required on the modern battlefield. This could lead to the attrition strategy evoked by the adherents of the maneuver school. But this was a misinterpretation of doctrine rather than its intention. DePuy stated that Active Defense offered the diversified tactics necessary to stop a massive Soviet attack in the first battle, but brigade commanders needed to keep a view of the entire defensive area in order to shift their battalions to critical points and tell battalion commanders what tactics to employ. Elastic defense was to counter Soviet breakthrough maneuvers, but static defense or counterattacks might be useful in other areas of the front. DePuy cited Bruce Clarke's defense of St. Vith in December 1944 as a classic example of elastic defense. He concluded that the critics overstated the role of attrition in Active Defense and overlooked the maneuver elements of the doctrine.[80]

Active Defense was an attempt to develop universal doctrine for land warfare in Central Europe. Some of the criticism that was extended in the late 1970s was certainly correct, but the critics missed the broader significance of DePuy's doctrinal manual. Until 1976, the army had treated doctrine as an expression of tactical and operational concepts. DePuy understood doctrine to be the first step toward creating an entirely new operational philosophy. While traditionalists argued that doctrine should tell commanders how to fight, DePuy designed a universal theory of the next war, which contained tactical and operational thought as the basis for research and development as well as organization of combat units and logistics. As a tactical manual, Active Defense was too narrowly focused on a particular battle in Europe. It was too reactive to Soviet operational concepts that had evolved beyond the breakthrough maneuver. This raised fear that USAREUR was well prepared for a particular kind of attack but could not cope with different Soviet operations. In short, Active Defense was too rigid, a blueprint that did not consider the agency of the enemy and imposed an assumption of predictable Soviet tactics and operations. But DePuy had little choice in the matter. While he inherently preferred a rigid doctrinal system, the climate of the mid-1970s would not have allowed for even bolder steps. In the end, DePuy succeeded in changing the mind-set and determining the future of the army. Active Defense fell short as an expression of tactics and operations, but it elevated doctrine to the core of the army's thinking about war and opened the door for AirLand Battle.[81]

AirLand Battle Doctrine and the Cold War Army

Parallel to the public debate of the late 1970s, General Donn Starry considered improvement of army doctrine. As commanding general of the Armor Center at Fort Knox, Starry had been intimately involved in the process of drafting Active Defense. But his tenure as commander of V Corps in Germany in 1976 and 1977 convinced him that further far-reaching changes to doctrine were necessary. Eventually, he came to consider Active Defense doctrine as "a false start" in the process of rebuilding the army.[82] Starry was convinced that the army and air force had the technological means to contain the attacker and engage his reserves before they could reach the battle area. As commander of TRADOC (1977–1981), Starry guided the army from the concept of the First Battle to the Extended Battlefield, where it was crucial to see and operate deep behind enemy lines. Between 1976 and 1982, he developed a doctrinal system that featured integration of armor, mobile infantry, artillery, missile forces, and airpower.[83]

Starry's crucial experience came in 1976 and 1977 when he commanded the forces that guarded the Fulda Gap and Hesse. His immediate adjustments to the General Defense Plan of V Corps were based on the lessons of the Yom Kippur War.[84] The new operational plan moved all available reserves to the corps commander in order to allow for greater depth in the defenses. By storing all ammunition and necessary equipment directly on tanks and other vehicles, speed and mobility of the force were increased.[85] Active Defense had eliminated the concept of prepared killing zones, with fortified defensive positions and well-defined fields of fire. This had been a staple of Central Army Group (CENTAG) plans in the early 1970s.[86] Moreover, there was confusion throughout the army about the mission of the covering force. Eventually, Starry's working definition became standard: "The covering force mission was usually described as a delay."[87] Starry expected that the covering force in his sector could not hold for more than one day if the enemy attacked en masse. Moreover, he estimated that V Corps would lose 70 M60 tanks and 120 M551 Sheridans during the covering-force battle. He assumed that the main battle would last less than ten days if the enemy's main effort were directed against V Corps, but that his forces could sustain operations for twenty days if faced by secondary attacks. Losses during the main battle would amount to sixty-two tanks per day, and the corps's 180 Sheridans would be destroyed after two days of combat. At the rate assumed by General Starry, V Corps would be out of tanks on the eleventh day of combat operations.[88]

During his tenure in Germany, Starry conducted a thorough study of corps operations in armored warfare, based on historical campaigns and battles and on war games for his particular sector of Central Region. He discovered that the traditional calculus, which prescribed at least a three-to-one force ratio in favor of the attacker, was flawed. Instead, the study of tank battles revealed that there was little difference in the outcome of battles fought with superior or inferior forces, as long as the attacker did not possess at least a six-to-one superiority.[89] In the mid-1970s, the Warsaw Pact had a two-to-one advantage in active divisions in Central Europe, but in ground-force personnel the advantage was less than 10 percent.[90]

From these studies, Starry concluded that the tension between the rather systemic nature of operational planning and the more random character of actual battle constituted a significant problem. War games were based on the assumption of predictable behavior of the commanders of friendly and enemy forces and could not replicate the uncertainty inherent to combat. To minimize this problem, Starry resolved that future operational doctrine should build a bridge between the general purpose of the battle and the chance events of actual combat. Instead of viewing the corps area as a front that had to be defended, Starry looked at it as both front and depth and he included the future as a second dimension of time. The maneuver in depth was closely linked to the elimination of rear echelons of the enemy that had not yet reached the battle zone. In essence, the corps had to destroy the enemy's future capability as well as its present one. The decisive battle in the defense of West Germany would thus not merely be fought against Soviet spearheads, but also against follow-on echelons in East Germany, Poland, or Czechoslovakia.[91]

Nevertheless, Starry still thought that Active Defense addressed the strategic and tactical situation in Central Europe and made good use of the terrain and the means that were at the army's disposal. But tactical-level commanders in Germany had failed to study terrain features and often were unfamiliar with their forward battle stations. During his command of V Corps, General Starry introduced his subordinate officers to the basic tenets of Active Defense doctrine, but he was less successful with neighboring VII Corps.[92] In an article in Military Review in August 1978, Starry defended the concept against its critics. He embraced the debate as a means to improve upon tactical concepts, but he counseled the proponents of maneuver warfare that Active Defense was not simply a new name for the traditional concepts of mobile defense and attrition by firepower. Instead, it allowed the defensive forces to concentrate rapidly at critical points and make best use of natural and man-made obstacles. It also offered some ability to observe the movement of enemy formations that were still far away from the battlefield. Most importantly, tactical doctrine now drove force design and the development of new weaponry and equipment.[93]

In practical terms for the defense of Germany, Starry emphasized the role of the covering force, which had to fight continuously rather than merely delay the enemy and retreat. The main functions of the covering force were to obfuscate enemy intelligence about the specific alignment of the defenders, draw the attacker away from its air defenses, and lead the enemy into terrain suitable for the defenders. For the main force, it was critical to achieve a very high rate of target destruction, possibly as many as 250 targets per battalion in a ten-minute period. The division might be called upon to destroy upward of 2,000 more targets, mainly artillery and second-echelon forces, in less than one day. The corps might have to engage an additional 3,000 targets, mainly enemy long-range artillery and rear-echelon formations, in three to five days. Division commanders had to be prepared to concentrate all but their air cavalry and helicopter units to prevent an enemy breakthrough, even though this would leave only two or three battalions for most of the approximately 40-kilometer-wide frontage of the division. Unlike in previous concepts of mobile defense, there was no centralized reserve for counterattacks once the Soviet offensive had been contained. In Active Defense, all units were needed immediately. The enemy had to be defeated in increasingly deep defensive areas and in counterattacks by divisions that were already engaged in the defensive battle. This was further indication that defensive, antitank weapons systems held a temporary advantage over armored vehicles.[94]

Starry conceded that the doctrinal emphasis on the first battle had to be broadened. His command tenure in Germany had illustrated the need to engage follow-on echelons of the attacking forces. Upon taking command of TRADOC, he developed a concept for corps operations that became known as Central Battle. U.S. ground forces in Germany were to be familiar with the terrain and could follow a particular "battle calculus," which was characterized by predetermined ranges for different weapons systems and by knowledge of how many and what kind of enemy units could advance in certain areas. Starry believed that the course of Central Battle could be expressed statistically, in terms of minutes into the battle, force ratios, specific weapons, rate of advance, visibility, rate of fire, number of command decisions, and time from request to delivery of tactical air support. The principal objective of U.S. ground forces was to destroy or suppress all enemy targets. Calculations for Central Battle specifically included the second echelon of

Warsaw Pact forces. For Starry, Central Battle "was the place where all the combat systems and combat support systems interacted on the battlefield."[95]

While considering adjustments to Active Defense, General Starry also initiated a force design study. He intended to combine Division 86 with the new doctrine that was slowly crystallizing. The Division 86 study was coordinated by the Command and General Staff College and tested in training schools. It became the most thorough division design effort since World War II. The heavy division, approved in principle by Army Chief of Staff Edward Meyer in October 1979, had 20,000 officers and men. It was to be as mobile and flexible as the ROAD division, but with air cavalry as a fourth brigade it would be better suited to counter Soviet deep operations on conventional or nuclear battlefields in Germany. Starry hoped that Division 86 would give tactical formations that could attack enemy rear echelons before the Warsaw Pact armies had an opportunity to concentrate their reserve forces. Following the concern of General Meyer that the army was too narrowly focused on war in Central Europe, Division 86 was combined in the Army 86 concept with studies of the corps, field army, and a nonmechanized infantry division for extra-European deployment. Eventually, the heavy division proved too costly, both in terms of manpower and resources.[96]

Just as General Starry was considering changes to the army's operational approach, army leaders and political officers in the United States and Western Europe tried to address the inherent imbalance in the quality and reliability of NATO forces along the projected front in Germany. Throughout the Cold War, military officers in Europe and North America had pointed at the weakness of German, British, Belgian, Dutch, and Canadian forces that were guarding northern Germany. In the event of a Soviet attack, they reasoned, the main effort was more likely to develop in the north German plain than against the stronger forces of CENTAG.[97] The latter had the additional advantage of more defensible terrain. By the mid-1970s, as USAREUR faced the redeployment of additional forces to the United States, U.S. officials were discussing deployment of a U.S. Army brigade in the vicinity of Bremerhaven, the American port of entry at the North Sea. In July 1978, after several years of negotiations that involved reconfiguration of defense plans as well as more mundane questions of proper facilities, housing, schools, and other troop services, 3rd Brigade of 2nd Armored Division was deployed from Ft. Hood, Texas, to Garlstedt in Lower Saxony. Despite concerns about logistics and the capacity of the Bremerhaven port, this brigade served as the nucleus of U.S. III Corps, a three-division force that was to strengthen the Northern Army Group (NORTHAG) in case of NATO mobilization.[98]

By the summer of 1979, TRADOC had resolved to publish a revised edition of Field Manual 100-5. But General Starry informed General Meyer that further study on global deployment, corps operations, and the role of firepower in defense and offense was needed. Meyer, who had just been promoted from deputy chief of staff for operations and plans to chief of staff, had noted that the base beliefs of Active Defense still were not universally accepted or even understood. The most glaring tactical problem was disagreement about the emphasis on firepower over maneuver. But Meyer was also concerned about the widespread interpretation of Field Manual 100-5 as a defensive doctrine. He acknowledged that this had not been the intention of the manual's authors, but it was nevertheless the impression of many field commanders. Starry perceived an intrinsic linkage between the two issues. He hoped that clearer language in a new manual would revive the offensive spirit of the army, but he cautioned Meyer not to accept the arguments of the maneuver school, which "ignore the very real problems with space and depth . . . in Europe, and with logistical support of highly mobile operations." Meyer pushed for greater consideration of global deployment. He was particularly concerned with the neglect of guerrilla warfare and counterinsurgency. Starry acknowledged that TRADOC had not made much progress in this area, but he stressed that "we cannot generalize too much and still be compatible with the Germans whose only mission is to fight in Europe, and whose doctrine will always reflect that." Starry was confident that TRADOC could design doctrine that worked in Europe, the Middle East, and Korea, but he did not believe that anything more was feasible.[99]

Interdiction of follow-on forces and the integrated battlefield formed the core of doctrinal considerations between 1979 and 1981. Traditionally, interdiction had been perceived as a disruptive technique, featuring attacks on enemy lines of communication, logistics, and reserves. But technological advances in communications systems, target acquisition systems, and long-range strike capability with missiles, helicopters, and jet planes permitted a more coordinated approach. Nuclear weapons in particular increased the need to plan for strikes on targets that were far removed from the front lines. Army planners began to consider whether a coordinated approach could negate the greatest Soviet advantage—numerical superiority. In order to win, the army had to manage the battle in depth, so that enemy forces would be put in a disadvantageous position. This included channeling enemy forces, opening gaps in their line, and delaying the arrival of Warsaw Pact reserves. Interdiction tactics could allow American forces to gain the initiative and dictate the location and course of what Starry referred to as Central Battle.[100]

The gradual emergence of army doctrine that placed greater emphasis on close air support coincided with a shift of power within the air force. For most of the Cold War, Strategic Air Command, with its emphasis on long-range bombers, missiles, and nuclear weapons, had defined the direction of the air force, but in the decade following the Vietnam War, a growing number of officers from Tactical Air Command rose to positions of leadership in the air force.[101] Since late 1973, Tactical Air Command and TRADOC had cooperated closely. General DePuy and Tactical Air Command commander General Dixon established an Air-Land Forces Application Directorate to discuss joint operational concepts.[102] In addition, new aircraft that became available during and after the Vietnam War enabled the air force to provide the kind of air support desired by army leaders, most importantly the A-10 attack jet, which could provide close fire support against enemy tanks and act as a force multiplier against the numerically superior Warsaw Pact armored formations.[103]

The experience of Vietnam itself, with practical cooperation between ground and tactical air forces, underscored the utility of air-land battle. Both army leaders and the new commanders of the air force came to the realization that the land battle could not be won without close cooperation of the two services. In Active Defense, this led to a general statement stressing the need for close air support. In the process of drafting AirLand Battle doctrine, a new understanding of joint operations was formed.[104] This emphasis on joint operations did not translate into agreement on proper doctrine, however. In the event, AirLand Battle doctrine and the air force conception of Follow-on Forces Attack were developed separately and placed primary emphasis on different targets. While army planners intended for a closely integrated battle of the corps, Tactical Air Command commanders earmarked targets of greater strategic importance deep behind enemy lines. Moreover, despite the Goldwater-Nichols Act of 1986, a congressional mandate to reorganize the defense establishment and improve cooperation among the armed services, army and air force leadership quarreled over who was to control tactical air assets.[105]

In December 1979, the Field Artillery School presented a proposal for the integrated battlefield. This concept entailed close cooperation of air and ground forces, mutually supporting employment of maneuver and firepower tactics, and integrated conventional and nuclear fire support. This became the foundation of AirLand Battle. It emphasized the need to interdict enemy forces before they could join the battle. Tactical nuclear weapons enhanced the interdiction capability of the army and permitted it to gain the initiative and go on the offensive. The depth of the integrated battlefield was defined in time. Brigade commanders were to be responsible for the delay or destruction of enemy rear-echelon forces that were less than 12 hours from the front. Division commanders had an area of responsibility of 24 hours, while corps commanders were to engage enemy forces that were within 72 hours from the front. The Field Artillery School recommended the use of tactical nuclear weapons against rear-area targets because it would force the enemy to disperse and would reduce the risk of a massed breakthrough maneuver. The best targets were command functions, rather than combat units, since the momentum of the enemy offensive depended on coordination of reinforcements. But integrated battle could only succeed if tactical nuclear war was minutely prepared for and release procedures were simplified. Still, the Field Artillery School could not conceive of a non-nuclear future battle.[106]

Doctrinal planners quickly accepted the concept of integrated battle, even though General Starry himself harbored serious doubts that tactical or operational-level commanders could use nuclear weapons effectively due to the lengthy process of acquiring release authority.[107] Force structure studies for Corps 86, an extension of the Division 86 study, in 1980, under the guidance of CAC, placed primary focus on interdiction of the second echelon of Warsaw Pact forces. General Starry maintained that the corps was the critical operational formation for air-land battle. Corps headquarters also were to coordinate nuclear fire support. CAC suggested forward defense in Germany with emphasis on deep battle against enemy rear echelons. Areas of interest supplemented the areas of responsibility of the integrated-battlefield concept: They extended to 24 hours, or 70 kilometers, for the brigade, 72 hours (150 kilometers) for the division, 96 hours (300 kilometers) for the corps, and up to 1,000 kilometers for field army and supreme command. On the defensive, the corps was to contain the enemy attack by destroying first-echelon forces, causing reinforcements to disperse, disrupting command and control, and generally slowing the momentum of the attack. On the offensive, it was critical to strike fast and attack command and control as well as logistics targets and reserve forces in the enemy's rear area. While dispersal in depth was to minimize the effect of enemy nuclear strikes on the corps in defensive operations, mass on target on the offensive was to be achieved by precisely timed arrival of attacking forces that advanced over different routes of approach.[108]

With the concepts for integrated battle and force structure of a heavy corps, the crucial pieces were in place to revise Field Manual 100-5, despite General Meyer's concern for worldwide contingencies. It was to be written at the Command and General Staff College, because General Starry recognized that opposition from army schools had impeded army-wide acceptance of Active Defense doctrine. He reasoned that returning doctrine to its traditional place of origin would allow for better integration of the schools as well as field commands in the writing process. TRADOC retained control, however, through the personal union of the offices of deputy commander TRADOC and commander CAC in Lieutenant General William R. Richardson. Starry himself exerted personal influence through close working relations with the principal authors of Field Manual 100-5, lieutenant colonels Huba Wass de Czege, L. D. Holder, and Richmond Henriques.[109]

General Starry provided the working title "Extended Battlefield" to drafts that were written in the course of 1980. "Extended Battlefield" adopted characteristics of integrated battlefield and stressed the deep attack. Since NATO ground forces could not contain a sustained Soviet offensive in protracted operations, it would be necessary to collapse the enemy's ability to fight. In other words, while doctrine and operational plans of the 1950s and 1960s had acknowledged the possibility of protracted war ending in a negotiated settlement, Starry's concept required winning the campaign as the only means of avoiding defeat. Starry expected that soon-to-be-available modern weapons systems would alter the balance between offense and defense. The army was close to producing the Bradley fighting vehicle and the Abrams tank; and improved target-acquisition and fire-direction systems, a remotely piloted vehicle, Pershing II missiles, a new attack helicopter, a multiple-launch rocket system, ground-launched cruise missiles, and a tactical communication satellite were also expected to be available before 1986.[110]

Starry's Extended Battlefield was based on TRADOC and CAC studies, but it also reflected the contributions of John Boyd to the debate of the late 1970s. Boyd had introduced the concept of the OODA loop—observation, orientation, decision, and action—to see beyond the narrow battlefield on which the enemy's first-echelon forces were engaged.[111] More important, Boyd had developed an operational concept that depended on speed, which would leave the enemy off balance and incapable of matching the pace of operations.[112] For Starry, Boyd's ideas had practical application in the delineation of specific battle areas and areas of interest for the operational units. Brigades were to engage the lead elements of Soviet first-echelon divisions but also stay alert to developments within a 10–15-hour march behind the enemy's front. Divisions were to engage follow-on forces close to the battlefield and stay alert to developments in the enemy's rear, at a distance of 16–48 hours from the front. Corps was to engage rear-area forces of the Soviet first echelon and stay alert to movements of the second and later echelons, approximately 72 hours removed from the front. Starry was optimistic that the army possessed sufficient target acquisition capability to engage targets this far in the enemy rear area.[113]

TRADOC historian John Romjue noted that the emphasis on initiative, which separated Extended-Battlefield doctrine from Central Battle, reflected the aggressive tactical philosophy that General Starry had developed during his TRADOC command. But much like the integrated battlefield, extended battlefield did not adequately illustrate the nature of air-land battle. Therefore, in January 1981, a new title for operational doctrine was announced: AirLand Battle. In March, TRADOC circulated a draft of AirLand Battle. It outlined operations against mechanized armies in Europe, Korea, and the Middle East. Unlike Active Defense, it emphasized the offensive. The operational concept reflected the fusion of integrated battlefield and Corps 86 concepts. AirLand Battle radically departed from the notion that the battle would be won in the main battle area. Instead, future battle should not be defined geographically and would not be restricted to traditional notions of front lines and rear areas.[114]

The draft of AirLand Battle doctrine was not universally embraced, although the response was favorable on balance. As a result of army-internal criticism and recommendations, TRADOC spent the next year working on revisions before the official version of Field Manual 100-5 was published in August 1982, one year after General Starry had moved from TRADOC to Readiness Command. Most noticeable among the changes was greater emphasis on the German concept of Auftragstaktik (mission-order tactics), which allowed for more decisions by tactical-level commanders. On a nonlinear, chaotic battlefield, division and brigade commanders could not expect to control all of their subordinate officers.[115] AirLand Battle doctrine also adopted the German concept of Schwerpunkt, which could be shifted according to the enemy situation and which required perfect understanding of command decisions by all inferior levels of command.[116] Finally, TRADOC included the operational level of war as an intermediate stage between strategy and tactics.[117]

Until 1976, doctrine had stressed that the primary mission of the army was to win the land battle. This was out of step with the strategic situation in Europe, and it did not reflect deterrence as the primary mission of the army. In 1982, the revised edition of Field Manual 100-5 stated: "The fundamental mission of the United States Army is to deter war."[118] Moreover, while Active Defense had outlined tactical operations of large formations, AirLand Battle recognized, and emphasized, operational art. Operational art was defined as proper application of military means "to attain strategic goals within a theater of war. Most simply, it is the theory of larger unit operations. It also involves planning and conducting campaigns." Tactics, on the other hand, were "the specific techniques smaller units use to win battles and engagements which support operational objectives."[119] In practical terms, it required theater commanders to coordinate multiple battles, utilize all available tactical units, and apportion resources in order to achieve the strategic objective of a campaign.[120] The U.S. Army's conception of operational art reflected the close study of Soviet operational capabilities that had been conducted throughout the 1970s.

Operational art had been developed as a theoretical concept in the Soviet Union prior to World War II. But its main practitioners were among the military officers purged after 1937, and the Red Army employed conservative operational doctrine at the beginning of the war. In the later stages of the war, particularly during the offensives of 1943–1945, crucial elements of operational art, such as deep battle and continuous attack with mobile, mechanized formations, were employed with great success. Operational art was largely neglected in the 1950s and early 1960s, as a result of emphasis on nuclear weapons. The Soviet army rediscovered it in the 1960s and 1970s.[121] To address the threat posed by Soviet deep-attack capabilities, AirLand Battle doctrine emphasized preparations to defeat multiple echelons of attacking forces before they could enter into close combat. It moved the thinking of senior commanders from the First Battle to the extended battlefield, reflecting the entirety of corps operations, the interdiction of enemy rear echelons, and the close integration of ground and air forces. AirLand Battle was specifically designed to defeat the numerically larger and technologically equal mechanized armies of the Warsaw Pact or Soviet client states. It was inspired by intellectual and operational concepts of the German Reichswehr in the 1920s and 1930s.[122]

AirLand Battle doctrine emphasized the central nature of operational art: "An Army's operational concept is the core of its doctrine. It is the way the Army fights its battles and campaigns, including tactics, procedures, organizations, support, equipment, and training."[123] Officers at TRADOC recognized that battlefield victories would not automatically translate into winning the war. Vietnam had demonstrated that political will and strategic objective were critical. Nevertheless, army doctrine had to concern itself with "winning battles and campaigns."[124] Field Manual 100-5 acknowledged the possibility of global deployments: The army had to be prepared to fight "light, well-equipped forces such as Soviet-supported insurgents or sophisticated terrorist groups," but its main focus had to be on the "areas of greatest strategic concern, [where] it must expect battles of greater scope and intensity than ever fought before." Moreover, while Field Manual 100-5 stressed conventional operations, the army "must anticipate battles fought with nuclear and chemical weapons." In future battle, it would be crucial to "retain the initiative and disrupt our opponent's fighting capability in depth with deep attack, effective firepower, and decisive maneuver."[125]

The authors of AirLand Battle placed a premium on leadership and command. Since the future battlefield would be nonlinear, that is, characterized by the absence of well-defined, coherent front lines, commanding officers would face a high degree of chaos and uncertainty. This had a precedent in the German armies of World War I, which shifted after 1916 from a tactical system based on strict and inflexible orders to mission-order tactics that permitted local commanders to decide upon the best method to achieve their objective.[126] The draft armies of Western democracies had not followed the German example, mainly because too many commanders came from reserve units or were too inexperienced for such a complex and sophisticated system that relied upon similar interpretation of doctrine on all levels of command and great familiarity with the mind of one's superior officer. The emergence of the all-volunteer army helped to address this problem. It was particularly important that all forward-deployed units were ready to fight on a few hours' notice and that their commanders had effective plans for the battle. Field Manual 100-5 concluded that "the fluid nature of modern war will place a premium on leadership, unit cohesion, and effective, independent operations."[127] To ensure preparedness, the doctrinal concept "must be broad enough to describe operations in all anticipated circumstances. Yet it must allow sufficient freedom for tactical variations in any situations. It must also be uniformly known and understood."[128]

Army operations were to be directed at destroying the enemy "by throwing the enemy off balance with powerful initial blows from unexpected directions and then following up rapidly to prevent his recovery."[129] Enemy forces were to be attacked in depth with "rapid, unpredictable, violent, and disorienting" operations. But while the pace of operations had to be fast enough to prevent effective countermeasures, it also had to be controllable in order to assure the cooperation of all arms. The basic tenets of AirLand Battle doctrine were initiative, depth, agility, and synchronization.[130] For the purpose of fighting the Soviets in Central Europe, field commanders had to assure close integration of maneuver and firepower in an effort to break the cohesion and disrupt command and control of enemy forces. This would allow them to isolate enemy units, which could then be defeated in detail. TRADOC had retained the emphasis on firepower that had characterized Active Defense doctrine, but the new manual was more successful in explaining the significance of maneuver. Firepower killed, but maneuver allowed one to create numerical superiority at critical points and contributed to retaining the tactical initiative and reducing vulnerability.[131]

Given the need to combat and disrupt elements of enemy force not yet on the battlefield, intelligence was a core ingredient of AirLand Battle doctrine. On the defensive, American commanders had the advantage of intimate familiarity with the terrain in West Germany. This advantage had not been fully exploited by tactical level commanders prior to the mid-1970s, but during his command tenure in V Corps, General Starry had emphasized that all of his officers needed to improve their knowledge about the geography, topography, and weather conditions in their assigned areas and beyond the assigned borders. Moreover, modern technology made it possible to gather and quickly analyze tactical intelligence about the area of operation, as well as the nature and capability of the enemy. It was necessary to see far beyond the battlefield and identify targets for conventional or nuclear strikes. For this purpose, AirLand Battle doctrine derived from integrated battle and extended battlefield the concept of clearly defined areas of interest and influence. Unlike in earlier editions of Field Manual 100-5, the chapter on tactical intelligence painstakingly explained how different command echelons could best take advantage of current capability to observe the entire battlefield, including a large portion of the area behind the enemy's front-line troops.[132]

The critical aspect of AirLand Battle operations was coordination of the combined arms. TRADOC planners warned that battles in future wars need not be short. They would certainly extend over greater distances than battles in the past. American armed forces would be outnumbered, particularly in war in Europe, but "complete unity of effort and thoroughly synchronized air and ground action . . . can defeat a much larger enemy force that is poorly coordinated."[133] Field Manual 100-5 delineated the role each branch of the army was to play in the combined-arms battle. Light infantry would be most useful in the defense or capture of urban areas, but it could also open gaps for mechanized and armored forces, defend strongpoints, and mop up enemy forces that had been bypassed by armored units. Mechanized infantry was to provide antitank fires and suppress enemy infantry and antitank guided missiles capability. Once IFVs became available, mechanized infantry could also accompany tanks in assault operations. The tank remained the primary offensive weapon, due to its lethal combination of firepower, speed, and armored protection, although it had obvious limitations in built-up or densely forested areas and could not easily traverse water obstacles. Field artillery provided vital fire support for the maneuver elements of the combined-arms fire team. It had become as mobile as armored and mechanized formations. Air defense artillery provided protection from enemy close air support and could secure command posts and logistics installations. Finally, army aviation—attack helicopters, air cavalry, and combat support—increased mobility and offered another dimension of firepower, on defense as well as offense.[134]

At first, army units would find themselves on the defensive. But AirLand Battle doctrine stressed the aggressive nature of defensive operations in future war. As in Active Defense, defense was to be elastic, that is, combine elements of strongpoint defense, delaying action, and particularly counterattack. In the event, the fundamental difference between defense and offense was one of purpose rather than type of combat operations.[135] Field Manual 100-5 acknowledged the inherent advantages of the defender. It was easier to deny success to the enemy than to seek a decision actively. The defender knew the terrain better than the attacker did. Also, the defender could fight under the cover of his artillery and air defense systems. But the attacker had the initiative, which was deemed at least equally valuable. Army leaders expected that in a protracted conventional war the Soviets would have the advantage because they could draw upon their vast reservoir of manpower and overwhelm NATO combat divisions. The U.S. Army could not enter into a campaign of attrition but had to seek a quick decision on the battlefield. Therefore, defensive operations had to be supplanted by offensive action at the earliest possible time.[136]

On the offensive, AirLand Battle stressed "rapid, violent operations that seek enemy soft spots, remain flexible in shifting the main effort, and exploit successes promptly."[137] Active Defense had intended to strike a balance between defensive and offensive operations, but the reception of the doctrine in the late 1970s had shown that it failed to state its case successfully. AirLand Battle doctrine reestablished that "the offense is the decisive form of war, the commander's only means of attaining a positive goal or of completely destroying an enemy force."[138] This was to be achieved through concentration of effort, surprise, speed of the attack, flexibility that allowed for pragmatic changes to initial planning, and audacity. On offense as well as defense, the army would face a numerically superior enemy, with great technological assets at his disposal. But numbers mattered less in future war than the ability to strike with all one's force at the critical moment. AirLand Battle doctrine assumed that the Soviet military could not wage a fast-paced combined-arms battle successfully. The audacity of army leaders may be admired or admonished, but short of building a much larger ground force, it is difficult to perceive a viable alternative.

From the perspective of interservice cooperation, AirLand Battle doctrine presented significant improvement over the deep-seated rivalries that characterized the bureaucratic and fiscal aspects of the defense establishment throughout the Cold War. It was not the end of interservice rivalry, but the army acknowledged that it "will seldom fight alone. . . . Joint operations will be the rule rather than the exception."[139] This terse acknowledgment of an obvious fact may be contrasted to the intense debates of the 1950s over strategy, control of missile programs, and the share of the defense budget. Field Manual 100-5 also paid greater attention to combined operations with NATO allies. This reflected both the army's primary area of deployment and General Starry's recent experiences in Germany.[140]

In 1985, a panel of retired senior commanders concluded that NATO ground forces were still too weak to defeat a Soviet attack with conventional means. Nevertheless, the deterrent value of the combat divisions in Central Region was high, because it now seemed likely that ACE forces could halt the initial attack of the Warsaw Pact. The problem was the inability to match the follow-on echelons of Soviet and Eastern European armies that would eventually overwhelm the alliance in a conventional war.[141] The follow-on echelons could include between 50 and 70 percent of the overall strength of the attacking force, giving the attacker the flexibility to exploit a breakthrough or penetration, or mass decisive force at a critical point of the front. These forces had to be delayed and degraded before they could reach the battlefield.[142] This concern of the panel had in fact been addressed in the most recent edition of Field Manual 100-5. AirLand Battle offered many of the improvements in target acquisition, tactics, operations, and the extended and integrated battlefield that General Goodpaster and his colleagues found necessary.

AirLand Battle doctrine completed the transition from the army of the world wars to the Cold War army. The process had been initiated by General Ridgway and his colleagues, who strove to create an atomic army, but it had been defined most of all by General Taylor, whose emphasis on limited nuclear war, deterrence, and the defense of Western Europe was the driving force behind reorganization and tactical and operational doctrine. The organizational structure of the Cold War army was largely in place prior to the Vietnam War. The war, however, delayed crucial aspects of mechanization of ground forces and the development of specific aircraft and missiles for combat in Central Europe. Moreover, tactical and operational doctrine could not be tailored to European war until after the withdrawal of American forces from Vietnam. At that point, TRADOC and its emphasis on doctrine as the centerpiece of the army became critical to the institution's recovery from the defeat in Vietnam and the breakdown in morale that had characterized the late 1960s and early 1970s. Active Defense doctrine, despite its shortcomings as tactical doctrine and its lack of consideration for operational art, was a milestone because the debate that followed the publication of the manual permitted TRADOC to revise doctrine to a more radical format. Simultaneously, the introduction of new weapons systems and communications and fire control technology allowed army leaders to consider seriously an entirely different system of battle over hundreds of miles in depth and behind the lines of the enemy front. AirLand Battle stood as the result of the marriage of organizational structure, technology, and altered understanding of tactics and operations. It reflected the primary mission of the army: deterrence of war and defense of West Germany.

Epilogue: The Cold War Army in the Persian Gulf

When war came in 1991, the enemy was not the Soviet army or any of the military forces of the Warsaw Pact. Instead, the U.S. Army, alongside airmen, sailors, and marines, was called upon to fight conventional forces of Iraq in the aftermath of the Iraqi occupation of Kuwait. This may be viewed as a fortuitous turn of events. It pitted the best-trained and best-equipped armed forces the United States had ever maintained in peacetime against the Iraqi military, a force that resembled that of the Soviet Union in terms of weaponry and doctrine but not in terms of combat power. Moreover, the terrain in the northern parts of the Arabian Peninsula was almost ideally suited to the type of operations that army and tactical air force had planned for under the doctrine of AirLand Battle. The result was a victory achieved within days of the beginning of the land campaign, following upon sustained strategic bombing of targets in Iraq and Kuwait.[143]

In covering the war, journalists and television cameras captured the technological superiority of the U.S. military and its coalition partners. This resulted in a lasting image of smart bombs and airpower—a push-button war. But that neglects the significant role played by ground forces and maneuver in mass. In the official history of VII Corps operations, army historian Stephen Bourque concludes that the differences in technology were insufficient to explain the one-sided outcome of the ground war. Instead, he suggests that U.S. Army units were better trained, moved at a faster pace, and retained the initiative throughout the short campaign.[144]

The apparent ease of victory in the Gulf War was largely the result of changes made in the army in the course of the Cold War. This book has argued that the Cold War U.S. Army came into its own with the introduction of AirLand Battle doctrine in 1982. But that doctrine had been further refined. The 1986 edition of Field Manual 100-5 (AirLand Battle) was more sophisticated, particularly in putting operational art at the center of a commander's decision-making process: "[It] involves fundamental decisions [of] when and where to fight and [whether] to accept or decline battle." Application of the new approach to operations would permit the commander to identify "the enemy's operational center of gravity—his source of strength or balance." Once that had been determined, the commander could concentrate "superior combat power against that point to achieve a decisive success." In other words, operational art provided the crucial link between tactical skill and strategic objective and enabled the army to apply its firepower and capacity to maneuver in a brief but violent war of movement.[145]

The result was "the most successful campaign in U.S. military history . . . [which] ranks with the great annihilation battles of all time." But Robert

Citino, a leading scholar of war of movement throughout modern history, also points out that the tactical and operational integration of air and land forces was incomplete.[146] There simply was not enough resistance to require complex joint-service operations, and AirLand Battle doctrine had been calibrated for the defensive and counteroffensive.[147] The experience of VII Corps at the left wing of the attacking force was perhaps more reminiscent of tank operations in World War II than of the deep and nonlinear battlefield anticipated in AirLand Battle doctrine. In the event, the collapse of the Soviet Union left the U.S. Army without an enemy that possessed sufficient conventional combat power to warrant application of the multidimensional operational concept that the army had developed since the end of the Vietnam War. But it had been the purpose of the Cold War army to persuade the enemy not to fight. Deterrence, rather than war fighting, had become the primary mission of the army. The end of the Cold War and the victory in the Persian Gulf confirmed the success of that mission, but it also foreshadowed new challenges that would force army leaders and the defense establishment to consider new ways of transformation of the military and novel approaches to doctrine.

Conclusion

The problem faced by the U.S. Army in the 1950s and onward was unprecedented in U.S. history: the creation and maintenance of a fighting force that was ready at the outset of a war. This posed a fundamental challenge to the American system of government and politics. Army leaders intended to transform their service from a conventional fighting force to a cold-war army that could operate on conventional and nuclear battlefields. The U.S. Army indeed found itself transformed in the 1980s as compared to 1953, but events in between belied the common usage of the term "military transformation." Instead, it was an evolutionary process, punctuated by changes in the nature and imminence of the threat, political and strategic developments in the United States, Europe, and Asia, the influence on American officers of operational and organizational thinking in European and Israeli militaries, and deliberate decisions by senior army officers to restructure their institution, introduce new weapon systems and equipment, and review doctrine.

Seventh Army was the largest and best-prepared field army the United States had ever maintained in peacetime. Its preparedness for the defense of West Germany and its contribution to the deterrence of conventional and limited nuclear war in Central Europe became the primary mission of the U.S. Army. Army leaders recognized that local conflicts outside of Europe were likely and that war between the superpowers was not, but they also recognized that a confrontation in Europe could escalate to general nuclear war, while war over less critically important territory elsewhere would be fought with conventional weapons. Political leaders of the nation expressed belief that an army that was prepared to fight against the Soviets in Germany could adapt quickly to circumstances in other regions of the world, but army leaders knew that different operational environments required different organizational structures, logistics, weapon systems, and doctrine. An ideal solution would have been to create and maintain separate forces for conflicts in Europe and elsewhere. But this was impossible within the budgetary and strategic premises of the United States. Therefore, army leaders chose to emphasize deterrence of war in Germany over the creation of general-purpose forces for global deployment. Although this led to a high state of preparedness for unlikely war and a much lower state of preparedness for likely war, it was nevertheless prudent, as only war in Europe by necessity would have escalated to nuclear war if the conventional battle was lost.

Maxwell Taylor identified the intermediate option of limited nuclear war, which would allow for a greater degree of graduated and extended deterrence. But he also realized that the army had to present an image of radical reform in order to prove its utility in the nuclear age. The focus on the North Atlantic Treaty Organization (NATO) commitment and the integration of tactical nuclear weapons permitted the army to recover its status as a premier armed service of the nation. Matthew Ridgway had opened the path for the army into the atomic age, but his approach had centered on new weapons and the best operational combat formations to integrate them. Taylor, on the other hand, introduced the pentomic division as a means to halt the decline of the army's budget relative to the other services and reestablish the army in the public mind as a modern and capable fighting force. Political leaders envisioned an army that would fight in peripheral regions and provide occupation forces for the time after nuclear war, but Taylor saw the army's future in Europe.

The pentomic division itself was an improvised response and, as a consequence, largely impractical. The strength of the concept rested upon its promise of dual capability for conventional and nuclear warfare. Taylor believed that altering the structure of combat divisions and adding tactical nuclear weapons to their arsenals would force the army to reconfigure tactical doctrine and result in transformation. As it were, most army officers perceived tactical nuclear weapons as a more powerful form of artillery and as a force multiplier, but specific concepts for their employment that clearly differentiated them from conventional artillery were not developed. Moreover, new conventional weapon systems and equipment, such as main battle tanks and improved armored personal carriers (APCs), did not enter into service in the Seventh Army until the final year of the pentomic division. Thus, the concept was abandoned just as the materiel components essential to effective function were beginning to arrive. Although the pentomic division has to be regarded as a failure from a purely operational perspective, it nevertheless fulfilled its political purpose. This was a structure designed to provide a platform for change and the political leverage required to get the resources necessary to accomplish it.

By the end of the 1950s, army planners returned operational considerations to the center of attention. Drawing upon their command experiences in Germany, senior army generals developed concepts for flexible combat divisions for the Cold War environment. Eventually, Clyde Eddleman emerged as the crucial figure in advocating the Reorganization Objective Army Division (ROAD), a unit that closely resembled the Bundeswehr combat division, which had recently been introduced. As a result, design of the new division was well advanced by the time John F. Kennedy entered the White House. It seemed suitable for the new strategy of Flexible Response. ROAD was based on the building-block principle, organized around three brigade headquarters to which a variable number of maneuver battalions could be attached. Thus, armored, airborne, mechanized, and infantry divisions could be tailored specifically to the strategic, operational, or tactical need. This was a significant step in the direction of creating general-purpose forces. It fell short of the expectations in political circles, largely because the danger of nuclear war in Europe continued to dictate the emphasis of army doctrine on large-scale conventional and tactical nuclear war. Ultimately, it was necessary to settle upon fixed structures with set numbers of maneuver battalions per division, thus negating the greatest inherent strength of ROAD.

Maxwell Taylor's most significant contribution to the Cold War army was not the initiation of reform of the combat division but the changes in national and alliance strategy that he helped to bring about. Under the nuclear-deterrence strategy of Massive Retaliation, the army had found its utility questioned, and its share of the defense budget declined in comparison to that of the air force. Army leaders could not publicly oppose the strategic concepts of the White House and the Defense Department without questioning the principle of civilian control of the military. Yet Taylor discovered that it was possible to uphold the principle while challenging the administration's perception of reality. His argument that the rapid approach of nuclear parity required greater flexibility and a deterrent for lesser forms of war than all-out nuclear exchange slowly won over his colleagues among the service chiefs, with the notable exception of the air force. His call for a strategy of Flexible Response, publicized shortly upon his retirement from the post of army chief of staff, won him the favor of the political opposition and eventually brought him into the inner circle of the Kennedy administration. The army, however, quickly discovered that the pendulum of strategic choices had swung too far. The service had found Massive Retaliation and its emphasis on strategic nuclear weapons unrealistic, but it also questioned the viability of conventional-war concepts that were embraced by government officials in the 1960s.

Army leadership noted that the strategic environment had not changed dramatically. The ideal army could indeed fulfill the commitment to NATO and maintain forces to intervene in local conflicts in the Third World, even if they took on the scale of the Korean or Vietnam wars. In reality, however, the generals knew that the means to do so were not available and would not be forthcoming. Thus, they maintained the emphasis on the deterrence of limited conventional and nuclear war in Europe, despite the theoretical capability to alter ROAD divisions according to the environment. Maxwell Taylor's warning that preparedness for large-scale war in Europe did not necessarily imply readiness for less intensive forms of warfare was proven correct by the course of events in Vietnam. Critically, the army had failed to adjust its tactical doctrine to antiguerrilla and counterinsurgency warfare. This was not mere oversight. It was impossible to do so without weakening the deterrent posture in Germany. In the 1960s, the army discovered that it could not function as both a territorial deterrent and a power projection force at the same time.

The defeat in Vietnam should not be blamed entirely on the lack of preparedness of the army to engage the enemy at hand. The war was not primarily a military conflict, and it remains unclear how it could have been won militarily. The United States never developed a strategy to address the issues that were central to the insurgency in South Vietnam and failed to separate insurgent and North Vietnamese military forces from the population at large. In essence, South Vietnam failed to build and sustain a South Vietnamese society. The army's own postwar defense, however, centered on the argument that the war had indeed been winnable and that it was the limitations imposed by the Johnson and Nixon administrations that prevented the U.S. military from doing so. This argument may have served its purpose as the army went through nearly an entire decade of recovery from the damage caused by the war, but it was a misleading rationalization of defeat. At heart, army generals must have realized that their prewar premonitions and their emphasis on Seventh Army as the most important fighting organization of the United States had been validated.

In a different sense, defeat was a blessing. It forced the army, now an all-volunteer force, to reconsider its tactical and operational conception of warfare. More important, it allowed full concentration on the defense of Western Europe, as military intervention at the periphery of the Cold War was no longer fashionable. As a result, the training and doctrine command (TRADOC) was created to rebuild the post-Vietnam army from the ground up. Generals William E. DePuy and Donn A. Starry recognized that the Arab-Israeli war of 1973 offered useful insight into advances in Soviet weapons technology, particularly in the field of armor. It was also recognized that the Soviets had perfected concepts of deep battle and operational art that had been under consideration since the 1920s. To counter Soviet numerical superiority and the imposing tank forces of the Warsaw Pact, TRADOC stressed the significance of the first battle and the extended battlefield that integrated frontline and enemy rear area and introduced the concept of Air-Land Battle, the first U.S. Army doctrine that emphasized operational art rather than grand tactics. It was at this point, in 1982, that the main threads of the transition—mission, technology, structure of the combat division, and operational doctrine—came together at last.

The transition process of the Cold War army was defined by external as well as internal pressures and considerations. The evolving strategies of the United States and NATO, and related budgetary policies, have been treated as the most visible phenomenon, but this was merely of political concern for army leadership. It did not alter fundamental operational concepts or the sense of purpose of the service. Nuclear weapons forced the army to adapt its mission to realities of the Cold War. This led to an emphasis on deterrence rather than on war fighting. It also caused the army to look upon a specific kind of deterrence in Europe as the most important reason for being. It did not fundamentally alter tactical or operational conceptions prior to the Vietnam War. Army transformation in the decade between 1955 and 1965 failed in the area of doctrine. The groundbreaking changes did not come until after the defeat in Vietnam. Given the mind-set of army leaders and the political and strategic circumstances of the early Cold War, it proved impossible to create operational doctrine to match the army's mission. Internally, the army understood its task to be the deterrence of limited types of war in Europe, but expressing so in public—by way of doctrinal changes—would have led to serious questions by political masters, who favored general-purpose forces that could operate outside of Europe when requested. Consequently, it was only after the nation turned away from direct interventions in the Third World that the army was able to focus its doctrine fully on the tactical and operational situation expected in a European war against the bulk of Warsaw Pact armies. The army of the 1980s was probably no more capable of operating against unconventional enemies than the army of the 1960s had been, but this was of little significance because the strategic dilemma of several global missions that required vastly different forces and doctrines had been suppressed.

Throughout the transition process, the army was greatly influenced by developments in Europe. Officers serving in Seventh Army cooperated closely with German armed forces. German corps were assigned to Seventh Army and joint maneuvers were conducted. Consequently, a degree of interoperability emerged out of practical concerns. The German divisional structure, featuring brigades and a great degree of mechanization, appealed to American commanders. As a result, the U.S. Army adopted the German combat division in 1960 and 1961, with only minor adjustments necessitated by global considerations. This was done despite the lack of armored vehicles, which critically hampered the effectiveness of the mechanized divisions. That problem was exacerbated by the requirements and cost of the Vietnam War, which prevented successful German-American cooperation in the development of main battle tanks and IFVs.

Tactical and operational doctrine was influenced accordingly by developments in Germany. In the 1950s, U.S. Army tactical doctrine closely resembled French concepts of the world wars. A greater degree of mechanization, however, allowed army planners to consider mobile defense and quick counterattacks in a more favorable light. The fundamental problems were the numerical superiority of enemy ground forces and the uncertainty about the use and effect of tactical nuclear weapons. Dispersion, mobility, and flexibility became the watchwords of the day, but the U.S. Army remained wedded to the application of massive firepower on a clearly defined battlefield as the fundamental principle of warfare. The reorientation toward the defense of Europe during the army's recovery from Vietnam changed this dynamic. In studying the lessons of the Yom Kippur War, army leaders realized that concepts of time, space, and lethality on the conventional battlefield had changed dramatically. Military intelligence added a clearer picture of Soviet capabilities and operational intentions. It was recognized that the enemy remained superior in numbers and had a vast arsenal of tanks and armored vehicles. The Soviets had perfected concepts of deep battle and operational art that had been considered since the decades prior to World War II. As a result, TRADOC developed doctrine that was geared at combating specific Soviet tactics and operations. To do so, DePuy and Starry, the principal authors of the 1976 and 1982 editions of Field Manual 100-5, turned to German operational doctrine. DePuy acknowledged that Active Defense was an attempt to adapt German concepts of mechanized warfare to the force structure of the U.S. Army. The result was not universally accepted. It was the beginning of a process of doctrinal change rather than its culmination.

Donn Starry, who had written several chapters on Active Defense, took the concept to V Corps, which he commanded in 1976 and 1977. He discovered that the emphasis on the first battle had to be altered in terms of time and space. Operations of the second, third, and even fourth echelon of Soviet forces had to be countered before they could engage American main forces in battle. Deep battle needed to be fought aggressively with strikes into the rear of the enemy. Starry resolved to refine tactical doctrine and elevate it to the level of operations. For this, he found precedent in pre–World War II Reichswehr doctrine of the 1920s and early 1930s. This in turn, of course, had been at the core of West German doctrinal considerations all along, as the architects of the Bundeswehr had gained their first command experience long before World War II. The amalgamation of pre- and postwar West German operational doctrine with American tactical and operational conceptions and necessities eventually led to the adoption of AirLand Battle doctrine in 1982. Previously, only fragments of German thinking had been adopted by the American armed forces. From the mid-1970s, the German army became the model for a new American army. Operational art, once a concept that existed only in the Soviet Union and to some extent in Germany, became a mainstay of the American military. Given the relative comparability of their strategic and operational circumstances, it is no surprise that American armed forces could learn much from the German and Israeli military experience. It is to their great credit that they did.

In addressing the history of the U.S. Army in the Cold War era, this book has raised questions about the history of the Cold War itself. It no longer seems fruitful to consider national policies and strategies isolated from alliances. Since the end of the Cold War, political, social, intellectual, economic, and cultural historians have investigated the dynamics of relationships in both camps of the Cold War divide. This study shows that NATO was not entirely dominated by American policy. NATO strategy did not always conform to the strategy of the United States, and the debates of Flexible Response throughout the 1960s contributed to a crisis within the alliance. But the need to maintain a strong deterrent overcame centrifugal forces that threatened to separate Western Europe from the United States, and Germany and France from Great Britain. The U.S. Army was strengthened greatly by what it learned and experienced in Germany. By the 1980s, it was a force that resembled more closely the Bundeswehr than the U.S. Army of World War II.

The Cold War U.S. Army was born not in rapid transformation, as Maxwell Taylor had hoped in the mid-1950s, but in a gradual process of transition. Taylor had assumed that changes to the structure of combat organizations and the introduction of modern conventional and nuclear weapon systems would lead to a radically different operational and doctrinal concept. But the pressure to deploy forces in Europe as well as outside of Europe negated the effect of structural change and locked doctrine in place. Only after the defeat in Vietnam, and the resulting changes in strategic outlook, did army leaders succeed in creating new operational doctrine for a new generation of conventional and nuclear weapon systems. The global nature of the Cold War appeared to require general-purpose forces, but the U.S. military was never capable of providing them. The defeat in Vietnam was a strong indicator of the weakness to project power into the Third World. The defeat of Soviet arms in Afghanistan served as a similar example. But while the protracted war in Afghanistan contributed to the collapse of the

Soviet Union, America's defeat in Vietnam did little to impede ultimate victory in the Cold War. Moreover, the deterrence of general war strongly implied that the choice of U.S. Army leaders to create and maintain a fighting force primarily designed for war in Germany was successful despite the initial failure to transform.

Beyond reevaluating U.S.-European defense relations and army transformation, this book considers the value and effect of military institutions in peacetime. John Keegan, the eminent military historian, has concluded that an army is defined by its actions on the field of battle.[1] The opposite is also true: Its character is determined by how it trains and thinks in peacetime. A large body of literature has emerged that discusses military doctrine, technology, strategy, and political culture in the interwar period.[2] A similar integrative effort is needed to address the history of the Cold War more comprehensively. Ultimately, the Cold War was a global competition for access to markets, resources, skilled labor, and strategically placed military bases. But Western Europe, with its industrial societies and vast economies, was the prize. Possession of Western Europe was the decisive factor in the Cold War. As a consequence, nuclear war could have resulted most easily from conflict in Europe. There, deterrence, the primary mission of the army, and containment, the critical objective of American strategy, were closely related. But in Vietnam they were not. The failure of containment on the periphery of the Cold War did not lead to general war or to a fundamental change in the socioeconomic and military balance of power. The army contributed greatly to the success of deterrence and of the containment strategy. The wars in Korea, Vietnam, Afghanistan, and elsewhere serve to remind us that the outcome of the Cold War was defined by more than the sum of its military battles.

Appendixes

Appendix 1. Army Strength by Region, 1951–1972

Year	Continental United States	Far East (Japan and Korea)	Vietnam	Europe	Total
1951	956,187	330,752		117,501	1,529,724
1952	857,248	343,726		250,651	1,594,693
1953	796,000	353,800		236,400	1,532,000
1954	739,806	295,069		247,912	1,404,598
1955	622,590	131,565		252,191	1,109,296
1956	616,547	98,617		239,558	1,025,778
1957	590,881	86,508		231,599	997,994
1958	536,250	56,333		224,155	898,925
1959	519,881	50,501		225,408	861,964
1960	526,464	53,962		225,099	873,078
1961	501,748	60,322		230,116	858,622
1962	652,918	53,978		277,583	1,066,404
1963	583,981	69,323		251,066	975,916
1964	581,009	80,559		235,612	973,238
1965	598,482	89,063		234,743	969,066
1966	696,263	66,894	149,604	204,784	1,199,784
1967	766,414	69,336	288,623	219,546	1,442,498
1968	855,011	71,591	351,024	192,963	1,570,343
1969	804,188	70,873	368,992	169,268	1,512,169
1970	684,239	60,740	361,838	176,697	1,322,549
1971	624,463	35,152	175,703	164,758	1,230,549
1972	488,390	37,239	71,048	172,307	801,081

Source: Courtesy of Dr. Robert S. Rush, Center of Military History.

Appendix 2. USAREUR Personnel Strength, 1945–1991

Date	Authorized	Actual
30 June 1945	Unknown	1,893,197
30 June 1946	300,000	289,896
30 June 1947	117,000	104,316
31 December 1948	93,856	90,740
31 December 1949	82,412	83,394
31 December 1950	88,593	86,146
31 December 1951	222,727	231,651
31 December 1952	258,869	252,137
30 June 1954	242,956	250,298
30 June 1955	238,428	245,675
30 June 1956	240,048	248,389
30 June 1957	230,219	232,686
30 June 1958	229,925	225,019
30 June 1959	226,039	225,373
30 June 1960	226,056	226,212
30 June 1961	225,732	232,658
30 June 1962	273,377	277,342
30 June 1963	253,170	251,615
30 June 1964	236,407	239,640
30 June 1965	229,258	235,330
30 June 1966	223,649	209,773
30 June 1967	222,821	222,566
30 June 1968	206,455	195,526
30 June 1969	185,668	180,895
30 June 1970	188,368	177,912
31 December 1970	189,105	169,144
31 December 1971	185,612	177,640
31 December 1972	182,599	182,843
31 December 1973	182,918	175,055
31 December 1974	180,708	176,568
31 December 1975	179,585	179,304
31 December 1976	179,855	182,096
31 December 1977	181,971	191,500
31 December 1978	193,106	198,664
31 December 1979	196,564	202,604
31 December 1980	198,514	199,146
31 December 1981	197,540	198,139
31 December 1982	199,464	200,584
31 December 1983	202,535	195,212
31 December 1984	198,345	200,544
31 December 1985	196,253	193,871
31 December 1986	197,616	194,567

31 December 1987	196,141	194,500
31 December 1988	197,092	197,147
31 December 1989	197,364	195, 989
31 December 1990	124,950	115,077
31 December 1991	140,993	143,479

Source: Courtesy of Headquarters, USAREUR, Historian's Office, Heidelberg, Germany.

Appendix 3. U.S. Army Force Structure, 1953–1982

Year	Divisions	Infantry	Armor	Airborne	Air Assault	Mech.	Other
1953	20	16	2	2	0	0	0
1954	19	14	3	2	0	0	0
1955	20	14	4	2	0	0	0
1956	19	12	4	3	0	0	0
1957	15	9	3	3	0	0	0
1958	15	9	3	3	0	0	0
1959	15	10	3	2	0	0	0
1960	14	9	3	2	0	0	0
1961	14	9	3	2	0	0	0
1962	18	7	5	2	0	4	0
1963	16	6	4	2	0	4	0
1964	16	6	4	2	0	4	0
1965	16	5	4	2	1	4	0
1966	17	6	4	2	1	4	0
1967	17	6	4	2	1	4	0
1968	19	8	4	2	1	4	0
1969	18	7	4	1	2	4	0
1970	16	5	4	1	2	4	0
1971	13	3	3	1	2	4	0
1972	13	3	3	1	1	4	1 TRICAP
1973	13	3	3	1	1	4	1 TRICAP
1974	13	3	4	1	1	4	0
1975	14	4	4	1	1	4	0
1976	16	5	4	1	1	5	0
1977	16	5	4	1	1	5	0
1978	16	5	4	1	1	5	0
1979	16	4	4	1	1	6	0
1980	16	4	4	1	1	6	0
1981	16	4	4	1	1	6	0
1982	16	4	4	1	1	6	0
1983	16	4	4	1	1	6	0
1984	16	4	4	1	1	6	0
1985	17	4	4	1	1	6	1 Motorized
1986	18	5	4	1	1	6	1 Motorized
1987	18	5	4	1	1	6	1 Motorized
1988	18	5	4	1	1	6	1 Motorized
1989	18	5	4	1	1	6	1 Motorized
1990	18	5	4	1	1	6	1 Motorized
1991	16	5	3	1	1	6	0

Source: Hawkins and Carafano, *Prelude to Army XXI*, A-1, A-2.

Appendix 4. U.S. Army, Europe, and Seventh Army Order of Battle (Select Years and Major Formations)

1951:
V Corps
1st Inf Div, 4th Inf Div, 2nd Armd Div, 2nd Armd Cav Regt, 6th Armd Cav Regt, 14th Armd Cav Regt

1952:
V Corps
1st Inf Div, 4th Inf Div, 2nd Armd Div, 14th Armd Cav Regt
VII Corps
28th Inf Div, 43rd Inf Div, 2nd Armd Cav Regt, 6th Armd Cav Regt

31 December 1953:

V Corps (Frankfurt)	VII Corps (Stuttgart)
1st Inf Div	28th Inf Div
4th Inf Div	43rd Inf Div
2nd Armd Div	2nd Armd Cav Regt
14th Armd Cav Regt	6th Armd Cav Regt
19th Armd Cav Gp	

Forces earmarked for assignment on mobilization:
350th Inf Regimental Combat Team (from Austria, Mobilization day); 351st Inf Regt (from Trieste, Mobilization day); 44th Inf Div (from U.S., M+30 days); 3 Inf Divs (from U.S., M+31 days); 3 Inf Divs (from Far East, M+31 days); 1st Armd Div (from U.S., M+30 days); 82nd Airborne Div (from U.S., M+30 days); 1 Airborne Div (from U.S., M+31 days); 2 Armd Cav Regts (from U.S., M+31 days); 1 Airborne RCT (from U.S., M+31 days); 1 Inf Regimental Combat Team (from Caribbean, M+31 days)

Source: JSPC 876/814, 18 February 1954, *Report by the Joint Strategic Plans Committee to the Joint Chiefs of Staff on Order of Battle Report for Earmarked Forces—Submission of Report*, Annex "A": *Army Order of Battle Report (SACEUR) as of 31 December 1953*, Section I: *Land Forces Order of Battle*, Part I: *Status Report as of 31 December 1953*. Joint Chiefs of Staff, Geographic File 1954–56, CCS092 Western Europe (3-12-48), Sec. 264, RG 218, NA.

31 December 1954:

V Corps (Frankfurt)	VII Corps (Stuttgart)
1st Inf Div	5th Inf Div
4th Inf Div	9th Inf Div
2nd Armd Div	2nd Armd Cav Regt
14th Armd Cav Regt	6th Armd Cav Regt
19th Armd Cav Gp	

Forces earmarked for assignment on mobilization:
350th Inf Regimental Combat Team (from Austria, D-day); 2nd Inf Div (U.S., D+30); 3 Inf Divs (U.S., D+91); 1 Inf Div (Pacific, D+91); 1st Armd Div (U.S., D+30); 1 Armd

Appendix 4. ***Continued***

Div (U.S., D+91); 82 Abn Div (U.S., D+30); 1 Abn Div (U.S., D+91); 3rd Armd Cav Regt (U.S., D+60); 1 Armd Gp (U.S., D+91); 1 Armd Cav Regt (U.S., D+91)

Source: JSPC 876/938, 12 January 1955, *Report by the Joint Strategic Plans Committee to the Joint Chiefs of Staff on Order of Battle Report for Earmarked Forces,* Annex "A": *Army Order of Battle Report (SACEUR) as of 31 December 1954,* Section I: *Land Forces Order of Battle,* Part I: *Status Report as of 31 December 1954.* Joint Chiefs of Staff, Geographic File 1954–56, CGS092 Western Europe (3-12-48), Sec. 2, RG 218, NA.

31 December 1955:

V Corps (Frankfurt)
10th Inf Div
4th Inf Div
2nd Armd Div
14th Armd Cav Regt
4th Armd Gp

VII Corps (Stuttgart-Möhringen)
5th Inf Div
9th Inf Div
3rd Armd Cav Regt
6th Armd Cav Regt

Forces earmarked for assignment on mobilization:
1st Armd Div (U.S., D+30); 1st Inf Div (U.S., D+30); 3rd Inf Div (U.S., D+30); 2nd Armd Cav Regt (U.S., D+60); 1 Armd Gp (U.S., D+91); 1 Armd Cav Regt (U.S., D+91); 82nd Abn Div (U.S., D+120); 4th Armd Div (U.S., D+150); 25th Inf Div (Pacific, D+150); 5 Inf Divs (U.S., D+180); 1 Armd Div (U.S., D+180)

Source: JCS 2073/1223, 30 January 1956, Report by the Joint Strategic Plans Committee to the Joint Chiefs of Staff on *Order of Battle Report to SACEUR for U.S. Forces Assigned, Earmarked for Assignment, and Earmarked for Assignment on Mobilization (as of 31 December 1955).* Records of the Joint Chiefs of Staff, Geographic File 1954–56, CGS092 Western Europe (3-12-48) (2), Sec. 49, RG 218, NA.

31 December 1956:

V Corps (Frankfurt)
10th Inf Div
2nd Armd Div
3rd Armd Div
4th Armd Gp
14th Armd Cav Regt

VII Corps (Stuttgart-Möhringen)
8th Inf Div
11th Abn Div
3rd Armd Cav Regt
6th Armd Cav Regt

Forces earmarked for assignment on mobilization:
1st Armd Div (U.S., D+30); 1st Inf Div (U.S., D+30); 4th Inf Div (U.S., D+30); 25th Inf Div (Pacific, D+60); 2nd Armd Cav Regt (U.S., D+60); 4th Armd Div (U.S., D+120); 82nd Abn Div (U.S., D+120); 3rd Inf Div (U.S., D+150); 4 Inf Divs (National Guard, D+180); 1 Armd Div (National Guard, D+180)

Source: JCS 2073/1346, 11 January 1957, Report by the Joint Strategic Plans Committee to the Joint Chiefs of Staff on *Order of Battle Report to SACEUR of U.S. Forces Assigned, Earmarked for Assignment, and Earmarked for Assignment on Mobilization (as of*

31 December 1956). Records of the Joint Chiefs of Staff, Geographic File 1957, CCS092 Western Europe (3-12-48) (2), Sec. 71, RG 218, NA.

31 December 1957:

V Corps (Frankfurt)
10th Inf Div
3rd Armd Div
4th Armd Div
4th Armd Gp
14th Armd Cav Regt

VII Corps (Stuttgart-Möhringen)
8th Inf Div
11th Abn Div
3rd Armd Cav Regt
11th Armd Cav Regt

Forces earmarked for assignment on mobilization:
1st Inf Div (U.S., D+30); 4th Inf Div (U.S., D+30); 101st Abn Div (U.S., D+30); 2nd Armd Cav Regt (U.S., D+60); 82nd Abn Div (U.S., D+90); 2nd Armd Div (U.S., D+120); 3rd Inf Div (D+150); 5 Inf Divs (National Guard, D+180); 1 Armd Div (National Guard, D+180)

Source: JCS 2073/1502, 8 January 1958, Report by the Joint Strategic Plans Committee to the Joint Chiefs of Staff on *Order of Battle Report to SACEUR of U.S. Forces Assigned, Earmarked for Assignment, and Earmarked for Assignment on Mobilization (as of 31 December 1957)*. Records of the Joint Chiefs of Staff, Geographic File 1958, CCS092 Western Europe (3-12-48) (2), Sec. 95, RG 218, NA.

1 January 1959:

V Corps (Frankfurt)
3rd Inf Div
3rd Armd Div
4th Armd Div
4th Armd Gp
14th Armd Cav Regt

VII Corps (Stuttgart-Möhringen)
8th Inf Div
24th Inf Div
2nd Armd Cav Regt
11th Armd Cav Regt

Forces earmarked for assignment on mobilization:
4th Inf Div (U.S., D+30); 82nd Abn Div (U.S., D+30); 101st Abn Div (U.S., D+30); 3rd Armd Cav Regt (U.S., D+30); 1st Inf Div (U.S., D+120); 2nd Armd Div (U.S., D+150); 2nd Inf Div (U.S., D+150); 2 Inf Divs (National Guard, D+150); 3 Inf Divs (National Guard, D+180); 1 Armd Div (National Guard, D+180)

Source: JCSM-49-59, Memorandum for the Secretary of Defense, 11 February 1959, *Order of Battle Report to SACEUR of U.S. Forces Assigned, Earmarked for Assignment, and Earmarked for Assignment on Mobilization as of 1 January 1959*. Records of the Joint Chiefs of Staff, Central Decimal File 1959, CCS9051/3400 Allied Commander Europe (11 February 1959), Box 113, RG 218, NA.

1 January 1960:

V Corps (Frankfurt)
3rd Inf Div
8th Inf Div
3rd Armd Div

VII Corps (Stuttgart-Möhringen)
24th Inf Div
4th Armd Div
2nd Armd Cav Regt

Appendix 4. ***Continued***

4th Armd Gp	11th Armd Cav Regt
14th Armd Cav Regt	

Forces earmarked for assignment on mobilization:
4th Inf Div (U.S., D+30); 82nd Abn Div (U.S., D+30); 101st Abn Div (U.S., D+30); 3rd Armd Cav Regt (U.S., D+30); 6th Armd Cav Regt (U.S., D+90); 1st Inf Div (U.S., D+120); 2nd Armd Div (U.S., D+150); 2nd Inf Div (U.S., D+150); 2 Inf Divs (National Guard, D+150); 3 Inf Divs (National Guard, D+180); 1 Armd Div (National Guard, D+180)

Source: JCSM-106-60, Memorandum for the U.S. Commander in Chief, Europe, 29 January 1960, *Order of Battle Report to SACEUR for Assigned Forces, Earmarked Forces, and Forces Earmarked for Assignment on Mobilization as of 1 January 1960*. Records of the Joint Chiefs of Staff, Central Decimal File 1960, CCS9051/3400 Allied Commander Europe (12 January 1960), Sec. 1, Box 66, RG 218, NA.

31 December 1963:

V Corps (Frankfurt)	VII Corps (Stuttgart-Möhringen)
3rd Inf Div	24th Inf Div
8th Inf Div	4th Armd Div
3rd Armd Div	2nd Armd Cav Regt
3rd Armd Cav Regt	11th Armd Cav Regt
14th Armd Cav Regt	

Source: Headquarters, USAREUR, 31 December 1963, *Station List, United States Army, Europe*. Accessible on the Web site of the USAREUR Military History Office, Heidelberg.

30 September 1965:

V Corps (Frankfurt)	VII Corps (Stuttgart-Möhringen)
8th Inf Div	3rd Inf Div
3rd Armd Div	24th Inf Div
3rd Armd Cav Regt (directly under Seventh Army)	4th Armd Div
14th Armd Cav Regt	2nd Armd Cav Regt

Source: Headquarters, USAREUR, 30 September 1965, *Station List, United States Army, Europe*. Accessible on the Web site of the USAREUR Military History Office, Heidelberg.

30 September 1966:

V Corps (Frankfurt)	VII Corps (Stuttgart-Möhringen)
8th Inf Div	3rd Inf Div
3rd Armd Div	24th Inf Div
3rd Armd Cav Regt (directly under Seventh Army)	4th Armd Div
14th Armd Cav Regt	2nd Armd Cav Regt

Source: Headquarters, USAREUR, 30 September 1966, *Station List, United States Army, Europe*. Accessible on the Web site of the USAREUR Military History Office, Heidelberg.

31 December 1967:

V Corps (Frankfurt)	VII Corps (Stuttgart-Möhringen)
8th Inf Div	3rd Inf Div
3rd Armd Div	24th Inf Div
3rd Armd Cav Regt (directly under Seventh Army)	4th Armd Div
14th Armd Cav Regt	2nd Armd Cav Regt

Source: Headquarters, USAREUR, 31 December 1967, *Station List, United States Army, Europe*. Accessible on the Web site of the USAREUR Military History Office, Heidelberg.

31 March 1973:

V Corps (Frankfurt)	VII Corps (Stuttgart-Möhringen)
8th Inf Div	3rd Inf Div
3rd Armd Div	1st Armd Div
11th Armd Cav Regt	1st Inf Div Fwd (and REFORGER)
	2nd Armd Cav Regt
	3rd Armd Cav Regt (REFORGER)

Source: Headquarters, USAREUR, 9 April 1973, *Station List, United States Army, Europe*. Accessible on the Web site of the USAREUR Military History Office, Heidelberg.

Appendix 5. U.S. Army Combat Divisions

For detailed tables of organization of U.S. Army divisions in the 1950s to 1980s in graphic form, see John B. Wilson, *Maneuver and Firepower: The Evolution of Divisions and Separate Brigades* (Washington, D.C.: U.S. Army, Center of Military History, 1998), chaps. 9–14, http://www.history.army.mil/books/Lineage/M-F/index.htm.

Notes

Additional Abbreviations Used in the Notes

BA-MA	Bundesarchiv-Militärarchiv, Freiburg, Germany
DDEL	Dwight D. Eisenhower Presidential Library, Abilene, KS
ESECS	European Security Study
FM 100-5	Department of the Army, *Field Manual 100-5: Field Service Regulations—Operations* (Washington, DC: Department of the Army, 1949–)
FRUS (year, volume)	*Foreign Relations of the United States* (Washington, DC: Government Printing Office)
GCML	George C. Marshall Research Library, Lexington, VA
HSTL	Harry S. Truman Presidential Library, Independence, MO
JFKL	John F. Kennedy Presidential Library, Boston
LBJL	Lyndon B. Johnson Presidential Library, Austin, TX
MACOV	*Mechanized and Armor Combat Operations in Vietnam*
MHI	U.S. Army Military History Institute, Carlisle Barracks, PA
NA	National Archives, Washington, DC
Norstad Papers	Lauris M. Norstad Papers, DDEL
NSA	National Security Archive, Washington, DC
NSC	National Security Council
PHP	Parallel History Project, Switzerland
Ridgway Papers	Matthew B. Ridgway Papers, MHI
Taylor Papers, NDU	Maxwell D. Taylor Papers, Digitized Collection, National Defense University, Washington, DC
TOE	Table of Organization and Equipment

Introduction

1. For a cultural history of U.S. military forces since World War II, see Adrian R. Lewis, *The American Culture of War: The History of U.S. Military Forces from World War II to Operation Iraqi Freedom* (New York: Routledge, 2007). The most comprehensive history of the U.S. Army during the Cold War remains Russell F. Weigley, *History of the United States Army* (rev. ed.; Bloomington: Indiana University Press, 1984), pp. 483–592.

2. The best study of conventional force levels in relation to NATO strategy is John S. Duffield, *Power Rules: The Evolution of NATO's Conventional Force Posture* (Stanford, CA: Stanford University Press, 1995). Duffield's political analysis is exhaustive, but he does not consider particular military questions of doctrine, institutional development, or technology.

3. Andrew F. Krepinevich Jr., *The Army and Vietnam* (Baltimore: Johns Hopkins University Press, 1986), argues that this decision was based on tradition and the desire of generals to retain the glory of past wars, but he viewed the Vietnam War in isolation from the Cold War and did not consider the legitimate need for a different force structure and doctrine in Europe. Drawing on Krepinevich's discussion, Lewis, *The American Culture of War*, pp. 226–227, agrees and concludes that constraints of institutional culture kept the army from developing proper counterinsurgency doctrine.

4. Among the best studies on nuclear deterrence with emphasis on Europe are Frederic Bozo, *Two Strategies for Europe: deGaulle, the United States, and the Atlantic Alliance* (Lanham, MD: Rowman and Littlefield, 2001); Bernard Brodie, *Strategy in the Missile Age* (Princeton, NJ: Princeton University Press, 1959); Lawrence Freedman, *The Evolution of Nuclear Strategy* (New York: St. Martin's, 1989); Beatrice Heuser, *NATO, Britain, France, and the FRG: Nuclear Strategies and Forces for Europe, 1949–2000* (Houndmills: Macmillan, 1997); Beatrice Heuser and Robert O'Neill, eds., *Securing Peace in Europe, 1945–1962* (New York: St. Martin's, 1992); Catherine McArdle Kelleher, *Germany and the Politics of Nuclear Weapons* (New York: Columbia University Press, 1975); Herman Kahn, *On Thermonuclear War* (Princeton, NJ: Princeton University Press, 1960); David Alan Rosenberg, "The Origins of Overkill: Nuclear Weapons and American Strategy, 1945–1960," *International Security* 7, no. 4 (Spring 1983): 3–71; David N. Schwartz, *NATO's Nuclear Dilemmas* (Washington, DC: Brookings Institution, 1983); and Robert Wampler, *NATO Strategic Planning and Nuclear Weapons, 1950–1957* (Nuclear History Program, Occasional Paper 6; University of Maryland: Center for International Security Studies, 1990). A comprehensive discussion of the nuclear strategists of the early Cold War period has been provided by Lawrence Freedman, "The First Two Generations of Nuclear Strategists," in *Makers of Modern Strategy: From Machiavelli to the Nuclear Age*, edited by Peter Paret (Princeton, NJ: Princeton University Press, 1986), pp. 735–778.

5. See, for instance, Richard K. Betts, *Conventional Deterrence: Predictive Uncertainty and Policy Confidence: Compound Deterrence vs. No-First-Use—What's Wrong Is What's Right* (Washington, DC: Brookings Institution, 1985); Thomas Boyd-Carpenter, *Conventional Deterrence into the 1990s* (New York: St. Martin's, 1989); Alexander L. George and Richard Smoke, *Deterrence in American Foreign Policy: Theory and Practice* (New York: Columbia University Press, 1974); James Reed Golden, Asa A. Clark, and Bruce E. Arlinghaus, *Conventional Deterrence: Alternatives for European Defense* (Lexington, MA: Lexington Books, 1984); Paul K. Huth, *Extended Deterrence and the Prevention of War* (New Haven, CT: Yale University Press, 1988); and John R. Mearsheimer, *Conventional Deterrence* (Ithaca, NY: Cornell University Press, 1983). None of these works pays much attention to the particular case of Central Europe in the first three decades of the Cold War.

6. An exception is Glenn H. Snyder, *Deterrence and Defense: Toward a Theory of*

National Security (Princeton, NJ: Princeton University Press, 1961), who does consider both nuclear and conventional deterrence in the context of NATO and the 1950s.

7. For the scholarship on limited and conventional war in the nuclear age, see, for instance, Michael Carver, "Conventional Warfare in the Nuclear Age," in Paret, *Makers of Modern Strategy*, pp. 779–814; Seymour J. Deitchman, *Limited War and American Defense Policy* (Cambridge, MA: MIT Press, 1964); Christopher M. Gacek, *The Logic of Force: The Dilemma of Limited War in American Foreign Policy* (New York: Columbia University Press, 1994); Morton H. Halperin, *Limited War in the Nuclear Age* (New York: John Wiley, 1963); Otto Heilbrunn, *Conventional Warfare in the Nuclear Age* (New York: Frederick A. Praeger, 1965); Henry Kissinger, *Nuclear Weapons and Foreign Policy* (Garden City, NY: Doubleday, 1957); and Robert Endicott Osgood, *Limited War: The Challenge to American Strategy* (Chicago: University of Chicago Press, 1957).

8. Maxwell Taylor, *The Uncertain Trumpet* (New York: Harper Brothers, 1959).

9. Lewis, *The American Culture of War*, pp. 201–227, discusses the different visions of how to fight limited wars that were held during the Kennedy and Johnson administrations by senior political leaders and army commanders.

10. Doctrine, in a broad sense, has been defined by army historian Paul Herbert as "an approved, shared idea about the conduct of warfare that undergirds an army's planning, organization, training, leadership style, tactics, weapons, and equipment." Paul Herbert, *Deciding What Has to Be Done: General William E. DePuy and the 1976 Edition of FM 100-5, Operations* (Leavenworth Paper No. 16; Ft. Leavenworth, KS: Command and General Staff College, 1988), p. 3.

11. For a theoretical model of punctuated equilibrium and evolution in nature as well as its recent application to historical studies, see Niles Eldredge and Stephen Jay Gould, "Punctuated Equilibria: An Alternative to Phyletic Gradualism," in *Models in Paleobiology*, edited by T. J. M. Schopf (San Francisco: Freeman, Cooper, 1972); Stephen Jay Gould, *The Structure of Evolutionary Theory* (Cambridge, MA: Harvard University Press, 2002); and Clifford J. Rogers, "Review Essay: The Field and the Forge," *Journal of Military History* 68, no. 4 (October 2004): 1233–1239.

12. Romie L. Brownlee and William J. Mullen III, *Changing an Army: An Oral History of General William E. DePuy* (Washington, DC: U.S. Army Center of Military History, 1986); Herbert, *Deciding What Has to Be Done*; Jonathan House, *Combined Arms Warfare in the Twentieth Century* (Lawrence: University Press of Kansas, 2001); John L. Romjue, *From Active Defense to AirLand Battle: The Development of Army Doctrine, 1973–1982* (Fort Monroe, VA: U.S. Army Training and Doctrine Command, Historical Office, 1984); Donn A. Starry, "A Tactical Evolution: FM 100-5," *Military Review* 58, no. 8 (August 1978): 2–11; Richard M. Swain, "AirLand Battle," in *Camp Colt to Desert Storm: The History of U.S. Armored Forces*, edited by George F. Hofmann and Donn A. Starry (Lexington: University Press of Kentucky, 1999), pp. 360–402.

13. See also David Alan Rosenberg, "Reality and Responsibility: Power and Process in the Making of United States Nuclear Strategy, 1945–1968," *Journal of Strategic Studies* 9, no. 1 (March 1986): 35–52.

14. Among the most prominent studies of American strategy in the Cold War are Robert R. Bowie and Richard H. Immerman, *Waging Peace: How Eisenhower Shaped an Enduring Cold War Strategy* (Oxford: Oxford University Press, 1998); Saki Dockrill,

Eisenhower's New Look National Security Policy, 1953–1961 (Houndmills: Macmillan, 1996); John Lewis Gaddis, *Strategies of Containment: A Critical Reappraisal of Postwar American National Security Policy* (Oxford: Oxford University Press, 1982); Melvyn P. Leffler, *A Preponderance of Power: National Security, the Truman Administration, and the Cold War* (Stanford, CA: Stanford University Press, 1992); and Marc Trachtenberg, *History and Strategy* (Princeton, NJ: Princeton University Press, 1991).

15. The recognition of operational art as a level of war between strategy and tactics is a fairly recent phenomenon in English-language scholarship. The concept was developed by the Soviets in the 1920s and 1930s. The German military practiced a comparable approach in the World War II era. See, for instance, Robert M. Citino, *The Path to Blitzkrieg: Doctrine and Training in the German Army, 1920–1939* (Boulder, CO: Lynne Rienner, 1999); Robert M. Citino, *Blitzkrieg to Desert Storm: The Evolution of Operational Warfare* (Lawrence: University Press of Kansas, 2004); David Glantz, *Soviet Military Operational Art: In Pursuit of Deep Battle* (London: Frank Cass, 1991); Mary R. Habeck, *Storm of Steel: The Development of Armor Doctrine in Germany and the Soviet Union, 1919–1939* (Ithaca, NY: Cornell University Press, 2003); Richard W. Harrison, *The Russian Way of War: Operational Art, 1904–1940* (Lawrence: University Press of Kansas, 2001); B. J. C. McKercher and Michael E. Hennesy, eds., *The Operational Art: Developments in the Theories of War* (Westport, CT: Praeger, 1996); Shimon Naveh, *In Pursuit of Military Excellence: The Evolution of Operational Theory* (London: Frank Cass, 1997); and R. Clayton Newell, *The Framework of Operational Warfare* (London: Routledge, 1991).

16. For a concise definition of operational art, see Kenneth E. Hamburger, "Operational Art," in *The Oxford Companion to American Military History*, edited by John Whiteclay Chambers II (Oxford: Oxford University Press, 1999), pp. 517–518.

17. For a more comprehensive discussion of the relationship of the German and U.S. armies, see Ingo Trauschweizer, "Learning with an Ally: The U.S. Army and the Bundeswehr in the Cold War," *Journal of Military History* 72, no. 2 (April 2008): 477–508.

18. Among the best works are A. J. Birtle, *Rearming the Phoenix: U.S. Military Assistance to the Federal Republic of Germany, 1950–1960* (New York: Garland, 1991); Hans Ehlert et al., *Die NATO Option*, vol. 3 of *Anfänge westdeutscher Sicherheitspolitik* (Munich: R. Oldenbourg Verlag, 1993); Heuser, *NATO, Britain, France, and the FRG*; Kelleher, *Germany and the Politics of Nuclear Weapons*; David Clay Large, *Germans to the Front: West German Rearmament in the Adenauer Era* (Chapel Hill: University of North Carolina Press, 1996); Robert McGeehan, *The German Rearmament Question: American Diplomacy and European Defense after World War II* (Chicago: University of Illinois Press, 1971); Roger Morgan, *The United States and West Germany 1945–1973: A Study in Alliance Politics* (London: Oxford University Press, 1974); and Hubert Zimmermann, *Money and Security: Troops, Monetary Policy, and West Germany's Relations with the United States and Britain, 1950–1971* (Cambridge: Cambridge University Press; for the German Historical Institute, Washington, DC, 2002).

19. On the opposite side of the argument, John Mueller contends that social, cultural, and intellectual dynamics rather than nuclear deterrence had made war obsolete. John E. Mueller, *Retreat from Doomsday: The Obsolescence of Major War* (New York: Basic Books, 1989). The difficulty of assessing the likelihood of war between the superpowers

is best illustrated by Cold War and disarmament scholar Christoph Bluth. In a single paragraph, he both disavowed and acknowledged the possibility of major war in Europe. He concluded that it "had to be deterred by military means and mitigated by political means." Christoph Bluth, *The Two Germanies and Military Security in Europe* (Houndmills: Palgrave Macmillan, 2002), p. 2.

20. Marc Trachtenberg, *A Constructed Peace: The Making of the European Settlement, 1945–1963* (Princeton, NJ: Princeton University Press, 1999). Trachtenberg claims that the Soviets ultimately tolerated German rearmament because West Germany was to be controlled within the confines of NATO. Vojtech Mastny has recently challenged this argument in his introductory essay "The Warsaw Pact as History," in Vojtech Mastny and Malcolm Byrne, eds., *A Cardboard Castle? An Inside History of the Warsaw Pact, 1955–1991* (Budapest: Central European University Press, 2005), p. 3.

21. Historians have thus far almost entirely ignored USAREUR and Seventh Army. The only comprehensive study has been provided by a political scientist, Daniel J. Nelson, *A History of U.S. Military Forces in Germany* (Boulder, CO: Westview Press, 1987).

22. David Miller, *The Cold War: A Military History* (New York: St. Martin's, 1998), is the rare exception, but his work is essentially journalistic in nature. Norman Friedman, *The Fifty-Year War: Conflict and Strategy in the Cold War* (Annapolis, MD: U.S. Naval Institute Press, 2000), offers a history of strategy but suffers from a somewhat polemic argumentation and overreliance on secondary sources. The pertinent chapters in Russell F. Weigley, *The American Way of War: A History of United States Military Strategy and Policy* (New York: Macmillan, 1973), remain the best work on the subject. Two recent books have opened a new line of inquiry in considering the Cold War and the post–Cold War periods as one era: Andrew J. Bacevich, ed., *The Long War: A New History of U.S. National Security Policy since World War II* (New York: Columbia University Press, 2007); and Lewis, *The American Culture of War.*

23. Among the best military histories of the Korean War are Roy E. Appleman, *South to the Naktong, North to the Yalu: June–November 1950* (Washington, DC: U.S. Army Center of Military History, 1961); Clay Blair, *The Forgotten War: America in Korea, 1950–1953* (New York: Times Books, 1987); Billy C. Mossman, *Ebb and Flow: November 1950–July 1951* (Washington, DC: U.S. Army Center of Military History, 1990); and David Rees, *Korea: The Limited War* (New York: St. Martin's, 1964).The most comprehensive studies on the army in Vietnam are Jeffrey Clarke, *Advice and Support: The Final Years, 1965–1973* (Washington, DC: U.S. Army Center of Military History, 1988); Douglas Kinnard, *The War Managers: American Generals Reflect on Vietnam* (Hanover, NH: University Press of New England, 1977); Krepinevich, *The Army and Vietnam*; Ronald H. Spector, *Advice and Support: The Early Years of the United States Army in Vietnam, 1941–1960* (Washington, DC: U.S. Army Center of Military History, 1983); Shelby L. Stanton, *The Rise and Fall of an American Army: U.S. Ground Forces in Vietnam, 1965–1973* (Novato, CA: Presidio Press, 1985); and Harry G. Summers Jr., *On Strategy: A Critical Analysis of the Vietnam War* (Novato, CA: Presidio Press, 1982).

24. A. J. Bacevich, *The Pentomic Era: The US Army between Korea and Vietnam* (Washington, DC: National Defense University Press, 1986).

25. John B. Wilson, *Maneuver and Firepower: The Evolution of Divisions and Separate Brigades* (Washington, DC: U.S. Army Center of Military History, 1998).

26. Robert A. Doughty, *The Evolution of U.S. Army Tactical Doctrine, 1946–1976* (Leavenworth Paper No. 1; Ft. Leavenworth, KS: Command and General Staff College, 1976).

27. John R. Midgley Jr., *Deadly Illusions: Army Policy for the Nuclear Battlefield* (Boulder, CO: Westview Press, 1986); John P. Rose, *The Evolution of U.S. Army Nuclear Doctrine, 1945–1980* (Boulder, CO: Westview Press, 1980).

28. G. C. Reinhardt and W. R. Kintner, *Atomic Weapons in Land Combat* (Harrisburg, PA: Military Service Publishing Company, 1953).

29. Theodore C. Mataxis and Seymour L. Goldberg, *Nuclear Tactics, Weapons, and Firepower in the Pentomic Division, Battle Group, and Company* (Harrisburg, PA: Military Service Publishing Company, 1958).

30. For World War II divisions and their wartime reorganization, see Wilson, *Maneuver and Firepower*, pp. 179–201.

31. For an overview of army reorganization in the early Cold War, see ibid., pp. 239–322.

32. The Armored Force was created in 1940. In the 1950s, armored infantry was a term used in the U.S. Army for infantry mounted on APCs. In the 1960s, similar formations were called mechanized infantry, even though that term implied the ability to fight mounted, which was in fact not achieved until the early 1980s.

33. John M. Collins, *U.S.-Soviet Military Balance: Concepts and Capabilities, 1960–1980* (New York: McGraw-Hill, 1980), p. 482.

34. Ibid., p. 484.

35. For history and specifications of the Bradley, see W. Blair Haworth Jr., *The Bradley and How It Got That Way: Technology, Institutions, and the Problem of Mechanized Infantry in the United States Army* (Westport, CT: Greenwood Press, 1999); R. P. Hunnicutt, *Bradley: A History of American Fighting and Support Vehicles* (Novato, CA: Presidio Press, 1999); and Diane L. Urbina, "'Lethal beyond All Expectations': The Bradley Fighting Vehicle," in Hofmann and Starry, *Camp Colt to Desert Storm*, pp. 403–431.

36. The best recent discussion of tanks and armored vehicles throughout the twentieth century is Bruce I. Gudmundsson, *On Armor* (Westport, CT: Praeger, 2004).

37. Christopher R. Gabel, "World War II Armor Operations in Europe," in Hofmann and Starry, *Camp Colt to Desert Storm*, pp. 144–184; R. P. Hunnicutt, *Sherman: A History of the American Medium Tank* (Novato, CA: Presidio Press, 1978); R. P. Hunnicutt, *Stuart: A History of the American Light Tank* (Novato, CA: Presidio Press, 1992).

38. FM 100-5: *Operations*, 1976, chap. 2, p. 3.

39. Gudmundsson, *On Armor*, p. 165.

40. Ibid., p. 169. For history and specifications of the Sheridan, see R. P. Hunnicutt, *Sheridan: A History of the American Light Tank* (Novato, CA: Presidio Press, 1995).

41. Main battle tanks of the 1960s and 1970s are usually perceived as improved Patton tanks because their design characteristics were similar. For history and specifications of medium-gun and main battle tanks, see Oscar C. Decker, "The Patton Tanks: The Cold War Learning Series," in Hofmann and Starry, *Camp Colt to Desert Storm*, pp. 298–323; and R. P. Hunnicutt, *Patton: A History of the American Main Battle Tank* (Novato, CA: Presidio Press, 1984).

42. Later model Abrams tanks had 120-mm guns. See Gudmundsson, *On Armor*, p. 165. For history and specifications of Abrams tanks, see R. P. Hunnicutt, *Abrams: A History of the American Main Battle Tank* (Novato, CA: Presidio Press, 1990); and Robert J. Sunell, "The Abrams Tank System," in Hofmann and Starry, *Camp Colt to Desert Storm*, pp. 432–473.

43. For specific characteristics of American and Soviet tanks, see Collins, *U.S.-Soviet Military Balance*, pp. 482–484.

44. Howitzers differ from other types of artillery pieces by their trajectory. They fire at higher angles and can drop projectiles on targets that are fortified or obscured.

45. For artillery in the European theater of operations, see Boyd L. Dastrup, *King of Battle: A Branch History of the U.S. Army's Field Artillery* (Fort Monroe, VA: Office of the Command Historian, U.S. Army Training and Doctrine Command, 1992), pp. 203–226, 237.

46. Ibid., p. 263.

47. For the development of field artillery from the mid-1950s to 1980, see ibid., pp. 265–304.

48. Ibid., p. 271.

49. For a concise discussion of artillery during the Cold War, see Bruce I. Gudmundsson, *On Artillery* (Westport, CT: Praeger, 1993), pp. 143–162. For design and performance of American self-propelled artillery, see Hunnicutt, *Sheridan*, pp. 198–224. See also Collins, *U.S.-Soviet Military Balance*, pp. 483–485, for performance characteristics of American and Soviet guns.

50. Dastrup, *King of Battle*, pp. 277, 290.

51. For developments from the 1960s to the 1990s, see Gudmundsson, *On Artillery*, pp. 151–162; and House, *Combined Arms Warfare*, pp. 231–286.

52. See Philip A. Karber, "Nuclear Weapons and the U.S. Army in Europe: 1953–1989," unpublished draft manuscript, January 1990, p. 7 (Nuclear History Database, Box 3, NSA); and David McKinley Walker, "Eisenhower's New Look, Tactical Nuclear Weapons, and Limited War with a Case Study of the Taiwan Strait Crisis of 1958" (Ph.D. diss., George Washington University, 2004), p. 116.

53. Sean M. Maloney, *War without Battles: Canada's NATO Brigade in Germany, 1951–1993* (Toronto: McGraw-Hill Ryerson, 1997), pp. 140–141.

54. Bacevich, *Pentomic Era*, pp. 82–96.

Chapter 1. The U.S. Army in National and Alliance Strategy

1. Richard W. Stewart, ed., *The United States Army in a Global Era, 1917–2003*, vol. 2 of *American Military History* (Washington, DC: U.S. Army Center of Military History, 2005), p. 211.

2. FM 100-5, 1949, p. 2.

3. Ibid., pp. 6–13.

4. See, for instance, ibid., p. 20.

5. Ibid., pp. 80–99.

6. Ibid., pp. 99–113.

7. Ibid., pp. 114–118.
8. Ibid., p. 120.
9. Ibid., p. 141.
10. In the wake of the Korean War, it was argued that individual soldiers, rather than entire divisions, had been unprepared for the war because occupation duty and life in Japan had softened them. See T. R. Fehrenbach, *This Kind of War: A Study in Unpreparedness* (New York: Macmillan, 1963). The recent work of Thomas E. Hanson, "The Eighth Army's Combat Readiness before Korea: A Reappraisal," *Armed Forces and Society* 29, no.2 (Winter 2003): 167–184, clearly demonstrates that individual soldiers were quite capable but lacked the necessary guns, tanks, and vehicles. Lack of tanks and antitank guns is also discussed in Gudmundsson, *On Armor*, p. 162.
11. Roy K. Flint, "Task Force Smith and the 24th Division: Delay and Withdrawal, 5–19 July 1950," in *America's First Battles: 1776–1965*, edited by Charles E. Heller and William A. Stofft (Lawrence: University Press of Kansas, 1986), pp. 266–299.
12. Kevin Soutor shows that the studies of German army officers conducted for the U.S. Army since the end of World War II had begun to resonate with their American counterparts. Kevin Soutor, "To Stem the Red Tide: The German Report Series and Its Effects on American Defense Doctrine, 1948–1954," *Journal of Military History* 57, no. 4 (October 1993): 653–688.
13. For the use of artillery in the Korean War, see Gudmundsson, *On Artillery*, pp. 144–147.
14. JSPC 902/381, 25 February 1954, *Report by the Joint Strategic Plans Committee to the Joint Chiefs of Staff on WSEG Staff Study No. 14*, Geographic File 1954–56, CGS092 Western Europe (3-12-48), sec. 261, RG 218, NA. The quotation is on p. 2.
15. JLPC 405/12/D, Joint Logistic Plans Committee, Directive, 18 June 1954, *Implications of Atomic Warfare*, Geographic File 1954–56, CGS092 Western Europe (3-12-48), sec. 282, RG 218, NA. The quotation is on p. 1.
16. FM 100-5, 1954, pp. 4–8. The quotations are, in order, on pp. 4, 5, and 7.
17. Ibid., p. 26.
18. Ibid., p. 40.
19. Ibid., p. 96.
20. Ibid., pp. 74–75.
21. Ibid., p. 77.
22. Ibid., pp. 78–87.
23. Ibid., pp. 87–89.
24. Ibid., p. 94.
25. A mere page count of the 1954 edition of FM 100-5 shows thirty-nine pages devoted to the offensive and only twenty-four to defensive operations. Ibid., pp. 74–112, 113–136.
26. Ibid., pp. 117–121.
27. Melbourne C. Chandler, "Notes on Defense," *Military Review* 34, no. 11 (February 1955): 38–49. Major Chandler served in the G-3 branch (Operations) of USAREUR headquarters.
28. FM 100-5, 1954, p. 113.
29. Ibid., pp. 114–115.

30. Ibid., pp. 120–121.

31. The political scientist Aaron Friedberg has introduced the terms "contract state" and "garrison state" for the two different types of economies and societies. He argues that a contract state generally possesses greater strength and flexibility. Aaron L. Friedberg, "Why Didn't the United States Become a Garrison State?" *International Security* 16, no. 4 (Spring 1992): 109–142.

32. See Kennan's "Long Telegram" of 1946, in *FRUS*, 1946, vol. 6: *Eastern Europe; The Soviet Union* (Washington, DC: Government Printing Office, 1969), pp. 696–709. His views were expressed with greater depth in the initially anonymous article, Mr. X, "The Sources of Soviet Conduct," in *Foreign Affairs* 25, no. 4 (July 1947): 566–582. For a discussion of Kennan's role in the formulation of containment, see Gaddis, *Strategies of Containment*, pp. 25–53.

33. There is some controversy, however, concerning whether the Marshall Plan was a necessary element to the recovery process of Western Europe. See, for instance, William I. Hitchcock, *France Restored: Cold War Diplomacy and the Quest for Leadership in Europe, 1944–1954* (Chapel Hill: University of North Carolina Press, 1998); Michael J. Hogan, *The Marshall Plan: America, Britain, and the Reconstruction of Western Europe, 1947–1952* (Cambridge: Cambridge University Press, 1987); and Alan S. Milward, *The Reconstruction of Western Europe, 1945–1951* (Berkeley: University of California Press, 1984).

34. For a comprehensive summary, see Steven T. Ross, *American War Plans, 1945–1950: Strategies for Defeating the Soviet Union* (London: Frank Cass, 1996). Some of the plans have been published by David Alan Rosenberg and Steven T. Ross, eds., *America's Plans for War against the Soviet Union, 1945–1950* (15 vols.; New York: Garland, 1989–1990). For the stockpile of atomic bombs, see David Alan Rosenberg, "U.S. Nuclear Stockpile, 1945–1950," *Bulletin of Atomic Scientists* 38 (May 1982): 25–30.

35. For Johnson's tenure as secretary of defense, as well as his previous career in the War Department, see the recent comprehensive biography by Keith D. McFarland and David L. Roll, *Louis Johnson and the Arming of America: The Roosevelt and Truman Years* (Bloomington: Indiana University Press, 2005).

36. David T. Fautua, "The 'Long Pull' Army: NSC-68, the Korean War, and the Creation of the Cold War Army," *Journal of Military History* 61, no. 1 (January 1997): 93–120, argues that NSC-68 allowed the army to sharpen its intellectual rationale for manpower, weapons, and structure for the Cold War. Given the dramatic developments of 1955 through 1961 in terms of personnel and budget cuts, as well as the apparent reorientation of the army under Taylor, the argument is not convincing. Rather, the halt of the downward slide was temporary, and the intellectual rationale remained open to significant change.

37. Paul H. Nitze, *From Hiroshima to Glasnost: At the Center of Decision* (New York: Grove Weidenfeld, 1989), p. 96.

38. Interim Report by the National Security Council, *The Program and Cost Estimates of NSC 68 and Their Implications for the United States*, undated, Part II: Tabulation of Cost Estimates, p. 1, George M. Elsey Papers, National Security folder, Box 89, HSTL.

39. The full text of NSC-68 can be found in *FRUS*, 1950, vol. 1, *National Security Af-*

fairs; Foreign Economic Policy (Washington, DC: Government Printing Office, 1977), pp. 234–292.

40. Robert W. Coakley, Karl E. Cocke, and Daniel P. Griffin, *Demobilization Following the Korean War* (Washington, DC: Histories Division, Office of the Chief of Military History, 1968), pp. 1–2.

41. For convenient summaries of the budgeting process, see Steven L. Rearden, *History of the Office of the Secretary of Defense: The Formative Years, 1947–1950* (Washington, DC: Historical Office, Office of the Secretary of Defense, 1984), pp. 309–384; and Doris M. Condit, *History of the Office of the Secretary of Defense: The Test of War, 1950–1953* (Washington, DC: Historical Office, Office of the Secretary of Defense, 1988), pp. 223–306. Both publications also contain several detailed tables on the defense budget and its component parts.

42. For estimates of Soviet military strength in the late 1940s and early 1950s, see John S. Duffield, "The Soviet Military Threat to Western Europe: U.S. Estimates in the 1950s and 1960s," *Journal of Strategic Studies* 15, no. 2 (June 1992): 208–227; Matthew A. Evangelista, "Stalin's Postwar Army Reappraised," *International Security* 7, no. 3 (Winter 1982–1983): 110–138; Raymond L. Garthoff, *Assessing the Adversary: Estimates by the Eisenhower Administration of Soviet Intentions and Capabilities* (Washington, DC: Brookings Institution, 1991); Philip A. Karber and Jerald A. Combs, "The United States, NATO, and the Soviet Threat to Western Europe: Military Estimates and Policy Options, 1945–1963," *Diplomatic History* 22, no. 3 (Summer 1998): 299–329; Scott A. Koch, ed., *Selected Estimates on the Soviet Union, 1950–1959* (Washington, DC: History Staff, Center for the Study of Intelligence, Central Intelligence Agency, 1993); and John Prados, *The Soviet Estimate: U.S. Intelligence Analysis and Soviet Strategic Forces* (Princeton, NJ: Princeton University Press, 1986). Evangelista contends that the military services deliberately overestimated the Soviet threat as leverage in the budgetary debates of the Truman administration. Duffield also expresses a degree of skepticism about the reliability of intelligence findings. Soviet and Eastern European records show that NATO indeed overestimated the threat emanating from the Warsaw Pact in the 1950s and early 1960s. See Mastny and Byrne, *A Cardboard Castle*. But Karber and Combs argued persuasively that this was not the result of deliberate actions by American intelligence agencies and military institutions. Raymond Garthoff, who served on various levels of intelligence assessment, evaluation, and policymaking throughout the Cold War, concluded that within the framework of containment "assessment of the adversary was realistic." Garthoff, *Assessing the Adversary*, p. 52.

43. Many European generals recognized this as early as 1949. Even within the French army there were voices that pointed at the need to rearm West Germany, at least in a limited fashion. This would bolster the alliance but was also necessary to tie West Germany to the West. Otherwise Germany might unite as a neutral or Communist country. French general Revers pointed out that it was crucial to allow rearmament only after the rest of Western Europe had recovered and rearmed. Translation of Memorandum No. 2 (from General Revers), *Overall Strategic Concepts*, 28 March 1949, Geographic File, 1948–50, CCS092 (3-12-48), Sec. 19, RG 218, NA.

44. In November 1950, the North Atlantic Council came to the conclusion that a German defense contribution was necessary. It was made clear, however, that a Ger-

man national army or even a general staff did not serve anyone's best interests. MC 30, 18 November 1950, *Report by the Standing Group to the Military Committee on Military Aspects of German Participation in the Defense of Western Europe*, International Military Staff, Records of the North Atlantic Military Committee, NATO Archives, Brussels.

45. For West German rearmament, the failure of the European Defense Community, and the decision to admit the Federal Republic into NATO proper, see Saki Dockrill, *Britain's Policy for West German Rearmament, 1950–1955* (Cambridge: Cambridge University Press, 1991); Ehlert et al., *Die NATO Option*; Roland G. Foerster et al., *Von der Kapitulation bis zum Pleven Plan*, vol. 1 of *Anfänge westdeutscher Sicherheitspolitik* (Munich: R. Oldenbourg Verlag, 1982); Edward Fursdon, *The European Defence Community: A History* (New York: St. Martin's, 1980); Lutz Köllner et al., *Anfänge westdeutscher Sicherheitspolitik*, vol. 2 of *Die EVG Phase* (Munich: R. Oldenbourg Verlag, 1989); Large, *Germans to the Front*; McGeehan, *The German Rearmament Question*; and Trachtenberg, *A Constructed Peace*, pp. 103–125.

46. JSPC 877/59, Joint Strategic Planning Committee, 26 May 1949, *Brief of Joint Outline Emergency War Plan (OFFTACKLE)*, Geographic File 1948–50, CCS381 USSR (3-2-46), sec. 32, RG 218; Anthony Cave Brown, *Dropshot: The United States Plan for War with the Soviet Union in 1957* (New York: Dial Press, 1978).

47. JMAC 73/2, Joint Munitions Allocation Committee, 18 August 1949, *U.S. Dollar Costs of Material, Bases, and Political Orientation to Support DROPSHOT*, Appendix A to Enclosure C: *Considerations Involved in Determining the Total Cost of Long-Range Foreign Military Assistance for Army Forces*, Central Decimal File 1948–50, 092 (8-22-46), RG 218.

48. PM-958, Joint Intelligence Group, Memorandum for the Joint Strategic Plans Committee, 11 October 1949, *Comparative Evaluation*, Enclosure A: Geographic File 1948–50, CCS092 (3-12-48), sec. 31, RG 218.

49. REAPER was accepted by the JCS on 25 November 1950. In January 1951, the plan was renamed GROUNDWORK but otherwise remained unaltered. See JCS 2143/6, 29 November 1950, *Joint Outline War Plan for a War Beginning 1 July 1954*, in Rosenberg and Ross, *Reaper*, vol. 15 in *America's Plans for War*; and Ross, *American War Plans, 1945–1950*, pp. 142–145.

50. Andrew M. Johnston has shown, however, that the British concept of nuclear deterrence and Eisenhower's New Look and Massive Retaliation were different and that Eisenhower's defense policy did not emulate that of Great Britain. Andrew M. Johnston, "Mr. Slessor Goes to Washington: The Influence of the British Global Strategy Paper on the Eisenhower New Look," *Diplomatic History* 22, no. 3 (Summer 1998): 361–398.

51. JP (52)108 (Final), Chiefs of Staff Committee, Joint Planning Staff, 27 November 1952, *Plan FAIRFAX: Report by the Joint Planning Staff*. The quotations are on p. 6. This document has been made available by the PHP, http://www.php.isn.ethz.ch/collections/colltopic.cfm?lng=en&id=18487&navinfo=14968 (accessed 15 November 2007). The original document is at the Public Record Office, Kew, London.

52. The shortfalls began to be noticeable as early as 1953. In the course of 1952, only three combat effective divisions ready at D-day had been added, and the forces for D-plus-thirty-days fell ten divisions short of the Lisbon commitments. Richard M.

Leighton, *Strategy, Money, and the New Look, 1953–1956*, vol. 3 of *History of the Office of the Secretary of Defense* (Washington, DC: Historical Office, Office of the Secretary of Defense, 2001), pp. 555–558.

53. Robert J. Watson, *The Joint Chiefs of Staff and National Policy, 1953–1954*, vol. 5 of *History of the Joint Chiefs of Staff* (Washington, DC: Historical Division, Joint Chiefs of Staff, 1986), pp. 14–21.

54. For a recent discussion of the antistatist foundation of the United States and its development in the Cold War, see Aaron L. Friedberg, *In the Shadow of the Garrison State: America's Anti-Statism and Its Cold War Grand Strategy* (Princeton, NJ: Princeton University Press, 2000).

55. The best recent discussions of the New Look and Massive Retaliation are Dockrill, *Eisenhower's New Look*; and Leighton, *Strategy, Money, and the New Look*. Marc Trachtenberg's essays, "A 'Wasting Asset': American Strategy and the Shifting Nuclear Balance, 1949–1954," and "The Nuclearization of NATO and U.S.–West European Relations," in his *History and Strategy*, pp. 100–168, also remain useful.

56. Bacevich, *Pentomic Era*, pp. 14–16. See also *FRUS*, 1952–1954, vol. 2, *National Security Affairs*, pt. 1 (Washington, DC: Government Printing Office, 1984), pp. 577–597, for the text of NSC-162/2. In addition, see pp. 562–564 of the same volume for the approval of the concept of Massive Retaliation by the JCS.

57. The last Truman budget proposal is discussed in detail in Condit, *History of Office of the Secretary of Defense: The Test of War*, pp. 285–306. The Eisenhower budgets from 1954 to 1957 are shown in Leighton, *Strategy, Money, and the New Look*, pp. 65–113, 231–276, 307–333, 359–378, 471–488, 605–630.

58. For the gradual but nevertheless drastic reduction of army forces, see Robert W. Coakley et al., *Demobilization Following the Korean War* (Washington, DC: Histories Division, Office of the Chief of Military History, 1968).

59. Watson, *Joint Chiefs of Staff and National Policy, 1953–54*, pp. 26–31.

60. Ibid., pp. 32–34. Ridgway's qualified consent to the force goals meant that the claim of unanimous approval by the JCS was technically correct. Admiral Carney, who also had reservations, assented without qualifications.

61. See Leighton, *Strategy, Money, and the New Look*, p. 260. In December 1953, approved service goals called for a fourteen-division, one-million-man army by 30 June 1956. In the service proposals of March 1954, this was elevated to 1,152,000 men and seventeen divisions.

62. Ridgway relates that General Bradley had inquired about his preference, whether to stay on as SACEUR or to serve as chief of staff. Ridgway Interview by Maurice Matloff, 18 April 1984, p. 41, Ridgway Papers, Box 34: Oral Histories, "Interview by Maurice Matloff."

63. Matthew B. Ridgway, *Soldier: The Memoirs of Matthew B. Ridgway* (New York: Harper, 1956), pp. 264–273. The quotations are on p. 271.

64. Andrew Bacevich argues that Ridgway challenged Eisenhower and Massive Retaliation because he feared the destruction of the military profession as a result of widespread belief that nuclear weapons made war inconceivable. He concludes that Ridgway's "almost mystical ideal of the warrior professional" trumped his belief in the need for civilian control. Andrew J. Bacevich, "The Paradox of Professionalism: Eisen-

hower, Ridgway, and the Challenge to Civilian Control, 1953–1955," *Journal of Military History* 61, no. 2 (April 1997): 303–333. The quotation is on p. 311.

65. Ridgway, *Soldier*, p. 234.

66. Ibid., p. 274. Ridgway detested Wilson for his lack of open-mindedness, his unwillingness to listen to positions he disliked, and his rather general criticism that the army had done little right, even in World War II. Ridgway Interview by Maurice Matloff, pt. 2, p. 1. Others agreed. General Gavin relates overhearing another service chief's assessment of Wilson as "the most uninformed man, and the most determined to remain so, that has ever been Secretary." James M. Gavin, *War and Peace in the Space Age* (New York: Harper, 1958), p. 155. But see E. Bruce Geelhoed, *Charles E. Wilson and Controversy at the Pentagon, 1953 to 1957* (Detroit: Wayne State University Press, 1979), for a more favorable account. Geelhoed depicts Wilson as a loyal secretary of defense in a crucial period of strategic change and as a hard-working and capable administrator.

67. Ridgway, *Soldier*, pp. 274–275.

68. Ridgway understood that Eisenhower needed to present himself as neutral toward the army to avoid charges of favoritism for his old service. But he suspected that the pendulum swung beyond neutral in the process. Ridgway Interview by Maurice Matloff, pt. 2, 19 April 1984, p. 6.

69. Ridgway, *Soldier*, p. 267. This was problematic, since Eisenhower and Ridgway had never been that friendly to begin with. An added difficulty in 1953 was that Ridgway believed in giving forthright and contrary advice if necessary, while Eisenhower thought that the role of the JCS was to create consensus among the service chiefs. See Jonathan Milton Soffer, *General Matthew B. Ridgway: From Progressivism to Reaganism, 1895–1993* (Westport, CT: Praeger, 1998), pp. 175–177.

70. Bacevich, *Pentomic Era*, pp. 20–21, 49–51.

71. Maxwell Taylor was among those who had supported the idea of an armed forces chief of staff. He returned the concept to the arena of discussions in the early 1960s. See Edgar F. Raines Jr. and David R. Campbell, *The Army and the Joint Chiefs of Staff: Evolution of Army Ideas on the Command, Control, and Coordination of the U.S. Armed Forces, 1942–1985* (Washington, DC: U.S. Army Center of Military History, 1986), pp. 70–116, particularly p. 86.

72. Lemnitzer is quoted in Bacevich, *Pentomic Era*, p. 21. He publicized the statement in his address "This Is a Significant Beginning," *Army Combat Forces Journal* 6, no. 4 (November 1955): 62.

73. See the transcript of the Senate hearing on 8 February 1956 and Ridgway's prepared statement, Ridgway Papers, "File Centering on His Testimony before the House of Representatives," Box 31: Retirement, MHI.

74. Ridgway, *Soldier*, pp. 286–294.

75. Leighton, *Strategy, Money, and the New Look*, p. 169.

76. Ibid., pp. 160–167. Leighton also states unequivocally that the ultimate defense manpower ceilings for FY 1955 were dictated wholly by economic considerations. Eisenhower's position is an example of the differences between the theory of the New Look and practical defense policy. In theory, Eisenhower wished to withdraw U.S. units from Europe, but he also knew that it was impracticable in the mid-1950s.

77. Ibid., p. 180.

78. Statement by General Matthew B. Ridgway, chief of staff, U.S. Army, before the Subcommittee on Armed Services of the Committee on Appropriations, House of Representatives, Relative to the Department of the Army Budget for Fiscal Year 1955, pp. 5–6, 12–13, Ridgway Papers, Box 36: Speeches, January 1951–August 1954, "Speech File—Gen. M. B. Ridgway, C/S, USA, No. 1 (Aug 53–Feb 54)," MHI. The quotation is on p. 6. See also Ridgway's draft statement to Congress for the 1956 Army budget, Statement of General Matthew B. Ridgway, chief of staff, U.S. Army, before the Subcommittee on Armed Services of the Committee on Appropriations, House of Representatives, Relative to the Department of the Army Budget for Fiscal Year 1956, p. 7, Ridgway Papers, Box 37: Speeches, 1954–1955, "Speech File, General Matthew B. Ridgway, C/S, USA, No. 4 (Jan–Jun 55)," MHI.

79. Maxwell Taylor later characterized these years as the army's "Babylonian captivity," a sentiment that Matthew Ridgway wholeheartedly endorsed. See Taylor, *The Uncertain Trumpet*, p. 108; and Ridgway Interview by Maurice Matloff, p. 45.

80. Ridgway, *Soldier*, pp. 303–308.

81. Ibid., pp. 311–316.

82. Robert J. Watson, *Into the Missile Age, 1956–1960*, vol. 4 of *History of the Office of the Secretary of Defense* (Washington, DC: Historical Office, Office of the Secretary of Defense, 1997), pp. 76–84.

83. Ridgway, *Soldier*, p. 296.

84. In 1984 Ridgway recalled that he and his predecessor, General J. Lawton Collins, had many discussions about the need to take the army into the atomic age. In the meantime, however, the notion that the army was no longer necessary in general war became so strong that he had to combat it first and foremost. Ridgway Interview by Maurice Matloff, pp. 43–44.

85. Ridgway, *Soldier*, pp. 296–300.

86. Bacevich, *Pentomic Era*, p. 28.

87. Special National Intelligence Estimate 11-54, Central Intelligence Agency, 15 February 1954, *Likelihood of General War through 1957*, National Intelligence Estimates Concerning the Soviet Union 1950–1961, Box 2, Folder 56, RG 263.

88. Ridgway, *Soldier*, pp. 317–321. See also pp. 323–332 for a reprint of the letter.

89. Soffer, *General Matthew B. Ridgway*, pp. 184–188.

90. A copy of Taylor's letter, dated 28 November 1955, is in Andrew J. Goodpaster Papers, Box 18, Folder 12, GCML.

91. Wilson is quoted in Taylor, *The Uncertain Trumpet*, p. 51. The statement was made in the presence of General Taylor at an NSC meeting on 25 July 1957.

92. Kenneth W. Condit, *The Joint Chiefs of Staff and National Policy, 1947–49*, vol. 2 of *The History of the Joint Chiefs of Staff* (Wilmington, DE: Michael Glazier, 1979), p. 402.

93. It is not entirely clear whether the ninety divisions would include the reserve. David Gates claims that the NATO planners called for ninety active divisions, to be supplemented upon mobilization. Gates furthermore contends that it was the governments of the NATO members that decided to read the force objectives in the way that was more convenient to them, i.e., as calling for ninety active and reserve divisions.

David Gates, *Non-Offensive Defense: An Alternative Strategy for NATO?* (New York: St. Martin's, 1991), p. 2. While Gates has received little support for his position, a U.S. Army officer writing in the 1980s claimed that regional planning groups in the late 1940s estimated a need for more than 300 combat divisions to defend continental Europe. Robert B. Killebrew, *Conventional Defense and Total Deterrence: Assessing NATO's Strategic Options* (Wilmington, DE: Scholarly Resources, 1986), pp. 3–4.

94. D.C. 13, 28 March 1950, *North Atlantic Treaty Organization Medium Term Plan*, in *NATO Strategy Documents, 1949–1969*, ed. Gregory W. Pedlow (Brussels: Historical Office, Supreme Headquarters Allied Powers Europe, 1998), pp. 111–177.

95. Memorandum from the Office of NAT Affairs for the Secretary of Defense, through Major General J. H. Burns, not dated (probably late 1951), *North Atlantic Treaty Organization Summary Report*, pp. 4–5, Office of the Secretary of Defense, Office of the Assistant Secretary (International Security Affairs), Decimal File 1951, CD 092.3 NATO General, RG 330.

96. *Statement by Gen. Alfred M. Gruenther, USA, Supreme Allied Commander, Europe, and United States Commander in Chief, Europe*, Hearing before the Committee on Foreign Relations, U.S. Senate, 26 March 1955 (Washington, DC: Government Printing Office, 1955), p. 2.

97. Memorandum for the Secretary of the Army, the Secretary of the Navy, the Secretary of the Air Force, and the Joint Chiefs of Staff by the Secretary of Defense, 29 March 1952, *Outline of NATO Force Goals as Accepted at the Lisbon Meeting of the North Atlantic Council, February 23, 1952*, Table I: Army Divisions, Office of the Secretary of Defense, Office of the Assistant Secretary (International Security Affairs), Decimal File 1952, CD 092.3 NATO General, RG 330.

98. Ibid., Table II: Breakdown by Type—Divisions.

99. Department of Defense, Office of the Comptroller, 11 April 1952, *Cost of Defense, Defense Expenditures, and External Financing for European NATO Nations and Germany, July 1950–June 1954*, Table 1: European NATO and Germany, Office of the Secretary of Defense, Office of the Assistant Secretary (International Security Affairs), Decimal File 1952, CD 092.3 NATO General, RG 330.

100. The incoming SACEUR, Matthew Ridgway, later stated that he was well aware of this. He was convinced that there was no prospect of receiving the divisions that had been promised. Ridgway Interview by Maurice Matloff, pp. 31–32.

101. Ridgway, *Soldier*, pp. 238–239.

102. Report to the Standing Group, 30 May 1953, *Report on Allied Command Europe, May 1952–May 1953*, p. 3, Ridgway Papers, Box 36: Speeches, January 1951–August 1954, "Speeches, Statements & Press, January 21, 1951–July 10, 1953," MHI.

103. Ibid., pp. 8–10.

104. Ibid., p. 15.

105. Ibid., p. 17.

106. SGM-600-54, Standing Group Modified, 1 July 1954, *Capabilities Plan Allied Command Europe 1957*, International Military Staff, Records of the Standing Group, NATO Archives, Brussels. The quotation is on p. 1.

107. See Peter J. Roman, "Ike's Hair Trigger: U.S. Nuclear Predelegation, 1953–60," *Security Studies* 7 (Summer 1998): 121–165; and Trachtenberg, *A Constructed Peace*, pp.

146–200. Documentary evidence in support has been published by the National Security Archive in the Electronic Briefing Book, "Eisenhower and Nuclear Predelegation" (http://www.gwu.edu/~nsarchiv/NSAEBB/NSAEBB45/#1) (accessed 15 November 2007).

108. SGM-600-54, pp. 10–11.

109. Ibid., Enclosure C: *Major Campaign No. 3 to Arrest the Soviet Land Advance in Central Europe*, pp. 1–2.

110. USEUCOM, 1955 (no more specific date on the document), *Outline Concept for the Conduct of Subsequent Operations*, Norstad Papers, Pre-SACEUR Subject Series, Box 46, "Requirements Study [atomic weapons & strategy]," DDEL.

111. SM-33-56, 17 January 1956, Memorandum for the Commander in Chief, U.S. European Command, *USEUCOM Joint Capabilities Plan 1-55* with Enclosure: Headquarters USEUCOM, Office of the Commander in Chief, 12 November 1955, *USEUCOM Joint Capabilities Plan, 1-55*, Central Decimal File 1954–56, CGS381 (11-15-48), sec. 10, RG 218. The quotations are on pp. 459 and 460 of the enclosure and p. 1 of the memorandum, respectively.

112. *Capabilities Plan Allied Command Europe, 1957*, Enclosure C, p. 3.

113. Ibid., p. 5.

114. SGM-1-55, North Atlantic Military Committee, Standing Group, 10 January 1955, *Memorandum for the Supreme Allied Commander Europe, the Supreme Allied Commander Atlantic, the Channel Committee, the Canada–United States Regional Planning Group*, Enclosure A: *Assignment of Land Forces*, International Military Staff, Records of the Standing Group, NATO Archives, Brussels.

115. The North Atlantic Council reluctantly approved French troop transfers out of Europe, but General Gruenther still complained to the French defense minister "that France was not keeping its commitments on the Rhine." Irwin M. Wall, *France, the United States, and the Algerian War* (Berkeley: University of California Press, 2001), p. 20. The full brunt of the war would be felt later, of course. In October 1957, John Foster Dulles and NATO general-secretary Paul-Henri Spaak noted that only four understrength French divisions out of a commitment of fourteen were in fact available. Two years later, France had sixteen army divisions in Algeria and only three in Germany. Ibid., pp. 91, 206–207.

116. SGM-1-55, Enclosure A, pp. 9–10. The quotation is on p. 9.

117. Personal Note for the Supreme Commander by Field Marshal Montgomery, 4 January 1954, Norstad Papers, Personal Name Series, Box 74, "Montgomery, Field Marshal (2)," DDEL.

118. SGM-1-55, Annex A to Appendix B to Enclosure J, pp. 38–39.

119. Ibid., pp. 40–41.

120. FM 100-5, 1954, pp. 178–196. It is certainly in part an expression of the army's global commitments, but that does not explain the level of detail afforded to the explanation of the concept.

121. This is not an entirely unprecedented phenomenon. Michael Geyer has argued that this happened in the German armies of the two world wars. Michael Geyer, "German Strategy in the Age of Machine Warfare, 1914–1945," in Paret, *Makers of Modern Strategy*, pp. 527–597. General-staff officers were convinced that no military strategy

could be developed to serve the political objectives of Kaiser or Führer. Hence, the political ends were taken out of the equation and the general staff focused its powers on its area of great expertise, campaign planning. Instead of strategists, the planners became managers of violence. There are obvious military similarities and striking political differences in the situation that SHAPE planners found themselves in, in the early 1950s.

122. Lawrence Freedman states that during two days of the CARTE BLANCHE exercise the explosion of 355 nuclear weapons was simulated, most of them over West Germany. The immediate civilian German casualties were 1.7 million dead and 3.5 million wounded, without consideration of the effects of radiation. Freedman, "First Two Generations of Nuclear Strategists," p. 747.

123. JP (54)76 (Final), Chiefs of Staff Committee, Joint Planning Staff, 2 September 1954, *Capabilities Study—Allied Command Europe, 1957: Report by the Joint Planning Staff*. PHP, http://www.php.isn.ethz.ch/collections/colltopic.cfm?lng=en&id=18485&navinfo=14968 (accessed 15 November 2007). JP (54)77 (Final), Chiefs of Staff Committee, Joint Planning Staff, 3 September 1954, *The Most Effective Pattern of NATO Military Strength for the Next Few Years: Report by the Joint Planning Staff*. PHP, http://www.php.isn.ethz.ch/collections/colltopic.cfm?lng=en&id=18484&navinfo=14968 (accessed 15 November 2007) . The original documents are located in the Public Record Office, Kew, London.

124. Norstad to Twining, 3 July 1954, Norstad Papers, Pre-SACEUR Message Correspondence Series, Box 39, "1 January 1954 thru 31 December 1954 (2)," DDEL.

125. MC 49, 18 November 1954, *Report by the Standing Group to the Military Committee on Capabilities Study Allied Command Europe (ACE) 1957*, International Military Staff, Records of the North Atlantic Military Committee, NATO Archives, Brussels. The quotation is on p. 13.

126. *Statement of Gen. Gruenther*, U.S. Senate, 26 March 1955, p. 6.

127. MC 49/1, 26 September 1955, *Report by the Standing Group to the Military Committee on SACEUR's 1955 Report on Future Capabilities Plan, 1957*, International Military Staff, Records of the North Atlantic Military Committee, NATO Archives, Brussels.

128. MC 39/5, 28 November 1955, *Report by the Military Committee to the North Atlantic Council on Military Comments on the 1955 Annual Review Report*, International Military Staff, Records of the North Atlantic Military Committee, NATO Archives, Brussels.

129. The most comprehensive discussion of the failed EDC remains Fursdon, *The European Defence Community*; but see also James McAllister, *No Exit: America and the German Problem, 1943–1954* (Ithaca, NY: Cornell University Press, 2002), pp. 171–244. A recent analysis of French policies is Hitchcock, *France Restored*. The British position is discussed by Spencer Mawby, *Containing Germany: Britain and the Arming of the Federal Republic* (London: Macmillan, 1999). For the German as well as the international perspective, the publications of the Militärgeschichtliches Forschungsamt are most useful.

130. JSPC 956/61, 20 September 1954, *Report by the Joint Strategic Plans Committee to the Joint Chiefs of Staff on Strategic Issues Confronting the U.S. in Europe*, Geographic File 1954–56, CGS092 Germany (5-4-49), sec. 24, RG 218, NA.

131. Ibid., pp. 17, 20–23, 25.

132. Ibid., p. 19.

133. JSPC 956/63, 4 October 1954, *Report by the Joint Strategic Plans Committee to the Joint Chiefs of Staff on Military Program for the Rearmament of West Germany*, Annex A to Appendix to Enclosure A: *Composition of Forces, Including Recommendations Regarding Tables of Organization and Equipment*, p. 13, Geographic File 1954–56, CGS092 Germany (5-4-49), sec. 25, RG 218, NA.

134. JSPC 956/63, Annex B to Appendix to Enclosure A, p. 18.

135. JSPC 956/63, Appendix to Enclosure A, Geographic File 1954–56, CGS092 Germany (5-4-49), sec. 25, RG 218, NA.

136. MC 48, 18 November 1954, *Report by the Military Committee to the North Atlantic Council on the Most Effective Pattern of NATO Military Strength for the Next Few Years*, in Pedlow, *NATO Strategy Documents*, pp. 231–250. The quotation is on p. 237.

137. Statement by Lauris Norstad, n.d., "The Shield," Norstad Papers, Pre-SACEUR Series, Box 46, DDEL.

138. Watson, *Into the Missile Age*, p. 499.

139. Ibid., p. 505.

Chapter 2. Atomic Weapons and Limited War

1. See, e.g., Russell F. Weigley, *History of the United States Army* (New York: Macmillan, 1967), pp. 537–540.

2. Bacevich, *Pentomic Era*; Midgley, *Deadly Illusions*, pp. 57–79; Wilson, *Maneuver and Firepower*, pp. 270–282.

3. Glen R. Hawkins, *United States Army Force Structure and Force Design Initiatives, 1939–1989* (Washington, DC: U.S. Army Center of Military History, 1991), pp. 27–28; Wilson, *Maneuver and Firepower*, p. 271. The Koreans "politely declined to engage in a program of division mobilization." Maxwell D. Taylor, *Swords and Plowshares* (New York: W. W. Norton, 1972), p. 153.

4. For Gavin's career and innovative ideas during and after World War II, see T. Michael Booth and Duncan Spencer, *Paratrooper: The Life of Gen. James Gavin* (New York: Simon and Schuster), 1994.

5. David C. Elliot, "Project Vista and Nuclear Weapons in Europe," *International Security* 11, no. 1 (Summer 1986): 163–183; David C. Elliot, *Project Vista: An Early Study of Nuclear Weapons in Europe* (Santa Monica: California Seminar on International Security and Foreign Policy, 1987).

6. Gavin, *War and Peace in the Space Age*, pp. 132–137.

7. Colonels Reinhardt and Kintner arrived at the same conclusion: dispersion of small battle groups offered the best available protection against destruction by atomic weapons. Reinhardt and Kintner, *Atomic Weapons in Land Combat*, pp. 201–211.

8. Gavin, *War and Peace in the Space Age*, pp. 137–139. For the battle-group principle, see also James Gavin, "New Divisional Organization," *Army-Navy-Air Force Register* 76, no. 3923 (12 February 1955): 1–2. For Gavin's thoughts on air cavalry, see "Cavalry, and I Don't Mean Horses," *Harper's Magazine*, April 1954, pp. 54–60.

9. Ridgway to Gruenther, 22 April 1954, Alfred M. Gruenther Papers, NATO Series, Box 4, "Ridgway, Matthew B., General, U.S.A., Chief of Staff [1954–56]," DDEL.

The use of the term "special weapons" is unexplained in this context, but it usually referred to atomic weapons.

10. Wilson, *Maneuver and Firepower*, pp. 264–265.

11. Ibid., pp. 265–266.

12. Ibid., pp. 267–268.

13. Ibid., pp. 268–269.

14. Headquarters, Department of the Army, TOE 7 ATFA, 10 August 1956. All TOEs used for this book are in the collection of MHI. General Taylor had rejected ATFA earlier that year, but he had decreed that ongoing projects, such as the drafting of TOEs, were to be completed.

15. Wilson, *Maneuver and Firepower*, pp. 269–270.

16. Summary of Remarks by General Maxwell D. Taylor, Chief of Staff, United States Army, at Quantico Conference, 23 June 1956, Taylor Papers, NDU.

17. Willard G. Wyman, "Let's Get Going on Our New Combinations for Combat," *Army* 6, no. 12 (July 1956): 39–43, 69. The quotations are on p. 69.

18. Wilson, *Maneuver and Firepower*, pp. 270–271; Glen R. Hawkins and James Jay Carafano, *Prelude to Army XXI: U.S. Army Division Design Initiatives and Experiments, 1917–1995* (Washington, DC: U.S. Army Center of Military History, 1997), p. 13.

19. Office of the Deputy Chief of Staff for Military Operations, Memorandum for Record, 15 May 1956, *Briefing for Chief of Staff on Army Organization, 1960–1970 (PENTANA)*, p. 4, MHI stacks. The author of the memorandum was Lieutenant General Clyde Eddleman, Deputy Chief of Staff for Operations.

20. Ibid., p. 3.

21. General Donn Starry, the principal architect of the AirLand Battle doctrine of the 1980s, believes that Taylor adopted the pentomic concept before it had been thoroughly considered. Starry to author, 4 October 2004.

22. Historian John McGrath argues that Taylor's command of an airborne division in Northern Europe during World War II conditioned his belief that five combat elements were better than three. Nominally, both the 82nd and the 101st Airborne Divisions had three regiments, but in the field two parachute regiments were added. John J. McGrath, *The Brigade: A History* (Ft. Leavenworth, KS: Combat Studies Institute Press, 2004), p. 59. Kalev Sepp goes beyond that and argues that the pentomic division was a reflection of the airborne experience of generals Gavin, Ridgway, and Taylor in World War II, rather than a response to the military and political circumstances of the 1950s. Kalev I. Sepp, "The Pentomic Puzzle: The Influence of Personality and Nuclear Weapons on U.S. Army Organization, 1952–1958," *Army History* 51 (Winter 2001): 1–13.

23. Bacevich, *Pentomic Era*, pp. 103–106, 115–119. It is unclear how the battle group in the center of the target area would have escaped the atomic attack.

24. James M. Shepherd, "Type Divisions for Atomic Warfare," *Military Review* 36, no. 8 (November 1956): 24–37, particularly pp. 24–27.

25. The Army Staff had published drafts of FM 101-31: *Tactical Use of Atomic Weapons* in 1951 and 1955, but it was clearly stated that the publications were to provide only temporary guidance while internal discussion continued. In addition, there was Reinhardt and Kintner, *Atomic Weapons in Land Combat*, a semiofficial monograph that originated at the Command and General Staff College.

26. General Westmoreland recalls how Eisenhower told Taylor that the army needed a more charismatic public image. He instructed Taylor to "sex up the Army." Hawkins, *United States Army Force Structure and Force Design Initiatives*, p. 35.

27. Headquarters, CONARC, TOE 57T ROTAD, 10 August 1956. See also Wilson, *Maneuver and Firepower*, pp. 271–273.

28. Captain Everett Royal, quoted in Bacevich, *Pentomic Era*, p. 68.

29. For the pentomic division as a failed attempt at transformation, see Arthur W. Connor, "The Army and Transformation, 1945–1991" (research paper, Carlisle Barracks, PA: U.S. Army War College, Strategy Research Project, 2002), pp. 10–14. The critical failure to develop suitable communications systems, particularly radios with enough channels for all elements of the pentomic division, is discussed in Paul C. Jussel, "Intimidating the World: The United States Atomic Army, 1956–1960" (Ph.D. diss., Ohio State University, 2004), pp. 147–154.

30. Headquarters, Department of the Army, TOE 57D, 31 July 1958. See also Wilson, *Maneuver and Firepower*, pp. 274–275.

31. Headquarters, CONARC, TOE 7T ROCID, 20 December 1956. The transitory nature of this proposal can be gauged from the handwritten substitution of battle groups for regiments on the organizational chart. See also Wilson, *Maneuver and Firepower*, pp. 276–277.

32. Headquarters, USAREUR, *Annual History United States Army, Europe, 1 January 1960–31 December 1960* (Heidelberg: Headquarters, USAREUR, 1961), pp. 11–12.

33. Headquarters, CONARC, TOE 17T ROCAD, 1 December 1956. See also Wilson, *Maneuver and Firepower*, p. 277.

34. McGrath, *The Brigade*, p. 62. For ROCID mechanization and transportation capacity, see also John K. Mahon and Romana Danysh, *Infantry*, pt. 1 of *Regular Army* (Washington, DC: Office of the Chief of Military History, U.S. Army, 1972), p. 92.

35. Proposed letter from General Taylor to CG CONARC, Tab D attachment to Chief of Information to Deputy Chief of Staff for Military Operations, 3 October 1956, *Atomic Army Demonstration*, Attachment: DCSOPS, Draft Summary Sheet, Atomic Army Demonstration, Records of the Army Staff, Records of the Office of the Chief of Information, Entry 45, Box 1, "Atomic Army 1956," RG 319, NA.

36. Ibid., Attachment DCSOPS, Draft Summary Sheet, Atomic Army Demonstration. The quotation is on p. 1.

37. Office of the Deputy Chief of Staff for Personnel, 15 August 1956, *Combat Arms Regimental System: Outline Plan (Draft)*, Records of the Army Staff, Records of the Office of the Chief of Information, Entry 45, Box 1: Security Classified Correspondence, 1956, "Combat Arms 1956," RG 319, NA.

38. The specific breakdown was seventy field artillery, forty-two infantry, thirty antiaircraft artillery, twenty-five cavalry and armor, ten airborne infantry, and eight armored infantry regiments. Ibid., Annex D.

39. Ibid., Annex B: Combat Arms Battalions, Active Army, FY 1957.

40. Mahon and Danysh, *Regular Army*, pp. 96–98.

41. Taylor, *Swords and Plowshares*, p. 171.

42. Bacevich, *Pentomic Era*, pp. 82–96.

43. Hunnicutt, *Patton*, pp. 149–150.

44. Wilson, *Maneuver and Firepower*, p. 286.

45. Headquarters, USAREUR, Office of the Commander in Chief, 13 September 1961, *Priorities Governing the Issue of New Equipment to Troops in USAREUR*, Norstad Papers, Personal Name File, Box 61, "Clarke, Bruce C. (4)," DDEL.

46. FM 100-5 did not have a new edition between 1954 and 1962. The 1956 supplement came too soon for the pentomic division, and the 1958 supplement did not address the new formation sufficiently. The Command and General Staff College submitted a draft manuscript to CONARC in 1958, but it was returned with the comment that it needed to be revised entirely. Col. Adam S. Buynoski to Commanding General, U.S. Continental Army Command, 20 December 1958, Final Manuscript of FM 100-5, FSR, *Operations*, Records of the United States Continental Army Command, U.S. Army Schools, Command and General Staff College, Fort Leavenworth, Kansas, Box 30, Manuals, RG 546, NA. Mataxis and Goldberg addressed atomic warfare in their 1958 monograph for infantry training, *Nuclear Tactics, Weapons, and Firepower in the Pentomic Division, Battle Group, and Company*, but a semiofficial publication was hardly the equivalent of a formal statement of doctrine.

47. Bacevich, *Pentomic Era*, pp. 108–110.

48. Taylor, "Mission of the United States Army," March 1956 discussion between Taylor and students of the Armed Forces Staff College, pp. 12–15, Taylor Papers, NDU (http://www.ndu.edu/library/taylor/mdt-0095.pdf) (accessed March 2006). Quotations are on p. 15.

49. House, *Combined Arms Warfare*, p. 206.

50. Taylor, *Swords and Plowshares*, p. 166.

51. Ibid., pp. 165–166. The document, as amended by the Army Staff and approved by the secretary of the army in October 1956, is reproduced in Taylor, *The Uncertain Trumpet*, pp. 30–34.

52. Taylor, *The Uncertain Trumpet*, p. 34.

53. See, for instance, *Notes for Remarks by General Maxwell Taylor, Chief of Staff, U.S. Army, before the Calvin Bullock Forum, New York, NY, 7 December 1955*, Taylor Papers, NDU (http://www.ndu.edu/library/taylor/mdt-0065.pdf) (accessed March 2006); *"The Army for Peace," Address by General Maxwell D. Taylor, Chief of Staff, U.S. Army, to the Dallas Council on World Affairs, Hotel Statler, Dallas, Texas, April 6, 1956*, Taylor Papers, NDU (http://www.ndu.edu/library/taylor/mdt-0082.pdf) (accessed March 2006); and *Address by General Maxwell Taylor to the National Strategy Seminar at the Army War College, Carlisle Barracks, Pennsylvania, 6 June 1956, "The Role of the Army in National Strategy,"* Taylor Papers, NDU (http://www.ndu.edu/library/taylor/mdt-0114a.pdf) (accessed March 2006).

54. The article, "Security through Deterrence," was not cleared for publication because of concerns raised by the defense and state departments. It is printed in the appendix to Taylor's *Uncertain Trumpet*, pp. 181–197.

55. Douglas Kinnard shows that the army's challenge to President Eisenhower's national security policy was the most pointed of all the services. He argues that Taylor's views provided the basis for the new strategic approach of the 1960s. He concludes, however, that Taylor's challenge was repelled by the administration prior to

Taylor's retirement in 1959. Douglas Kinnard, "Civil-Military Relations: The President and the General," *Parameters* 15, no. 2 (Summer 1985): 19–29.

56. He did, however, acknowledge that the greater need for supporting units would not allow for significant overall manpower reductions. Taylor, "Mission of the United States Army," March 1956 discussion between Taylor and students of the Armed Forces Staff College, pp. 13–14, Taylor Papers, NDU (http://www.ndu.edu/library/taylor/mdt-0095.pdf) (accessed March 2006).

57. Senior Officers Debriefing Program, *Conversations between General Maxwell D. Taylor (USA, ret.) and Col. Richard A. Manion, USAWC [1972–1973]*, pt. 4, 16 February 1973, pp. 8–9, Maxwell D. Taylor Papers, MHI.

58. Maxwell D. Taylor, "The World-Wide Role and Capability of the Army," *Army Combat Forces Journal* 6, no. 2 (September 1955): 24–26. The quotations are on p. 25.

59. *Address by General Maxwell Taylor, Chief of Staff, United States Army, at the Tenth Annual Reunion of 101st Airborne Division Association, Sheraton Plaza Hotel, Boston, Massachusetts, Saturday, September 3, 1955*, Maxwell D. Taylor Papers, Box 2: Speeches 1955–1959, "Speeches 1955," MHI.

60. This was a theme that Taylor struck on several occasions. Airmobility was a key part of his argument to the 101st Airborne Association, and he reiterated it six weeks later in a speech to the National Defense Transportation Association. But Taylor also told the transportation industry executives that sea transport remained vital. He expressed great expectations for the helicopter, which he thought had performed admirably in Korea. *Address by General Maxwell Taylor, Chief of Staff, United States Army, at the Tenth Annual Convention, National Defense Transportation Association, Sheraton Plaza Hotel, Boston, Massachusetts, Thursday, October 13, 1955*, Maxwell D. Taylor Papers, Box 2: Speeches 1955–1959, "Speeches 1955," MHI.

61. For Andrew Bacevich, the transition from Ridgway to Taylor symbolized a new era of politicization rather than traditional military professionalism. Bacevich, "The Paradox of Professionalism," pp. 332–333.

62. Leighton, *Strategy, Money, and the New Look*, pp. 613–615. Representative Mahon and Taylor are quoted on p. 614. For Taylor's prepared remarks in the House of Representatives, see *Statement of General Maxwell D. Taylor, Chief of Staff, U.S. Army, before the Subcommittee on Department of Defense Appropriations, House of Representatives, Relative to the Department of the Army Budget for Fiscal Year 1957*, Taylor Papers, NDU (http://www.ndu.edu/library/taylor/mdt-0054.pdf) (accessed March 2006). Here, Taylor stressed deterrence through balanced forces, the need for a versatile army, the deterrence mission of the overseas-deployed forces and the need to provide a sufficient strategic reserve to back them up, and the army's role in training and assisting 200 divisions in 44 nations. Taylor reiterated these points in the Senate in May 1956, *Statement of General Maxwell D. Taylor, Chief of Staff, U.S. Army, before the Subcommittee of the Committee on Appropriations, United States Senate, Relative to the Department of the Army Budget for Fiscal Year 1957*, Taylor Papers, NDU (http://www.ndu.edu/library/ taylor/mdt-0073.pdf) (accessed March 2006).

63. Unattributed report, probably 17 September 1956, *Discussion of Major Issues*, sec. 1, pp. 1–2, Records of the Army Staff, Records of the Office of the Chief of Information, Entry 45, Box 1: Security Classified Correspondence, 1956, "Current Army

Thinking on Major Issues 1956," RG 319, NA. The bulk of the report was submitted on 9 May 1956, but there is a handwritten date of 17 September on the cover sheet.

64. Leighton, *Strategy, Money, and the New Look*, pp. 39–40.

65. General Maxwell Taylor, *Address to the National War College, 18 November 1960, "Limited War,"* particularly p. 6, Taylor Papers, NDU (http://www.ndu.edu/library/taylor/mdt-0138.pdf) (accessed March 2006).

66. Robert S. Jordan, *Norstad, Cold War NATO Supreme Commander: Airman, Strategist, Diplomat* (Houndmills: Macmillan, 2000), p. 208.

67. Unattributed report, probably 17 September 1956, *Discussion of Major Issues*, sec. 1, pp. 3–5, Records of the Army Staff, Records of the Office of the Chief of Information, Entry 45, Box 1: Security Classified Correspondence, 1956, "Current Army Thinking on Major Issues 1956," RG 319, NA. The quotation is on p. 5. Sec. 2, pp. 1–3, discusses the suggested National Military Program in detail.

68. Ibid., sec. 3, pp. 3–8. The quotation is on p. 3.

69. Ibid., sec. 8, pp. 1–6. The quotations are on p. 1.

70. Ibid., Appendix B: Statement by General Maxwell D. Taylor, Chief of Staff, United States Army, before the Subcommittee on Department of Defense Appropriations of the Committee on Appropriations, House of Representatives, Relative to the DA Budget, FY 1957, pp. 3, 8.

71. Ross, *American War Plans, 1945–1950*, offers the best available synopsis. Several of the plans have been published in Rosenberg and Ross, *America's Plans for War against the Soviet Union, 1945–1950*.

72. Kenneth W. Condit, *The Joint Chiefs of Staff and National Policy, 1955–1956*, vol. 6 of *History of the Joint Chiefs of Staff* (Washington, DC: Historical Office, Joint Staff, 1992), pp. 25–32. For Taylor's argumentation in the debates, see also Taylor, *The Uncertain Trumpet*, pp. 38–39.

73. Maxwell Taylor, "A Military Strategy for NATO" (speech before the Council on Foreign Relations, 12 April 1961), Taylor Papers, NDU (http://www.ndu.edu/library/taylor/mdt-0165.pdf) (accessed March 2006).

74. The ensuing limited war debate and the crucial role played by Maxwell Taylor has been discussed recently by Walker, "Eisenhower's New Look," pp. 172–228, 339–366. For Taylor and the army, see especially pp. 182–212. Walker concludes that Maxwell Taylor intended to design an army for limited nuclear war and that the pentomic division offered a useful organization for this purpose. He asserts that the army developed coherent doctrine for tactical nuclear war but cites only semiofficial monographs as examples, e.g., Mataxis and Goldberg, *Nuclear Tactics*; and Reinhardt and Kintner, *Atomic Weapons in Land Combat.*

75. Watson, *Into the Missile Age*, pp. 661–664; Condit, *The Joint Chiefs of Staff, 1955–56*, pp. 32–37. For the 24 May meeting, see *FRUS*, 1955–1957, vol. 19: *National Security Policy* (Washington, DC: Government Printing Office, 1990), pp. 311–315; and Colonel A. J. Goodpaster, Memorandum of Conference with the President, 24 May 1956, Nuclear History/Berlin Crisis, 1956 TNF Copies, Box 3, NSA. Eisenhower's attitude toward limited war at that time is discussed further by Trachtenberg, *A Constructed Peace*, pp. 160–162.

76. The next two paragraphs rely mainly on Leighton, *Strategy, Money, and the New*

Look, pp. 664–666. For a discussion of the Radford Plan and its effects on the army, see also Taylor, *The Uncertain Trumpet*, pp. 39–42.

77. A proposal to withdraw American troops from Germany had been raised before. In May 1955, General Gruenther advised against such a step in a cable to the JCS. He argued that the balance of military power presented a credible deterrent in Central Europe. He warned that any withdrawal would endanger the political and diplomatic position of the West and implied that the foundations of containment could be shaken. Gruenther to JCS, 25 May 1955, Norstad Papers, Pre-SACEUR Subject Series, Box 44, "German Withdrawal," DDEL.

78. Trachtenberg, *A Constructed Peace*, pp. vi–x, 146–200. Trachtenberg's argument may be questioned on the grounds that a policy of troop withdrawals would have destroyed NATO, thus pulling the rug out from under Eisenhower's feet.

79. Taylor, *The Uncertain Trumpet*, pp. 40–41.

80. Byron R. Fairchild and Walter S. Poole, *The Joint Chiefs of Staff and National Policy, 1957–1960*, vol. 7 of *The History of the Joint Chiefs of Staff* (Washington, DC: Office of Joint History, Office of the Chairman of the Joint Chiefs of Staff, 2000), pp. 31–42.

81. Maxwell Taylor based his concept of Flexible Response upon the assumption that requirements of the services needed to be evaluated carefully and soundly. He hoped that this would eventually lead to military requirements being determined by the mission rather than the budget. Taylor, *The Uncertain Trumpet*, pp. 149–150.

82. Watson, *Into the Missile Age*, pp. 75–101.

83. In the course of 1958, the army position was reinforced by a detailed study conducted for the Senate Committee on Foreign Relations. It concluded that strategic nuclear deterrence had to be strongly supplemented by tactical nuclear and conventional ground forces that could deter or stop any Soviet attack with limited means but that need not escalate into general war. *Developments in Military Technology and Their Impact on United States Strategy and Foreign Policy* (a study prepared at the request of the Committee on Foreign Relations, U.S. Senate, by the Washington Center of Foreign Policy Research, Johns Hopkins University; Washington, DC: Government Printing Office, 1959). See particularly the recommendations on pp. 10–12.

84. Watson, *Into the Missile Age*, pp. 127–155.

85. Taylor, "Mission of the United States Army," March 1956 discussion between Taylor and students of the Armed Forces Staff College, pp. 6–8 (the quotation is from p. 8), Taylor Papers, NDU (http://www.ndu.edu/library/taylor/mdt-0095.pdf) (accessed March 2006).

86. Watson, *Into the Missile Age*, pp. 292–322.

87. Ibid., pp. 323–360.

88. NATO commanders strongly suggested that NATO had to employ atomic and nuclear weapons at the outset of general war with the Soviets, even if the enemy did not do so first, or Europe would be overrun. The initial intensive atomic exchange might have to be followed by a subsequent period of operations to ensure victory. SM-109-57, 8 February 1957, Appendix to Enclosure A to JCS 2073/1353, *Over-all Strategic Concept for the Defense of the NATO Area*, Geographic File 1957, CCS092 Western Europe (3-12-48) (2), sec. 73, RG 218, NA.

89. This was expressed in official army doctrine in 1962, but Taylor and his staff had worked on this assumption since the mid-1950s. Department of the Army, *FM 100-5: Field Service Regulations: Operations* (Washington, DC: Headquarters, Department of the Army, February 1962), pp. 5, 12.

90. Nathan F. Twining, *Neither Liberty nor Safety: A Hard Look at U.S. Military Policy and Strategy* (New York: Holt, Rinehart and Winston, 1966), p. 115. For Twining's general argumentation against limited war, see pp. 102–120.

91. The debates of 1957 through 1959 are summarized in Fairchild and Poole, *The Joint Chiefs of Staff and National Policy, 1957–1960*, pp. 11–29. See also pp. 95–112 for strategic planning in NATO.

92. Taylor had opposed the reduction to 870,000 men, indicating that 925,000 men were necessary to fulfill the army's objectives within the tasks dictated by national security policy. See Department of the Army, Office, Chief of Information, *Minutes of Press Conference Held by General Maxwell D. Taylor, Chief of Staff, Friday, 14 November 1958*, p. 4, Maxwell D. Taylor Papers, Box 2: Speeches, 1955–1959, "Speeches 1958," MHI.

93. See Maxwell D. Taylor, *Military Objectives of the Army, 1960–1962*, pp. 1–5, Chart I, Address to the Secretaries' Conference, Quantico, VA, 21 June 1958. A copy of the speech can be found in the stacks of the MHI. It appears that this is not technically a published source, even though it is bound and cataloged.

94. Ibid., p. 6.

95. Office of European Regional Affairs, Memorandum of Conversation, 4 May 1960, *NATO Military Concept*, Records of the Department of State, Office of European Regional Affairs, Politico-Military Numerical Files 1953–1962, Box 8, "Strategic Doctrine," RG 59, NA. The document is also available online at PHP, http://www.php.isn.ethz.ch/collections/colltopic.cfm?lng=en&id=18450&navinfo=14968 (accessed 15 November 2007). The author of the memorandum was John Millar. The recipient was Russell Fessenden.

96. Trachtenberg, *A Constructed Peace*, pp. 147–156.

97. General Eisenhower estimated that between sixty-five and ninety-five divisions were needed to defend Central Region at the Rhine River. By 1957, due to the integration of tactical nuclear weapons into NATO planning, the requirement had been reduced to thirty divisions, and General Norstad argued that the line of defense could be moved forward to the Iron Curtain once that objective had been reached. *Summary of SACEUR's Presentation to the Permanent Representatives of the NATO Council—28 May 57*, Norstad Papers, Policy Files Series, Box 87, "Forces (5)," DDEL.

98. Bradley is quoted in Trachtenberg, *A Constructed Peace*, pp. 100–101.

99. The debate is discussed in Duffield, *Power Rules*, pp. 122–126.

100. This led to more serious talks about Franco-German defense relations. See Wall, *France, the United States, and the Algerian War*, p. 78. When combined with the Radford Plan, Adenauer's paranoia becomes more understandable, albeit no more logical. It was, in fact, the U.S. Army's position in the strategy debates that would have offered the greatest likelihood of a territorial defense of West Germany, yet the chancellor essentially sided with General Norstad's modified conception of Massive Retaliation.

101. Taylor, *Swords and Plowshares*, pp. 166–167.

102. JP (56)133 (Final), 28 August 1956, Chiefs of Staff Committee, Joint Planning Staff, *SACEUR's Emergency Defence Plan—1957: Report by the Joint Planning Staff*, PHP, http://www.php.isn.ethz.ch/collections/colltopic.cfm?lng=en&id=18482&nav info=14968 (accessed 15 November 2007). The original is at the Public Record Office, Kew, London, in DEFE 4/90. SHAPE has not released the actual EDPs. The quotation, drawing on EDP 1-57, is on p. 2.

103. The Weser-Lech line was the main line of defense for Central Region from 1957 to 1963. Maloney, *War without Battles*, pp. 133–135.

104. Norstad to Heusinger, n.d. (probably July 1957), Norstad Papers, Country Files, Box 48, "Germany 1956–1960 (9)," DDEL.

105. SG 184/7 (Final), 14 January 1957, Decision on SG 184/7, A Report by the International Planning Team on *SACEUR's Emergency Defense Plan, 1957*, International Military Staff, Records of the Standing Group, NATO Archives, Brussels.

106. Valluy to Norstad, n.d. (probably February 1958), Norstad Papers, Subject Series, Box 95, "AFCENT (7)," DDEL.

107. Deputy SACEUR to Norstad, 6 January 1959, *Report on Conversation with Generals Valluy and Speidel on Command Structure, Central Europe, on 22 December 1958*, Norstad Papers, Subject Series, Box 104, "Memorandum for Record 1957–1958–1959 (3)," DDEL.

108. COS (57)244, 14 November 1957, Chiefs of Staff Committee, *NATO Minimum Force Studies: Note by the Secretary*, PHP, http://www.php.isn.ethz.ch/collections/colltopic.cfm?lng=en&id=18470&navinfo=14968 (accessed 15 November 2007). The original is in the Public Record Office, Kew, London, at DEFE 5/79.

109. MC 14/2 (revised) (Final Decision), 23 May 1957, *Final Decision on MC 14/2 (Revised): A Report by the Military Committee on Overall Strategic Concept for the Defense of the North Atlantic Treaty Organization Area*, in Pedlow, *NATO Strategy Documents*, pp. 277–314.

110. Ibid., p. 291. Marc Trachtenberg nevertheless sees MC 14/2 as a significant step to Flexible Response. It certainly shows the growing awareness of approaching nuclear parity and its consequences. Trachtenberg, *A Constructed Peace*, pp. 188–191. John Duffield concurs. Duffield, *Power Rules*, pp. 112–150. Neither author had access to MC 14/2, however. Christian Greiner, in "Die Entwicklung der Bündnisstrategie, 1949 bis 1958," pp. 163–171, in *Die NATO als Militärallianz: Strategie, Organization und nukleare Kontrolle im Bündnis, 1949 bis 1959*, edited by Christian Greiner et al. (Munich: R. Oldenbourg Verlag, 2003), pp. 17–174, interprets MC 14/2 as the further codification of Massive Retaliation.

111. DSAC 1705/7, Standing Group, *CPX Seven—Notes for the Exercise Staff: No. 5, Points to Be Included in a New Directive Which Might Well Be Given to NATO Commands*, Norstad Papers, Subject Series, Box 99, "CPX Seven, 15–18 April 1958," DDEL.

112. MC 14/2 (revised) (Final Decision), 23 May 1957, *Final Decision on MC 14/2 (Revised): A Report by the Military Committee on Overall Strategic Concept for the Defense of the North Atlantic Treaty Organization Area*, in Pedlow, *NATO Strategy Documents*, p. 294.

113. Hans Speidel, *Aus Unserer Zeit: Erinnerungen* (Frankfurt/Main: Verlag Ullstein, 1977), pp. 361–362. Speidel states that he had opposed Massive Retaliation since its inception because it posed a grave danger to Germany.

114. Headquarters, USAREUR, Office of A/C of S, G-2, Special Intelligence Estimate 1-59, 1 February 1959, *Soviet/Satellite Military Courses of Action in Europe through 1960*, pp. 46–47.

115. Enclosure to JCS 2099/733, n.d. (probably August 1957), *Status of National Security Program on 30 June 1957*, and Enclosure to Decision on JCS 2099/733, 18 September 1957, Memorandum for the Secretary of Defense, *Status of National Security Programs on 30 June 1957*, Central Decimal File 1957, CGS092 (8-22-46) (2), sec. 44, RG 218, NA.

116. CSAM 12-58, Memorandum by the Chief of Staff, U.S. Army, 29 January 1958, *NATO Minimum Essential Force Requirements, 1958–1963 (MC 70)*, Geographic File 1958, CCS092 Western Europe (3-12-48) (2), sec. 97, RG 218, NA.

117. MC 70, A Report by the Military Committee to the North Atlantic Council, 29 January 1958, *The Minimum Essential Force Requirements, 1958–1963*, International Military Staff, Records of the North Atlantic Military Committee, NATO Archives, Brussels.

118. Ibid., pp. 37–38.

119. Ibid., pp. 44–45.

120. Ibid., p. 50.

121. Ibid., p. 51.

122. Ibid., p. 52. This is discussed in greater depth in chapter 3.

123. Annex 1 to Appendix A, MC 70, *Total Force Requirements: Land Forces.*

124. In anticipation of the German buildup, Great Britain had already reduced its ground forces in British Army of the Rhine from about 100,000 officers and men in 1955 to about 80,000 by 1957 and had also withdrawn 31 squadrons and 362 aircraft of the tactical air force. Thus, British Army of the Rhine was one division short of its four-division requirement. Memorandum on U.K. forces, 29 April 1958, Norstad Papers, Box 87, "Forces (5)," DDEL.

125. Annex 1 to Appendix E, MC 70, *Country Breakdown.*

126. JCS 2285/2, Memorandum by the Chief of Staff, U.S. Army, 18 June 1958, *Strategic Mobility for U.S. Forces*, Central Decimal File 1958, CCS381 (11-22-57), sec. 2, RG 218, NA. See also Enclosure A: *Joint Chiefs of Staff Approved Contingency Plans for Limited War Which Provide for Movement of Forces from CONUS.* Besides the four-division contingency plan for Europe, three divisions and two armored cavalry regiments were slated for Korea, one airborne or infantry division accompanied by two battle groups were slated for Indonesia, two battle groups of infantry or airborne infantry were slated for the Caribbean, and two divisions were slated for the Middle East. Handling several crises at a time would have been very difficult, yet plans for general war always assumed operations in several theaters.

127. Submission by the United States of America in Response to the Questionnaire for the Annual Review 1958, 12 August 1958, *General Memorandum, Part II: Service Sections—Army*, Geographic File 1958, CCS092 Western Europe (3-12-48) (2), B.P. 21, RG 218, NA.

128. Central Intelligence Agency, Office of National Estimates, Staff Memorandum No. 52-57, 22 November 1957, *The NATO Defense Problem*, CIA Records, Electronic Database, NA.

129. MC 39/10, A Report by the Military Committee to the North Atlantic Council, 24 October 1958, *Analysis of Military Implications of 1958 Annual Review*, International Military Staff, Records of the North Atlantic Military Committee, NATO Archives, Brussels. Both quotations are on p. 4.

130. Ibid., pp. 13, 17; Enclosure 1: *Shortfalls and Deficiencies in NATO Forces*.

131. SHAPE, Paris, 31 October 1961, Norstad Papers, Subject Series, Box 112, "Strategy, NATO (2)," DDEL.

132. Hans Speidel, "Mission and Needs of NATO's Shield," *Army* 11, no. 2 (September 1960): 33–38. The quotation is on p. 36.

133. Memorandum of Conversation, 1 February 1961, in *FRUS*, 1961–1963, vol. 13, *Western Europe and Canada* (Washington, DC: Government Printing Office, 1994), pp. 253–256.

134. MC 43/6, A Report by the Standing Group to the Military Committee, 20 May 1959, *NATO Exercises 1958*, Appendix E: *Report on Exercise HOSTAGE BLEU*, International Military Staff, Records of the North Atlantic Military Committee, NATO Archives, Brussels.

135. Ibid., pp. 3–4.

136. Ibid., pp. 4–5.

137. Ibid., pp. 5–6.

138. MC 92 (Revised), A Report by the Military Committee to the North Atlantic Council, 21 April 1960, *An Overall Evaluation of the MC 70 Country Studies*, sec. 3: *Evaluation by Major Command*, International Military Staff, Records of the North Atlantic Military Committee, NATO Archives, Brussels. The quotation is on p. 10.

139. Robert R. Bowie, *The North Atlantic Nations: Tasks for the 1960's—A Report to the Secretary of State, August 1960* (Bowie Report) (Nuclear History Program: Occasional Paper 7; University of Maryland: Center for International Security Studies, 1991). This publication contains the report itself and a new foreword by Bowie.

140. Even the secretary of defense, Thomas Gates, admitted that he thought the Bowie Report constituted the first "reasonable approach…to the problem of reduced confidence in the concept of massive retaliation." Memorandum of Conversation, 16 September 1960, *Meeting between Secretary of Defense, United States, and General Norstad*, Norstad Papers, Policy File Series, Box 91, "US Support of NATO, 1958–60 (2)," DDEL.

141. *SACEUR's Comments on the Bowie Report*, n.d., Norstad Papers, Subject Series, Box 98, "Bowie Report (2)," DDEL. The quotations are on p. 2.

142. SACEUR to Major Subordinate Commands, 13 December 1960, *Basic Strategic Guidance for Allied Command Europe*, Norstad Papers, Policy File Series, Box 90, "Strategy—General (2)," DDEL.

143. Norstad to Irwin, 16 November 1960, Norstad Papers, Subject Series, Box 96, "Assistant Secretary of Defense/ISA (5)," DDEL.

144. Taylor, *Swords and Plowshares*, p. 169.

145. JCS 2305/263, 28 October 1960, *NATO Long-Range Planning*, Central Decimal File 1960, CCS9050/3000 NATO (29 August 1960), sec. 4, Box 61, RG 218, NA.

Chapter 3. The Pentomic Army in Germany

1. JCS 2073/61, 3 September 1950, *Report by the Joint Strategic Plans Committee to the Joint Chiefs of Staff on U.S. Participation in the Defense of Western Europe*, Appendix to Enclosure A: *United States Views on Measures for the Defense of Western Europe*, p. 436, Geographic File 1948–50, CCS092 (3-12-48), sec. 55, RG 218, NA.

2. SM-2597-50, Memorandum for the U.S. Representative to the Standing Group, North Atlantic Military Committee, 18 October 1950, *Proposed Increases in Military Forces Readily Available by 1 July 1951 for North Atlantic Treaty Area (Report on Medium Term Defense Plan)*, Appendix A: *Buildup of National Contributions to Meet NATO Force Objectives*, Geographic File 1948–50, CCS092 (3-12-48), sec. 61, RG 218, NA.

3. JSPC 876/814, 18 February 1954, *Report by the Joint Strategic Plans Committee to the Joint Chiefs of Staff on Order of Battle Report for Earmarked Forces—Submission of Report*, Annex A: *Army Order of Battle Report (SACEUR) as of 31 December 1953*, sec. 1: *Land Forces Order of Battle*, pt. 1: *Status Report as of 31 December 1953*, Geographic File 1954–56, CCS092 Western Europe (3-12-48), sec. 264, RG 218, NA.

4. JSPC 876/938, 12 January 1955, *Report by the Joint Strategic Plans Committee to the Joint Chiefs of Staff on Order of Battle Report for Earmarked Forces*, Annex A: *Army Order of Battle Report (SACEUR) as of 31 December 1954*, sec. 1: *Land Forces Order of Battle*, pt. 1: *Status Report as of 31 December 1954*, Geographic File 1954–56, CGS092 Western Europe (3-12-48), sec. 2, RG 218, NA.

5. Karber, "Nuclear Weapons and the U.S. Army in Europe: 1953–1989," p. 7.

6. SM-357-55, Memorandum for the Joint Chiefs of Staff, 5 May 1955, *Order of Battle Report for Earmarked Forces*, Geographic File 1954–56, CGS092 Western Europe (3-12-48) (2), sec. 15, RG 218, NA.

7. Ibid., Appendix to Enclosure A: *Draft: Memorandum for the Supreme Allied Commander, Europe.*

8. JCS 2073/1223, 30 January 1956, Report by the Joint Strategic Plans Committee to the Joint Chiefs of Staff on *Order of Battle Report to SACEUR for U.S. Forces Assigned, Earmarked for Assignment, and Earmarked for Assignment on Mobilization (as of 31 December 1955)*, Geographic File 1954–56, CGS092 Western Europe (3-12-48) (2), sec. 49, RG 218, NA.

9. Karber, "Nuclear Weapons and the U.S. Army in Europe: 1953–1989," p. 13.

10. By nature of the subject, this book is mainly concerned with the American and West German forces in CENTAG. For maneuvers and exercises in NORTHAG in this time period, see Maloney, *War without Battles*, pp. 85–93.

11. Headquarters, VII Corps, 9 June 1955, *CPX WOLF CALL, 19–22 July 1955*, pp. 1–6, VII Corps 1953–1966, Box 32, RG 338, NA.

12. Ibid., Annex B (Boundaries) to Initial Instructions, CPX "WOLF CALL."

13. Ibid., Operation Order 1—CPX "WOLF CALL."

14. Ibid., Annex A (Task Organization) to Operation Order 1—CPX "WOLF CALL."

15. Ibid., Annex J (Counterattack Plans—Seventh Army Reserve) to Operation Order 1 CPX "WOLF CALL."

16. Headquarters, Central Army Group, 22 September 1955, Internal Press Release

for CENTAG Use Only, FTX CORDON BLEU, VII Corps 1953–1966, 354 Maneuver "CORDON BLEU" October 1955, Box 30, RG 338, NA.

17. Headquarters, VII Corps, 12 October 1955, *Operation Order 1—FTX "CORDON BLEU,"* Appendix 1 (Troop List) to Annex A (Task Organization) to Operations Order 1 FTX "CORDON BLEU," VII Corps 1953–1966, Box 32, RG 338, NA.

18. Ibid., Operation Order 1—FTX "CORDON BLEU."

19. Ibid., Annex B (Intelligence) to Operation Order 1—FTX "CORDON BLEU."

20. Ibid., Operation Order 1—FTX "CORDON BLEU."

21. MC 43/3, 28 May 1956, Report by the Standing Group to the North Atlantic Military Committee on *NATO Exercises, 1955*, Enclosure A: SHAPE/70/56, 28 February 1956, *Report on NATO Exercises 1955*, pp. 30–33, International Military Staff, Records of the North Atlantic Military Committee, NATO Archives, Brussels. The quotation is on p. 32.

22. Theoretically, any use of nuclear weapons would have had to be approved by President Eisenhower. Marc Trachtenberg claims that predelegation of nuclear weapons use from Eisenhower to SACEUR had indeed been arranged. But even if that was the case, it would still not explain how field army, corps, and division commanders could get the green light from Paris in time before the tactical situation had changed. Trachtenberg, *A Constructed Peace*, pp. 165–173.

23. Headquarters, VII Corps, 12 November 1956, *FTX "WAR HAWK," 5–12 Dec 56*, Annex M (Counter Offensive Plan) 1-56—FTX "WAR HAWK," U.S. Army Commands, VII Corps 1953–1966, Box 28, RG 338, NA.

24. Headquarters, Seventh Army, 18 January 1957, *Operation Plan 1-57, CPX "LION NOIR"* and Appendix I (Barrier Trace) to Annex G (Barrier Plan) to Operation Plan 1-57 CPX "LION NOIR," U.S. Army Commands, Seventh Army 1954–65, 250/6 Perm Record Set—Ops Plan 1-57—CPX "LION NOIR," RG 338, NA.

25. Ibid., Operation Plan 1-57, CPX "LION NOIR."

26. Ibid., Annex A (Task Organization) to Operation Plan 1-57 CPX "LION NOIR."

27. Frank Buchholz, *Strategische und Militärpolitische Diskussionen in der Gründungsphase der Bundeswehr, 1949–1960* (Frankfurt/Main: Peter Lang, 1991), pp. 244–245.

28. Headquarters, Seventh Army, 18 March 1957, Operations Plan 2-57, CPX "LION NOIR," and Annex A (Task Organization) to Operation Plan 2-57, CPX "LION NOIR," Seventh Army 1954–65, 250/6 Perm Record Set—Ops Plan 2-57—CPX LION NOIR, Box 57, RG 338, NA.

29. Headquarters, Seventh Army, 26 March 1957, Operation Plan 3-57, CPX "LION NOIR," Seventh Army 1954–65, 250/6 Perm Record Set—Opn Plan 3-57—CPX LION NOIR, Box 57, RG 338, NA.

30. JCS 2073/1346, 11 January 1957, Report by the Joint Strategic Plans Committee to the Joint Chiefs of Staff on *Order of Battle Report to SACEUR of U.S. Forces Assigned, Earmarked for Assignment, and Earmarked for Assignment on Mobilization (as of 31 December 1956)*, Geographic File 1957, CCS092 Western Europe (3-12-48) (2), sec. 71, RG 218, NA.

31. Taylor, *The Uncertain Trumpet*, pp. 143–144, 151–152, 168.

32. Karber, "Nuclear Weapons and the U.S. Army in Europe: 1953–1989," p. 18.

33. JCS 2124/183, 26 February 1957, Decision on JCS 2124/183, A Memorandum by the Chief of Staff, U.S. Army, on *U.S. Forces in Germany*, Geographic File 1957, CCS092 Germany (5-4-49), sec. 32, RG 218, NA.

34. Memorandum for Captain Blouin, Joint Staff, from Colonel Twitchell, Deputy for NATO Affairs, European Region, I.S.A., 20 June 1957, *Seventh Army Re-Stationing Plan and Acquisition of NIKE Sites*, Chairman's File, Admiral Radford 1953–1957, Box 9, 091 Germany, RG 218, NA.

35. Memorandum for Record, 24 January 1957, *Gen. Valluy's Proposals Bearing on Re-Stationing and New Operational Plans*, Assistant Chief of Staff, G-3 Operations, Plans and Policy Branch, Policy Section Organizational Files 1954–58, Box 158, "Organization Planning Files 1957," RG 549, NA. CINCUSAREUR General Hodes liked the proposed Franco-German army south of the Danube, but his preference for the Koblenz-Trier area was a three-division German corps.

36. Historical Division, Headquarters, USAREUR, *Annual Historical Report, 1 July 1957–30 June 1958*, p. 1.

37. General Clarke to General O'Meara, 4 October 1957, Seventh Army 1954–65, Box 51, 250/16 Organization Planning Files, RG 338, NA.

38. Minutes, 8 October 1957, *Seventh Army Commanders Conference*, Seventh Army 1954–65, Box 57, 250/16 Organization Planning Files (Plans), RG 338, NA.

39. Karber, "Nuclear Weapons and the U.S. Army in Europe: 1953–1989," p. 28.

40. Headquarters, USAREUR, *Annual Report, 1957–58*, pp. 115–119.

41. Speidel, *Aus Unserer Zeit*, pp. 359–402, recalls his tenure as commanding general of LANDCENT.

42. Ibid., p. 361.

43. Headquarters, USAREUR, *Annual History, United States Army, Europe, 1 July 1958–30 June 1959*, pp. 48–51.

44. JCS 2073/1502, 8 January 1958, Report by the Joint Strategic Plans Committee to the Joint Chiefs of Staff on *Order of Battle Report to SACEUR of U.S. Forces Assigned, Earmarked for Assignment, and Earmarked for Assignment on Mobilization (as of 31 December 1957)*, Geographic File 1958, CCS092 Western Europe (3-12-48) (2), sec. 95, RG 218, NA.

45. Headquarters, USAREUR, *Annual Report, 1957–58*, p. 134.

46. Ibid., p. 135.

47. Trachtenberg, *A Constructed Peace*, p. 191.

48. Headquarters, USAREUR, *Annual Report, 1957–58*, pp. 155–156.

49. Ibid., p. 166.

50. Ibid., pp. 168–169.

51. Ibid., p. 169.

52. Ibid., p. 171.

53. JCSM-49-59, Memorandum for the Secretary of Defense, 11 February 1959, *Order of Battle Report to SACEUR of U.S. Forces Assigned, Earmarked for Assignment, and Earmarked for Assignment on Mobilization as of 1 January 1959*, Central Decimal File 1959, CCS9051/3400 Allied Command Europe (11 February 1959), Box 113, RG 218, NA.

54. JCSM-106-60, Memorandum for the U.S. Commander in Chief, Europe, 29 January 1960, *Order of Battle Report to SACEUR for Assigned Forces, Earmarked Forces and*

Forces Earmarked for Assignment on Mobilization as of 1 January 1960, Central Decimal File 1960, CCS9051/3400 Allied Command Europe (12 January 1960), sec. 1, Box 66, RG 218, NA.

55. Karber, "Nuclear Weapons and the U.S. Army in Europe: 1953–1989," p. 33.

56. Bruce C. Clarke, "The Why of STRAC," Robert F. Sink, "The What of STRAC," and William C. Westmoreland, "The How of STRAC," *Army* 9, no. 5 (December 1958): 59–62. See also Draft Study prepared by Department of the Army, Office of the Chief of Military History, "The Development of the STRAF," 1963, pp. 20–30, MHI library.

57. Headquarters, Seventh United States Army, Memorandum for Assistant Chief of Staff, G4, 3 June 1959, *Staff Study Field Army Logistics*, MHI library.

58. Senior Officer Oral History Program, General Donald V. Bennett interview by Lieutenant Colonel Smith and Lieutenant Colonel Hatcher, vol. 1, tape 5, 21 April 1976, pp. 10–12, Donald V. Bennett Papers, Oral History, Box 1, MHI. Bennett oversaw the evaluation of the pentomic divisions in Seventh Army as Chief of Plans, Operations, Organization, and Equipment (G-3). He was particularly critical of the limited staying power and the limited mobility of the infantry division.

59. Brigadier General J. K. Wilson, Artillery Commander, to Assistant Commandant, Artillery and Missile School, Fort Sill, 1 May 1958, U.S. Army Schools, Artillery and Guided Missile School, Fort Sill, Box 9, Organization and Planning Files: Reorganization of the Inf Div Arty, RG 546, NA.

60. Memorandum for Record, 5 November 1958, *General Palmer's Discussion with SACEUR, 1100 hrs, 5 Nov, on the Subject Review of USAREUR's Strength*, Norstad Papers, Subject Series, Box 104, "Memorandum for Record 1957–1958–1959 (4)," DDEL.

61. *Staff Study Field Army Logistics*, MHI Library, pp. 4–8.

62. Submission by the United States of America in Response to the Questionnaire for the Annual Review 1959, 24 July 1959, *General Memorandum*, pt. 2: *Service Section: Army*, II-A-3, Central Decimal File 1959, CCS9050/3410 NATO (15 July 1959), Box 105, RG 218, NA.

63. Headquarters, Department of the Army, TOE 7D, 1 February 1960.

64. Address by Lieutenant General Harold K. Johnson, Deputy Chief of Staff for Military Operations, to Canadian National Defense College, 10 January 1964, *Modern Land Weaponry and Methods of Warfare*, p. 4, Harold K. Johnson Papers, Speech Reference File—Personal (4 of 4), through 1968, Box 56, MHI.

65. Anthony B. Herbert, *Soldier* (New York: Holt, Rinehart and Winston, 1973), pp. 77–79.

66. Memorandum for Record, 19 September 1963, *Organizational Concept for a New Type Airborne Division*, General Staff, ODCSOPS/OACSFOR, Security Classified Correspondence 1963, 201-45 Services, Box 15, RG 319, NA.

67. Doughty, *Evolution of U.S. Army Tactical Doctrine*, p. 19.

68. Headquarters, USAREUR, *Annual Report, 1958–59*, p. 2.

69. Ibid., pp. 44–45.

70. Ibid., pp. 24–25, 30–31.

71. Central Intelligence Agency, SNIE 100-6-59, 6 April 1959, *Soviet and Other Reactions to Various Courses of Action in the Berlin Crisis*, National Intelligence Estimates In-

volving the Soviet Union, 1957–1983, Box 8, Folder 2, RG 263, NA; National Intelligence Council Memoranda, March 1982–April 1983, Box 8, Folder 2, RG 263, NA.

72. Taylor, *The Uncertain Trumpet*, p. 137.

73. Headquarters, USAREUR, *Annual Report, 1958–59*, pp. 33–36. For a history of military operations in Lebanon, see Roger J. Spiller, *"Not War but Like War": The American Intervention in Lebanon* (Leavenworth Paper No. 3; Fort Leavenworth, KS: U.S. Army Command and General Staff College, 1981).

74. Memorandum of Conversation, General Norstad, General Eddleman, Major General Jark, Colonel Downey, 26 August 1960, Norstad Papers, Subject Series, Box 105, "Memorandum for Record II 1960–1961 (7)," DDEL.

75. ORO-S-1647, Staff Memorandum, 25 April 1961, *Trip Report: NATO FTX* WINTERSHIELD II, by Edward W. Girard, Command and General Staff College, Combined Arms Research Library, Archive 16454.900. See also Robert B. Asprey, "Wintershield 2: War in a Nuclear Climate," *Army* 11, no. 10 (May 1961): 40–46.

76. Headquarters, USAREUR, Office of the Commander in Chief, 22 October 1961, *Synopsis of General Clarke's Remarks to the Division Chiefs, Headquarters, USAREUR, 21 October 1961*, Norstad Papers, Personal Name File, Box 61, "Clarke, Bruce C. (3)," DDEL.

77. Headquarters, USAREUR, Office of the Commander in Chief, 5 March 1962, *Summary of Opening Conference with Dr. Peck and Colonel Irby (Members of Ailes Committee)*, p. 4, Norstad Papers, Personal Name File, Box 61, "Clarke, Bruce C. (2)," DDEL.

78. Operations Coordinating Board, 17 May 1956, Progress Report, *United States Policy toward the Federal Republic of Germany*, pp. 1, 4, Records Relating to State Department Participation in the Operations Coordinating Board and the National Security Council, 1947–1963, Lot File 62D430: Operations Coordinating Board, Box 18, "Germany 2," RG 59, NA.

79. *Meeting of the Standing Group with General Heusinger in the Standing Group Conference Room, the Pentagon, at 10:00 A.M. on 27 July 1956*, International Military Staff, Records of the Standing Group, NATO Archives, Brussels. See p. 4 for the discussion of the implications of the Radford Plan.

80. Memorandum for Lieutenant General Fox, 15 February 1957, *Variations in Strauss Statements on German Buildup*, Chairman's File: Admiral Radford 1953–1957, Box 9, 091 Germany, RG 218, NA. See also Department of State, Memorandum of Conversation, 18 February 1957, *The German Military Buildup*, Chairman's File: Admiral Radford 1953–1957, Box 9, 091 Germany, RG 218, NA.

81. National Security Council, Memorandum for the NSC Planning Board, 7 November 1957, *U.S. Policy toward Germany*, Geographic File 1958, CCS092 Germany (5-4-49), sec. 34, RG 218, NA.

82. For the positive attitude of the Eisenhower administration toward sharing atomic weapons with the German armed forces, as part of more general nuclear sharing with NATO partners, see Trachtenberg, *A Constructed Peace*, pp. 195, 209–210. See also the notes for the NSC meetings of 16 July and 30 July 1959, in *FRUS*, 1958–1960, vol. 3, *National Security Policy* (Washington, DC: Government Printing Office, 1996), pp. 260–261, 288–289.

83. Operations Coordinating Board, n.d. (probably August 1957), Progress Report,

United States Policy toward the Federal Republic of Germany (NSC-160/1), *United States Policy toward East Germany* (Supplement to NSC-160/1), *United States Policy toward Berlin* (NSC-5404/1), p. 3. Records Relating to State Department Participation in the Operations Coordinating Board and the National Security Council, 1947–1963: Operations Coordinating Board, Germany 2, Box 18, RG 59, NA.

84. National Security Council, Memorandum for the NSC Planning Board, 25 October 1957, *U.S. Policy toward Germany*, p. 1, Geographic File 1958, CCS092 Germany (5-4-49), sec. 34, RG 218, NA.

85. Christian Greiner, "Die Militärische Eingliederung der Bundesrepublik Deutschland in die WEU und die NATO, 1954 bis 1957," pp. 711–712, in Ehlert et al., *Die NATO Option*, pp. 561–850.

86. A comprehensive discussion of the evolution of German military attitudes toward atomic war can be found in Bruno Thoss, *NATO-Strategie und nationale Verteidigungsplanung: Planung und Aufbau der Bundeswehr unter den Bedingungen einer massiven atomaren Vergeltungsstrategie, 1952–1960* (Munich: R. Oldenbourg Verlag, 2006), pp. 108–150.

87. Buchholz, *Strategische und Militärpolitische Diskussionen*, pp. 137–139.

88. The reorganization of the division and introduction of the brigade was central to the Bundeswehr's *Heeresstruktur* 2, the reform that was implemented in 1959. For a recent comprehensive discussion, see Martin Rink, "Strukturen brausen um die Wette: Zur Organization des deutschen Heeres," pp. 435–455, in Helmut Hammerich et al., *Das Heer 1950 bis 1970: Konzeption, Organisation, Aufstellung* (Munich: R. Oldenbourg, 2006), pp. 353–483. There is some debate about the size of the proposed divisions. Christian Tuschhoff, *Deutschland, Kernwaffen und die NATO, 1949–1967* (Baden-Baden: Nomos Verlagsgesellschaft, 2002), pp. 54–56; Birtle, *Rearming the Phoenix*, pp. 77–79; and Rink, "Strukturen," p. 380, discuss proposals for an armored division of only 10,000 officers and men. Buchholz has it at a much larger size.

89. General John Heintges, who had served as the commander of Military Assistance Advisory Group, Germany, was convinced that the German divisional organization subsequently became the model for the ROAD division of the U.S. Army. In his view, General Clyde Eddleman, the father of ROAD, merely copied the German division that he had encountered during his tenure as CINCUSAREUR from 1958 to 1960. Debriefing of John A. Heintges by Major J. A. Pellicci, 6 May 1974, tape 8, pp. 28–29, John A. Heintges Papers, Recollections and Reflections: Transcripts of the Debriefing of John A. Heintges by Major J. A. Pellicci, Oral History Transcripts, tape 8, Box 1, MHI.

90. Headquarters, USAREUR, *Annual History, United States Army, Europe, 1 July 1958–30 June 1959*, pp. 70–71. See also Robert B. Asprey, "Building the Bundeswehr," *Army* 12, no. 2 (September 1961): 30–36 and 82; Buchholz, *Strategische und Militärpolitische Diskussionen*, pp. 155–162; and General Alfred Zerbel, inspector general of the Bundeswehr, "The Modern Army," *NATO's Fifteen Nations* 6, no. 6 (December 1961–January 1962): 40–43.

91. Birtle, *Rearming the Phoenix*, pp. 327–329.

92. Buchholz, *Strategische und Militärpolitische Diskussionen*, p. 158.

93. Robert S. McNamara, secretary of defense under Kennedy and Johnson, agreed.

McNamara to President Kennedy, 10 May 1961, *Reappraisal of Capabilities of Conventional Forces*, attached report, "Appraisal of Capabilities of Conventional Forces," pp. 63–74, National Security Files, Departments and Agencies, Box 273, "Department of Defense, General, DOD Study on Conventional Forces 5/61," JFKL.

94. Buchholz, *Strategische und Militärpolitische Diskussionen*, pp. 154–162; Rink, "Strukturen," pp. 435–455. See also Robert B. Asprey, "Building the Bundeswehr," *Army* 12, no. 2 (September 1961): 30–36 and 82; and Zerbel, "The Modern Army."

95. Headquarters, USAREUR, *Annual Report, 1958–59*, pp. 70–71.

96. Hawkins, *United States Army Force Structure and Force Design Initiatives*, pp. 43–44.

97. SGWM-638-59, Note for the Record, 13 November 1959, *Meeting with General Heusinger—Chief of German Armed Forces Staff*, pp. 1–5, International Military Staff, Records of the Standing Group, NATO Archives, Brussels.

98. Ibid., pp. 5–6.

99. SGM-554-60, North Atlantic Military Committee, Standing Group, 15 September 1960, *1960 Annual Review: Military Comments and Final Military Recommendations—Germany*, International Military Staff, Records of the Standing Group, NATO Archives, Brussels. There was some confusion about the maximum number of brigades per division. The Military Committee stated four, while AFCENT understood that there could be five.

100. German National Military Representative to SACEUR, 24 August 1960, *1. WEU Recommendations; 2. Pamphlet Issued by the Armed Forces Staff on "Requirements for Effective Defense,"* Norstad Papers, Country Files Series, Box 48, "Germany 1956–60 (1)," DDEL.

101. This line was taken, for instance, by General Valluy, commander of LANDCENT, in 1955. Lemnitzer to Gruenther, 8 January 1955, Enclosure: Brigadier General Moorman to Ridgway, Office Memorandum, 6 January 1955, *Conversation with Valluy*, Gruenther Papers, NATO Series, Box 3, "Lemnitzer, L. L., Lt. General, GS, U.S.A., Deputy Chief of Staff for Plans and Research [1954–1956]," DDEL.

102. Speidel, "Mission and Needs of NATO's Shield," p. 37.

103. Valluy to Norstad, 25 January 1960, Norstad Papers, Subject Series, Box 95, "AFCENT (4)," DDEL.

104. MC 91, A Report by the Standing Group to the Military Committee, 22 January 1960, *Divisional Compatibility Study*, International Military Staff, Records of the North Atlantic Military Committee, NATO Archives, Brussels.

105. Ibid., sec. 2.

106. For Clarke's fight at St. Vith, see J. D. Morelock and Martin Blumenson, *Generals of the Ardennes: American Leadership in the Battle of the Bulge* (Washington, DC: National Defense University, 1994), pp. 275–344.

107. Gordon L. Rottman, *Korean War Order of Battle: United States, United Nations, and Communist Ground, Naval, and Air Forces, 1950–1953* (Westport, CT: Praeger, 2002), p. 11.

108. William D. Ellis and Thomas J. Cunningham, *Clarke of St. Vith: The Sergeant's General* (Cleveland: Dillon and Liederbach, 1974), pp. 254–269.

109. Ibid. The quotation is on p. 101. Clarke's operational philosophy is described in a series of statements that are quoted on pp. 165–167.

110. Bruce C. Clarke to Major General L. L. Doan, Chief, Armor Section, Continental Army Command, 3 January 1957, Seventh Army 1954–65, Box 51, "250/16 Organization Planning Files," RG 338, NA.

111. Clarke to Major General Murphy, Chief, Artillery Section, Continental Army Command, 15 April 1958, Seventh Army 1954–65, Box 60, "250/15 Organization Planning Files," RG 338, NA.

112. Bruce C. Clarke, "Design for An Atomic Army," *Army* 8, no. 6 (January 1958): 20–26. The quotation is on p. 20.

113. Clarke continued to argue this point from retirement. He was not particularly pleased with the ROAD division, but his bigger concern was the excessive number of command echelons. Johnson to Clarke, 31 January 1963, and Daley to Johnson, 22 January 1963, Harold K. Johnson Papers, 1962–63 (6 of 15), Box 91, MHI.

114. *MOMAR-I*, Headquarters, United States Continental Army Command, *Modern Mobile Army 1965–70* (Fort Monroe, VA: United States Continental Army Command, 1960).

115. Ibid., pp. 1-1–1-3.

116. Ibid., pp. 1-3–1-5.

117. James H. Polk, "Elements of Command," 24 October 1974, pp. 8–10, James K. Polk Papers, Elements of Command, 1971–1974 (unnumbered box), MHI. The quotations are on p. 10.

118. Wilson, *Maneuver and Firepower*, pp. 291–292. See also Hawkins, *United States Army Force Structure and Force Design Initiatives*, pp. 38–41. Wilson mentions the task force headquarters, essentially brigade-type units. There is no specific mention of such entities in the actual *MOMAR-I* study, but, given the development of ad hoc brigades in Seventh Army, it is altogether likely that they were supposed to be maintained as informal structures.

119. *MOMAR-I*, pp. 2-1, 3-1.

120. Ibid., pp. 2-2–2-3, 3-3.

121. Wilson, *Maneuver and Firepower*, p. 292. General Eddleman is quoted in Hawkins and Carafano, *Prelude to Army XXI*, p. 15.

122. For MOMAR as an advanced evolutionary stage of the pentomic concept, see Doughty, *Evolution of U.S. Army Tactical Doctrine*, p. 21.

123. An unnamed officer claimed that "the entire organization could have been designed by reading the battle of St. Vith." Hawkins and Carafano, *Prelude to Army XXI*, p. 15. The papers of General Clarke at MHI and at the Historian's Office, U.S. Chief of Engineers, are full of examples of Clarke mentally or physically returning to St. Vith while considering plans for the defense of CENTAG.

124. See especially Krepinevich, *The Army and Vietnam.*

125. Hodes to Eddleman, 14 October 1958, Seventh Army 1954–65, Box 60, "250/15 Organization Planning Files," RG 338, NA.

126. Headquarters, USAREUR, Office of the Secretary of the General Staff, Memorandum for Record, 24 December 1959, *Commander in Chief's Comments to Staff Division Chiefs on 23 December 1959*, Entry 2002, Office of the Commanding General, Administration Branch, Operations Planning Files, 1960–62, Box 194, RG 549, NA.

127. For Eddleman's early thoughts on what would soon become the ROAD concept, see Wilson, *Maneuver and Firepower*, pp. 293–296.

128. Ibid., p. 293.

Chapter 4. The ROAD Army and Flexible Response

1. Gaddis, *Strategies of Containment*, pp. 198–236, argues that the Kennedy administration intended to implement a strategy that was capable of deterring aggression of any kind, regardless of the cost. Gaddis regards Flexible Response as the antithesis of Massive Retaliation. Francis J. Gavin, on the other hand, finds little practical difference in the strategies of the Eisenhower and Kennedy administrations. Francis J. Gavin, "The Myth of Flexible Response: United States Strategy in Europe during the 1960s," *International History Review* 23, no. 4 (December 2001): 847–875.

2. Wilson, *Maneuver and Firepower*, pp. 296–297. See also McGrath, *The Brigade*, p. 61, for the universal nature of the ROAD division in theory. For the sake of clarity, I will use the terms "mechanized" and "infantry" to express the distinction between mechanized infantry and infantry units, even though mechanized divisions remained listed as infantry divisions.

3. Wilson, *Maneuver and Firepower*, pp. 296–297.

4. Like the pentomic division, ROAD was not tested by a major experimental force. Hawkins and Carafano, *Prelude to Army XXI*, p. 17.

5. Wilson, *Maneuver and Firepower*, pp. 298–303.

6. McNamara to President Kennedy, 10 May 1961, *Reappraisal of Capabilities of Conventional Forces*, attached report, "Appraisal of Capabilities of Conventional Forces," p. 74, National Security Files, Departments and Agencies, Box 273, "Department of Defense, General, DOD Study on Conventional Forces 5/61," JFKL.

7. Ibid.

8. Robert S. McNamara, Memorandum for the President, 10 May 1961, *Reappraisal of Capabilities of Conventional Forces*, pp. 2–3, National Security Files, Departments and Agencies, Box 173, "Department of Defense, General, DoD Study on Conventional Forces 5/61," JFKL. See also pp. 64–73 of the attached report, "Appraisal of Capabilities of Conventional Forces," for McNamara's reasoning, particularly p. 68, on the relationship of the ROAD and LANDCENT divisions.

9. Wilson, *Maneuver and Firepower*, pp. 306–307. Decker is cited on p. 307.

10. For the complexity of reorganizing an airborne division according to the ROAD concept, see Headquarters, 82nd Airborne Division, 21 February 1964, *Reorganization Plan All American ROAD*, Command and General Staff College, Combined Arms Research Library, Archive N-16289.29. The 82nd Airborne actually received nine infantry battalions and one tank battalion.

11. Wilson, *Maneuver and Firepower*, pp. 308–310. Doughty, *Evolution of U.S. Army Tactical Doctrine*, p. 21, also discusses the standardization of ROAD divisions.

12. Alain C. Enthoven, Memorandum for Bundy, Gordon, and Wiesner, 16 November 1963, *Recommended FY1965–FY1969 Army and Marine Corps General Purpose*

Forces, p. 45, Lyndon B. Johnson Papers, President, 1963–1969, National Security File, Agency File, Box 15, Defense Budget—1965, sec. 2, LBJL.

13. Freeman to Wheeler, 30 December 1962, and Parker to Freeman, 11 January 1963, *Reorganization of USAREUR Units under ROAD*, General Staff, ODCSOPS/OACSFOR, Security Classified Correspondence, 1963, 201-45 Series, Box 13, RG 319, NA.

14. Polk to Girard, 3 May 1965, James K. Polk Papers, Correspondence V Corps 1964/65, 1965 (unnumbered box), MHI.

15. John Steadman, Memorandum for Robert E. Kintner, 26 July 1966, *Weekly Report for the President*, Lyndon B. Johnson Papers, President, Confidential File, Agency Reports, Department of Defense, July 1966, Box 118, LBJL.

16. Director of Budget, Comptroller of the Army, 13 November 1968, *FY 62–FY 79, Five Year Defense Program, Program II: General Purpose Forces*, Entry 71B-003, Comptroller of the Army, Director of Army Budget, Program and Budget Systems Division, Program Branch, Box 1, RG 319, NA.

17. *Oregon Trail* is discussed in Midgley, *Deadly Illusions*, pp. 115–123.

18. Headquarters, USAREUR, and Seventh Army, *Annual Historical Summary*, 1 January to 31 December 1966 (Headquarters, USAREUR, and Seventh Army: Office of the Deputy Chief of Staff, Operations, Military History Branch, 1967), pp. 85–88.

19. Midgley, *Deadly Illusions*, pp. 121–123.

20. Flexible Response thus has no signature document comparable to NSC-68 or NSC-162/2. The annual Basic National Security Policy reviews continued through 1963, but Kennedy did not approve the draft reports. See Philip Nash, "Bear *Any* Burden? John F. Kennedy and Nuclear Weapons," p. 126, in *Cold War Statesmen Confront the Bomb: Nuclear Diplomacy since 1945*, edited by John Lewis Gaddis et al. (Oxford: Oxford University Press, 1999), pp. 120–140. The best comprehensive study of Flexible Response remains Jane E. Stromseth, *The Origins of Flexible Response: NATO's Debate over Strategy in the 1960s* (New York: St. Martin's, 1988). But for a more recent account based on greater access to government documents, see Lawrence S. Kaplan et al., *The McNamara Ascendancy, 1961–1965*, vol. 5 of *History of the Office of the Secretary of Defense* (Washington, DC: Historical Office, Office of the Secretary of Defense, 2006), pp. 293–322.

21. Taylor, *The Uncertain Trumpet*, p. 146.

22. Taylor quotes from a letter sent by Kennedy in his interview for the Kennedy Oral History Project. John F. Kennedy Oral History Project, Taylor interview by Elspeth Rostow, 12 April 1964, p. 4, JFKL. For Kennedy's thinking on nuclear weapons prior to his presidency, see Nash, "Bear *Any* Burden?" pp. 121–124.

23. John Lewis Gaddis argues in *We Now Know: Rethinking Cold War History* (Oxford: Clarendon Press, 1997), pp. 221–259, that Massive Retaliation was a strategy of war avoidance but carried tremendous risks. Flexible Response reopened the possibility of war fighting, even in Europe, but in doing so it elevated the credibility of deterrence.

24. Dean Acheson, for the Democratic Advisory Council, "The Military Forces We Need and How to Get Them: Our Object Which Lies Beyond War and Weapons," p. 8, Roswell L. Gilpatric Papers, Box 8, "Analysis of D.O.D. Budget for FY 1961 (A)," JFKL.

25. Seymour Weiss to Henry Owen, 14 February 1964, *Attached Paper on National*

Strategy, pp. 6–10, Records of the Policy Planning Council (S/PC) 1963–64, Europe 1963–1964, Box 281, RG 59, NA.

26. McNamara to Kennedy, 5 May 1961, *Military Planning for a Possible Berlin Crisis*, in *FRUS*, 1961–1963, vol. 14, *Berlin Crisis, 1961–1962* (Washington, DC: Government Printing Office, 1993), pp. 61–63.

27. Policy Directive, 20 April 1961, in *FRUS*, 1961–1963, vol. 13, pp. 285–291. The quotation is on p. 286.

28. McNamara to Kennedy, 20 February 1961, table 2, pp. 10–11. Records of Robert S. McNamara, Defense Programs and Operations, "Report to the President, FY 1962 Budget," Box 10, RG 200, NA.

29. Ibid., Annex A, Attachment 2: Limited War Proposals.

30. For the differences in thinking between General Norstad and the White House, see Jordan, *Norstad*, pp. 167–172, 189–190, 208–212.

31. Senior Officers Debriefing Program, General Paul Freeman interviewed by Colonel James Ellis, sec. 2, p. 20, Paul Freeman Papers, Oral History, Box 1, MHI.

32. Taylor to Rostow, 14 May 1962, President Kennedy Papers, National Security Files, Subject Series, Box 294, "Basic National Security Policy 6/22/62 and undated [Folder 1 of 2]," JFKL.

33. Department of Defense, 3 October 1964, *Military Strength Increase since FY1961*, Schedule A: *Strategic Retaliatory Forces*, Lyndon B. Johnson Papers, President, 1963–1969, National Security File, Agency File, Box 11, "Defense, Department of, vol. 1 [1 of 2], 11/63," LBJL.

34. Ibid., Schedule C: *General Purpose Forces*.

35. *President Kennedy's Remarks before the Military Committee of the North Atlantic Treaty Organization, Washington, D.C., on 10 April 1961*, Norstad Papers, Personal Name File Series, Box 70, "Kennedy, John F. (President, USA) (1)," DDEL. At the same meeting, General Norstad reiterated that conventional forces might be sufficient to deal with a transgression and that nuclear weapons would only be introduced in well-defined cases of self-defense or after a thorough, established decision-making process that ensured that commanders of basic combat units could not make such a decision. USM-120-61, Office of the U.S. Military Representative to Joint Chiefs of Staff, 13 April 1961, *Summary Report of the Twenty-sixth Session, NATO Military Committee in Chiefs of Staff Session (MC/CS), Washington, D.C., 10 April 1961*, Enclosure 6: *SACEUR's Criteria for Developing End-1966 Force Requirements*, Assistant Secretary of Defense (International Security Affairs), Secret and Below General Files, 1961, 334 NATO, 1–15 April, Box 17, RG 330, NA.

36. Rusk to USRO Paris, 19 April 1961, Norstad Papers, Policy File Series, Box 91, "US Support of NATO 1961 thru 30 June (1)," DDEL. See also Rusk to Finletter, 26 April 1961, ibid.

37. Dean Acheson, March 1961, *A Review of North Atlantic Problems for the Future*, National Security Files, Regional Security Series, Box 220, "NATO—General, Acheson Report, 3/61," JFKL; National Security Action Memorandum No. 40, 24 April 1961, *Policy Directive Regarding NATO and the Atlantic Nations*, National Security Files, Meetings and Memoranda, Box 329, "NSAM 40," JFKL. See also Lawrence Freedman,

Kennedy's Wars: Berlin, Cuba, Laos, and Vietnam (New York: Oxford University Press, 2000), pp. 49–50; and Nash, "Bear *Any* Burden?" pp. 125–126.

38. Acheson, *Review of North Atlantic Problems*, p. 5.

39. Dean Acheson, *A Partnership with Europe*, McEnerney Lecture at the University of California, Berkeley, 24 October 1962, 3rd draft, 12 October 1962, pp. 18–22, President Kennedy Papers, President's Office Files, Special Correspondence, "Acheson, Dean, 8/1/60–10/12/62," Box 27, JFKL.

40. JCSM-175-61, Burke to Acheson, 20 March 1961 (but apparently sent on 25 March), Nuclear History/Berlin Crisis Collection, Box 54, NSA.

41. Memorandum of Conference with the President, 27 July 1961, p. 2, President Kennedy Papers, National Security Files, Chester V. Clifton, Conferences with the President, Joint Chiefs of Staff, Box 345, JFKL.

42. 4 April 1961, *Chancellor Adenauer's Visit, Washington, April 12–13, 1961*, Assistant Secretary of Defense (International Security Affairs), Secret and Below General Files, 333 Germany, January–June 1961, Box 33, RG 330, NA. For a recent discussion of West German attitudes toward Flexible Response, see Bluth, *The Two Germanies and Military Security in Europe*, pp. 55–64.

43. Secret Memorandum by Robert Magill, 8 June 1961, *Draft Comments on German Memorandum Regarding NATO Defense Strategy and Planning*, Assistant Secretary of Defense (International Security Affairs), Secret and Below General Files 1961, 334 NATO, 1–15 June 1961, Box 17, RG 330, NA; Memorandum of Conversation, 12 June 1961, *Visit of Minister of Defense Strauss to SHAPE*, ibid., 333 Germany, January–June 1961, Box 33. In particular, Norstad's concept implied the loss of Hamburg prior to negotiations. See Elizabeth Pond, *Beyond the Wall: Germany's Road to Unification* (Washington, DC: Brookings Institution, 1993), p. 36; and Frank A. Mayer, *Adenauer and Kennedy: A Study in German-American Relations, 1961–1963* (New York: St. Martin's, 1996), p. 21.

44. Comments by the Government of the Federal Republic of Germany on the Statement made by the United States Permanent Representative on Defence matters to the NATO Council on 26 April 1961, p. 1, Norstad Papers, Country File, Box 49, "Germany 1961–1962 (5)," DDEL.

45. *Strauss-McNamara Conversation, 14 July 1961*, p. 2, Central Decimal File 1961, CCS 9165/5420 Germany (West), Box 177, RG 218, NA.

46. Memorandum of Conversation, Fessenden and Dr. Ulrich Sahm, 10 May 1961, *NATO Defense Problems*, Norstad Papers, Policy File Series, Box 88, "Germany—Problems (2)," DDEL.

47. Strauss believed that the West would have to undergo three years of vigorous military buildup to achieve a force posture with which nuclear war could be avoided even if deterrence failed. *Notes on Conversation with Defense Minister Franz Josef Strauss at Mr. Paul Nitze's Place in Southern Maryland, Saturday and Sunday, July 29 and 30, 1961* (author not specified, probably Dean Acheson, dated 1 August 1961), Assistant Secretary of Defense (International Security Affairs), Secret and Below General Files 1961, 333 Germany, July–December 1961, Box 33, RG 330, NA.

48. That division was never actually deployed. It is possible that the augmentation during the Berlin Crisis, which included the pre-positioning of equipment for two divisions in Europe, changed the force deployment planning.

49. JCSM-306-61, JCS to Secretary of Defense, 5 May 1961, *NATO Requirements Study (Project 106 C)*, Appendix A: *1966 NATO Nonnuclear Capability Requirements and Costs:* TAB A to Annex B to Appendix A: *Army Force Requirements for 1966*, and Annex A to Appendix B: *Army: NATO Force Requirements, 1961–1966*, Central Decimal File 1961, 9050/3410 NATO (29 April 1961), sec. 1, Box 140, RG 218, NA.

50. SHAPE/118/61, *SACEUR's SHAPEX Presentation, 26 May 1961*, pp. 5–6, Norstad Papers, Subject Series, Box 111, "SHAPEX 59-60-61-62 (2)," DDEL.

51. Jacquot to Norstad, 26 April 1961, Norstad Papers, Subject Series, Box 95, "AFCENT (3)," DDEL.

52. National Intelligence Estimate 11-4-61, 24 August 1961, *Main Trends in Soviet Capabilities and Policies, 1961–1966*, Historical Review Group, National Intelligence Estimates Concerning Soviet Military Power, 1950–1984, Box 16, Folder 9, RG 263, NA. See also Raymond Garthoff, "Estimating Soviet Military Force Levels: Some Light from the Past," *International Security* 14, no. 4 (Spring 1990): 93–116.

53. MC 96, 30 November 1961, Report by the Military Committee to the North Atlantic Council, *NATO Force Requirements for End-1966 and Tentative Individual Country Breakdown Thereof*, and MC 26/4, 11 December 1961, Report by the Military Committee to the North Atlantic Council, *Force Requirements for End-1966*, International Military Staff, Records of the North Atlantic Military Committee NATO Archives, Brussels.

54. MC 39/13 (Military Decision), 1 December 1961, *Military Decision on MC 39/13:* A Report by the Military Committee, *An Analysis of the Military Implications of the 1961 Interim Review*, pp. 6, 15, International Military Staff, Records of the North Atlantic Military Committee, NATO Archives, Brussels.

55. Cold War–era standard accounts of the Berlin Crisis are Norman Gelb, *The Berlin Wall: Kennedy, Khrushchev, and a Showdown in the Heart of Europe* (New York: Simon and Schuster, 1986); Jack M. Schick, *The Berlin Crisis, 1958–1962* (Philadelphia: University of Pennsylvania Press, 1971); and Robert M. Slusser, *The Berlin Crisis of 1961: Soviet-American Relations and the Struggle for Power in the Kremlin, June–November 1961* (Baltimore: Johns Hopkins University Press, 1973). Since the end of the Cold War, historians, political scientists, and participants in the crisis have added to the record. See, for instance, John C. Ausland, *Kennedy, Khrushchev, and the Berlin-Cuba Crisis, 1961–1964* (Oslo: Scandinavian University Press, 1996); Gaddis, *We Now Know*, pp. 113–151, 221–259; W. R. Smyser, *From Yalta to Berlin: The Cold War Struggle over Germany* (New York: St. Martin's, 1999), pp. 137–192; Trachtenberg, *History and Strategy*, pp. 169–234; and Trachtenberg, *A Constructed Peace*, pp. 251–351. Particular military options are discussed by Sean M. Maloney, "Berlin Contingency Planning: Prelude to Flexible Response, 1958–63," *Journal of Strategic Studies* 25, no. 1 (March 2002): 99–134; and Gregory W. Pedlow, "Flexible Response before MC 14/3: General Lauris Norstad and the Second Berlin Crisis, 1958–1962," *Storia delle Relazioni Internazionali* 13, no. 1 (1995): 235–268.

56. This ran counter to NATO planning for much smaller military operations along the autobahn that should be conducted by battalion-size units. In the spring of 1959, General Norstad had been appointed director of a tripartite American, British, and French staff within ACE that prepared contingency scenarios for imminent crises in

and on the road to Berlin. For the history and operations of the LIVE OAK group, see Gregory W. Pedlow, "Allied Crisis Management for Berlin: The LIVE OAK Organization, 1959–1963," in *International Cold War Military Records and History: Proceedings of the International Conference on Cold War Records and History Held in Washington, D.C., 21–26 March 1994*, ed. William W. Epley (Washington, DC: Center for Military History, 1996), pp. 87–116.

57. Owen to Bundy, 17 May 1961, *Berlin and Conventional Forces*, President Kennedy Papers, National Security Files, Country Series, Box 81, "Germany—Berlin General 5/61," JFKL.

58. Michael Beschloss, *The Crisis Years: Kennedy and Khrushchev, 1960–1963* (New York: HarperCollins, 1991), pp. 211–236.

59. Bundy to the President et al., 13 July 1961, *Military Choices in Berlin Planning*, President Kennedy Papers, National Security Files, Country Series, Box 81A, "Germany—Berlin General 7/13/61," JFKL.

60. *National Security Action Memorandum No. 62*, 24 July 1961, National Security Action Memorandum (NSAM), RG 273, NA.

61. *President's Report to the Nation on the Berlin Crisis, Delivered July 25, 1961*, made available by the John F. Kennedy Presidential Library at http://www.jfklibrary.org/Historical+Resources/Archives/Reference+Desk/Speeches/JFK/003POF03BerlinCrisis07251961.htm (accessed 15 November 2007).

62. Norstad to Lemnitzer and Clarke, 13 August 1961, Norstad Papers, Subject Series, Box 103, "Joint Chiefs of Staff 1957 thru Oct 1961, vol. I (5)," DDEL.

63. As we have seen in the previous chapter, these weapons systems were only then arriving in USAREUR. Moreover, new equipment, such as the M113 APC, did not automatically translate into improved performance of a mechanized unit in practice. Henry Gole, a platoon commander in Germany in 1961, recalled that the new APCs posed technical and tactical problems, as proper maintenance and use of the vehicles had to be learned and tactical doctrine had to be adjusted. Gole claimed that the army fared poorly with the latter, and that company commanders tended to equate the APC either with a tank or with a truck. Henry G. Gole, *Soldiering: Observations from Korea, Vietnam, and Safe Places* (Dulles, VA: Potomac Books, 2005), pp. 115–117.

64. National Security Action Memorandum No. 103, 10 October 1961, *Deployment of U.S. Military Forces*, National Security Action Memo Files 1961–1968, Box 2, "NSAM 91-115," RG 59, NA.

65. Wilson, *Maneuver and Firepower*, pp. 303–305. In September 1962, General Norstad inquired whether USAREUR thought it would be feasible to pre-position equipment for a third division and, if so, what type of division would be best suited. He specifically excluded airborne divisions. USCINCEUR to CINCUSAREUR, 8 September 1962, Norstad Papers, Subject Series, Box 113, "USAREUR Apr 1962 (1)," DDEL.

66. JCSM-508-61, Lemnitzer to McNamara, 29 July 1961, *Allied Military Planning on Berlin*, Defense Programs and Operations, "Misc., 1961," Box 81, RG 200, NA.

67. See, for instance, Policy Planning Staff, OASD (ISA), 26 June 1961, *A New Approach to Berlin*, Secret and Below General Files 1961, 092 Germany, 21–30 June 1961, Box 33, RG 330, NA: "It is probable that in the coming fall or winter Khrushchev will

bring about a crisis designed to result eventually in the expulsion of the Western garrisons from Berlin and in a GDR capability to isolate West Berlin."

68. Memorandum by Paul Nitze, summarized in Lemnitzer to Norstad, 26 August 1961, Norstad Papers, Subject Series, Box 103, "Joint Chiefs of Staff 1957 thru Oct 1961, vol. I (4)," DDEL.

69. Norstad to Lemnitzer, 18 August 1961, Norstad Papers, Policy Files Series, Box 86, "Berlin—LIVE OAK 1961 thru 30 Aug. (1)," DDEL. Chancellor Adenauer later told Dean Acheson that negotiations were the only option because NATO was too weak conventionally, and he rejected the idea of using nuclear weapons in the Berlin Crisis. Acheson to Marshall Shulman, 23 November 1961, Dean Acheson Papers, Post Administration Files, State Department and White House Advisor, 1960–68, Box 99, "State Department and White House Advisor, 1961, October–December," HSTL.

70. Wall, *France, the United States, and the Algerian War*, p. 251.

71. Memorandum for Record, 25 March 1961, *SACEUR's Meeting with Minister of Defense Strauss, 24 March 1961*, Norstad Papers, Subject Series, Box 105, "Memorandum for Record II 1960–1961 (4)," DDEL.

72. See Maloney, "Berlin Contingency Planning," for a detailed discussion of Norstad's options in 1961.

73. Norstad to McNamara, 29 May 1961, Norstad Papers, Policy Files Series, Box 86, "Berlin—LIVE OAK 1961 thru 30 Aug. (4)," DDEL.

74. Wall, *France, the United States, and the Algerian War*, p. 242.

75. *Address by General Bruce C. Clarke, Commander in Chief, United States Army, Europe, and Commander, Central Army Group (NATO), before the Staff, Faculty and Students, United States Army War College, 28 November 1961, Carlisle Barracks, Pennsylvania*, Norstad Papers, Subject Series, Box 112, "USAREUR Dec. 57–30 Apr. 62 (5)," DDEL. For a study on NATO logistics, see James A. Huston, *One for All: NATO Strategy and Logistics through the Formative Period* (Newark: University of Delaware Press, 1984).

76. Clarke was pessimistic about the state of American air- and sealift. He thought that pre-positioning equipment for two combat divisions was a wasteful exercise, because the transportation capacities for the units were lacking. Clarke interview by Francis Kish, vol. 2, pp. 199–203. Bruce Clarke Papers, Oral History, Box 3, MHI.

77. *Address by General Bruce C. Clarke before the United States Army War College, 28 November 1961*, p. 10.

78. Clarke interview by Francis Kish, vol. 2, pp. 212–213.

79. McGeorge Bundy had considered an overall mobilization of one million men. General Lemnitzer thought that the army would then receive 564,000 new recruits. Seven additional combat divisions could be sent to Germany and France within five months of mobilization. JCSM-179-61, Lemnitzer to McNamara, 13 July 1961, *Mobilization (Berlin Situation)*, Assistant Secretary of Defense (International Security Affairs), Secret and Below General Files 1961, 092 Germany, 1–20 July 1961, Box 33, RG 330, NA.

80. Maxwell Taylor, Memorandum for Record, 18 September 1961, *Meeting with the President on the Military Build Up and Possible Action in Europe*, Nuclear History—Berlin Crisis Files, Taylor Papers, Box 28, NSA.

81. SNIE 2-5-61, 14 September 1961, *Soviet Reactions to Certain U.S. Courses of Action*,

National Intelligence Estimates Concerning the Soviet Union 1950–1961, Box 4, Folder 126, RG 263, NA.

82. Jacquot to Norstad, 3 August 1961, Norstad Papers, Subject Series, Box 95, "AFCENT (2)," DDEL.

83. Norstad to Jacquot, 4 September 1961, ibid.

84. Stoessel to Fessenden, 1 December 1961, Entry 5301, Bureau of European Affairs, NATO and Atlantic Political-Military Affairs (EUR/RPM), Records Relating to NATO Affairs 1959–1966, Organization and Administration SACEUR, Box 5, RG 59, NA.

85. McNamara to Norstad, 13 September 1961, Norstad Papers, Policy Files Series, Box 91, "US Support of NATO, 1961, 1 July thru 31 Dec. (2)," DDEL. McNamara attached a statement by General Lemnitzer that largely supported his assessment. See also McNamara to President Kennedy, 18 September 1961, *Military Build-Up and Possible Action in Europe*, National Security Action Memo Files 1961–1968, Box 2, "NSAM 91-115," RG 59, NA.

86. The Berlin Crisis eventually led to moderate improvements. In April 1961, SACEUR had about twenty-three division equivalents for Central Region, but actual combat equivalent strength stood at only sixteen. By April 1962, this had increased to a combat-equivalent twenty divisions out of a total of twenty-four. Nitze to Norstad, 25 April 1962, Norstad Papers, Subject Series, Box 109, "Secretary of Defense (2)," DDEL.

87. SHAPE 188/61, Norstad to Dirk Stikker, 15 September 1961, Norstad Papers, Policy Files Series, Box 87, "Forces (1)," DDEL.

88. Notes on a meeting following the Chiefs of Staff session on 21 November 1961. Present at the meeting were Kennedy, Adenauer, Strauss, and generals Lemnitzer and Schnez, pp. 4–6, Bestand BW 2, Aktenband 12265, BA-MA, Freiburg. In the course of the discussion, Kennedy assured Adenauer that the United States would respond with nuclear weapons to a Soviet seizure of Berlin.

89. Norstad to JCS and Deputy USCINCEUR, 21 September 1961, Norstad Papers, Subject Series, Box 103, "Joint Chiefs of Staff 1957 thru Oct 1961, vol. I (3)," DDEL.

90. Draft, HWF, 6 October 1961, *General Norstad's Discussions with the JCS on Monday, 2 October*, Norstad Papers, Subject Series, Box 105, "Memorandum for Record II 1960–1961 (2)," DDEL.

91. Taylor to John F. Kennedy, 3 October 1961, *General Norstad's Proposal for U.S. Reinforcements to NATO*, President Kennedy Papers, President's Office Files, Subjects, Box 103, "NATO—Norstad Meetings," JFKL.

92. Robert McNamara, Memorandum for the President, 6 October 1961, *Recommended Department of Defense FY '63 Budget and 1963–67 Programs*, pp. 9–12, President Kennedy Papers, National Security Files, Departments and Agencies, Box 175, "Department of Defense, Recommended DOD FY63 Budget 10/6/61," JFKL. The recommendation and McNamara's rationale are still based on fourteen divisions, but two more divisions and an eighth brigade were added in pencil.

93. Maxwell Taylor, Memorandum for the President, 22 November 1961, *Support of Conventional Forces in the 1963 Budget*, President Kennedy Papers, National Security Files, Departments and Agencies, Box 175, "Department of Defense, Defense Budget FY63 11/61–12/61," JFKL.

94. The president was aware that the "timing and scale of nuclear weapons use" was

only partially controlled by the allies. Kennedy to Norstad, 20 October 1961, Norstad Papers, Policy Files Series, Box 86, "Berlin—LIVE OAK 1961, 1 Sep–31 Dec (2)," DDEL. See also *National Security Action Memorandum No. 109*, 23 October 1961, National Security Action Memorandum (NSAM), RG 273, NA.

95. Pedlow, "Flexible Response before MC 14/3," pp. 256–260. There is some question concerning whether Kennedy had transmitted the directive through the appropriate chain of command, i.e., to CINCUSAREUR, or whether he had attempted to give direct orders to SACEUR. Norstad felt that the latter was the case.

96. Dean Rusk had argued that the purpose of the buildup of forces was to attain capability to fight the Soviets conventionally for several weeks by the end of 1961. See, for instance, Minutes of National Security Council Meeting, 19 July 1961, in *FRUS, 1961–1963*, vol. 14, pp. 219–222. Sean Maloney argues in "Berlin Contingency Planning: Prelude to Flexible Response," *Journal of Strategic Studies* 25, no. 1 (March 2002): 99–134, that the Berlin contingency plans constituted a critical step in the development of the strategy of Flexible Response for the NATO alliance.

97. SNIE-2-6-61, 19 October, *Probable Soviet and Other Reactions to Certain US Military Measures in the Berlin Crisis*, National Intelligence Estimates Concerning the Soviet Union 1950–1961, Box 4, Folder 127, RG 263, NA.

98. Norstad to Kennedy, 16 November 1961, Norstad Papers, Policy Files Series, Box 86, "Berlin—LIVE OAK 1961, 1 Sep–31 Dec (1)," DDEL. Three months earlier, Norstad had, in fact, ordered AFCENT to provide plans for such limited offensive operations. Norstad to Jacquot, 17 August 1961, *Operations in the Central Region*, Norstad Papers, Policy Files Series, Box 90, "Strategy—General (1)," DDEL.

99. Maloney, "Berlin Contingency Planning," pp. 121–128.

100. The Army Reserve and the National Guard in the early 1960s and beyond are discussed in James T. Currie and Richard B. Crossland, *Twice the Citizen: A History of the United States Army Reserve, 1908–1995* (Washington, DC: Office of the Chief, Army Reserve, 1997); and Department of the Army, Office of the Chief of Military History, "The Development of the STRAF," pp. 36–62. The attempts to activate National Guard divisions are addressed in Robert W. Coakley and Walter G. Hermes, *Mobilization of a Two Division National Guard Force—1961: Decisions at Headquarters, Department of Army Level* (Washington, DC: Department of the Army, Office of the Chief of Military History, 1962). The reform proposal of 1962 and ensuing controversy are captured in Kaplan et al., *The McNamara Ascendancy*, pp. 107–117.

101. For the debate, see Stromseth, *Origins of Flexible Response.*

102. CINCENT to Norstad, 8 February 1961, Norstad Papers, Subject Series, Box 95, "AFCENT (3)," DDEL, pp. 2–3; quotation on p. 3.

103. Norstad to Jacquot, 4 September 1961, Norstad Papers, Subject Series, Box 95, "AFCENT (2)," DDEL.

104. Headquarters, USAREUR, Office of the Commander in Chief, 22 October 1961, *Synopsis of General Clarke's Remarks to the Division Chiefs, Headquarters, USAREUR, 21 October 1961*, Norstad Papers, Personal Name File, Box 61, "Clarke, Bruce C. (3)," DDEL.

105. For this, as well as the overall expansion of the army and increased readiness in response to the Berlin Crisis, see Robert W. Coakley et al., *U.S. Army Expansion and Readiness, 1961–1962* (Washington, DC: Office of the Chief of Military History, 1963).

106. Among the requests of General Norstad to the JCS in the discussions of October were 240,000 men and one armored cavalry regiment. Draft, HWF, 6 October 1961, *General Norstad's Discussions with the JCS on Monday, 2 October*, Norstad Papers, Subject Series, Box 105, "Memorandum for Record II 1960–1961 (2)," DDEL.

107. On 26 February, he underscored his criticism in an angry message to General Lemnitzer: "I could think of few things less acceptable to our Allies at this point…than the presentation on the part of the United States of a study of 'The Conventional Situation on the Central Front.'" Norstad to Lemnitzer, 26 February 1962, Norstad Papers, Subject Series, Box 103, "Joint Chiefs of Staff Nov 1961–Dec 1962, vol. II (4)," DDEL.

108. Acting Secretary of State to the President, 24 January 1962, *Your Meeting with General Norstad on Thursday, January 25*, Norstad Papers, Subject Series, Box 112, "Strategy, NATO (2)," DDEL.

109. McNamara's address at the NATO meeting in Athens is also discussed in Kaplan et al., *The McNamara Ascendancy*, pp. 305–308.

110. C-M(62)55, 5 May 1962, *Defense Policy*, Statement made on Saturday, 5 May, by Secretary McNamara at the NATO Ministerial Meeting in Athens, p. 1, International Military Staff, Records of the North Atlantic Military Committee, NATO Archives, Brussels. This document is also available at the National Security Archive, Electronic Briefing Book 159, Document 16C (http://www.gwu.edu/~nsarchiv/NSAEBB/NSAEBB159/index.htm) (accessed July 2005).

111. National Security Archive, Electronic Briefing Book No. 159, 1 July 2005, "'Consultation Is Presidential Business': Secret Understandings on the Use of Nuclear Weapons, 1950–1974."

112. Statement made on Saturday, 5 May, by Secretary McNamara at the NATO Ministerial Meeting in Athens, pp. 9–13, International Military Staff, Records of the North Atlantic Military Committee, NATO Archives, Brussels.

113. By December 1962, the German defense ministry had come to the conclusion that the new American concept favored conventional defense that was "doomed to failure." Bluth, *The Two Germanies and Military Security in Europe*, p. 58.

114. C-VR(62)25, 21 May 1962, Joint Meeting of the Foreign and Defense Ministers, Verbatim Record of the meeting of the Council held on Saturday, 5 May 1962, at 5 P.M., International Military Staff, Records of the North Atlantic Military Committee, NATO Archives, Brussels. This document is also available at the National Security Archive, Electronic Briefing Book 159, Document 16B (http://www.gwu.edu/~nsarchiv/NSAEBB/NSAEBB159/index.htm) (accessed July 2005). For Rusk's opening remarks, see pp. 2–6. For Messmer's objections, see pp. 10–11. For McNamara's reply, see p. 12.

115. Statement made on Saturday, 5 May, by Secretary McNamara at the NATO Ministerial Meeting in Athens, p. 9, International Military Staff, Records of the North Atlantic Military Committee, NATO Archives, Brussels.

116. Eventually, the events of the Cuban Missile Crisis led to an adjustment in the timetable, and Norstad remained in Paris until the end of the year. His retirement was hardly voluntary. Norstad was only fifty-six years old, and although he had suffered from heart disease, he had recovered by the time of his retirement.

117. For meetings between Norstad and Adenauer in August and September 1962, see

Embassy, Bonn, to Secretary of State, 17 August 1962, Norstad Papers, Policy Files Series, Box 91, "U.S. Support of NATO 1962 (1)," DDEL; and Memorandum for Record, 17 September 1962, *Notes on Luncheon Meeting at Lovena di Menaggio, 16 September 1962*, Norstad Papers, Subject Series, Box 105, " Memorandum for Record 1962," DDEL.

118. Interview with General Lemnitzer, SACEUR (1963–1969), 11 February 1970, by Dr. David Nunnerley, pp. 6–7, Oral History Collection, JFKL.

119. Remarks by General A. J. Goodpaster, SACEUR, Imperial Defence College, SHAPE, Belgium, on 17 October 1969, Andrew J. Goodpaster Papers, Box 35, Folder 6, GCML.

120. Remarks by Secretary McNamara, 17 December 1963, Lyndon B. Johnson Papers, President, 1963–1969, National Security File, Agency File, Box 38, "NATO—Rusk-Min. Mtg. Paris 12/63 and Other Conversations (DeGaulle, Couve, etc.)," LBJL.

121. See, for instance, the analysis of Defense Department officials, in Alain C. Enthoven and K. Wayne Smith, *How Much Is Enough? Shaping the Defense Program, 1961–1969* (New York: Harper and Row, 1971), pp. 117–164. At the end of the Johnson administration, the Defense Department estimated that 677,000 NATO troops faced only 619,000 Warsaw Pact troops in Central Region. In addition, with the notable exception of tanks, the NATO forces had more and better equipment. Ibid., p. 148.

122. Headquarters, USAREUR, Office of the Deputy Chief of Staff, Intelligence, 1 January 1962, *USAREUR Intelligence Estimate 1962*, pp. 31–36, PHP, http://www.php.isn.ethz.ch/collections/colltopic.cfm?lng=en&id=18690&navinfo=14968 (accessed 15 November 2007).

123. National Intelligence Estimate 11-14-62, 5 December 1962, *Capabilities of the Soviet Theater Forces*, Historical Review Group, National Intelligence Estimates Concerning Soviet Military Power 1950–1984, Box 16, Folder 12, RG 263, NA.

124. CM-966-62, Lemnitzer to McGeorge Bundy, 20 September 1962, *Joint Chiefs of Staff Briefing, NATO Nuclear Capabilities and Problem Areas*, pp. 8–9, Chairman's File, General Lemnitzer, 1960–62, CM 940-62–995-62, RG 218, NA.

125. MC 39/14 (Military Decision), 29 November 1962, *Military Decision on MC39/14:* A Report by the Military Committee, *An Analysis of the Military Implications of the 1962 Triennial Review*, Enclosure 1: *Evaluation of Allied Command Europe*, p. 13, International Military Staff, Records of the North Atlantic Military Committee, NATO Archives, Brussels.

126. MC 39/15 (Military Decision), 29 November 1963, *Military Decision on MC39/15: A Report by the Military Committee, An Analysis of the Military Implications of the 1963 Intermediate Review*, and MC 39/16 (Military Decision), 1 December 1964, *Military Decision on MC39/16:* A Report by the Military Committee, *An Analysis of the Military Implications of the 1964 Annual Review*, International Military Staff, Records of the North Atlantic Military Committee, NATO Archives, Brussels.

127. CM-647-62, Lemnitzer to the Secretary of Defense and the Deputy Secretary of Defense, 16 April 1962, *Study Group Terms of Reference for Strategic Appraisal of Requirements for General Purpose Forces*, pp. 4–5, Chairman's File, General Lemnitzer, 1960–62, CM 630-62–673-62, Box 2, RG 218, NA.

128. CM-966-62, Lemnitzer to McGeorge Bundy, 20 September 1962, *Joint Chiefs of*

Staff Briefing, NATO Nuclear Capabilities and Problem Areas, p. 3, Chairman's File, General Lemnitzer, 1960–62, CM 940-62–995-62, RG 218, NA.

129. National Intelligence Estimate 11-14-63, 8 January 1964, *Capabilities of the Soviet General Purpose Forces, 1963–1969*, Historical Review Group, National Intelligence Estimates Concerning Soviet Military Power 1950–1984, Box 16, Folder 14, RG 263, NA.

130. National Intelligence Estimate 11-14-64, 10 December 1964, *Capabilities of Soviet General Purpose Forces, 1964–1970*, Historical Review Group, National Intelligence Estimates Concerning Soviet Military Power 1950–1984, Box 16, Folder 17, RG 263, NA.

131. SGM-674-62, Standing Group to Secretary General, 23 November 1962, *Assignment of German Army Forces to SACEUR*, International Military Staff, Records of the Standing Group, NATO Archives, Brussels.

132. SGM-1-63, Standing Group Memorandum, 14 January 1963, *The Assignment of Forces Available to NATO: End-1962 and End-1963*, International Military Staff, Records of the Standing Group, NATO Archives, Brussels.

133. SGM-1-64, Standing Group Memorandum, 17 January 1964, *The Assignment of Forces Available to NATO: End-1963 and End-1964*, International Military Staff, Records of the Standing Group, NATO Archives, Brussels.

134. U. Alexis Johnson to Secretary of State, 8 February 1963, *The Strategic Confrontation in NATO over U.S. Views on Conventional Strategy*, p. 1, Records of the Policy Planning Council (S/PC), 1963–64, Europe, January–February 1963, Box 259, RG 59, NA.

135. Henry Kissinger, Memorandum of Conversation with General Speidel in Fontainebleau, 10 January 1963, President Kennedy Papers, National Security Files, Robert W. Komer, Box 417, "Germany (Berlin) 1961–1962 [Folder 1 of 2]," JFKL.

136. Aide Memoire for Mr. Stikker, 19 January 1962, *NATO Strategy*, Norstad Papers, Subject Series, Box 110, "Secretary General—NATO (4)," DDEL.

137. The German military representative to NATO argued that eastward movement of the main line of defense meant that "the deterrence will also be moved forward." In particular, it meant that the cities of Hamburg and Munich could not easily be taken by Soviet troops and used as pawns in negotiations. NMR-Germany, 12 November 1962, Norstad Papers, Country File, Box 49, "Germany 1961–1962 (1)," DDEL.

138. Führungsstab des Heeres, Bonn, February 1960, *Lage ILLMENAU* mit Anlagen: *Korpsbefehl für die Verteidigung zwischen Elbe und Aller*, und *BRV für die Verteidigung zwischen Elbe und Aller*, Bestand BH 1, Aktenband 1684, BA-MA, Freiburg.

139. Maloney, *War without Battles*, pp. 199–202. Maloney points out that many of the German soldiers in NORTHAG came from areas close to the border. He states that Canadian officers were convinced that I and III German corps had contingency plans for forward operations east of the border. In that case, entire brigades would be moved into East Germany in order to engage the Soviet spearheads on enemy territory and begin the attrition of Soviet forces before they could reach the forward-defense line.

140. Taylor to Walt Rostow, 23 April 1962, President Kennedy Papers, National Security Files, Box 294, "Basic National Security Policy 6/22/62 and Undated [Folder 1 of 2]," JFKL. U.S. doctrine did not distinguish categorically between small nuclear warheads of 0.4 kilotons that were to be launched by Davy Crocketts and nuclear bombs of several hundred kilotons that were to be delivered by tactical air forces. Tay-

lor suggested that tactical nuclear forces should be divided into battlefield forces for direct use against enemy formations and interdiction forces for use against enemy reserves and installations in the rear.

141. Memorandum of Conversation, *Secretary McNamara's Meeting with Defense Minister von Hassel on Strategic Subjects, Bonn, July 31, 1963*, pp. 2, 5–6, General Staff, ODCSOPS/OACSFOR, Security Classified Correspondence 1963, 201-45 Germany, Box 5, RG 319, NA; Memorandum for Record, 24 October 1963, *Discussions between General Speidel and Chief of Staff, U.S. Army*, p. 4, General Staff, ODCSOPS/OACSFOR, Security Classified Correspondence 1963, 201-45 Services, Box 15, RG 319, NA.

142. Memorandum for Record, 24 October 1963, *Discussions between General Speidel and Chief of Staff, U.S. Army*, pp. 2–3, 7, General Staff, ODCSOPS/OACSFOR, Security Classified Correspondence 1963, 201-45 Services, Box 15, RG 319, NA.

143. Ibid., Enclosure 1, p. 6.

144. Rostow and Tyler to Rusk, 13 November 1963, *New Nuclear Dangers*, with an attached undated letter from Rusk to McNamara, Records of the Policy Planning Staff (S/PC) 1963–64, Germany, Box 281, RG 59, NA.

145. Rusk to McNamara, 20 February 1964, Lyndon B. Johnson Papers, President, 1963–1969, National Security File, Agency File, Box 35, "NATO—General, vol. 1, 12/63–7/64 [1 of 3]," LBJL. The quotation is on p. 1. Rusk's criticisms were supported by consultants of the Policy Planning Staff, including Dean Acheson, Robert Bowie, and Allen Dulles, who had met on 8 January to discuss problems facing NATO. Walt Rostow to Secretary Rusk, *Consultant's Meeting*, 11 January 1964, Lyndon B. Johnson Papers, President, 1963–1969, National Security File, Agency File, Box 35, "NATO—General, vol. 1, 12/63–7/64 [3 of 3]," LBJL.

146. Weiss to Owen, 14 February 1964, *Attached Paper on National Strategy*, pt. 2: *Key Issues Concerning Various Aspects of US and Allied Views on NATO Strategy*, Records of the Policy Planning Council (S/PC) 1963–64, Europe 1963–1964, Box 281, RG 59, NA.

147. Project I d, First Interim Report, 18 May 1964, pt. 3: *Evaluation of UK, FRG, and French Views on NATO Strategy*, pp. 1–5, Defense Programs and Operations, Tactical Nuclear Study, Box 41, RG 200, NA.

148. Memorandum of Conversation, 9 December 1963, *Meeting with FRG MOD von Hassel, Washington, 3 December 1963*, pp. 6–7. PHP, http://www.php.isn.ethz.ch/collections/colltopic.cfm?lng=en&id=18687&navinfo=14968 (accessed 15 November 2007).

149. Ibid., pp. 7–8.

150. Rostow to Rusk, 11 December 1963, *Defense Proposal for NATO Military Strategy*, Records of the Policy Planning Council (S/PC) 1963–64, Europe September–December 1963, Box 259, RG 59, NA.

151. Duffield, *Power Rules*, pp. 156–168; Lawrence S. Kaplan, *NATO and the United States: The Enduring Alliance* (Boston: Twayne Publishers, 1988), pp. 94–101; Stromseth, *Origins of Flexible Response*, pp. 121–150. For the resulting political crisis in NATO, see also Helga Haftendorn, *NATO and the Nuclear Revolution: A Crisis of Credibility, 1966–1967* (Oxford: Clarendon Press, 1996).

152. Gathright to Weiss, 11 February 1964, *AIAS Studies of Tactical Nuclear Warfare*, Records of the Policy Planning Council (S/PC) 1963–64, Military and Naval Policy

(National Security), Box 280, RG 59, NA. For the rejection of limited nuclear war, see also Weiss to Owen, 14 February 1964, *Attached Paper on National Strategy*, pt. 3: *Key Issues Concerning Various Aspects of US and Allied Views on NATO Strategy*, pp. 6–11, Records of the Policy Planning Council (S/PC) 1963–64, Europe 1963–1964, Box 281, RG 59, NA.

153. CM-1324-64, Taylor to Service Chiefs, 16 April 1964, *Military Strategy for NATO*, Chairman's File, General Taylor 1962–64, CM-1324-64, Box 2, RG 218, NA. All quotations are on p. 2.

154. Weiss to Johnson, 27 May 1964, Attachment: Johnson to Rusk, *Meetings in Paris with Bohlen, Finletter, Lemnitzer and McConnell*, Records of the Deputy Assistant Secretary for Politico-Military Affairs, Subject Files 1961–63, Memoranda (File 1 of 5), Box 1, RG 59, NA.

155. Llewelyn Thompson, Memorandum, 30 October 1964, *NATO Force Planning*, Records of the Policy Planning Council (S/PC) 1963–64, Europe, October–December 1964, Box 258, RG 59, NA.

156. Memorandum of Conversation, 13 November 1964, *Secretary McNamara's Meeting with FRG MOD von Hassel, 12–13 November, Doctrine and Strategy*, pp. 3–5, Memcons with Germany, vol. 1, sec. 1, Box 133, RG 200, NA.

157. Ibid., pp. 5–6.

158. Ibid., p. 12.

159. MCM-161-64, Memorandum for the Members of the Military Committee, 2 December 1964, *Transmission of Additional Information to NATO Authorities*, International Military Staff, Records of the North Atlantic Military Committee, NATO Archives, Brussels.

160. Record-MC 150, 14 January 1965, *Summary Record: 150th Meeting of the Military Committee*, International Military Staff, Records of the North Atlantic Military Committee, NATO Archives, Brussels. The quotations are on pp. 14–15 and 17, respectively.

161. For the shift in the official German position in 1966 and the still-continued adherence to strict nuclear deterrence by the Mediterranean countries, see American Embassy, Paris to State Department, 26 November 1966, *December Ministerial Meeting—Defense Planning*, PHP, http://www.php.isn.ethz.ch/collections/colltopic.cfm?lng=en&id=18770&navinfo=14968 (accessed 15 November 2007).

162. DPC/D(67)23, 11 May 1967, *Defence Planning Committee: Decisions of the Defence Planning Committee in Ministerial Session*; and MC 14/3 (Final), 16 January 1968, *Final Decision on MC 14/3:* A Report by the Military Committee to the Defence Planning Committee on *Overall Strategic Concept for the Defense of the North Atlantic Treaty Organization Area*, in Pedlow, *NATO Strategy Documents*, pp. 333–370. The JCS protested that this was nothing but nuclear deterrence differently phrased. JCSM-313-67, 2 June 1967, *NATO Force Structure, 10 May 1967*, PHP, http://www.php.isn.ethz.ch/collections/colltopic.cfm?lng=en&id=18768&navinfo=14968 (accessed 15 November 2007).

163. MC 39/18 (Military Decision), 15 February 1967, *Military Decision on MC 39/18:* A Report by the Military Committee, *An Assessment of the Overall Military Situation of NATO*, International Military Staff, Records of the North Atlantic Military Committee, NATO Archives, Brussels.

164. Stromseth, *Origins of Flexible Response*.

Chapter 5. The ROAD Army in Germany and Vietnam

1. See, for instance, Thomas A. Schwartz, *Lyndon Johnson and Europe: In the Shadow of Vietnam* (Cambridge, MA: Harvard University Press, 2003). See also George C. Herring, *LBJ and Vietnam: A Different Kind of War* (Austin: University of Texas Press, 1996), for the deliberate decision to fight a limited war in Vietnam.

2. FM 100-5, 1962, p. 5.

3. Hawkins, *United States Army Force Structure and Force Design Initiatives*, A-1.

4. FM 100-5, 1962, p. 5.

5. Ibid., p. 46.

6. Ibid., pp. 75–76.

7. Gavin, "Cavalry, and I Don't Mean Horses."

8. Hamilton H. Howze, *A Cavalryman's Story: Memoirs of a Twentieth-Century Army General* (Washington, DC: Smithsonian Institution Press, 1996), pp. 233–234.

9. The best works on airmobility are the recollections of practitioners, such as John R. Galvin, *Air Assault: The Development of Airmobile Warfare* (New York: Hawthorne Books, 1969); and John J. Tolson, *Airmobility, 1961–1971* (Washington, DC: Department of the Army, 1973). Krepinevich, *The Army and Vietnam*, pp. 112–127, offers a convenient survey. A recent scholarly study by Christopher C. S. Cheng, *Air Mobility: The Development of a Doctrine* (Westport, CT: Praeger, 1994), suffers from an incomplete source base and failure to consider airmobility in the context of broader institutional reform. Finally, Frederic A. Bergerson, *The Army Gets an Air Force: Tactics of Insurgent Bureaucratic Politics* (Baltimore: Johns Hopkins University Press, 1980), addresses the bureaucratic politics of planning and acquiring the means for tactical airmobility. For a broader discussion of close air support and the competition of army and air force, see John Schlight, *Help from Above: Air Force Close Air Support of the Army, 1946–1973* (Washington, DC: Air Force History and Museums Program, 2003). See particularly pp. 233–298 for the debate of close air support in army, air force, and administration in the first half of the 1960s.

10. Tolson, *Airmobility*, pp. 8–12.

11. For the formation of the Howze Board, which was stacked with airmobility advocates, its recommendations, and its difficult relationship with the more conservative army leadership, see Thomas L. Hendrix et al., "Air Assault on the Pentagon: Army Airmobility, the Howze Board, and Implementing Change" (Historical Study No. 1; Carlisle, PA: U.S. Army Military History Institute, 1997).

12. Ibid., pp. 22–24.

13. Hamilton H. Howze, "Tactical Employment of the Air Assault Division," *Army* 14, no. 2 (September 1963): 35–53.

14. For a discussion of the development of the airmobile division, see Wilson, *Maneuver and Firepower*, pp. 314–317; and Hawkins, *United States Army Force Structure and Force Design Initiatives*, pp. 49–52. See also the recollections of Hamilton Howze, *A Cavalryman's Story*, pp. 233–257.

15. See FM 100-5, 1962, pp. 99–109. Andrew Krepinevich argues that the army aviation community emphasized the compatibility of airmobile forces to war in Central Europe in order to increase the chances that the Army Staff would accept their design. Krepinevich, *The Army and Vietnam*, pp. 115–127.

16. Hamilton H. Howze, "The Land Battle in Atomic War," *Army* 11, no. 12 (July 1961): 28–36.

17. Ibid., p. 34.

18. Ibid., p. 35.

19. Ibid.

20. Memorandum for Record, 14 November 1963, *Visit of Major General Karl Wilhelm Thilo to the Vice Chief of Staff*, General Staff, ODCSOPS/OACSFOR, Security Classified Correspondence 1963, 201-45 Germany, Box 5, RG 319, NA. A fourth German corps was deployed in the northern state of Schleswig-Holstein, which was part of NATO's Northern Region.

21. *Strauss-McNamara Conversation*, 14 July 1961, pp. 9–10, Central Decimal File 1961, CCS 9165/5420 Germany (West), Box 177, RG 218, NA; Memorandum of Conversation, 15 July 1961, *Meeting between Secretary of the Treasury and German Defense Minister, Strauss*, 15 July 1961, p. 3, Assistant Secretary of Defense (ISA), Secret and Below General Files, 1961, 092 Germany, 1–20 July 1961, Box 33, RG 330, NA.

22. *Strauss-McNamara Conversation*, 14 July 1961, pp. 9–10. See also Hunnicutt, *Patton*, p. 439, for characteristics of the M60 tank.

23. Memorandum for Record, 18 November 1963, *FY 65 Tank Procurement*, General Staff, ODCSOPS/OACSFOR, Security Classified Correspondence 1963, 1401-01, Box 49, RG 319, NA.

24. Agreement between the Government of the United States of America and the Government of the Federal Republic of Germany for a Cooperative Tank Development Program, Bonn, 1 August 1963, President Kennedy Papers, National Security Files, Country Series, Box 80a, "McNamara Visit to Germany, 1963," JFKL. Strangely, however, the minutes of the discussion between McNamara and von Hassel reveal that there was no joint-venture agreement drafted at that point, and the two defense ministers concurred that an intergovernmental agreement could be worked out by the staffs of the finance ministries. Secretary McNamara's Meeting with Defense Minister von Hassel on Logistics Subjects, 1 August 1963, General Staff, ODCSOPS/OACSFOR, Security Classified Correspondence, 1963, 201-45 Germany, Box 5, RG 319, NA.

25. For the development of the MBT-70 and its ultimate rejection, see Hunnicutt, *Abrams*, pp. 117–142.

26. Memorandum of Conversation, 23 July 1968, in *FRUS*, 1964–1968, vol. 15, *Germany and Berlin* (Washington, DC: Government Printing Office, 1999), pp. 721–727.

27. Statement of Secretary of Defense Elliot L. Richardson before the Committee on Appropriations, House of Representatives, Subcommittee on Department of Defense on the FY 1974 Defense Budget and FY 1974–1978 Program, 3 April 1973, p. 71, Joint Secretariat, Central File 1973, 565 (27 March 1973), Box 16, RG 218, NA.

28. James H. Polk, "We Need a New Tank," *Army* 22, no. 6 (June 1972): 8–14; Royce R. Taylor Jr., "The Abrams XM 1 Main Battle Tank," *NATO's Fifteen Nations* 25, no. 5 (October–November 1980): 65–71.

29. Wolfgang Flume and Paul Denning, "Main Battle Tanks for the Eighties," *NATO's Fifteen Nations* 25, no. 1 (February–March 1980): 48–57.

30. For German mechanized doctrine and equipment in the 1950s and 1960s, see Dieter H. Kollmer, *Rüstungsgüterbeschaffung in der Aufbauphase der Bundeswehr: Der*

Schützenpanzer HS 30 als Fallbeispiel (1953–1961) (Stuttgart: Franz Steiner Verlag, 2002). For a more general discussion of German army materiel, see Dieter H. Kollmer, "Klotzen, nicht kleckern! Die materielle Aufrüstung des Heeres von den Anfängen bis Ende der sechziger Jahre," in Hammerich et al., *Das Heer*, pp. 485–614. For German reservations about American weapon systems and equipment, see also Birtle, *Rearming the Phoenix*, pp. 264–266.

31. The Bundeswehr already had an armored infantry fighting vehicle in service in the early 1960s, the *Schützenpanzer* 12-3. This, as W. Blair Haworth argues, came in response to the difficulty of maintaining infantry support for armor on the Eastern Front in World War II. The Germans did not have much experience in World War II with armored infantry, but they did analyze the need for it and addressed it early on in their rearmament effort. Haworth, *The Bradley*, pp. 39–41.

32. Joseph Califano, Memorandum for Jack Valenti, 1 December 1964, *Weekly Report for the President*, Lyndon B. Johnson Papers, President, Confidential File, Agency Reports, Department of Defense, December 1964, Box 112, LBJL.

33. Lieutenant Colonel Walter Arnold, 20 November 1963, *US/FRG Armored Personnel Carrier Co-Production Proposal*, General Staff, ODCSOPS/OACSFOR, Security Classified Correspondence 1963, 1401-01, Box 49, RG 319, NA. For the rejection of the XM701, the AIFV-65 prototype, see Haworth, *The Bradley*, pp. 43–44.

34. Andrew Krepinevich argues that army generals contributed to the attitude that "any good soldier can handle guerillas." He points at a statement made to this effect by General Decker to President Kennedy, and he implies that Lyman Lemnitzer, Earle Wheeler, and Maxwell Taylor agreed with Decker. Krepinevich, *The Army and Vietnam*, p. 37. This account, apparently based on an interview with Maxwell Taylor in 1982, does not reflect the opinion Taylor had expressed as army chief of staff, that armed forces trained and equipped for combat against the Soviets were not necessarily suited for conflict of lesser intensity. Moreover, McMaster relates that General Decker was asked to retire in 1962 because he did not believe that the United States could win a conventional war in Southeast Asia. H. R. McMaster, *Dereliction of Duty: Lyndon Johnson, Robert McNamara, the Joint Chiefs of Staff, and the Lies That Led to Vietnam* (New York: HarperCollins, 1997), p. 22.

35. Krepinevich argues that the Army Staff's opposition to counterinsurgency doctrine was an expression of a deeply ingrained "Army Concept," which favored large-scale conventional war, based on the experience of the two world wars and the Korean War. He concedes that deterrence of war in Europe was the primary concern of the army but concludes that this was a mistake because sub-limited war in Vietnam was more likely to occur. Krepinevich was aware of the prevailing attitude among senior army officers that failure in Europe was too costly while defeat in Vietnam could be tolerated, but he nevertheless blames army leaders for transplanting the "Army Concept" to Vietnam.

36. CM-1294-64, Memorandum for the Director, Joint Staff, 14 April 1964, *Logistic Capability Study of CINCPAC OPLAN 32–64, Phase IV*, Chairman's File, General Taylor 1962–64, CM 1294-64, Box 2, RG 218, NA.

37. Memorandum for the Secretary of the Army, 3 April 1963, *Recommended Force Structure for FY 1965*, General Staff, Security Classified Correspondence 1963, Box 1,

RG 319, NA. In 1966 and 1967, the army had seventeen divisions; there were two more in 1968 and eighteen in 1969. By 1970 it was back to the sixteen divisions of 1965, even though one airborne division had been converted into an air assault division. Since the number of armored and mechanized divisions remained steady, it appears obvious that the fluctuation was a direct result of the combat in Vietnam. See Hawkins and Carafano, *Prelude to Army XXI*, A-1, A-2.

38. Memorandum for the Secretary of the Army, 3 April 1963, *Recommended Force Structure for FY 1965*.

39. Memorandum from the Chairman of the Joint Chiefs of Staff (Taylor) to Secretary of Defense McNamara, 20 March 1964, *Joint Strategic Objectives Plan for FY 1969–1971 (JSOP-69) Part VI—Force Tabs and Analysis*, in *FRUS*, 1964–1968, vol. 10, *National Security Policy* (Washington, DC: Government Printing Office, 2002), pp. 60–64. The quotations are on p. 62.

40. President Kennedy approved the shift of emphasis in LONG THRUST from 101st Airborne Division to 4th Infantry Division on 10 October 1961. See McGeorge Bundy, Minutes of Meeting, 10 October 1961, in *FRUS*, 1961, vol. 14, pp. 487–489.

41. TNT/D-15, Position Paper for NATO Ministerial Meeting, Paris, 16–18 December 1963, 6 December 1963, *U.S. Military Force Levels in Europe*, Lyndon B. Johnson Papers, President, 1963–1969, National Security File, Agency File, Box 38, "NATO: Ministerial Meeting—Paris, December 16–18, 1963 (Briefing Book)," LBJL. See also Joseph Califano, Memorandum for Bill Moyers, 28 April 1964, *Weekly Report for the President*, Lyndon B. Johnson Papers, President, Confidential File, Agency Reports, Department of Defense, April 1964, Box 111, LBJL.

42. US CINCEUR to JCS, 29 December 1961, Norstad Papers, Subject Series, Box 103, "Joint Chiefs of Staff, Nov 1961–Dec 1962, vol. II (4)," DDEL.

43. National Security Action Memorandum No. 270, 29 October 1963, *Meeting with the President, Thursday, October 26, on European Matters*, National Security Action Memorandum (NSAM), Box 3, RG 273, NA. For the concerns in Europe, see Memorandum for Record, *Meeting of General Speidel, FRG, and General Taylor, CJCS [on October 28, 1963]*, PHP, http://www.php.isn.ethz.ch/collections/colltopic.cfm?lng=en&id=18684&navinfo=14968 (accessed 15 November 2007). See also Duffield, *Power Rules*, p. 170.

44. Rusk to American embassies in Europe, 23 December 1964, *Secretary McNamara's Remarks to NATO Ministerial Meeting, December 15–17, Paris*, Formerly Top Secret Foreign Policy Files 1964–66, NATO, Box 22, RG 59, NA.

45. Department of Defense, 1963–1969, Military Programs, pt. 3: Mobility Forces, pp. 7–8, 17, Administrative History for the Department of Defense, Box 1, LBJL.

46. Memorandum for the Secretary of the Army, 3 April 1963, *Recommended Force Structure for FY 1965*, Enclosure 4: *Rationale for an 18 Division Active Army in FY 65*, ibid.

47. Background Paper, The Under Secretary's Trip to Europe, November 1963, 30 October 1963, *U.S. Troop Strength in Europe*, Records of the Policy Planning Council (S/PC) 1963–64, Europe, September–December 1963, Box 259, RG 59, NA.

48. Vance to Assistant Secretary of Defense (ISA), 31 October 1963, *U.S. Force Adjustments and Modernization*, General Staff, ODCSOPS/OACSFOR, Security Classified

Correspondence 1963, 201-45 Services, Box 15, RG 319, NA. The M109 155-mm howitzer had a range of 18,000 meters, versus 15,000 for the 105-mm howitzer. The downside was in the drop of the rate of fire from ten to three rounds per minute. Ammunition for the 155-mm howitzer had tested as up to five times more effective on target than ammunition for the 105-mm guns. White House Fact Sheet, 19 November 1963, *USAREUR Artillery Reorganization*, General Staff, ODCSOPS/OACSFOR, Security Classified Correspondence 1963, 1401-01, Box 49, RG 319, NA.

49. Memorandum for Record, *Meeting of General Speidel, FRG, and General Taylor, CJCS [on October 28, 1963]*, pp. 4–5, PHP, http://www.php.isn.ethz.ch/collections/colltopic.cfm?lng=en&id=18684&navinfo=14968 (accessed 15 November 2007).

50. *A Study of The Management and Termination of War with the Soviet Union*, prepared by the Staff of the Net Evaluation Subcommittee of the National Security Council, 15 November 1963, Records of the Policy Planning Council (S/PC) 1963–64, War Aims, Box 280, RG 59, NA. Also available online at National Security Archive, 24 May 2000, "U.S. Planning for War in Europe, 1963–64," Electronic Briefing Book No. 31, Document 1 (http://www.gwu.edu/~nsarchiv/NSAEBB/NSAEBB31/index.html) (accessed August 2005).

51. Ibid., pp. 21–25.

52. Ibid., pp. 25–27.

53. Ibid., pt. 4: *Analysis of SACEUR EDP*, pp. 13–15.

54. Ibid., p. 21.

55. MC 43/17, 8 November 1965, A Report by the Military Committee to the North Atlantic Council, *Exercise FALLEX-64*, International Military Staff, Records of the North Atlantic Military Committee, NATO Archives, Brussels.

56. Kitchen to Lindley, 19 October 1964, *Cromley's Article on Conventional Weapons Deficiency*, Attachment: Memorandum of Conversation, 30 September 1964, *Summary of Briefing by Dr. Enthoven on General Purpose Forces*, Records of the Policy Planning Council (S/PC) 1963–64, Military and Naval Policy (National Security), Box 280, RG 59, NA; Department of Defense Draft for the NATO Ministerial Meeting, Paris—December 1964, 4 December 1964, *The Role of Tactical Nuclear Forces in NATO Strategy*, PHP, http://www.php.isn.ethz.ch/collections/colltopic.cfm?lng=en&id=18607&navinfo=14968 (accessed 15 November 2007).

57. Colbert to Gatright, 28 October 1964, *Attached Correspondence re US Conventional Weapons Deficiency*, Records of the Policy Planning Staff (S/PC) 1963–64, Military and Naval Policy (National Security), Box 280, RG 59, NA.

58. Rusk to American embassies in Europe, 23 December 1964, *Secretary McNamara's Remarks to NATO Ministerial Meeting, December 15–17, Paris*, Formerly Top Secret Foreign Policy Files 1964–66, NATO, Box 22, RG 59, NA.

59. Thompson to Weiss, 29 December 1964, *Implications of a Major Soviet Conventional Attack in Central Europe*, Records of Ambassador-at-Large Llewellyn Thompson, 1961–1970, Chron—July 1964, Box 21, RG 59, NA.

60. Kissinger, *Nuclear Weapons and Foreign Policy*; Osgood, *Limited War*. See also Weigley, *The American Way of War*, pp. 410–418.

61. Project KALIUM (I), Study 98.1, ORO-S-1632, 4 March 1961, Group 1—Strategies, Major Tactics and Operational Concepts, by G. J. Higgins, *Realignment of NATO*

Ground Forces in the Defense of Central Europe and *Some Aspects of the Problem of Providing a "Dual Capability,"* Command and General Staff College, Combined Arms Research Library, Archive N-16454.910.

62. The JCS indeed advised President Kennedy in 1961 that among the military requirements for a ground war in Laos were nuclear weapons. See McMaster, *Dereliction of Duty*, p. 7. See also Gacek, *The Logic of Force*, pp. 158–178, for an interesting discussion of army opposition to an invasion of Laos.

63. Project KALIUM (I), Study 98.1, pp. 3–5.

64. Ibid., pp. 9–14.

65. FM 100-5, 1962, pp. 91–95. In 1961, the army had published FM 31-15, *Operations against Irregular Forces*, but, in the assessment of the Command and General Staff College, that manual was merely an initial step in the direction of proper doctrine, and it remained "broad in scope and general in content." See U.S. Army Command and General Staff College, *A Detailed Concept for Employment of U.S. Army Combat Units in Military Operations against Irregular Forces* (Ft. Leavenworth, KS: Command and General Staff College, 1962), pp. A-11, 12.

66. FM 100-5, 1962, pp. 127–135.

67. Ibid., pp. 136–154.

68. Heilbrunn, *Conventional Warfare in the Nuclear Age*; Helmut Schmidt, *Verteidigung oder Vergeltung: Ein deutscher Beitrag zum strategischen Problem der NATO* (Stuttgart: Verlag Seewald, 1961); Helmut Schmidt, *Defense or Retaliation: A German View* (New York: Praeger, 1962).

69. For the improvement of the Bundeswehr, see, for instance, American Embassy, Bonn to State Department, 18 May 1961, *Defense Minister Strauss' Views on Defense Policy and Related Matters*, President Kennedy Papers, National Security Files, Countries, Box 74, "Germany, 5/3/61–7/31/61," JFKL; and William Bundy to Secretary of the Army, 17 June 1961, *Alleged Superiority of West German over United States Conventional Equipment*, Assistant Secretary of Defense (International Security Affairs), Secret and Below General Files 1961, 400 Germany 1961, Box 33, RG 330, NA.

70. Wheeler to Secretary of the Army, 12 December 1962, *Theater Type Division Forces*, General Staff, Security Classified Correspondence 1963, 201-22 Series, Box 2, RG 319, NA. See also Command and General Staff College, *A Detailed Concept for Employment of U.S. Army Combat Units in Military Operations against Irregular Forces*, Annex B: Organizational Concept.

71. Combat Developments Command, *Review and Analysis of the Evaluation of Army Combat Operations in Vietnam*, 30 April 1966, pp. 2–3, Record 85966, Virtual Vietnam Archive, Texas Tech University, http://star.vietnam.ttu.edu (accessed December 2005).

72. Kermit B. Blaney, "Is the Infantry Ready?" *Army* 15, no. 13 (August 1965): 28–33, offers a good example.

73. Donn A. Starry, *Mounted Combat in Vietnam* (Washington, DC: Department of the Army, 1989), pp. 3–4. This official history of armored operations in Vietnam was originally published in 1978. For a recent discussion of armored combat in Vietnam, see also Lewis Sorley, "Adaptation and Impact: Mounted Combat in Vietnam," in Hofmann and Starry, *Camp Colt to Desert Storm*, pp. 324–359.

74. Starry, *Mounted Combat in Vietnam*, p. 7. General Starry pointed out that tactical field manuals for armor units largely ignored combat in woods, swamps, and jungles and near lakes.

75. See, for instance, John Hay Jr., *Tactical and Materiel Innovations* (Washington, DC: Department of the Army, 1974), pp. 3–6, 97–106; and Doughty, *Evolution of U.S. Army Tactical Doctrine*, pp. 36–37.

76. Hay, *Tactical and Materiel Innovations*, p. 180.

77. Doughty, *Evolution of U.S. Army Tactical Doctrine*, p. 38.

78. For recent analysis of the U.S. Army in Vietnam, as caught between organization and operational planning for big-unit war and the need to adapt to guerrilla warfare and implement a comprehensive counterinsurgency policy and strategy, see John A. Nagl, *Learning to Eat Soup with a Knife: Counterinsurgency Lessons from Malaya to Vietnam* (Chicago: University of Chicago Press, 2005), pp. 151–187.

79. *MACOV*. See also Starry, *Mounted Combat in Vietnam*, pp. 9, 52–54, for Marine Corps tank battalions.

80. Starry, *Mounted Combat in Vietnam*, pp. 62–78. The quotation is on p. 65. For armor tactics, organization, and equipment in Vietnam, see also U.S. Army Armor School, *Armor in Vietnam* (Fort Knox, KY, October 1970).

81. *MACOV*, pp. 53–54, 60–67.

82. Ibid., p. 56.

83. Ibid., pp. 68–70.

84. Shelby L. Stanton, *Vietnam Order of Battle* (New York: Galahad Books, 1987), pp. 93–94, 141–160.

85. For a typical tank battalion in Vietnam, see Stanton, *Vietnam Order of Battle*, p. 48. For the ROAD division standard tank battalion, see Headquarters, Department of the Army, TOE 17E, 31 March 1966. The changes to armor battalions are detailed in U.S. Army Armor School, *Armor in Vietnam*, pp. 3-1–3-55.

86. The army had intended to arm the M48A3 with a 105-mm gun, but funding for the program was reduced because of the overall cost of the Vietnam War. By 1967, the demand for medium-gun tanks was so great that the obsolescent M48A1 was converted to the M48A3 standard. Hunnicutt, *Patton*, p. 227.

87. U.S. Army Armor School, *Armor in Vietnam*, p. 3-1.

88. For the design, production, and reception of the Sheridan, see Haworth, *The Bradley*, pp. 67–69. For the ACAV model of the M113, essentially the APC with additional machine guns, see ibid., p. 32.

89. The deployment of Sheridans to USAREUR armored cavalry was completed in the spring of 1971. Headquarters, USAREUR, and Seventh Army, *Annual Historical Summary*, 1 January–31 December 1971, p. 45. The ACAV had very limited anti-armor capability, but the Sheridan could destroy enemy tanks at 3,000 meters. Headquarters, USAREUR, and Seventh Army, *Report of Major Activities, 1 January to 31 December 1973*, pp. 1–26.

90. Haworth, *The Bradley*, p. 69.

91. Stanton, *Vietnam Order of Battle*, pp. 72–89.

92. Headquarters, Combat Development Command, TOE 77-100 T (Tentative), 25 October 1965, and Headquarters, Department of the Army, TOE 7E, 15 July 1963.

93. Headquarters, Department of the Army, TOE 77-100G, 29 May 1968.

94. Stanton, *Vietnam Order of Battle*, p. 53. See also Mahon and Danysh, *Regular Army*, pp. 111–121.

95. U.S. Army, Vietnam, *Evaluation of U.S. Army Combat Operations in Vietnam (ARCOV)*, vol. 3, *Annex B—Mobility*, 25 April 1966, pp. B-11, B1-10. Record 86418, Virtual Vietnam Archive, Texas Tech University, http://www.star.vietnam.ttu.edu (accessed December 2005).

96. U.S. Army, Vietnam, *ARCOV*, vol. 4, *Annex C—Firepower*, 25 April 1966, pp. C-4–C-16, Record 86742, Virtual Vietnam Archive, Texas Tech University, http://www.star.vietnam.ttu.edu (accessed December 2005).

97. ROCID battle groups had four rifle companies; ROAD infantry battalions had only three. Mahon and Danysh, *Regular Army*, pp. 91, 102, and 115.

98. For the change from three to four rifle companies in an infantry battalion, see the 25 April 1966 and 30 October 1966 editions of U.S. Army, Vietnam, *ARCOV*, vol. 1: *Basic Report*, Records 85966 and 86164, Virtual Vietnam Archive, Texas Tech University, http://www.star.vietnam.ttu.edu. Pages II-9–II-17 of the April edition still show three rifle companies in an infantry battalion, although battalions in an airborne division already had four line companies. In the October edition, CONARC recommended the general change to four rifle companies. See ibid., pp. 2–3 (accessed December 2005).

99. Hay, *Tactical and Materiel Innovations*, p. 6. Lieutenant General Hay served as commander of Command and General Staff College when he conducted this study.

100. Ibid., p. 3.

101. Tolson, *Airmobility*, p. 254. For a detailed operational account of air cavalry in Vietnam, see First Air Cavalry Division, *Memoirs of the First Team: August 1965–December 1969* (Tokyo: Nippon Printing Company, 1970).

102. Charles J. V. Murphy, "The New Multi-Purpose U.S. Army," *Army* 16, no. 7 (July 1966): 21–33.

103. For a summary of adjustments to tactics and materiel innovations in Vietnam, see Hay, *Tactical and Materiel Innovations*.

104. Ibid., particularly pp. 78–106.

105. For signal communications in Vietnam, see Major General Thomas Matthew Rienzi, *Communications-Electronics, 1962–1970* (Washington, DC: Department of the Army, 1972).

106. FM 100-5, 1968.

107. John Nagl concludes that the primary reason for the army's inability to adopt comprehensive counterinsurgency doctrine after 1965 lay in "the organizational culture of the United States Army [that] precluded organizational learning on counterinsurgency during the Vietnam War." Nagl, *Learning to Eat Soup with a Knife*, p. 180.

108. Lyman Lemnitzer interviewed by Ted Gittinger, 3 March 1982, pp. 35–37, LBJL.

109. JCSM-130-66, Memorandum for the Secretary of Defense, 1 March 1966, *CY 1966 Deployments to Southeast Asia and World-Wide US Military Posture*, Chairman's File, General Wheeler 1964–70, JCSM 130-66, Box 183, RG 218, NA. The quotation is on p. 5.

110. Memorandum from the Chairman of the Joint Chiefs of Staff (Taylor) to Sec-

retary of Defense McNamara, 20 March 1964, *Joint Strategic Objectives Plan for FY 1969–1971 (JSOP-69), Part VI—Force Tabs and Analysis*, and Letter from the Chairman of the Joint Chiefs of Staff (Taylor) to Secretary of Defense McNamara, 1 July 1964, in *FRUS*, 1964–1968, vol. 10, pp. 60–64, 97–101.

111. Wartime allotment of personnel slots for support forces in U.S. Army divisions was 32,644; a German division had to make do with 16,528 and a British division with only 14,393. See Draft Memorandum for the President, *Redeployment of U.S. Forces from Europe*, p. 14, attached to McNamara to Rostow, 19 January 1967, Lyndon B. Johnson Papers, President, 1963–1969, National Security File, Agency File, Box 12, Defense, Department of, vol. 4, 6/66 (2 of 2), LBJL.

112. JCSM-130-66, Memorandum for the Secretary of Defense, 1 March 1966, *CY 1966 Deployments to Southeast Asia and World-Wide US Military Posture*, Chairman's File, General Wheeler 1964–70, JCSM 130-66, Box 183, RG 218, NA.

113. JCSM-646-66, Memorandum for the Secretary of Defense, 7 October 1966, *World-Wide US Military Posture*, Chairman's File, General Wheeler 1964–70, JCSM 646-66, Box 183, RG 218, NA.

114. JCSM-22-67, Memorandum for the Secretary of Defense, 20 May 1967, *World-wide US Military Posture*, Chairman's File, General Wheeler 1964–70, JCSM 288-67, Box 184, RG 218, NA.

115. USAREUR, *Annual Historical Summary*, 1966, pp. 22–30.

116. Statement of Secretary of Defense Robert S. McNamara before a Joint Session of the Senate Armed Services Committee and the Senate Subcommittee on Department of Defense Appropriations on the FY 1968–1972, Defense Programs and Defense Budget, 23 January 1967, p. 68, Lyndon B. Johnson Papers, President, 1963–1969, National Security File, Agency File, Box 17, DOD FY1967 Budget book (1 of 2), LBJL.

117. MC 39/17 (Military Decision), 2 December 1965, *Military Decision on MC 39/17:* A Report by the Military Committee, *Analysis of the Military Implications of the 1965 Annual Review*, International Military Staff, Records of the North Atlantic Military Committee, NATO Archives, Brussels. The quotation is on p. 14.

118. The Red Army Faction evolved out of the Baader-Meinhof Gang. The two names are often used together in American historiography. For a brief history of terrorist attacks, see Daniel J. Nelson, *Defenders or Intruders? The Dilemmas of U.S. Forces in Germany* (Boulder, CO: Westview Press, 1987), pp. 164–177.

119. Robert H. Scales, *Certain Victory: The U.S. Army in the Gulf War* (Washington, DC: Office of the Chief of Staff, U.S. Army, 1993), p. 6, states that "forty percent of the Army in Europe confessed to drug use, mostly hashish"; 7 percent admitted to heroin addiction.

120. The best account on the turbulent years from 1966 to 1973 is Nelson, *History of U.S. Military Forces in Germany*, pp. 87–130. For a sociological analysis of USAREUR in the 1970s and 1980s, see also Nelson, *Defenders or Intruders.*

121. National Intelligence Estimate 11-14-65, 21 October 1965, *Capabilities of Soviet General Purpose Forces*, Historical Review Group, National Intelligence Estimates Concerning Soviet Military Power, 1950–1984, Box 16, Folder 21, RG 263, NA.

122. Mastny and Byrne, *A Cardboard Castle.*

123. National Intelligence Estimate 11-14-66, 9 November 1966, *Capabilities of Soviet General Purpose Forces*, Historical Review Group, National Intelligence Estimates Concerning Soviet Military Power, 1950–1984, Box 16, Folder 25, RG 263, NA.

124. See Draft Memorandum for the President, *Redeployment of U.S. Forces from Europe*, p. 2, attached to McNamara to Rostow, 19 January 1967, Lyndon B. Johnson Papers, President, 1963–1969, National Security File, Agency File, Box 12, Defense, Department of, vol. 4, 6/66 (2 of 2), LBJL. But Otto Heilbrunn pointed out that such an interpretation of doctrine was in the interest of Soviet leaders. He assumed that the Soviet army was in fact prepared for purely conventional or limited nuclear war. Heilbrunn, *Conventional Warfare in the Nuclear Age*, p. 12. See also House, *Combined Arms Warfare*, pp. 191–196, for the gradual reorientation in Soviet doctrinal thinking after 1964, from nuclear war to conventional spearheads. Nevertheless, recently declassified records from the Warsaw Pact states show that the Soviet Union planned for first use of nuclear weapons and expected conventional war to escalate to nuclear war. See Mastny and Byrne, *A Cardboard Castle.*

125. Headquarters, USAREUR, Training Pamphlet 525-1, 15 July 1966, *Combat Operations: Small Unit Tactics in Nuclear Warfare*, Command and General Staff College, Combined Arms Research Library, Archive.

126. Ibid., p. iii.

127. Five French active divisions had been committed to NATO prior to the withdrawal. The French army retained two combat divisions, 65,000 men, in southern Germany. See Draft Memorandum for the President, *Redeployment of U.S. Forces from Europe*, p. 2, attached to McNamara to Rostow, 19 January 1967, Lyndon B. Johnson Papers, President, 1963–1969, National Security File, Agency File, Box 12, Defense, Department of, vol. 4, 6/66 (2 of 2), LBJL.

128. For the evacuation of support and supply functions, see Headquarters, United States European Command, *FRELOC Final Report (Phase I)*, Lyndon B. Johnson Papers, President, 1963–1969, National Security File, Agency File, Box 36, LBJL.

129. Ibid., p. 100.

130. See Draft Memorandum for the President, *Redeployment of U.S. Forces from Europe*, p. 2, attached to McNamara to Rostow, 19 January 1967. There is evidence to suggest that French forces would have been available to NATO in the event of a war. In 1970, the French Ministry of Defense approved operations plan NANCY, outlining a counterattack of French II Corps against Warsaw Pact force penetration in the corridor from Frankfurt to Eisenach. Plan NANCY also determined French support for the CENTAG rear area and counterattack or blocking operations at the Danube between Donauwörth and Ingolstadt in Bavaria. See Headquarters, USAREUR, *Annual Historical Summary*, 1 January–31 December 1970, p. 34.

131. IMSWM-85-67 (2nd ed.), Memorandum for the Members of the Military Committee, 7 July 1967, *Force Proposals 1968–1972*, International Military Staff, Records of the Military Committee, NATO Archives, Brussels.

132. For recent studies of the international financial system and its effects on the alliance, see Francis J. Gavin, *Gold, Dollars, and Power: The Politics of International Monetary Relations, 1958–1971* (Chapel Hill: University of North Carolina Press, 2004); and Zimmermann, *Money and Security*.

133. For political reasons, that name was later changed to Redeployment of Forces to Germany.

134. The REFORGER concept awaits proper historical evaluation. This paragraph is based on the USAREUR annual histories of 1967 and 1968, which discuss the initial movement to the United States, and subsequent annual histories that address the annual exercises in which parts of the REFORGER units returned to Germany for maneuvers. The best narrative source is Nelson, *History of U.S. Military Forces in Germany*, pp. 89–90, 151–154.

135. IMSWM-85-67 (2nd ed.), Appendix 1, Annex A: *Allied Command Europe: Land Force—Comparison between Forces for 1970 and 1972*, Memorandum for the Members of the Military Committee, 7 July 1967, *Force Proposals 1968–1972*, International Military Staff, Records of the Military Committee, NATO Archives, Brussels.

136. General Graf Kielmansegg, Address to the Atlantic Channel Symposium, 4 October 1967, *The Military Challenge to the Central Region*, Chairman's File, General Wheeler 1964–70, 092.2. NATO (August 1967–February 1968), Box 71, RG 218, NA.

137. Draft, Memorandum for the President, revised 16 January 1968, *NATO Strategy and Force Structure*, Draft Memo to the President, vol. 1, Box 77, RG 200, NA.

138. Ivo Daalder, *The Nature and Practice of Flexible Response: NATO Strategy and Theater Nuclear Forces since 1967* (New York: Columbia University Press, 1991).

139. Draft, Memorandum for the President, revised 16 January 1968, *NATO Strategy and Force Structure*, pp. 5–7, Draft Memo to the President, vol. 1, Box 77, RG 200, NA.

140. JCSM-221-68, Memorandum for the Secretary of Defense, 10 April 1968, *Worldwide US Military Posture*, Chairman's File, General Wheeler 1964–70, JCSM 221-68, Box 184, RG 218, NA.

141. Headquarters, USAREUR, and Seventh Army, *Annual Historical Summary*, 1 January–31 December 1972, p. 32. By the end of 1972, USEUCOM and USAREUR officers had convinced ACE planners that the two divisions would arrive within one month of mobilization—or that it was politically necessary to pretend they would.

142. Headquarters, USAREUR, and Seventh Army, *Annual Historical Summary*, 1 January–31 December 1968 (Headquarters, USAREUR, and Seventh Army: Office of the Deputy Chief of Staff, Operations, 1969), pp. 2–5.

143. J-5 BP, Background Paper for the Chairman, JCS, 22 August 1968, *US Military Posture*, Hanson W. Baldwin Papers, Box 10, Folder 24, GCML.

144. General Spivy to General Wheeler, 25 September 1968, *The Military Implications for the Alliance of the Invasion of Czechoslovakia*, Appendix A to MCM-68, dated September 1968, *Suggested Measured to Achieve Short Term Improvements in European Conventional Forces*, Chairman's File, General Wheeler 1964–70, 337 NATO MC/CS Meeting (September 1968), Box 96, RG 218, NA.

145. Special National Intelligence Estimate 11-17-68, 8 October 1968, *Capabilities of Warsaw Pact Forces against NATO*, Historical Review Group, National Intelligence Estimate Concerning Soviet Military Power 1950–1984, Box 17, Folder 34, RG 263, NA.

146. National Intelligence Estimate 11-14-68, 12 December 1968, *Soviet and East European General Purpose Forces*, Historical Review Group, National Intelligence Estimates Concerning Soviet Military Power 1950–1984, Box 17, Folder 36, RG 263, NA.

147. Attachment to Clark Clifford to Walt Rostow, 11 July 1968, p. 3, Lyndon B.

Johnson Papers, President, 1963–1969, National Security File, Agency File, Box 37, "NATO General, vol. 6, 2/68–9/68," LBJL.

148. Paul Warnke, Memorandum for the Secretary of Defense, 8 July 1968, *Discussion with JCS on July 8 of US Troop Levels in Europe*, Clark Clifford Papers, Box 17, "[Troops in Europe and Balance of Payments]," LBJL.

149. Draft Memorandum for the President, 6 June 1968, *The Balance-of-Payments and Forces in Europe*, ibid.

150. CM-3702-68, Memorandum for the Secretary of Defense, 4 October 1968, *Report of Visit to Europe*, Lyndon B. Johnson Papers, President, 1963–1969, National Security File, Agency File, Box 13, Defense, Department of, vol. 6 (1 of 6), April 1968, LBJL.

151. CM-3792-68, General Earle Wheeler, Memorandum for the Secretary of Defense, 4 October 1968, *Report of Visit to Europe*, p. 2, Lyndon B. Johnson Papers, President, 1963–1969, National Security File, Agency File, Box 13, Defense, Department of, vol. 6, April 1968 (1 of 6), LBJL.

152. Wheeler to Clifford and Nitze, 8 November 1968, *Statement by General Wheeler at Meeting of NATO Military Committee in Chiefs of Staff Session, Brussels, 13 November 1968* (2nd rev.), Records of the Joint Chiefs of Staff, Chairman's File, General Wheeler 1964–70, 337 NATO Meeting (Nov 68), Box 96, RG 218, NA.

153. AGAM-P (M) (23 May 69), Adjutant General of the Army, 28 May 1969, *After Action Report Exercise REFORGER I*, Command and General Staff College, Combined Arms Research Library, Archive N-17211.29.

154. For a comprehensive study of revisions to nuclear strategy in the Nixon-Kissinger years, see Terry Terriff, *The Nixon Administration and the Making of U.S. Nuclear Strategy* (Ithaca, NY: Cornell University Press, 1995).

155. [National Security Council], January 1969, *Pilot Study of Alternative Military Objectives, Forces, and Budgets for General Purpose Forces*, National Security Study Memorandum (NSSM), NSSM 3, Box 3, RG 273, NA; National Security Council, Memorandum for the Office of the Vice President, 6 September 1969, *Response to NSSM 3: U.S. Military Posture and the Balance of Power*, pp. 10–13, General Records of the Department of State, Executive Secretariat, NSC Meeting Files 1969–1970, NSC Meeting 9/10/69, Box 5, RG 59, NA.

156. This was expressed in National Security Decision Memorandum 27. See Henry Kissinger, Memorandum for the Vice President, 26 January 1970, *Background Papers on Europe for NSC Meeting, January 28*, p. 14, Executive Secretariat, NSC Meeting Files 1969–1970, NSC Meeting, 28 January 1970, Box 6, RG 59, NA.

157. NSSM 84, Inter-Departmental Steering Committee, National Security Study Memorandum 84 Report, n.d., *US Strategies and Forces for NATO*, National Security Study Memorandum (NSSM), NSSM 84, Box 8, RG 273, NA.

158. The most publicized proposals for force withdrawals came from Senator Mike Mansfield, but Senator Stuart Symington, a former air force secretary and longtime advocate of airpower, was also quite outspoken on the subject. The best survey of Senate policy and U.S. troops in Germany is Phil Williams, *The Senate and U.S. Troops in Europe* (New York: St. Martin's, 1985). For Mansfield, see the excellent recent biography by Don Oberdorfer, *Senator Mansfield: The Extraordinary Life of a Great American*

Statesman and Diplomat (Washington, DC: Smithsonian Books, 2003). For Symington, see Linda McFarland, *Cold War Strategist: Stuart Symington and the Search for National Security* (Westport, CT: Praeger, 2001), pp. 4, 146.

159. National Security Council, National Security Decision Memorandum 95, 25 November 1970, *U.S. Strategy and Forces for NATO*, National Security Decision Memorandum (NSDM), NSDM 95, Box 1, RG 273, NA. The quotations are on p. 1.

160. National Security Council, National Security Decision Memorandum 133, 22 September 1971, *U.S. Strategy and Forces for NATO; Allied Force Improvements*, National Security Decision Memorandum (NSDM), NSDM 133, Box 2, RG 273, NA. The quotations are on pp. 2 and 3.

161. National Intelligence Estimate 11-14-71, 9 September 1971, *Warsaw Pact Forces for Operations in Eurasia*, Historical Review Group, National Intelligence Estimates Concerning Soviet Military Power, 1950–1984, Box 17, Folder 41, RG 263, NA.

162. Blanchard to Aaron, 16 April 1973, *Tactical Intelligence Resources*, George S. Blanchard Papers, CG VII Corps: Messages, January–December 1973, Box 2, MHI. The quotations are on pp. 2–3 and 5, respectively.

163. Davison to Weyand, 12 September 1973, p. 3, Michael Davison Papers, CINCUSAREUR Declassified Documents, 4 September–26 December 1973, Box 2, MHI.

164. Dwight D. Eisenhower had made that observation in late March 1945: "The so-called 'good ground' in northern Germany is not really good at this time of year. That region is not only cut up with waterways, but in it the ground during this time of year is wet and not so favorable for rapid movement. . . . Moreover, if, as we expect, the German continues the widespread destruction of bridges, experience has shown that it is better to advance across the headwaters than to be faced by the main streams." Cited in Stephen G. Fritz, *Endkampf: Soldiers, Civilians, and the Death of the Third Reich* (Lexington: University Press of Kentucky, 2004), p. 19. Nearly forty years later, a major on duty with 2nd Armored Division in a REFORGER maneuver reinforced Eisenhower's outlook, adding that the area was now built up to such a degree that Soviet tank formations would have to fight their way through towns and cities. Michael A. Andrews, "Back on the Northern Plain, "*Army* 31, no. 1 (January 1981): 16–22.

165. USAREUR, *Annual Historical Summary*, 1970, pp. 12, 98–100.

166. Ibid., p. 35.

167. Ibid., pp. 18–19, 38–39, 63. At the same time, the combat developments command of CONARC introduced a reorganization study for area defense based on the future availability of mechanized fighting vehicles and high-tech antitank missiles. General Polk realized, however, that his corps could not hold their assigned area and that he would have to fight with the available means if war broke out.

168. For the history of the Bradley and the complex developments surrounding the MICV in the decade from 1965 to 1975, see the excellent study of Haworth, *The Bradley*, pp. 47–93; and Hunnicutt, *Bradley*, pp. 274–281. See also Eric C. Ludvigsen, "IFV: Gestation Long, Painful, but Product Is Superior," *Army* 29, no. 6 (June 1979): 26–30.

169. See Schmidt, *Verteidigung oder Vergeltung*.

170. Collins to Davison, 12 July 1971, Arthur S. Collins Jr. Papers, USAREUR 1971–1972, Box 7, MHI. The quotations are on pp. 2 and 3, respectively. For Collins's doubts

about tactical nuclear war, see his articles "The Other Side of the Atom," *Army* 10, no. 4 (November 1959): 18–19; "Tactical Nuclear Weapons: Are They a Real Option?" *Army* 32, no. 7 (July 1982): 36–39; and "Tactical Nuclear Weapons and NATO: Viable Strategy or Dead End?" *NATO's Fifteen Nations* 21, no. 3 (June–July 1979): 73–82.

171. Collins to Davison, 2 January 1973, Arthur S. Collins Jr. Papers, USAREUR 1973–1974, Box 7, MHI.

172. Collins to Davison, 30 June 1972, Arthur S. Collins Jr. Papers, USAREUR 1971–1972, Box 7, MHI.

Chapter 6. The Cold War Army

1. General Donn Starry, the second commanding general of TRADOC, succinctly describes its central role in the process of reorganizing the army after Vietnam, in "To Change an Army," *Military Review* 63, no. 3 (March 1983): 20–27.

2. See, for instance, Andrew J. Bacevich, *The New American Militarism: How Americans Are Seduced by War* (Oxford: Oxford University Press, 2005), pp. 44–47. The critical long-term implications beyond the Cold War of the repression of recent history and memory are discussed in Conrad Crane, "Avoiding Vietnam: The U.S. Army's Response to Defeat in Southeast Asia" (Carlisle Barracks, PA: U.S. Army War College, Strategic Studies Institute, 2002).

3. In his recent study of operational-level war of movement, Robert Citino points out that the army and the Marines could take pride in their effectiveness in battles at Khe Sanh and Hue. Citino draws parallels between operations in Vietnam and operational doctrine that evolved after the war. Citino, *Blitzkrieg to Desert Storm*, pp. 237–266. James Kitfield, *Prodigal Soldiers: How the Generation of Officers Born of Vietnam Revolutionized the American Style of War* (New York: Simon and Schuster, 1995), also points at the generation of army generals who gained senior command experience in Vietnam. But other scholars have shown that army leaders intended to put Vietnam behind themselves and that they instead devised operational doctrine based on the specific situation in Central Europe and their professional experience before Vietnam. See Richard Lock-Pullan, "How to Rethink War: Conceptual Innovation and AirLand Battle Doctrine," *Journal of Strategic Studies* 28, no. 4 (August 2005): 679–702; and Roger J. Spiller, "In the Shadow of the Dragon: Doctrine and the US Army after Vietnam," *RUSI Journal* 142, no. 6 (December 1997): 41–54.

4. See, for instance, William C. Cromwell, *The United States and the European Pillar: The Strained Alliance* (New York: St. Martin's, 1992). Argyris G. Andrianopoulos, *Western Europe in Kissinger's Global Strategy* (New York: St. Martin's, 1988), argues that a fundamental misreading of Kissinger's academic writings led Western European leaders to question whether the United States still intended to maintain a close relationship. Gaddis, *Strategies of Containment*, 332–333, adds that Kissinger's inattention to NATO contributed greatly to the crisis. For the different interpretations of détente and its effect on alliance relationships, see especially Lawrence S. Kaplan, *NATO Divided, NATO United: The Evolution of an Alliance* (Westport, CT: Praeger, 2004), pp. 57–85.

5. See particularly Cromwell, *The United States and the European Pillar*, pp. 79–100.

6. Geir Lundestad, *The United States and Western Europe since 1945: From "Empire" by Invitation to Transatlantic Drift* (Oxford: Oxford University Press, 2003), p. 169 (emphasis in original).

7. Ibid., p. 201.

8. Larry Berman, *No Peace, No Honor: Nixon, Kissinger, and Betrayal in Vietnam* (New York: Free Press, 2001). For U.S. policy under Nixon, see also Jeffrey Kimball, *Nixon's Vietnam War* (Lawrence: University Press of Kansas, 1998). For U.S. casualties, see Stanton, *Vietnam Order of Battle*, p. 346.

9. Several army officers addressed this crisis in confidence: William L. Hauser, *America's Army in Crisis: A Study in Civil-Military Relations* (Baltimore: Johns Hopkins University Press, 1973); Edward L. King, *The Death of an Army: A Pre-Mortem* (New York: Saturday Review Press, 1972); and Michael Lee Lanning, *The Battles of Peace* (New York: Ballantine Books, 1992). But Lanning, reporting with hindsight, was already more upbeat, as were Zeb Bradford Jr. and Frederic J. Brown, *The United States Army in Transition* (Beverly Hills, CA: Sage Publications, 1973). Specific symptoms were also noted by General Starry, who, after more than three decades, was still upset at the state of affairs in the army in general and in Germany in particular. Author's interview with General Starry, 27 April 2004, and Starry's unpublished address of April 2002, "Historical Perspectives on the Army of the Future: A Case Study in Change (aka Transformation): The United States Army from 1973 to 1991" (in author's possession, courtesy of General Starry).

10. General Starry viewed the army's war in Vietnam as a prolonged period of being away from Germany, its Cold War home. Author's interview with General Starry, 27 April 2004.

11. Remarks by General A. J. Goodpaster, SACEUR, National Defence College, Latimer, England, 26 April 1974, p. 3, Andrew J. Goodpaster Papers, Box 37, Folder 4, GCML. This was one of several speeches Goodpaster made in 1973 and 1974 in which he stressed Soviet conventional superiority.

12. Ibid., p. 6.

13. Ibid., p. 9.

14. Ibid., p. 10. A Lance missile could fire a nuclear warhead seventy-five miles or a conventional warhead forty-five miles. It first appeared in USAREUR in September 1973.

15. Ibid., pp. 14–15.

16. Ibid., p. 15.

17. For Abrams's tenure as chief of staff, see Lewis Sorley, *Thunderbolt: General Creighton Abrams and the Army of His Times* (New York: Simon and Schuster, 1992), pp. 350–378. For Total Force and the integration of Active Army, Army Reserve, and National Guard, see also Lewis Sorley, "Creighton Abrams and Active-Reserve Integration in Wartime," *Parameters* 21, no. 2 (Summer 1991): 35–50.

18. For discussion of the heavy division as the intended substitute for both armored and mechanized divisions, see Wilson, *Maneuver and Firepower*, pp. 380–390. In the early 1980s, the concept was softened and the army retained ROAD armored and mechanized divisions, fortified with new heavy weapons systems such as the Abrams tank and the Bradley IFV. The army also converted four active infantry divisions to

light divisions in the mid-1980s: the 6th, 7th, and 25th Infantry Divisions and the 10th Mountain Division. Ibid., pp. 390–395.

19. Hawkins and Carafano, *Prelude to Army XXI*, p. 19.

20. Ibid., pp. 19–20.

21. For the political considerations that led to the all-volunteer force and initial army opposition, see George Q. Flynn, *The Draft, 1940–1973* (Lawrence: University Press of Kansas, 1993), pp. 224–274. More specific on army policy is Robert Griffith, *U.S. Army's Transition to the All-Volunteer Force, 1968–1974* (Washington, DC: Center for Military History, 1997).

22. See DePuy's keynote address to the TRADOC Leadership Conference, Fort Benning, Georgia, 22 May 1974, in Richard M. Swain, ed., *Selected Papers of General William E. DePuy* (Ft. Leavenworth, KS: Combat Studies Institute, 1994), pp. 113–120. See particularly pp. 114–115. DePuy feared that raw recruits of the all-volunteer army were of much poorer quality than Israeli recruits.

23. FM 100-5: *Operations*, 1976, chap. 1, p. 5.

24. See particularly ibid., chap. 3 ("How to Fight"), p. 2. This reflected DePuy's method—to express every tactical problem as a formula. Richard Swain, the editor of DePuy's personal papers, concluded that "DePuy was the ultimate Cartesian [who] sought to reduce all combat functions to their lowest denominator, define them with precision, and then regurgitate them." Swain, "AirLand Battle," p. 363.

25. For the "training revolution" of the U.S. Army, see, for instance, Scales, *Certain Victory*, pp. 10–25; and Stewart, *United States Army in a Global Era*, pp. 389–392.

26. For DePuy's tenure as commander of TRADOC, see the excellent study by Paul Herbert, *Deciding What Has to Be Done*. See especially pp. 21–50 for DePuy's first year in office. General Starry also stressed the trinity of organization, technological requirements, and training that was to be defined by doctrine. Author's interview with General Starry, 27 April 2004.

27. Herbert, *Deciding What Has to Be Done*, pp. 61–68.

28. The most compelling reason to maintain the division base was logistics. Although there was a group of army officers that favored independent brigades, General Starry expressed the opinion of the majority when he explained that brigades would need similar numbers of support units as divisions required. He cited the example of the Vietnam War, in which three separate brigades had been combined to form 23rd Division, resulting in a division that was 7,000 officers and men larger than the next-largest division. Starry to Lieutenant Colonel Dale Brudvig, 10 March 1976, Donn A. Starry Papers, Box 4: Personal Correspondence, January–April 1976, "Personal Correspondence Files, Mar–Apr 1976," MHI.

29. Headquarters, 1st Infantry Division Fwd, n.d. [1975], *NATO Tactical Doctrine Comparison Study: Panzer Brigade 30 and 1st Inf Div Fwd*, Command and General Staff College, Combined Arms Research Library, Archive N-17439.49.

30. FM 100-5, 1976, chap. 1, p. 2.

31. Military historians have recently renewed the discussion of the effect of the Yom Kippur War on the U.S. Army. Lewis, *The American Culture of War*, pp. 300–301, restates the traditional argument of a direct relationship of the lessons of the Yom Kippur War to subsequent U.S. Army doctrine. But an important revisionist study by

the Israeli scholar Saul Bronfeld, "Fighting Outnumbered: The Impact of the Yom Kippur War on the U.S. Army," *Journal of Military History* 71, no. 2 (April 2007): 465–498, shows that DePuy and other proponents of doctrinal change used the lessons of the Yom Kippur War selectively in order to advocate reforms that were based on their own experiences prior to the Vietnam War.

32. This is best expressed in the report by Avigdor Kahalani, *The Heights of Courage: A Tank Leader's War on the Golan* (Westport, CT: Greenwood Press, 1984). Kahalani's account was made available to American visitors to Israel soon after the war. Donn Starry, who wrote the foreword for the 1984 and 1992 editions of the memoir, suggests that Kahalani's experience in fending off a vastly superior armored enemy force had great effect on DePuy and his colleagues.

33. Chaim Herzog, *The War of Atonement: October 1973* (Boston: Little, Brown, 1975), remains the best account of the war, combining discussion of strategy, operations, and tactics. The recollections of General Avraham Adan, *On the Banks of the Suez* (San Francisco: Presidio Press, 1980), are useful for the southern theater. For the Israeli army, see also Martin Van Creveld, *The Sword and the Olive: A Critical History of the Israeli Defense Force* (New York: Public Affairs, 1998), pp. 217–243. Herzog's book was mandatory reading at the Armor Center, and General Starry noted that it helped to shape the final version of army doctrine in 1976. Starry to Lieutenant Colonel Michael D. Mahler, 28 April 1976, Donn A. Starry Papers, Box 4: Personal Correspondence, January–April 1976, "Personal Correspondence Files, Mar–Apr 1976," MHI.

34. DePuy to General Creighton Abrams, 14 January 1974, in Swain, *DePuy Papers*, pp. 69–74. The quotations are on p. 71.

35. *Implications of the Middle East War on U.S. Army Tactics, Doctrine and Systems*, a presentation by General William E. DePuy, Commander, U.S. Army Training and Doctrine Command, n.d. (most likely April or May 1974), in Swain, *DePuy Papers*, pp. 75–111, particularly pp. 78–79. See also DePuy to Senator Culver, 12 May 1975, in ibid., pp. 165–169.

36. Gudmundsson, *On Armor*, p. 167.

37. DePuy to Weyand, 18 February 1976, enclosure to Starry to Simmons, 20 April 1976, Donn A. Starry Papers, "Personal Correspondence Files, Mar–Apr 1976," Box 4, MHI.

38. Decker, "The Patton Tanks," p. 317.

39. DePuy, *Implications of the Middle East War on U.S. Army Tactics, Doctrine and Systems*, in Swain, *DePuy Papers*, pp. 93–94.

40. DePuy to Abrams, 14 January 1974, in ibid., p. 72.

41. DePuy to Weyand, 29 April 1975, in ibid., pp. 161–163.

42. DePuy to Robert Komer, 24 April 1975, in ibid., pp. 157–158. Quotations are on p. 158.

43. DePuy to Major General Gordon Sumner, 25 April 1975, in ibid., pp. 159–160. Quotation is on p. 159. See also DePuy to Weyand, 29 April 1975, in ibid.

44. FM 100-5, 1976, chap. 2, pp. 7–17.

45. DePuy to Weyand, 18 February 1976, enclosure to Starry to Simmons, 20 April 1976, Donn A. Starry Papers, "Personal Correspondence Files, Mar–Apr 1976," Box 4, MHI.

46. DePuy to Komer, 24 April 1975, in Swain, *DePuy Papers*, p. 157.

47. DePuy, *Implications of the Middle East War on U.S. Army Tactics, Doctrine and Systems*, in ibid., pp. 98–99.

48. Herbert, *Deciding What Has to Be Done*, pp. 51–58. General Cushman is quoted on p. 55. See also Romjue, *From Active Defense to AirLand Battle*, p. 5; and Swain, "AirLand Battle," pp. 370–372.

49. See DePuy's handwritten notes on "Modern Battle Tactics," 17 August 1974, in Swain, *DePuy Papers*, pp. 137–139.

50. William E. DePuy, "Technology and Tactics in the Defense of Europe," *Army* 29, no. 4 (April 1979): 14–23.

51. William E. DePuy, "One Up and Two Back?" *Army* 30, no. 1 (January 1980): 20–25. The quotation is on p. 25.

52. Not coincidentally, the army historical community underwrote a series of studies on opening battles of American wars, which were eventually published as Heller and Stofft, *America's First Battles.*

53. For detailed discussions of Active Defense, see Herbert, *Deciding What Has to Be Done*, pp. 75–93; and Romjue, *From Active Defense to AirLand Battle*, pp. 3–11.

54. FM 100-5, 1976, chap. 1, pp. 1–5.

55. Ibid., chap. 2, pp. 1–32.

56. By DePuy's own count, "Active Defense" appeared only once in the entire manual. William E. DePuy, "FM 100-5 Revisited," *Army* 30, no. 11 (November 1980): 12–17.

57. FM 100-5, 1976, chap. 3, p. 1. The significantly shorter tenth chapter of the manual outlined tactical nuclear operations.

58. Ibid., chap. 3, pp. 3–4, and chap. 5, pp. 1–14. See also chap. 3, p. 17, for the four bold keywords: cover, concealment, suppression, teamwork.

59. Ibid., chap. 3, p. 5.

60. Ibid., chap. 3, p. 6, and chap. 4, pp. 1–12.

61. Ibid., chap. 3, pp. 6–7.

62. Ibid., chap. 4.

63. DePuy to Sumner, 25 April 1975, in Swain, *DePuy Papers*, pp. 159–160. The quotations are from p. 159. DePuy to Weyand, 29 April 1975, in ibid., pp. 161–163.

64. FM 100-5, 1976, chap. 5, pp. 1–14.

65. For USAREUR's authorship of portions of the manual, see Romjue, *From Active Defense to AirLand Battle*, p. 5.

66. FM 100-5, 1976, chap. 13, pp. 1–16. The quotation is on p. 16.

67. Ibid., chap. 14, pp. 15–28. The quotation is on p. 19.

68. DePuy, "FM 100-5 Revisited," p. 12.

69. DePuy's personal opinion in favor of three or four tanks per platoon as a means to improve command and control was expressed in conversations with General Starry. See Starry to Colonel Edward P. Davis, 10 May 1976, Donn A. Starry Papers, Box 5: Personal Correspondence, May–October 1976, "Personal Correspondence Files, May–June 1976," MHI.

70. DePuy to Weyand, 18 February 1976, in Swain, *DePuy Papers*, p. 182.

71. Speech of General William E. DePuy, AFTCON IV, 24 May 1977, *The Army Training System Overview*, in Swain, *DePuy Papers*, pp. 225–237. See especially p. 226.

72. FM 100-5, 1976, chap. 8, pp. 1–7.

73. This is expressed most clearly in William S. Lind, "Some Doctrinal Questions for the United States Army," *Military Review* 57, no. 3 (March 1977): 54–65. For Boyd's theory of war and his impact on the American defense establishment during and after the Cold War, see Robert Coram, *Boyd: The Fighter Pilot Who Changed the Art of War* (Boston: Little, Brown, 2002).

74. Naveh, *In Pursuit of Military Excellence*, pp. 256–276. The quotation is on p. 263. For a more extensive treatment of the discussion within the army, see Richard M. Swain, "Filling the Void: The Operational Art and the U.S. Army," pp. 154–156, in McKercher and Hennesy, *The Operational Art*.

75. Romjue, *From Active Defense to AirLand Battle*, pp. 14–17.

76. Ibid., pp. 17–20.

77. Excerpts from General Haig's letter to DePuy are quoted in Herbert, *Deciding What Has to Be Done*, pp. 96–97.

78. Ibid., p. 97.

79. Ibid., pp. 96–98.

80. DePuy, "FM 100-5 Revisited."

81. The British scholar Richard Lock-Pullan has recently offered an important discussion of Active Defense and AirLand Battle doctrine. He shows that internal processes and intellectual inquiry, more than a new strategic environment or new technology, shaped U.S. Army doctrine after the Vietnam War. See Richard Lock-Pullan, "An Inward Looking Time: The U.S. Army, 1973–76," *Journal of Military History* 67, no. 2 (April 2003): 483–511; and Lock-Pullan, "How to Rethink War." But particularly in his discussion of AirLand Battle, Lock-Pullan seems to underestimate to what extent weapons technology and intellectual engagement and study of military history were integrated into the doctrinal manual.

82. Author's interview with General Starry, 27 April 2004.

83. The best summary on Starry's operational thought prior to the drafting of AirLand Battle is Romjue, *From Active Defense to AirLand Battle*, pp. 23–39. See also Naveh, *In Pursuit of Military Excellence*, pp. 287–288, 292–299. For a recent account of Starry's career after Vietnam and his impact on the Cold War army, see also the outstanding West Point senior thesis by Martin J. D'Amato, "Vigilant Warrior: General Donn A. Starry's AirLand Battle and How It Changed the Army," *Armor* 109, no. 3 (May–June 2000): 18–22, 45, which General Starry considers to be the best work on the subject.

84. Starry to Lieutenant Colonel Michael D. Mahler, 28 April 1976, Donn A. Starry Papers, Box 4: Personal Correspondence, January–April 1976, "Personal Correspondence Files, Mar–Apr 1976," MHI.

85. Starry to Colonel Erwin Brigham, 8 June 1977, Donn A. Starry Papers, Box 7: Personal Correspondence, March–July 1977, "Personal Correspondence Files, May–June 1977," MHI.

86. Starry to Lieutenant Colonel Samuel D. Wilder, 23 August 1976, Donn A. Starry Papers, Box 5: Personal Correspondence, May–October 1976, "Personal Correspondence Files, August 1976," MHI.

87. Quoted in Lieutenant Colonel Edwin G. Scribner to General Starry, 25 June 1976, Donn A. Starry Papers, Box 5: Personal Correspondence, May–October 1976, "Personal Correspondence Files, July 1976," MHI.

88. See Starry's answers of 2 June 1976 to a questionnaire provided by the Analysis and Gaming Agency for the JCS. Rear Admiral R. H. Cormley to General Starry, 21 May 1976, Donn A. Starry Papers, Box 5: Personal Correspondence, May–October 1976, "Personal Correspondence Files, May–June 1976," MHI.

89. Donn A. Starry, "A Tactical Evolution—FM 100-5," *Military Review* 58, no. 8 (August 1978): 2–11. See particularly pp. 6–7 for a brief discussion of the calculation method and a mathematical figure expressing Starry's conclusion.

90. Robert Lucas Fischer, *Defending the Central Front: The Balance of Forces* (Adelphi Paper No. 127; London: International Institute for Strategic Studies, 1976), pp. 8–15.

91. Naveh, *In Pursuit of Military Excellence*, pp. 288–289.

92. Author's interview with General Starry, 27 April 2004.

93. Starry, "FM 100-5," pp. 2–11. Starry, as commander of the Armor Center, had written the chapters on offense and defense.

94. Ibid., pp. 8–9, and author's interview with General Starry, 27 April 2004.

95. Romjue, *From Active Defense to AirLand Battle*, pp. 23–24. General Starry is quoted on p. 24.

96. Hawkins and Carafano, *Prelude to Army XXI*, pp. 20–24. Division 86 resembled Bruce Clarke's heavy MOMAR division, with the obvious exception of airmobility.

97. An interesting and not entirely fanciful scenario is presented in Sir John Hackett et al., *The Third World War: A Future History* (New York: Macmillan, 1978). Evidence unearthed since the dissolution of the Warsaw Pact and the opening of Eastern European government archives supports the notion that Soviet commanders were well aware of the vulnerability of NORTHAG.

98. The history of the debate as well as the actual deployment is documented in Headquarters, USAREUR, *Strengthening NATO: Stationing of the 2nd Armored Division (Forward) in Northern Germany* (Heidelberg: Headquarters, USAREUR, Historian's Office, 1980). See also Andrews, "Back on the Northern Plain."

99. Meyer to Starry, 13 June 1979, and Starry to Meyer, 26 June 1979, Donn A. Starry Papers, Box 17: Personal Correspondence, June–September 1979, "Personal Correspondence Files, June 1979," MHI. See also Romjue, *From Active Defense to AirLand Battle*, pp. 31–32.

100. Romjue, *From Active Defense to AirLand Battle*, pp. 33–34.

101. Mike Worden, *The Rise of the Fighter Generals: The Problem of Air Force Leadership, 1945–1982* (Maxwell Air Force Base, AL: Air University Press, 1997), pp. 211–234.

102. Benjamin S. Lambeth, *The Transformation of American Air Power* (Ithaca, NY: Cornell University Press, 2000), pp. 83–85.

103. Ibid., pp. 72–73. Schlight, *Help from Above*, p. 383, concludes that air force commanders considered the A-10 as a means of retaining centralized control of close air support functions while also freeing up capabilities to invest in expensive new fighter jets.

104. Worden, *Rise of the Fighter Generals*, p. 222. For a general discussion of airpower and war of movement, see also Martin Van Creveld, *Air Power and Maneuver Warfare*

(Maxwell Air Force Base, AL: Air University Press, 1994), particularly pp. 193–211, for the Cold War era.

105. Lambeth, *Transformation of Air Power*, pp. 88–89.

106. Romjue, *From Active Defense to AirLand Battle*, pp. 34–37.

107. Starry's doubts dated back to 1960–1964, when he served as brigade operations officer and armor battalion commander in Germany. In the late 1970s, he found that the release procedure had not been improved. Author's interview with General Starry, 27 April 2004; D'Amato, "Vigilant Warrior," p. 19. In his unpublished essay "Fifty Years at the Business End of the Bomb," Starry stated that he found tactical nuclear weapons to be useful if the release procedure could be simplified (in author's possession, courtesy of General Starry).

108. Romjue, *From Active Defense to AirLand Battle*, pp. 80–82.

109. D'Amato, "Vigilant Warrior," p. 21.

110. Romjue, *From Active Defense to AirLand Battle*, pp. 42–44. For new equipment, see ibid., p. 47. General Starry believed that new communications systems and tactical missiles made deep-attack concepts possible in the 1980s. Author's interview with General Starry, 27 April 2004.

111. Naveh, *In Pursuit of Military Excellence*, pp. 257–259. Boyd and Wass de Czege frequently discussed the development of army doctrine. In the event, the uncompromising John Boyd dismissed AirLand Battle doctrine because it retained an element of synchronization of forces. This led Boyd to believe that the slowest unit would determine the pace of operations. Coram, *Boyd*, pp. 370–371.

112. Coram, *Boyd*, pp. 317–419.

113. Donn A. Starry, "Extending the Battlefield," *Military Review* 61, no. 3 (March 1981): 31–50. The discussion of the battle areas and areas of interest for the operational units is on pp. 35–44. See also Naveh, *In Pursuit of Military Excellence*, p. 298.

114. Romjue, *From Active Defense to AirLand Battle*, pp. 44–50.

115. The need for individual initiative and synchronization on the battlefield is discussed in Lock-Pullan, "How to Rethink War," pp. 689–692.

116. *Schwerpunkt* is commonly translated as "center of gravity," but this does not capture the meaning of the German concept entirely accurately. A better translation would be "point of emphasis of operations."

117. Romjue, *From Active Defense to AirLand Battle*, pp. 57–61. The German army, which had recognized the operational level of war in official doctrine since the 1870s, had recently dropped the term from its central doctrinal manual, HDV 100/100 (1973).

118. FM 100-5: *Operations*, 1982, p. i.

119. Ibid., chap. 2, p. 3. L. D. Holder, one of the principal authors of FM 100-5 (1982), explained that the second edition of AirLand Battle, FM 100-5 (1986), developed the subject in more detail. L. D. Holder, "Training for the Operational Level," *Parameters* 16, no. 1 (Spring 1986): 7–13.

120. See Hamburger, "Operational Art."

121. See Glantz, *Soviet Military Operational Art*; Harrison, *The Russian Way of War*; Frederick W. Kagan, "The Rise and Fall of Soviet Operational Art, 1917–1941"; and Frederick W. Kagan, "The Great Patriotic War: Rediscovering Operational Art," in

The Military History of the Soviet Union, edited by Robin Higham and Frederick W. Kagan (Houndmills: Palgrave, 2002), pp. 79–92, 137–151.

122. Author's interview with General Starry, 27 April 2004. General Starry pointed at the recent translation of *Truppenführung* to support his argument. See Bruce Condell and David T. Zabecki, eds., *On the German Art of War: Truppenführung* (Boulder, CO: Lynne Rienner, 2001). For concise discussions of Reichswehr doctrine, see Citino, *The Path to Blitzkrieg*; and James S. Corum, *The Roots of Blitzkrieg: Hans von Seeckt and German Military Reform* (Lawrence: University Press of Kansas, 1992). A useful comparative study of prewar German and Soviet doctrine for war of movement is Habeck, *Storm of Steel*.

123. FM 100-5, 1982, chap. 2, p. 1.

124. Ibid., chap. 1, p. 1.

125. All quotations are from ibid., 1982, chap. 1, p. 1. For the stated emphasis on conventional operations, see p. i.

126. The German tactical system of the last years of World War I are discussed by Timothy Lupfer, *The Dynamics of Doctrine: The Changes in German Tactical Doctrine during the First World War* (Leavenworth Paper No. 4; Forth Leavenworth, KS: U.S. Army Command and General Staff College, 1981); and Martin Samuels, *Command or Control? Command, Training and Tactics in the British and German Armies, 1888–1918* (London: Frank Cass, 1995).

127. FM 100-5, 1982, chap. 1, p. 3.

128. Ibid., chap. 2, p. 1.

129. Ibid.

130. Ibid., chap. 2, p. 1–3.

131. Ibid., chap. 2, p. 4.

132. Ibid., chap. 6, pp. 1–9.

133. Ibid., chap. 7, p. 1.

134. Ibid., chap. 7, pp. 4–7.

135. Ibid., chap. 10, p. 1.

136. Ibid., chaps. 8 and 10.

137. Ibid., chap. 7, p. 2.

138. Ibid., chap. 8, p. 1.

139. Ibid., chap. 15, p. 1. The entire chapter contains only two pages of text and one detailed organizational chart.

140. Ibid., chap. 17, pp. 1–7. Pages 8–13 addressed combined operations with Korean or Japanese forces.

141. Andrew J. Goodpaster et al., *Strengthening Conventional Deterrence in Europe: A Program for the 1980s* (Boulder, CO: Westview Press, 1985), p. 67. This was the second report of the European Security Study (ESECS). Besides General Goodpaster, the panel included General Franz-Josef Schulze, a former CINCENT; Air Chief Marshal Sir Alastair Steedeman; and former Pentagon analyst—and future secretary of defense—William Perry.

142. Ibid., pp. 67–82, 130–131.

143. For comprehensive accounts of the Persian Gulf War, see, for instance, Stephen P. Gehring, *From the Fulda Gap to Kuwait: U.S. Army, Europe, and the Gulf War* (Wash-

ington, DC: Department of the Army, 1998); Michael R. Gordon and Bernard E. Trainor, *The Generals' War: The Inside Story of the Conflict in the Gulf* (Boston: Little, Brown, 1995); and Scales, *Certain Victory*.

144. Stephen A. Bourque, *Jayhawk! The VII Corps in the Persian Gulf War* (Washington, DC: Department of the Army, 2002), pp. 455–461.

145. FM 100-5, 1986, p. 10. See also Lock-Pullan, "How to Rethink War," pp. 685–687.

146. Citino, *Blitzkrieg to Desert Storm*, p. 288.

147. Stephen Bourque agrees with the assessment that the campaign in the desert did not represent a direct application of all facets of AirLand Battle. Bourque, however, faults the air force for its reluctance to embrace the concept. Bourque, *Jayhawk*, p. 460.

Conclusion

1. John Keegan, *The Face of Battle* (New York: Penguin Books, 1978), p. 28.

2. Among the best examples are Citino, *The Path to Blitzkrieg*; David French, *Raising Churchill's Army: The British Army and the War against Germany, 1919–1945* (Oxford: Oxford University Press, 2000); Habeck, *Storm of Steel*; Eugenia C. Kiesling, *Arming against Hitler: France and the Limits of Military Planning* (Lawrence: University Press of Kansas, 1996); Roger R. Reese, *Stalin's Reluctant Soldiers: A Social History of the Red Army, 1925–1941* (Lawrence: University Press of Kansas, 1996); David Stone, *Hammer and Rifle: The Militarization of the Soviet Union, 1926–1933* (Lawrence: University Press of Kansas, 2000); and Harold R. Winton and David R. Mets, eds., *The Challenge of Change: Military Institutions and New Realities, 1918–1941* (Lincoln: University of Nebraska Press, 2000).

Bibliography

Archival Sources

Bundesarchiv/Militärarchiv, Freiburg, Germany

Bestand BH 1
Bestand BW 1
Bestand BW 2

Command and General Staff College, Combined Arms Research Library, Archive, Ft. Leavenworth, KS

Dwight D. Eisenhower Presidential Library, Abilene, KS

J. Lawton Collins Papers
Joseph M. Dodge Papers
Dwight D. Eisenhower Papers
  Pre-Presidential
  White House Central Files
  Ann Whitman File
Gordon Gray Papers
Alfred M. Gruenther Papers
C. D. Jackson Papers
Neil H. McElroy Papers
Lauris Norstad Papers
Donald A. Quarles Papers
Walter Bedell Smith Papers
Oral histories
  Robert R. Bowie
  Lucius D. Clay
  Andrew Goodpaster
  Gordon Gray
  Alfred Gruenther
  Lyman Lemnitzer
  Neil McElroy
  Lauris Norstad
  Nathan Twining

Lyndon B. Johnson Presidential Library, Austin, TX
Administrative History for the Department of Defense
Francis M. Bator Papers
Clark Clifford Papers
Lyndon B. Johnson Papers
    Vice-Presidential Papers
    White House Central File
    White House Central File, Confidential File
National Security File
Office Files of the White House Aides
Oral histories
    Harlan Cleveland
    Clark Clifford
    Alain Enthoven
    Thomas K. Finletter
    Andrew Goodpaster
    Lyman Lemnitzer
    John J. McCloy
    George C. McGhee
    Robert S. McNamara
    Frank Pace Jr.
    Maxwell D. Taylor

John F. Kennedy Presidential Library, Boston
George W. Ball Papers
Harlan Cleveland Papers
Roswell L. Gilpatric Papers
William Kaufmann Papers
President Kennedy Papers
    Kennedy Oral History Project
    National Security Files
    President's Office Files
    White House Central Files
Arthur M. Schlesinger Jr. Papers
Theodore C. Sorensen Papers
Adam Yarmolinsky Papers
Oral histories
    Dean Acheson
    Lucius D. Clay
    Alain C. Enthoven
    Thomas K. Finletter
    Roswell Gilpatric
    Lyman Lemnitzer
    Robert S. McNamara
    Elvis J. Stahr
    Dirk Stikker

Maxwell Taylor
Earle Wheeler

Library of Congress, Manuscript Collection, Washington, DC
Nathan F. Twining Papers

George C. Marshall Research Library, Lexington, VA
Hanson W. Baldwin Papers
Lucius D. Clay Papers
Andrew J. Goodpaster Papers
Thomas T. Handy Papers

National Archives, College Park, MD
RG 59 Records of the Department of State
RG 200 Donated Material of Robert S. McNamara
RG 218 Records of the Joint Chiefs of Staff
RG 263 Records of the Central Intelligence Agency
RG 273 Records of the National Security Council
RG 319 Records of the Army Staff
RG 330 Records of the Office of the Secretary of Defense
RG 338 Records of Army Commands
RG 546 Records of the United States Continental Army Command
RG 549 Records of U.S. Army, Europe
RG 553 Records of the U.S. Army Training and Doctrine Command

National Defense University, Washington, DC
Maxwell D. Taylor Papers (digitized collection)

National Security Archive, Washington, DC
Nuclear History Project Files
Nuclear History—Berlin Crisis Files
Nuclear History Project Database Files
Digital National Security Archive (http://nsarchive.chadwyck.com/)
The Berlin Crisis, 1958–1962
The Soviet Estimate: U.S. Analysis of the Soviet Union, 1947–1991
U.S. Nuclear History: Nuclear Arms and Politics in the Missile Age, 1955–1968

NATO Archives, Brussels, Belgium
Future Tasks of the Alliance, Harmel Report (http://www.nato.int/archives/harmel/harmel.htm)
International Military Staff: Records of the North Atlantic Military Committee, 1949–1965
International Military Staff: Records of the Standing Group, 1949–1966

Harry S. Truman Presidential Library, Independence, MO
Dean Acheson Papers
Lucius D. Battle Papers

George M. Elsey Papers
Thomas K. Finletter Papers
John M. Ohly Papers
Howard Trivers Papers
Harry S. Truman Papers
Staff Member and Office Files
White House Central Files

U.S. Army Chief of Engineers, Historian's Office, Ft. Belvoir, VA
Bruce C. Clarke Papers

U.S. Army Military Academy, Archives and Manuscripts Division, West Point, NY
Williston B. Palmer Papers

U.S. Army Military History Institute, Carlisle Barracks, PA
Donald V. Bennett Papers
George S. Blanchard Papers
Bruce C. Clarke Papers
Arthur S. Collins Jr. Papers
John H. Cushman Papers
Garrison H. Davidson Papers
Michael Davison Papers
William E. DePuy Papers
Clyde D. Eddleman Papers
Paul Freeman Papers
John A. Heintges Papers
Hamilton H. Howze Papers
Harold K. Johnson Papers
Lyman Lemnitzer Papers
Frank T. Mildren Papers
Andrew P. O'Meara Papers
James K. Polk Papers
Matthew B. Ridgway Papers
George Seneff Papers
Donn A. Starry Papers
Maxwell D. Taylor Papers
Earle G. Wheeler Papers

Published Primary Sources

Bowie, Robert R. *The North Atlantic Nations: Tasks for the 1960's—A Report to the Secretary of State, August 1960*. Nuclear History Program: Occasional Paper 7. University of Maryland: Center for International Security Studies, 1991.
Brownlee, Romie L., and William J. Mullen III. *Changing an Army: An Oral History*

of General William E. DePuy. Washington, DC: U.S. Army Center of Military History, 1986.
Bundesministerium der Verteidigung. *Übung Prellbock*. Bonn: Bundesministerium der Verteidigung, 1966.
———. *Drei Jahrzehnte Armee im Bündnis, 1955–1985*. Bonn: Bundesministerium der Verteidigung, 1985.
Bundeswehr, Heer, I. Korps. *30 Jahre I. Korps 1956–1986: Geschichte und Chronik der Heeresverbände im nordwestdeutschen Raum*. Osnabrück: Biblio Verlag, 1986.
Department of the Army. *Field Manual, FM 100-5: Field Service Regulations—Operations*. Washington, DC: Department of the Army, 1949–.
———. *The Armoured Infantry Battalion (APC)*. Washington, DC: Headquarters, Department of the Army, Assistant Chief of Staff for Intelligence, 1963.
———. *USAREUR and Seventh Army After Action Report for Exercise REFORGER 75*. Heidelberg: Headquarters USAREUR and Seventh Army, 1975.
Department of State. *Foreign Relations of the United States*. Washington, DC: Government Printing Office, 1861–.
Developments in Military Technology and Their Impact on United States Strategy and Foreign Policy. A Study Prepared at the Request of the Committee on Foreign Relations, U.S. Senate, by the Washington Center of Foreign Policy Research, Johns Hopkins University. Washington, DC: Government Printing Office, 1959.
First Air Cavalry Division. *Memoirs of the First Team: August 1965–December 1969*. Tokyo: Nippon Printing Company, 1970.
Headquarters, U.S. Army, Europe. *Annual Historical Summary*, 1953–1965.
Headquarters, U.S. Army, Europe and Seventh Army. *Annual Historical Summary*, 1966 and 1968.
———. *Strengthening NATO: Stationing of the 2nd Armored Division (Forward) in Northern Germany*. Heidelberg: Headquarters, U.S. Army, Europe, Historian's Office, 1980.
Koch, Scott A., ed. *Selected Estimates on the Soviet Union, 1950–1959*. Washington, DC: History Staff, Center for the Study of Intelligence, Central Intelligence Agency, 1993.
Mastny, Vojtech, and Malcolm Byrne, eds. *A Cardboard Castle? An Inside History of the Warsaw Pact, 1955–1991*. Budapest: Central European University Press, 2005.
Rosenberg, David Alan, and Steven T. Ross, eds. *America's Plans for War against the Soviet Union, 1945–1950*. 15 vols. New York: Garland, 1989–1990.
Sokolovskii, V. D., ed. *Soviet Military Strategy*. Translated by Herbert S. Dinerstein, Leon Gouré, and Thomas D. Wolfe. Santa Monica, CA: Rand Corporation, 1963.
Steury, Donald P., ed. *On the Front Lines of the Cold War: Documents on the Intelligence War in Berlin, 1946 to 1961*. Washington, DC: CIA History Staff, Center for the Study of Intelligence, 1999.
Swain, Richard M., ed. *Selected Papers of General William E. DePuy*. Ft. Leavenworth, KS: Combat Studies Institute, 1994.
United States Army Vietnam. *Mechanized and Armor Combat Operations in Vietnam*. 28 March 1967. N.p.

U.S. Seventh Army. *Post Exercise Report: Exercise Grand Slam I.* N.p.: Headquarters, Seventh Army, 1962.

———. *Operation Big Lift: After Action Report.* N.p.: Big Lift Joint Visitors Bureau, 1963.

Service Journals Consulted

Armor
Army
Army Combat Forces Journal
Army-Navy-Air Force Register
Military Review
NATO's Fifteen Nations
Parameters

Books and Articles

Abenheim, Donald. *Reforging the Iron Cross: The Search for Tradition in the West German Armed Forces.* Princeton, NJ: Princeton University Press, 1988.

Adan, Avraham. *On the Banks of the Suez.* San Francisco: Presidio Press, 1980.

Aliano, Richard A. *American Defense Policy from Eisenhower to Kennedy: The Politics of Changing Military Requirements, 1957–1961.* Athens: Ohio University Press, 1975.

Andrianopoulos, Argyris G. *Western Europe in Kissinger's Global Strategy.* New York: St. Martin's, 1988.

Appleman, Roy E. *South to the Naktong, North to the Yalu: June–November 1950.* Washington, DC: U.S. Army Center of Military History, 1961.

Arenth, Joachim. *Der Westen tut nichts! Transatlantische Kooperation während der zweiten Berlin-Krise (1958–1962) im Spiegel neuer amerikanischer Quellen.* Frankfurt/Main: Peter Lang, 1993.

———. *Johnson, Vietnam und der Westen: Transatlantische Belastungen, 1963–1969.* Munich: Olzog Verlag, 1994.

Armacost, Michael H. *The Politics of Weapons Innovation: The Thor-Jupiter Controversy.* New York: Columbia University Press, 1969.

Ausland, John C. *Kennedy, Khrushchev, and the Berlin-Cuba Crisis, 1961–1964.* Oslo: Scandinavian University Press, 1996.

Bacevich, A. J. *The Pentomic Era: The US Army between Korea and Vietnam.* Washington, DC: National Defense University Press, 1986.

———. "The Paradox of Professionalism: Eisenhower, Ridgway, and the Challenge to Civilian Control, 1953–1955." *Journal of Military History* 61, no. 2 (April 1997): 303–333.

———. *The New American Militarism: How Americans Are Seduced by War.* Oxford: Oxford University Press, 2005.

———. ed. *The Long War: A New History of U.S. National Security Policy since World War II.* New York: Columbia University Press, 2007.

Bald, Detlef. *Die Atombewaffnung der Bundeswehr: Militär, Öffentlichkeit und Politik in der Ära Adenauer*. Bremen: Edition Temmen, 1994.

Bergerson, Frederic A. *The Army Gets an Air Force: Tactics of Insurgent Bureaucratic Politics*. Baltimore: Johns Hopkins University Press, 1980.

Bering, Henrik. *Outpost Berlin: The History of the American Military Forces in Berlin, 1945–1994*. Chicago: Edition Q, 1995.

Berman, Larry. *No Peace, No Honor: Nixon, Kissinger, and Betrayal in Vietnam*. New York: Free Press, 2001.

Beschloss, Michael R. *The Crisis Years: Kennedy and Khrushchev, 1960–1963*. New York: HarperCollins, 1991.

Betts, Richard K. *Conventional Deterrence: Predictive Uncertainty and Policy Confidence; Compound Deterrence vs. No-First-Use—What's Wrong Is What's Right*. Washington, DC: Brookings Institution, 1985.

Binder, L. James. *Lemnitzer: A Soldier for His Time*. Washington, DC: Brassey's, 1997.

Birtle, A. J. *Rearming the Phoenix: U.S. Military Assistance to the Federal Republic of Germany, 1950–1960*. New York: Garland, 1991.

Black, Robert W. *A Ranger Born: A Memoir of Combat and Valor from Korea to Vietnam*. New York: Ballantine Books, 2002.

Blair, Clay. *The Forgotten War: America in Korea, 1950–1953*. New York: Times Books, 1987.

Bland, Douglas. *The Military Committee of the North Atlantic Alliance: A Study of Structure and Strategy*. New York: Praeger, 1991.

Blaufarb, Douglas S. *The Counterinsurgency Era: U.S. Doctrine and Performance, 1950 to the Present*. New York: Free Press, 1977.

Blechman, Barry M., and Stephen S. Kaplan. *Force without War: US Armed Forces as a Political Instrument*. Washington, DC: Brookings Institution, 1978.

Blume, Peter. *US Army, 1945–1995: Von der Besatzungstruppe zur verbündeten Armee—50 Jahre US Army in Deutschland*. Illertissen: Flugzeug Publikationen, 1999.

Blumenson, Martin. *Reorganization of the Army, 1962*. Washington, DC: Department of the Army, Histories Division, Office of the Chief of Military History, n.d.

Bluth, Christoph. "Reconciling the Irreconcilable: Alliance Politics and the Paradox of Extended Deterrence in the 1960s." *Cold War History* 1, no. 2 (January 2001): 73–102.

———. *The Two Germanies and Military Security in Europe*. Houndmills: Palgrave Macmillan, 2002.

Boog, Horst. *Operatives Denken und Handeln in deutschen Streitkräften im 19. und 20. Jahrhundert*. Herford: Mittler, 1988.

Booth, T. Michael, and Duncan Spencer. *Paratrooper: The Life of Gen. James Gavin*. New York: Simon and Schuster, 1994.

Bourque, Stephen A. *Jayhawk! The VII Corps in the Persian Gulf War*. Washington, DC: Department of the Army, 2002.

Bowie, Robert R., and Richard H. Immerman. *Waging Peace: How Eisenhower Shaped an Enduring Cold War Strategy*. Oxford: Oxford University Press, 1998.

Boyd-Carpenter, Thomas. *Conventional Deterrence into the 1990s*. New York: St. Martin's, 1989.

Bozo, Frederic. *Two Strategies for Europe: DeGaulle, the United States, and the Atlantic*

Alliance. Translated by Susan Emanuel. Lanham, MD: Rowman and Littlefield, 2001.

Bradford, Zeb, Jr., and Frederic J. Brown. *The United States Army in Transition*. Beverly Hills, CA: Sage Publications, 1973.

Brauch, Hans-Günter, and Robert Kennedy, eds. *Alternative Conventional Defense Postures in the European Theater*. 3 vols. New York: Crane Russak, 1990–1993.

Brodie, Bernard. *Strategy in the Missile Age*. Princeton, NJ: Princeton University Press, 1959.

Bronfeld, Saul. "Fighting Outnumbered: The Impact of the Yom Kippur War on the U.S. Army." *Journal of Military History* 71, no. 2 (April 2007): 465–498.

Brown, Anthony Cave. *Dropshot: The United States Plan for War with the Soviet Union in 1957*. New York: Dial Press, 1978.

Brown, Neville. *Strategic Mobility*. New York: F. A. Praeger, 1964.

———. *Nuclear War: The Impending Strategic Deadlock*. New York: Praeger, 1965.

Buchholz, Frank. *Strategische und Militärpolitische Diskussionen in der Gründungsphase der Bundeswehr, 1949–1960*. Frankfurt/Main: Peter Lang, 1991.

Bull, Hedley. *Strategy and the Atlantic Alliance: A Critique of United States Doctrine*. Princeton, NJ: Center of International Studies, Woodrow Wilson School of Public and International Affairs, 1964.

Burrell, Raymond. *Strategic Nuclear Parity and NATO Defense Doctrine*. Washington, DC: National Defense University Press, 1978.

Canby, Stephen L. *NATO Military Policy: Obtaining Conventional Comparability with the Warsaw Pact*. Santa Monica, CA: Rand Corporation, 1973.

Carver, Michael. "Conventional Warfare in the Nuclear Age." In *The Makers of Modern Strategy from Machiavelli to the Nuclear Age*, edited by Peter Paret, pp. 779–814. Princeton, NJ: Princeton University Press, 1986.

Chambers, John Whiteclay II, ed. *The Oxford Companion to American Military History*. Oxford: Oxford University Press, 1999.

Cheng, Christopher C. S. *Air Mobility: The Development of a Doctrine*. Westport, CT: Praeger, 1994.

Cimbala, Stephen J. *Extended Deterrence: The United States and NATO Europe*. Lexington, MA: Lexington Books, 1987.

Citino, Robert M. *The Path to Blitzkrieg: Doctrine and Training in the German Army, 1920–1939*. Boulder, CO: Lynne Rienner, 1999.

———. *From Blitzkrieg to Desert Storm: The Evolution of Operational Warfare*. Lawrence: University Press of Kansas, 2004.

Clarfield, Gerard. *Security with Solvency: Dwight D. Eisenhower and the Shaping of the American Military Establishment*. Westport, CT: Praeger, 1999.

Clark, Ian. *Limited Nuclear War: Political Theory and War Conventions*. Princeton, NJ: Princeton University Press, 1982.

Clausewitz, Carl von. *On War*. Edited and translated by Michael Howard and Peter Paret. Princeton, NJ: Princeton University Press, 1976.

Cliffe, Trevor. *Military Technology and the European Balance*. London: International Institute for Strategic Studies, 1972.

Clifford, Clark. *Counsel to the President: A Memoir*. New York: Random House, 1991.

Close, Robert. *The Feasibility of a Surprise Attack against Western Europe*. Rome: NATO Defense College, 1975.

Clotfelter, James. *The Military in American Politics*. New York: Harper and Row, 1975.

Coakley, Robert W., and Walter G. Hermes. *Mobilization of a Two Division National Guard Force—1961: Decisions at Headquarters, Department of Army Level*. Washington, DC: Department of the Army, Office of the Chief of Military History, 1962.

Coakley, Robert W., Walter G. Hermes, James F. Schnabel, and Earl F. Ziemke. *U.S. Army Expansion and Readiness, 1961–1962*. Washington, DC: Office of the Chief of Military History, 1963.

Coakley, Robert W., Karl E. Cocke, and Daniel P. Griffin. *Demobilization Following the Korean War*. OCMH Study 29. Washington, DC: Histories Division, Office of the Chief of Military History, 1968.

Coffey, Kenneth J. *Strategic Implications of the All-Volunteer Force: The Conventional Defense of Central Europe*. Chapel Hill: University of North Carolina Press, 1979.

Cohen, Eliot A. "Change and Transformation in Military Affairs." *Journal of Strategic Studies* 27, no.3 (September 2004): 395–407.

Cohen, Michael Joseph. *Fighting World War Three from the Middle East: Allied Contingency Plans, 1945–1954*. London: Frank Cass, 1997.

Collins, J. Lawton. *War in Peacetime: The History and Lessons of Korea*. Boston: Houghton Mifflin, 1969.

Collins, John M. *U.S.-Soviet Military Balance: Concepts and Capabilities, 1960–1980*. N.p.: McGraw-Hill Publications, 1980.

Condell, Bruce, and David T. Zabecki, eds. *On the German Art of War: Truppenführung*. Boulder, CO: Lynne Rienner, 2001.

Condit, Doris M. *History of Office of the Secretary of Defense: The Test of War, 1950–1953*. Washington, DC: Historical Office, Office of the Secretary of Defense, 1988.

Condit, Kenneth W. *The Joint Chiefs of Staff and National Policy, 1947–49*. Vol. 2 of *The History of the Joint Chiefs of Staff*. Wilmington, DE: Michael Glazier, 1979.

———. *The Joint Chiefs of Staff and National Policy, 1955–56*. Vol. 6 of *The History of the Joint Chiefs of Staff*. Washington, DC: Historical Office, Joint Staff, 1992.

Connor, Arthur W. "The Army and Transformation, 1945–1991." Carlisle Barracks, PA: U.S. Army War College, Strategy Research Project, 2002.

Cooling, B. Franklin, and John A. Hixson. *Interoperability of Allied Forces in Europe: Some Peacetime Realities*. Carlisle Barracks, PA: U.S. Army Military History Institute, 1977.

Coram, Robert. *Boyd: The Fighter Pilot Who Changed the Art of War*. Boston: Little, Brown, 2002.

Corum, James S. *The Roots of Blitzkrieg: Hans von Seeckt and German Military Reform*. Lawrence: University Press of Kansas, 1992.

———. "Building A New Luftwaffe: The United States Air Force and Bundeswehr Planning for Rearmament, 1950–1960." *Journal of Strategic Studies* 27, no. 1 (March 2004): 89–113.

Craig, Gordon A. *NATO and the New German Army*. Princeton, NJ: Princeton University Press, 1955.

Crane, Conrad. "Avoiding Vietnam: The U.S. Army's Response to Defeat in Southeast Asia." Carlisle Barracks, PA: U.S. Army War College, Strategic Studies Institute, 2002.

Cromwell, William C. *The United States and the European Pillar: The Strained Alliance*. New York: St. Martin's, 1992.

Currie, James T., and Richard B. Crossland. *Twice the Citizen: A History of the United States Army Reserve, 1908–1995*. 2nd ed. Washington, DC: Office of the Chief, Army Reserve, 1997.

Daalder, Ivo. *The Nature and Practice of Flexible Response: NATO Strategy and Theater Nuclear Forces since 1967*. New York: Columbia University Press, 1991.

Dastrup, Boyd L. *King of Battle: A Branch History of the U.S. Army's Field Artillery*. Ft. Monroe, VA: Office of the Command Historian, U.S. Army Training and Doctrine Command, 1992.

Davis, Lynn Etheridge. *Limited Nuclear Options: Deterrence and the New American Doctrine*. Adelphi Paper 121. London: International Institute for Strategic Studies, 1976.

Decker, Oscar C. "The Patton Tanks: The Cold War Learning Series." In *Camp Colt to Desert Storm: The History of U.S. Armored Forces*, edited by George F. Hofmann and Donn A. Starry, pp. 298–323. Lexington: University Press of Kentucky, 1999.

Deitchman, Seymour J. *Limited War and American Defense Policy*. Cambridge, MA: MIT Press, 1964.

de Maizière, Ulrich. *Führen im Frieden: 20 Jahre Dienst für Bundeswehr und Staat*. Munich: Bernard und Graefe Verlag für Wehrwesen, 1974.

———. *Verteidigung in Europa-Mitte*. Munich: J. F. Lehmanns Verlag, 1975.

———. *In der Pflicht: Lebensbericht eines deutschen Soldaten im 20. Jahrhundert*. Herford: Verlag E. S. Mittler, 1989.

Dinter, Elmar, and Paddy Griffith. *Not Over by Christmas: NATO's Central Front in World War III*. Chichester, Sussex: Antony Bird Publications, 1983.

Dittgen, Herbert. *Deutsch-amerikanische Sicherheitsbeziehungen in der Ära Helmut Schmidt: Vorgeschichte und Folgen des NATO-Doppelbeschlusses*. Munich: Wilhelm Fink Verlag, 1991.

Dockrill, Saki. *Britain's Policy for West German Rearmament, 1950–1955*. Cambridge: Cambridge University Press, 1991.

———. *Eisenhower's New Look National Security Policy, 1953–1961*. Houndmills: Macmillan, 1996.

Dormann, Manfred. *Demokratische Militärpolitik: Die alliierte Militärstrategie als Thema deutscher Politik, 1949–1968*. Freiburg: Verlag Rombach, 1970.

Doughty, Robert A. *The Evolution of U.S. Army Tactical Doctrine, 1946–1976*. Leavenworth Paper No. 1. Ft. Leavenworth, KS: Command and General Staff College, 1976.

Duffield, John S. "The Soviet Military Threat to Western Europe: U.S. Estimates in the 1950s and 1960s." *Journal of Strategic Studies* 15, no. 2 (June 1992): 208–227.

———. *Power Rules: The Evolution of NATO's Conventional Force Posture*. Stanford, CA: Stanford University Press, 1995.

Duke, Simon. *United States Military Forces and Installations in Europe*. Oxford: Oxford University Press, 1989.
Duke, Simon, and Wolfgang Krieger, eds. *U.S. Military Forces in Europe: The Early Years, 1945–1970*. Boulder, CO: Westview Press, 1993.
Dunnigan, James F., and Raymond M. Macedonia. *Getting It Right: American Military Reform after Vietnam to the Persian Gulf and Beyond*. New York: William Morrow, 1993.
Edinger, Lewis Joachim. *West German Armament*. Maxwell Air Force Base, AL: Air University, Research Studies Institute, 1955.
Ehlert, Hans, Christian Greiner, Georg Meyer, and Bruno Thoss. *Die NATO Option*. Vol. 3 of *Anfänge westdeutscher Sicherheitspolitik*. Munich: R. Oldenbourg Verlag, 1993.
Eisenhower, Dwight D. *The White House Years: Mandate for Change, 1953–1956*. Garden City, NY: Doubleday, 1963.
———. *The White House Years: Waging Peace, 1956–1961*. Garden City, NY: Doubleday, 1965.
Eldredge, Niles, and Stephen Jay Gould. "Punctuated Equilibria: An Alternative to Phyletic Gradualism." In *Models in Paleobiology*, edited by T. J. M. Schopf. San Francisco: Freeman, Cooper, 1972.
Elliot, David C. "Project Vista and Nuclear Weapons in Europe." *International Security* 11, no. 1 (Summer 1986): 163–183.
———. *Project Vista: An Early Study of Nuclear Weapons in Europe*. Santa Monica: California Seminar on International Security and Foreign Policy, 1987.
Ellis, William D., and Thomas J. Cunningham. *Clarke of St. Vith: The Sergeant's General*. Cleveland: Dillon and Liederbach, 1974.
Enders, Thomas. *Franz Josef Strauss—Helmut Schmidt und die Doktrin der Abschreckung*. Coblenz: Bernard und Graefe, 1984.
English, John A., J. Addicott, and P. J. Kramers. *The Mechanized Battlefield: A Tactical Analysis*. Washington, DC: Pergamon Press, 1985.
English, John A., and Bruce I. Gudmundsson. *On Infantry*. Rev. ed. Westport, CT: Praeger, 1994.
Enthoven, Alain C., and K. Wayne Smith. *How Much Is Enough? Shaping the Defense Program, 1961–1969*. New York: Harper and Row, 1971.
Epley, William W. *America's First Cold War Army, 1945–1950*. Arlington, VA: Institute of Land Warfare, Association of the United States Army, 1999.
———. ed. *International Cold War Military Records and History: Proceedings of the International Conference on Cold War Military Records and History Held in Washington, D.C., 21–26 March 1994*. Washington, DC: Office of the Secretary of Defense, 1996.
Evangelista, Matthew A. "Stalin's Postwar Army Reappraised." *International Security* 7, no.3 (Winter 1982–83): 110–138.
Fairchild, Byron R., and Walter S. Poole. *The Joint Chiefs of Staff and National Policy, 1957–1960*. Vol. 7 of *The History of the Joint Chiefs of Staff*. Washington, DC: Office of Joint History, Office of the Chairman of the Joint Chiefs of Staff, 2000.
Fautua, David T. "The 'Long Pull' Army: NSC 68, the Korean War, and the Cre-

ation of the Cold War Army." *Journal of Military History* 61, no. 1 (January 1997): 93–120.

Fehrenbach, T. R. *This Kind of War: A Study in Unpreparedness*. New York: Macmillan, 1963.

Finlayson, Kenneth. *An Uncertain Trumpet: The Evolution of U.S. Army Infantry Doctrine, 1919–1941*. Westport, CT: Greenwood, 2001.

Fischer, Alexander. *Entmilitarisierung und Aufrüstung in Mitteleuropa 1945 bis 1956*. Herford: E. S. Mittler, 1983.

Fischer, Robert Lucas. *Defending the Central Front: The Balance of Forces*. Adelphi Paper No. 127. London: International Institute for Strategic Studies, 1976.

Flint, Roy K. "Task Force Smith and the 24th Division: Delay and Withdrawal, 5–19 July 1950." In *America's First Battles, 1776–1965*, edited by Charles E. Heller and William A. Stofft, pp. 266–299. Lawrence: University Press of Kansas, 1986.

Flynn, George Q. *The Draft, 1940–1973*. Lawrence: University Press of Kansas, 1993.

Flynn, Gregory, ed. *Soviet Military Doctrine and Western Policy*. London: Routledge, 1989.

Foerster, Roland G., Christian Greiner, Georg Meyer, Hans-Jürgen Rautenberg, and Norbert Wiggershaus. *Von der Kapitulation bis zum Pleven Plan*. Vol. 1 of *Anfänge westdeutscher Sicherheitspolitik*. Munich: R. Oldenbourg Verlag, 1982.

Freedman, Lawrence. "The First Two Generations of Nuclear Strategists." In *The Makers of Modern Strategy from Machiavelli to the Nuclear Age*, edited by Peter Paret, pp. 735–778. Princeton, NJ: Princeton University Press, 1986.

———. *The Evolution of Nuclear Strategy*. New York: St. Martin's, 1989.

———. *Kennedy's Wars: Berlin, Cuba, Laos, and Vietnam*. New York: Oxford University Press, 2000.

French, David. *Raising Churchill's Army: The British Army and the War against Germany, 1919–1945*. Oxford: Oxford University Press, 2000.

Friedberg, Aaron L. "Why Didn't the United States Become a Garrison State?" *International Security* 16, no. 4 (Spring 1992): 109–142.

———. *In the Shadow of the Garrison State: America's Anti-Statism and Its Cold War Grand Strategy*. Princeton, NJ: Princeton University Press, 2000.

Friedman, Norman. *The Fifty-Year War: Conflict and Strategy in the Cold War*. Annapolis, MD: U.S. Naval Institute Press, 2000.

Fritz, Stephen G. *Endkampf: Soldiers, Civilians, and the Death of the Third Reich*. Lexington: University Press of Kentucky, 2004.

Fursdon, Edward. *The European Defence Community: A History*. New York: St. Martin's, 1980.

Gabel, Christopher R. "World War II Armor Operations in Europe." In *Camp Colt to Desert Storm: The History of U.S. Armored Forces*, edited by George F. Hofmann and Donn A. Starry, pp. 144–184. Lexington: University Press of Kentucky, 1999.

Gablik, Axel F. *Strategische Planungen in der Bundesrepublik Deutschland, 1955–1967: Politische Kontrolle oder militärische Notwendigkeit?* Baden-Baden: Nomos, 1996.

Gacek, Christopher M. *The Logic of Force: The Dilemma of Limited War in American Foreign Policy*. New York: Columbia University Press, 1994.

Gaddis, John Lewis. *Strategies of Containment: A Critical Reappraisal of Postwar American National Security Policy*. Oxford: Oxford University Press, 1982.

———. *The Long Peace: Inquiries into the History of the Cold War*. New York: Oxford University Press, 1987.

———. *We Now Know: Rethinking Cold War History*. Oxford: Clarendon Press, 1997.

———. *Strategies of Containment: A Critical Appraisal of American National Security Policy during the Cold War*. Rev. ed. Oxford: Oxford University Press, 2005.

Gaddis, John Lewis, Philip Gordon, Ernest May, and Jonathan Rosenberg, eds. *Cold War Statesmen Confront the Bomb: Nuclear Diplomacy since 1945*. Oxford: Oxford University Press, 1999.

Galvin, John R. *Air Assault: The Development of Airmobile Warfare*. New York: Hawthorn Books, 1969.

Garthoff, Raymond L. "Estimating Soviet Military Force Levels: Some Light from the Past." *International Security* 14, no. 4 (Spring 1990): 93–116.

———. *Assessing the Adversary: Estimates by the Eisenhower Administration of Soviet Intentions and Capabilities*. Washington, DC: Brookings Institution, 1991.

———. *A Journey through the Cold War: A Memoir of Containment and Coexistence*. Washington, DC: Brookings Institution Press, 2001.

Gavin, Francis J. "The Myth of Flexible Response: United States Strategy in Europe during the 1960s." *International History Review* 23, no. 4 (December 2001): 847–875.

———. *Gold, Dollars, and Power: The Politics of International Monetary Relations, 1958–1971*. Chapel Hill: University of North Carolina Press, 2004.

Gavin, James M. "Cavalry, and I Don't Mean Horses." *Harper's Magazine*, April 1954, pp. 54–60.

———. *War and Peace in the Space Age*. New York: Harper, 1958.

Geelhoed, E. Bruce. *Charles E. Wilson and Controversy at the Pentagon, 1953 to 1957*. Detroit: Wayne State University Press, 1979.

Gehring, Stephen P. *From the Fulda Gap to Kuwait: U.S. Army, Europe, and the Gulf War*. Washington, DC: Department of the Army, 1998.

Geiling, Martin. *Aussenpolitik und Nuklearstrategie: Eine Analyse des konzeptionellen Wandels der amerikanischen Sicherheitspolitik gegenüber der Sowjetunion, 1945–1963*. Cologne: Böhlau Verlag, 1975.

George, Alexander L., and Richard Smoke. *Deterrence in American Foreign Policy: Theory and Practice*. New York: Columbia University Press, 1974.

Gerber, Johannes. *Die Bundeswehr im Nordatlantischen Bündnis*. Regensburg: Wallhalla und Praetoria Verlag, 1985.

Geyer, Michael. *Deutsche Rüstungspolitik, 1860–1980*. Frankfurt/Main: Verlag Suhrkamp, 1984.

———. "German Strategy in the Age of Machine Warfare, 1914–1945." In *The Makers of Modern Strategy from Machiavelli to the Nuclear Age*, edited by Peter Paret, pp. 527–597. Princeton, NJ: Princeton University Press, 1986.

Giauque, Jeffrey Glenn. *Grand Designs and Visions of Unity: The Atlantic Powers and the Reorganization of Western Europe, 1955–1963*. Chapel Hill: University of North Carolina Press, 2002.

Glantz, David. *Soviet Military Operational Art: In Pursuit of Deep Battle*. London: Frank Cass, 1991.
Golden, James Reed, Asa A. Clark, and Bruce E. Arlinghaus. *Conventional Deterrence: Alternatives for European Defense*. Lexington, MA: Lexington Books, 1984.
Gole, Henry G. *Soldiering: Observations from Korea, Vietnam, and Safe Places*. Dulles, VA: Potomac Books, 2005.
Goodpaster, Andrew J. *For the Common Defense*. Lexington, MA: Lexington Books, 1977.
———. *Strengthening Conventional Deterrence in Europe: A Program for the 1980s*. Boulder, CO: Westview Press, 1985.
Gordon, Michael R., and Bernard E. Trainor. *The Generals' War: The Inside Story of the Conflict in the Gulf*. Boston: Little, Brown, 1995.
Gould, Stephen Jay. *The Structure of Evolutionary Theory*. Cambridge, MA: Harvard University Press, 2002.
Graham, Leonard Thomas. *The West German Territorial Army in Support of NATO*. Ft. Leavenworth, KS: Command and General Staff College, 1975.
Grathwol, Robert P., and Donita Moorhus. *American Forces in Berlin: Cold War Outpost, 1945–1994*. Washington, DC: Department of Defense, Legacy Resource Management Program, 1994.
———. *Berlin and the American Military: A Cold War Chronicle*. New York: New York University Press, 1999.
Greiner, Christian, Klaus A. Maier and Heinz Rebhan. *Die NATO als Militärallianz: Strategie, Organization und nukleare Kontrolle im Bündnis, 1949 bis 1959*. Munich: R. Oldenbourg Verlag, 2003.
Griffith, Robert. *U.S Army's Transition to the All-Volunteer Force, 1968–1974*. Washington, DC: U.S. Army Center of Military History, 1997.
Gudmundsson, Bruce I. *On Artillery*. Westport, CT: Praeger, 1993.
———. *On Armor*. Westport, CT: Praeger, 2004.
Habeck, Mary R. *Storm of Steel: The Development of Armor Doctrine in Germany and the Soviet Union, 1919–1939*. Ithaca, NY: Cornell University Press, 2003.
Hackett, Sir John. *The Third World War: A Future History*. New York: Macmillan, 1978.
Haffa, Robert P., Jr. *The Half War: Planning U.S. Rapid Deployment Forces to Meet a Limited Contingency, 1960–1983*. Boulder, CO: Westview Press, 1984.
Haftendorn, Helga. *Security and Détente: Conflicting Priorities in German Foreign Policy*. New York: Praeger, 1985.
———. *Kernwaffen und die Glaubwürdigkeit der Allianz: Die NATO-Krise von 1966/67*. Baden-Baden: Nomos Verlag, 1994.
———. *NATO and the Nuclear Revolution: A Crisis of Credibility, 1966–1967*. Oxford: Clarendon Press, 1996.
Halperin, Morton H. *Limited War in the Nuclear Age*. New York: John Wiley, 1963.
Hamburger, Kenneth E. "Operational Art." In *The Oxford Companion to American Military History*, edited by John Whiteclay Chamber II, pp. 517–518. Oxford: Oxford University Press, 1999.
Hammerich, Helmut, Dieter H. Kollmer, Martin Rink, and Rudolf Schlaffer. *Das*

Heer, 1950 bis 1970: Konzeption, Organisation, Aufstellung. Munich: R. Oldenbourg Verlag, 2006.

Hanson, Thomas E. "The Eighth Army's Combat Readiness before Korea: A Reappraisal." *Armed Forces and Society* 29, no. 2 (Winter 2003): 167–184.

Harrison, Richard W. *The Russian Way of War: Operational Art, 1904–1940*. Lawrence: University Press of Kansas, 2001.

Hauser, William L. *America's Army in Crisis: A Study in Civil-Military Relations*. Baltimore: Johns Hopkins University Press, 1973.

Hawkins, Glen R. *United States Army Force Structure and Force Design Initiatives, 1939–1989*. Washington, DC: U.S. Army Center of Military History, 1991.

Hawkins, Glen R., and James Jay Carafano. *Prelude to Army XXI: U.S. Army Division Design Initiatives and Experiments, 1917–1995*. Washington, DC: U.S. Army Center of Military History, 1997.

Hawkins, John Palmer. *Army of Hope, Army of Alienation: Culture and Contradiction in the American Army Communities of Cold War Germany*. Westport, CT: Praeger, 2001.

Haworth, W. Blair, Jr. *The Bradley and How It Got That Way: Technology, Institutions, and the Problem of Mechanized Infantry in the United States Army*. Westport, CT: Greenwood Press, 1999.

Hay, John H. *Tactical and Materiel Innovations*. Washington, DC: Department of the Army, 1974.

Heilbrunn, Otto. *Conventional Warfare in the Nuclear Age*. New York: Praeger, 1965.

Heller, Charles E., and William A. Stofft, eds. *America's First Battles, 1776–1965*. Lawrence: University Press of Kansas, 1986.

Hendrix, Thomas L. "Air Assault on the Pentagon: Army Airmobility, the Howze Board, and Implementing Change." USAMHI Historical Study No. 1. Carlisle, PA: U.S. Army Military History Institute, 1997.

Herbert, Anthony B. *Soldier*. New York: Holt, Rinehart and Winston, 1973.

Herbert, Paul. *Deciding What Has to Be Done: General William E. DePuy and the 1976 Edition of FM 100-5, Operations*. Leavenworth Paper No. 16. Ft. Leavenworth, KS: Command and General Staff College, 1988.

Herring, George C. *LBJ and Vietnam: A Different Kind of War*. Austin: University of Texas Press, 1996.

Herzog, Chaim. *The War of Atonement: October 1973*. Boston: Little, Brown, 1975.

Heuer, Uwe. *Reichswehr, Wehrmacht, Bundeswehr: Zum Image deutscher Streitkräfte in den Vereinigten Staaten von Amerika: Kontinuität und Wandel im Urteil amerikanischer Experten*. Frankfurt/Main: P. Lang Verlag, 1990.

Heuser, Beatrice. *NATO, Britain, France, and the FRG: Nuclear Strategies and Forces for Europe, 1949–2000*. Houndmills: Macmillan, 1997.

Heuser, Beatrice, and Robert O'Neill, eds. *Securing Peace in Europe, 1945–1962*. New York: St. Martin's, 1992.

Heusinger, Adolf. *Reden, 1956–1961*. Boppard: Harald Boldt Verlag, 1961.

Hickman, Donald J. *The U.S. Army in Europe, 1953–1963*. Heidelberg: U.S. Army Europe, Historian's Office, 1964.

Higham, Robin, and Frederick W. Kagan, eds. *The Military History of the Soviet Union*. Houndmills: Palgrave, 2002.

Hitchcock, William I. *France Restored: Cold War Diplomacy and the Quest for Leadership in Europe, 1944–1954*. Chapel Hill: University of North Carolina Press, 1998.

Hoag, Malcolm. *Rationalizing NATO Strategy*. Santa Monica, CA: Rand Corporation, 1964.

Hofmann, Daniel. *Truppenstationierung in der Bundesrepublik Deutschland: Die Vertragsverhandlungen mit den Westmächten, 1951–1959*. Munich: R. Oldenbourg Verlag, 1997.

Hofmann, George F., and Donn A. Starry, eds. *Camp Colt to Desert Storm: The History of U.S. Armored Forces*. Lexington: University Press of Kentucky, 1999.

Hogan, Michael J. *The Marshall Plan: America, Britain, and the Reconstruction of Western Europe, 1947–1952*. Cambridge: Cambridge University Press, 1987.

Hoppe, Christoph. *Zwischen Teilhabe und Mitsprache: Die Nuklearfrage in der Allianzpolitik Deutschlands, 1959–66*. Baden-Baden: Nomos Verlagsgesellschaft, 1993.

House, Jonathan. *Toward Combined Arms Warfare: A Survey of 20th Century Tactics, Doctrine, and Organization*. Ft. Leavenworth, KS: Command and General Staff College, 1985.

———. *The U.S. Army in Joint Operations, 1950–1983*. Washington, DC: U.S. Army Center of Military History, 1992.

———. *Combined Arms Warfare in the Twentieth Century*. Lawrence: University Press of Kansas, 2001.

Howze, Hamilton H. "Tactical Employment of the Air Assault Division." *Army* 14, no. 2 (September 1963): 35–53.

———.*A Cavalryman's Story: Memoirs of a Twentieth-Century Army General*. Washington, DC: Smithsonian Institution Press, 1996.

Hunnicutt, R. P. *Sherman: A History of the American Medium Tank*. Novato, CA: Presidio Press, 1978.

———. *Patton: A History of the American Main Battle Tank*. Novato, CA: Presidio Press, 1984.

———. *Abrams: A History of the American Main Battle Tank*. Novato, CA: Presidio Press, 1990.

———. *Stuart: A History of the American Light Tank*. Novato, CA: Presidio Press, 1992.

———. *Sheridan: A History of the American Light Tank*. Novato, CA: Presidio Press, 1995.

———. *Bradley: A History of American Fighting and Support Vehicles*. Novato, CA: Presidio Press, 1999.

Hunt, Kenneth. *The Alliance and Europe, Part II: Defense with Fewer Men*. London: International Institute for Strategic Studies, 1973.

Huntington, Samuel P. *The Soldier and the State: The Theory and Politics of Civil-Military Relations*. Cambridge, MA: Belknap Press, 1957.

———. *The Common Defense: Strategic Programs in National Politics*. New York: Columbia University Press, 1961.

———. "Conventional Deterrence and Conventional Retaliation in Europe." *International Security* 8, no. 3 (Winter 1983–84): 32–56.

Huston, James A. *One for All: NATO Strategy and Logistics through the Formative Period, 1949–1969*. Newark: University of Delaware Press, 1984.

Huth, Paul K. *Extended Deterrence and the Prevention of War*. New Haven, CT: Yale University Press, 1988.

Isby, David C., and Charles Kamps Jr. *Armies of NATO's Central Front*. London: Jane's, 1985.

Ismay, Lord Hastings. *NATO: The First Five Years*. Utrecht: Bosch, 1954.

Johnston, Andrew M. "Mr. Slessor Goes to Washington: The Influence of the British Global Strategy Paper on the Eisenhower New Look." *Diplomatic History* 22, no. 3 (Summer 1998): 361–398.

———. *Hegemony and Culture in the Origins of NATO Nuclear First-Use, 1945–1955*. New York: Palgrave Macmillan, 2005.

Jordan, Robert S. *Norstad: Cold War NATO Supreme Commander: Airman, Strategist, Diplomat*. Houndmills: Macmillan, 2000.

———. ed. *Generals in International Politics: NATO's Supreme Commander Europe*. Lexington: University Press of Kentucky, 1987.

Junker, Detlef, ed. *Germany and the United States in the Era of the Cold War, 1945–90*. 2 vols. Cambridge: Cambridge University Press for the German Historical Institute, Washington, DC, 2004.

Jurika, Stephen, Jr., ed. *From Pearl Harbor to Vietnam: The Memoirs of Admiral Arthur W. Radford*. Stanford, CA: Hoover Institute Press, 1980.

Kagan, Frederick W. "The Rise and Fall of Soviet Operational Art, 1917–1941." In *The Military History of the Soviet Union*, edited by Robin Higham and Frederick W. Kagan, pp. 79–92. Houndmills: Palgrave, 2002.

———. "The Great Patriotic War: Rediscovering Operational Art." In *The Military History of the Soviet Union*, edited by Robin Higham and Frederick W. Kagan, pp. 137–151. Houndmills: Palgrave, 2002.

Kahn, Herman. *On Thermonuclear War*. Princeton, NJ: Princeton University Press, 1960.

———. *On Escalation: Metaphors and Scenarios*. New York: Praeger, 1965.

Kaplan, Lawrence S. *NATO and the Policy of Containment*. Boston: Heath, 1968.

———. *The United States and NATO: The Formative Years*. Lexington: University Press of Kentucky, 1984.

———. *NATO and the United States: The Enduring Alliance*. Boston: Twayne, 1988.

———. *The Long Entanglement: NATO's First Fifty Years*. Westport, CT: Praeger, 1999.

———. "The MLF Debate." In *John F. Kennedy and Europe*, edited by Douglas Brinkley and Richard T. Griffiths, pp. 51–65. Baton Rouge: Louisiana State University Press, 1999.

———. *NATO Divided, NATO United: The Evolution of an Alliance*. Westport, CT: Praeger, 2004.

Kaplan, Lawrence S., Ronald D. Landa, and Edward J. Drea. *The McNamara Ascendancy, 1961–1965*. Vol. 5 in *History of the Office of the Secretary of Defense*. Washington, DC: Historical Office, Office of the Secretary of Defense, 2006.

Karanowski, Stanley. *The German Army and NATO Strategy*. Washington, DC: National Defense University Press, 1982.

Karber, Philip A., and Jerald A. Combs. "The United States, NATO, and the Soviet

Threat to Western Europe: Military Establishments and Policy Options, 1945–1963." *Diplomatic History* 22, no. 3 (Summer 1998): 299–329.

Kedzior, Richard W. *Evolution and Endurance: The U.S. Army Division in the Twentieth Century*. Santa Monica, CA: Rand Corporation, 2000.

Keegan, John. *The Face of Battle*. New York: Penguin Books, 1978.

Kelleher, Catherine McArdle. *Germany and the Politics of Nuclear Weapons*. New York: Columbia University Press, 1975.

Kennan, George F. "The Sources of Soviet Conduct." *Foreign Affairs* 25, no. 4 (July 1947): 566–582.

Kiesling, Eugenia C. *Arming against Hitler: France and the Limits of Military Planning*. Lawrence: University Press of Kansas, 1996.

Killebrew, Robert B. *Conventional Defense and Total Deterrence: Assessing NATO's Strategic Options*. Wilmington, DE: Scholarly Resources, 1986.

Kimball, Jeffrey. *Nixon's Vietnam War*. Lawrence: University Press of Kansas, 1998.

King, Edward L. *The Death of an Army: A Pre-Mortem*. New York: Saturday Review Press, 1972.

Kinnard, Douglas. *President Eisenhower and Strategy Management*. Lexington: University Press of Kentucky, 1977.

———. *The War Managers: American Generals Reflect on Vietnam*. Hanover, NH: University Press of New England, 1977.

———. "Civil-Military Relations: The President and the General." *Parameters* 15, no. 2 (Summer 1985): 19–29.

———. "A Soldier in Camelot: Maxwell Taylor in the Kennedy White House." *Parameters* 18, no. 4 (December 1988): 13–24.

Kirkpatrick, Charles E. *The Army and the A-10: The Army's Role in Developing Close Air Support Aircraft, 1961–1971*. Washington, DC: U.S. Army Center of Military History, 1988.

Kissinger, Henry. *Nuclear Weapons and Foreign Policy*. Garden City, NY: Doubleday, 1957.

———. *The Troubled Partnership: A Re-Appraisal of the Atlantic Alliance*. New York: McGraw-Hill, 1965.

———. *White House Years*. Boston: Little, Brown, 1979.

———. *Years of Upheaval*. Boston: Little, Brown, 1982.

———. *Years of Renewal*. New York: Simon and Schuster, 1999.

Kitfield, James. *Prodigal Soldiers: How the Generation of Officers Born of Vietnam Revolutionized the American Style of War*. New York: Simon and Schuster, 1995.

Kokoshin, Andrei A. *Soviet Strategic Thought, 1917–91*. Cambridge, MA: MIT Press, 1998.

Kollmer, Dieter H. *Rüstungsgüterbeschaffung in der Aufbauphase der Bundeswehr: Der Schützenpanzer HS 30 als Fallbeispiel (1953–1961)*. Stuttgart: Franz Steiner Verlag, 2002.

Köllner, Lutz, Klaus Maier, Wilhelm Meier-Dörnberg, and Hans-Erich Volkmann. *Die EVG Phase*. Vol. 2 of *Anfänge westdeutscher Sicherheitspolitik*. Munich: R. Oldenbourg Verlag, 1989.

Krause, Michael D., and R. Cody Phillips, eds. *Historical Perspectives of the Operational Art*. Washington, DC: U.S. Army Center of Military History, 2005.

Krepinevich, Andrew F., Jr. *The Army and Vietnam*. Baltimore: Johns Hopkins University Press, 1986.

Lambeth, Benjamin S. *The Transformation of American Air Power*. Ithaca, NY: Cornell University Press, 2000.

Landry, John R. *Strategic and Doctrinal Implications of Deep Attack Concepts for the Defense of Central Europe*. Washington, DC: National Defense University, 1983.

Lanning, Michael Lee. *The Battles of Peace*. New York: Ballantine Books, 1992.

Large, David Clay. *Germans to the Front: West German Rearmament in the Adenauer Era*. Chapel Hill: University of North Carolina Press, 1996.

Lawrence, Richard D., and Jeffrey Record. *U.S. Force Structure in NATO*. Washington, DC: Brookings Institution, 1974.

Leffler, Melvyn P. *A Preponderance of Power: National Security, the Truman Administration, and the Cold War*. Stanford, CA: Stanford University Press, 1992.

Leighton, Richard M. *Strategy, Money, and the New Look, 1953–1956*. Vol. 3 of *History of the Office of the Secretary of Defense*. Washington, DC: Historical Office, Office of the Secretary of Defense, 2001.

Lepgold, Joseph. *The Declining Hegemon: The United States and European Defense, 1960–1990*. New York: Greenwood Press, 1990.

Lewis, Adrian R. *The American Culture of War: The History of U.S. Military Forces from World War II to Operation Iraqi Freedom*. New York: Routledge, 2007.

Lider, Julian. *West Germany in NATO*. Warsaw: Zachodnia Agencja Prasowa, 1965.

———. *Origins and Development of West German Military Thought, 1949–1969*. Aldershot: Gower, 1986.

Lind, Michael. *Vietnam: The Necessary War*. New York: Simon and Schuster, 1999.

Linn, Brian McAlister. "Peacetime Transformation in the U.S. Army, 1865–1965." In *Transforming Defense*, edited by Conrad Crane, pp. 3–29. Carlisle, PA: U.S. Army War College, Strategic Studies Institute, 2001.

———. "Eisenhower, the Army, and the American Way of War." The Dwight D. Eisenhower Lectures in War and Peace, no. 10. Manhattan: Kansas State University, 2003.

Lock-Pullan, Richard. "An Inward Looking Time: The U.S. Army, 1973–76." *Journal of Military History* 67, no. 2 (April 2003): 483–511.

———. "How to Rethink War: Conceptual Innovation and AirLand Battle Doctrine." *Journal of Strategic Studies* 28, no. 4 (August 2005): 679–702.

———. *US Intervention Policy and Army Innovation: From Vietnam to Iraq*. London: Routledge, 2005.

Lowry, Montecue J. *The Forge of West German Rearmament: Theodor Blank and the Amt Blank*. New York: Peter Lang, 1990.

Lundestad, Geir. *The United States and Western Europe since 1945: From "Empire" by Invitation to Transatlantic Drift*. Oxford: Oxford University Press, 2003.

Mahncke, Dieter. *Nukleare Mitwirkung: Die Bundesrepublik Deutschland in der atlantischen Allianz, 1954–1970*. Berlin: Walter de Gruyter, 1972.

Mahon, John K., and Romana Danysh. *Regular Army*. Pt. 1 of *Infantry*. Washington, DC: Office of the Chief of Military History, U.S. Army, 1972.

Mai, Gunther. *Westliche Sicherheitspolitik im Kalten Krieg: Der Korea-Krieg und die deutsche Wiederbewaffnung 1950*. Boppard: H. Boldt Verlag, 1977.

Mako, William P. *U.S. Ground Forces in the Defense of Central Europe*. Washington, DC: Brookings Institution, 1983.
Mallin, Maurice A. *Tanks, Fighters, and Ships: U.S. Conventional Force Planning since WWII*. Washington, DC: Brassey's, 1990.
Maloney, Sean M. *War without Battles: Canada's NATO Brigade in Germany, 1951–1993*. Toronto: McGraw-Hill Ryerson, 1997.
———. "Berlin Contingency Planning: Prelude to Flexible Response, 1958–63." *Journal of Strategic Studies* 25, no. 1 (March 2002): 99–134.
Mark, Edward. *Aerial Interdiction: Air Power and the Land Battle in Three American Wars*. Washington, DC: Center for Air Force History, 1994.
Martin, Laurence W. *NATO and the Defense of the West: An Analysis of America's First Line of Defense*. New York: Holt, Rinehart and Winston, 1985.
———, ed. *Strategic Thought in the Nuclear Age*. Baltimore: Johns Hopkins University Press, 1979.
Mataxis, Theodore C., and Seymour L. Goldberg. *Nuclear Tactics, Weapons, and Firepower in the Pentomic Division, Battle Group, and Company*. Harrisburg, PA: Military Service Publishing Company, 1958.
Mayer, Frank A. *Adenauer and Kennedy: A Study in German-American Relations, 1961–1963*. New York: St. Martin's, 1996.
McAllister, James. *No Exit: America and the German Problem, 1943–1954*. Ithaca, NY: Cornell University Press, 2002.
McFarland, Keith D., and David L. Roll. *Louis Johnson and the Arming of America: The Roosevelt and Truman Years*. Bloomington: Indiana University Press, 2005.
McFarland, Linda. *Cold War Strategist: Stuart Symington and the Search for National Security*. Westport, CT: Praeger, 2001.
McGeehan, Robert. *The German Rearmament Question: American Diplomacy and European Defense after World War II*. Chicago: University of Illinois Press, 1971.
McGrath, John J. *The Brigade: A History*. Ft. Leavenworth, KS: Combat Studies Institute Press, 2004.
McKercher, B. J. C., and Michael E. Hennesy, eds. *The Operational Art: Developments in the Theories of War*. Westport, CT: Praeger, 1996.
McLin, John B. *Rationalising Defense Production in NATO*. Hanover, NH: American Universities Field Staff, 1968.
McMaster, H. R. *Dereliction of Duty: Lyndon Johnson, Robert McNamara, the Joint Chiefs of Staff, and the Lies That Led to Vietnam*. New York: HarperCollins, 1997.
McNamara, Robert S. *The Essence of Security: Reflections in Office*. New York: Harper and Row, 1968.
———. "The Military Role of Nuclear Weapons: Perceptions and Misperceptions." In *The Nuclear Controversy: A Foreign Affairs Reader*, edited by William P. Bundy, pp. 73–98. New York: New American Library, 1985.
Mearsheimer, John J. "Why the Soviets Can't Win Quickly in Central Europe." *International Security* 7, no. 1 (Summer 1982): 3–39.
———. *Conventional Deterrence*. Ithaca, NY: Cornell University Press, 1983.
Mellenthin, Friedrich von, and R. H. S. Stolfi, with E. Sobik. *NATO under Attack: Why the Western Alliance Can Fight Outnumbered and Win in Central Europe without Nuclear Weapons*. Durham, NC: Duke University Press, 1984.

Mendershausen, Horst. *Troop Stationing in Germany: Value and Cost*. Santa Monica, CA: Rand Corporation, 1968.

———. *The Defense of Germany and the German Defense Contribution*. Santa Monica, CA: Rand Corporation, 1981.

Meredith, David S. *The Bundeswehr in NATO: A Changing Role*. Carlisle Barracks, PA: Army War College, 1971.

Meyer, Georg. *Vom Kriegsgefangenen zum Generalinspekteur: Adolf Heusinger*. Potsdam: Militärgeschichtliches Forschungsamt, 1997.

———. *Adolf Heusinger: Dienst eines deutschen Soldaten, 1915 bis 1964*. Hamburg: E. S. Mittler, 2001.

Midgley, John R., Jr. *Deadly Illusions: Army Policy for the Nuclear Battlefield*. Boulder, CO: Westview Press, 1986.

Militärgeschichtliches Forschungsamt. *Verteidigung im Bündnis: Planung, Aufbau und Bewährung der Bundeswehr, 1950 bis 1972*. Munich: Bernard und Graefe, 1975.

Miller, David. *The Cold War: A Military History*. New York: St. Martin's, 1998.

Miller, Steven E., ed. *Conventional Forces and American Defense Policy: An International Security Reader*. Princeton, NJ: Princeton University Press, 1986.

Milward, Alan S. *The Reconstruction of Western Europe, 1945–1951*. Berkeley: University of California Press, 1984.

Morelock, J. D., and Martin Blumenson. *Generals of the Ardennes: American Leadership in the Battle of the Bulge*. Washington, DC: National Defense University, 1994.

Morgan, Roger. *The United States and West Germany, 1945–1973: A Study in Alliance Politics*. London: Oxford University Press, 1974.

Mossman, Billy C. *Ebb and Flow: November 1950–July 1951*. Washington, DC: U.S. Army Center of Military History, 1990.

Mueller, John E. *Retreat from Doomsday: The Obsolescence of Major War*. New York: Basic Books, 1989.

Nagl, John A. *Learning to Eat Soup with a Knife: Counterinsurgency Lessons from Malaya and Vietnam*. Chicago: University of Chicago Press, 2005.

Nash, Philip. "Bear *Any* Burden? John F. Kennedy and Nuclear Weapons." In *Cold War Statesmen Confront the Bomb: Nuclear Diplomacy since 1945*, edited by John Lewis Gaddis et al., pp. 120–140. Oxford: Oxford University Press, 1999.

Naveh, Shimon. *In Pursuit of Military Excellence: The Evolution of Operational Theory*. London: Frank Cass, 1997.

Nelson, Daniel J. *A History of U.S. Military Forces in Germany*. Boulder, CO: Westview Press, 1987.

———. *Defenders or Intruders? The Dilemmas of U.S. Forces in Germany*. Boulder, CO: Westview Press, 1987.

Nelson, Walter Henry. *Germany Rearmed*. New York: Simon and Schuster, 1972.

Neustadt, Richard E. *Alliance Politics*. New York: Columbia University Press, 1970.

Newell, R. Clayton. *The Framework of Operational Warfare*. London: Routledge, 1991.

Newell, R. Clayton, and Michael D. Krause, eds. *On Operational Art*. Washington, DC: U.S. Army Center of Military History, 1994.

Newhouse, John. *U.S. Troops in Europe: Issues, Costs, and Choices*. Washington, DC: Brookings Institution, 1971.

Ney, Virgil. *Evolution of the U.S. Army Division, 1939–1968*. Ft. Belvoir, VA: Technical Operations Incorporated, 1969.

Nitze, Paul H. *From Hiroshima to Glasnost: At the Center of Decision*. New York: Grove Weidenfeld, 1989.

Oberdorfer, Don. *Senator Mansfield: The Extraordinary Life of a Great American Statesman and Diplomat*. Washington, DC: Smithsonian Books, 2003.

Ogorkiewicz, Richard M. *Armoured Forces: A History of Armoured Forces and Their Vehicles*. New York: Arco Books, 1970.

Ojserkis, Raymond P. *Beginnings of the Cold War Arms Race: The Truman Administration and the U.S. Arms Build-Up*. Westport, CT: Praeger, 2003.

Osgood, Robert Endicott. *Limited War: The Challenge to American Strategy*. Chicago: University of Chicago Press, 1957.

Pach, Chester J. *Arming the Free World: The Origins of the United States Military Assistance Program*. Chapel Hill: University of North Carolina Press, 1991.

Paret, Peter, ed. *The Makers of Modern Strategy from Machiavelli to the Nuclear Age*. Princeton, NJ: Princeton University Press, 1986.

Park, William. *Defending the West: A History of NATO*. Boulder, CO: Westview Press, 1986.

Paul, Roland A. *American Military Commitments Abroad*. New Brunswick, NJ: Rutgers University Press, 1973.

Pedlow, Gregory W. "Flexible Response before MC 14/3: General Lauris Norstad and the Second Berlin Crisis, 1958–1962." *Storia delle Relazioni Internazionali* 13, no. 1 (1995): 235–268.

———. "Allied Crisis Management for Berlin: The LIVE OAK Organization, 1959–1963." In *International Cold War Military Records and History*, edited by William W. Epley, pp. 87–116. Washington, DC: Office of the Secretary of Defense, 1996.

———. ed. *NATO Strategy Documents, 1949–1969*. Brussels: Historical Office, Supreme Headquarters Allied Powers Europe, 1998.

Pond, Elizabeth. *Beyond the Wall: Germany's Road to Unification*. Washington, DC: Brookings Institution, 1993.

Poole, Walter S. *The Joint Chiefs of Staff and National Policy, 1950–1952*. Vol. 4 of *History of the Joint Chiefs of Staff*. Washington, DC: Historical Division, Joint Chiefs of Staff, 1979.

Posen, Barry R. *Inadvertent Escalation: Conventional War and Nuclear Risks*. Ithaca, NY: Cornell University Press, 1991.

Pöttering, Hans-Gert. *Adenauers Sicherheitspolitik, 1955–1963: Ein Beitrag zum deutsch-amerikanischen Verhältnis*. Düsseldorf: Droste Verlag, 1975.

Powaski, Ronald E. *The Entangling Alliance: The United States and European Security, 1950–1993*. Westport, CT: Greenwood Press, 1994.

Prados, John. *The Soviet Estimate: U.S. Intelligence Analysis and Soviet Strategic Forces*. Princeton, NJ: Princeton University Press, 1986.

———. *Keepers of the Keys: A History of the National Security Council from Truman to Bush*. New York: William Morrow, 1991.

Raines, Edgar F., and David R. Campbell. *The Army and the Joint Chiefs of Staff: Evolution of Army Ideas on the Command, Control, and Coordination of the U.S. Armed*

Forces, 1942–1985. Washington, DC: U.S. Army Center of Military History, 1986.
Raj, Christopher S. *American Military in Europe: Controversy over NATO Burden Sharing*. New Delhi: ABC Publishing House, 1983.
Raven, Wolfram von, ed. *Armee gegen den Krieg: Wert und Wirkung der Bundeswehr*. Stuttgart: Verlag Seewald, 1966.
Record, Jeffrey. *U.S. Nuclear Weapons in Europe: Issues and Alternatives*. Washington, DC: Brookings Institution, 1974.
———. "Operational Brilliance, Strategic Incompetence: The Military Reformers and the German Model." *Parameters* 16, no. 3 (Autumn 1986): 2–8.
Reed, John A., Jr. *Germany and NATO*. Washington, DC: Government Printing Office, 1987.
Reese, Roger R. *Stalin's Reluctant Soldiers: A Social History of the Red Army, 1925–1941*. Lawrence: University Press of Kansas, 1996.
Reinhardt, G. C., and W. R. Kintner. *Atomic Weapons in Land Combat*. Harrisburg, PA: Military Service Publishing Company, 1953.
Richardson, J. L. *Germany and the Atlantic Alliance: The Interaction of Strategy and Politics*. Cambridge, MA: Harvard University Press, 1966.
Ridgway, Matthew B. *Soldier: The Memoirs of Matthew B. Ridgway*. New York: Harper, 1956.
Riemann, Horst. *Deutsche Panzergrenadiere*. Herford: E. S. Mittler, 1989.
Romjue, John L. *From Active Defense to AirLand Battle: The Development of Army Doctrine, 1973–1982*. Fort Monroe, VA: U.S. Army Training and Doctrine Command, Historical Office, 1984.
Rose, John P. *The Evolution of U.S. Army Nuclear Doctrine, 1945–1980*. Boulder, CO: Westview Press, 1980.
Rosenberg, David Alan. "A Smoking Radiating Ruin at the End of Two Hours: Documents on American Plans for Nuclear War with the Soviet Union, 1954–1955." *International Security* 6, no. 3 (Winter 1981–1982): 3–38.
———. "U.S. Nuclear Stockpile, 1945–1950." *Bulletin of Atomic Scientists* 38 (May 1982): 25–30.
———. "The Origins of Overkill: Nuclear Weapons and American Strategy, 1945–1960." *International Security* 7, no. 4 (Spring 1983): 3–71.
———. "Reality and Responsibility: Power and Process in the Making of United States Nuclear Strategy, 1945–1968." *Journal of Strategic Studies* 9, no. 1 (March 1986): 35–52.
Ross, Steven T. *American War Plans, 1945–1950: Strategies for Defeating the Soviet Union*. London: Frank Cass, 1996.
Rottman, Gordon L. *Korean War Order of Battle: United States, United Nations, and Communist Ground, Naval, and Air Forces, 1950–1953*. Westport, CT: Praeger, 2002.
Scales, Robert H. *Certain Victory: The U.S. Army in the Gulf War*. Washington, DC: Office of the Chief of Staff, U.S. Army, 1993.
Schlight, John. *Help from Above: Air Force Close Air Support of the Army, 1946–1973*. Washington, DC: Air Force History and Museum Program, 2003.

Schmidt, Helmut. *Verteidigung oder Vergeltung: Ein deutscher Beitrag zum strategischen Problem der NATO*. Stuttgart: Verlag Seewald, 1961.

———. *Defense or Retaliation: A German View*. Translated by Edward Thomas. New York: Praeger, 1962.

Schulz, Siegfried. *Das Neue Heer: Die grösste Teilstreitkraft der Bundeswehr*. Coblenz: Wehr und Wissen, 1979.

Schwartz, David N. *NATO's Nuclear Dilemmas*. Washington, DC: Brookings Institution, 1983.

Schwartz, Thomas A. *Lyndon Johnson and Europe: In the Shadow of Vietnam*. Cambridge, MA: Harvard University Press, 2003.

Sepp, Kalev I. "The Pentomic Puzzle: The Influence of Personality and Nuclear Weapons on U.S. Army Organization, 1952–1958." *Army History* 51 (Winter 2001): 1–13.

Shimshoni, Jonathan. *Israel and Conventional Deterrence: Border Warfare from 1953 to 1970*. Ithaca, NY: Cornell University Press, 1988.

Simkin, Richard E. *Tank Warfare: An Analysis of Soviet and NATO Tank Philosophy*. London: Brassey's, 1979.

———. *Mechanized Infantry*. Oxford: Brassey's, 1980.

Simon, Jeffrey. *NATO–Warsaw Pact Force Mobilization*. Washington, DC: National Defense University Press, 1988.

Simpson, Keith. *History of the Germany Army: 1648–Present*. London: Bison Books, 1985.

Skinner, Michael. *USAREUR: The United States Army in Europe*. Novato, CA: Presidio Press, 1989.

Smyser, W. R. *From Yalta to Berlin: The Cold War Struggle over Germany*. New York: St. Martin's, 1999.

Snyder, Glenn H. *Deterrence and Defense: Toward a Theory of National Security*. Princeton, NJ: Princeton University Press, 1961.

Soffer, Jonathan M. *General Matthew B. Ridgway: From Progressivism to Reaganism, 1895–1993*. Westport, CT: Praeger, 1998.

Sorley, Lewis. "Creighton Abrams and Active-Reserve Integration in Wartime." *Parameters* 21, no. 2 (Summer 1991): 35–50.

———. *Thunderbolt: General Creighton Abrams and the Army of His Times*. New York: Simon and Schuster, 1992.

———. *Honorable Warrior: General Harold K. Johnson and the Ethics of Command*. Lawrence: University Press of Kansas, 1998.

———. "Adaptation and Impact: Mounted Combat in Vietnam." In *Camp Colt to Desert Storm: The History of U.S. Armored Forces*, edited by George F. Hofmann and Donn A. Starry, pp. 324–359. Lexington: University Press of Kentucky, 1999.

Soutor, Kevin. "To Stem the Red Tide: The German Report Series and Its Effects on American Defense Doctrine, 1948–1954." *Journal of Military History* 57, no. 4 (October 1993): 653–688.

Spector, Ronald H. *Advice and Support: The Early Years of the United States Army in Vietnam, 1941–1960*. Washington, DC: U.S. Army Center of Military History, 1983.

Index